T0202917

Communications
in Computer and Information Science   **1555**

More information about this series at https://link.springer.com/bookseries/7899

Sergio Nesmachnow ·
Luis Hernández Callejo (Eds.)

Smart Cities

4th Ibero-American Congress, ICSC-Cities 2021
Cancún, Mexico, November 29 – December 1, 2021
Revised Selected Papers

 Springer

Editors
Sergio Nesmachnow ⓘ
Universidad de la República
Montevideo, Uruguay

Luis Hernández Callejo ⓘ
University of Valladolid
Soria, Spain

ISSN 1865-0929   ISSN 1865-0937 (electronic)
Communications in Computer and Information Science
ISBN 978-3-030-96752-9   ISBN 978-3-030-96753-6 (eBook)
https://doi.org/10.1007/978-3-030-96753-6

This Springer imprint is published by the registered company Springer Nature Switzerland AG
The registered company address is: Gewerbestrasse 11, 6330 Cham, Switzerland

Preface

This CCIS volume presents selected articles from the 4th edition of the Ibero-American Congress on Smart Cities (ICSC-CITIES 2021), held from November 29 to December 1, 2021, in Cancún, México, in a mixed modality, with in-person and online talks and article presentations. This event followed the successful three previous editions of the congress, held in Soria, Spain, in 2018 and 2019 and in San José, Costa Rica, in 2020.

The main goal of ICSC-CITIES 2021 was to provide a forum for researchers, scientists, teachers, decision-makers, postgraduate students, and practitioners from different countries in Ibero-America and worldwide to share their current initiatives related to Smart Cities. Articles in this volume address four relevant topics (energy efficiency and sustainability; infrastructures and environment; mobility and IoT; and governance and citizenship) covering several areas of research and applications.

The main program consisted of six keynote talks, 65 oral presentations, and 15 poster presentations from international speakers highlighting recent developments in different areas. Over two hundred distinguished participants from 26 countries gathered in person or virtually for the congress. The Program Committee of ICSC-CITIES 2021 received 112 manuscripts, of which 65 submissions were accepted for oral presentation and the best 22, whose contents were within the computer and information science areas, were selected to be published in this CCIS volume. All articles underwent careful single-blind peer-review by at least three subject-matter experts before being selected for publication.

We would like to express our deep gratitude to all contributors to ICSC-CITIES 2021, including the congress organizers and the authors and reviewers for their endeavors that made the paper reviewing process run efficiently. We also thank the participants of the congress, our government and industry sponsors, and the readers of the proceedings.

December 2021

Sergio Nesmachnow
Luis Hernández Callejo

Organization

General Chairs

Luis Hernández Callejo	Universidad de Valladolid, Spain
Sergio Nesmachnow	Universidad de la República, Uruguay

Track Chairs

Luis Hernandez Callejo	Universidad de Valladolid, Spain
Sergio Nesmachnow	Universidad de la República, Uruguay
Santiago Iturriaga	Universidad de la República, Uruguay
Adriana Correa-Guimaraes	Universidad de Valladolid, Spain
Alfredo Cristobal-Salas	Universidad Veracruzana, México
Ana Ruiz	San Jorge University, Spain
Ana Carolina Olivera	Universidad Nacional de Cuyo, Argentina
Andrés Adolfo Navarro Newball	Pontificia Universidad Javeriana, Colombia
Bernabe Dorronsoro	University of Cadiz, Spain
Daniel Rossit	Universidad Nacional del Sur, Argentina
Diego Gabriel Rossit	Universidad Nacional del Sur and CONICET, Argentina
Fabian Castillo Peña	Universidad Libre, Cali, Colombia
Irene Lebrusán	Harvard University, USA
Jamal Toutouh	Massachusetts Institute of Technology, USA
Jorge Mírez	Universidad Nacional de Ingeniería, Perú
Lorena Parra	Universitat Politècnica de València, Spain
Luis Tobon	Pontificia Universidad Javeriana, Cali, Colombia
Luis Manuel Navas-Gracia	Universidad de Valladolid, Spain
Luiz Angelo Steffenel	Université de Reims Champagne-Ardenne, France
Oscar Duque-Perez	University of Valladolid, Spain
Paulo Gondim	Universidade de Brasilia, Brasil
Pedro Moreno	Universidad Autónoma del Estado de Morelos, México
Ponciano Jorge	Escamilla-Ambrosio, CIC-IPN, México
Renzo Massobrio	Universidad de la República, Uruguay
Roberto Villafafila	Universitat Politècnica de Catalunya, Spain
Sara Gallardo-Saavedra	Universidad de Valladolid, Spain
Teodoro Calonge	Universidad de Valladolid, Spain
Víctor Alonso Gómez	Universidad de Valladolid, Spain

Publication Chairs

Luis Hernández Callejo   Universidad de Valladolid, Spain
Sergio Nesmachnow   Universidad de la República, Uruguay

Submission and Conference Management Chair

Santiago Iturriaga   Universidad de la República, Uruguay

Program Committee

Abiagil Parra Parra   Universidad Autonoma del Estado de Morelos,
    México
Adrian Toncovich   Universidad Nacional del Sur, Argentina
Adriana Correa-Guimaraes   Universidad de Valladolid, Spain
Agustín Laguarda   Universidad de la República, Uruguay
Alberto López Casillas   Diputación de Ávila, Spain
Alejandro Otero   UBA/CSC-CONICET, Argentina
Alejandro Paz Parra   Pontificia Universidad Javeriana, Cali, Colombia
Alessandra Bussador   UDC, Brasil
Alex Cano   Universidad de Quintana Roo, México
Alexander Shemetev   VSE, Czech Republic
Alexander Vallejo Díaz   Santo Domingo Institute of Technology,
    Dominican Republic
Alfredo Cristobal-Salas   Universidad Veracruzana, México
Alice Monteiro   UFMG, Brasil
Alicia Martinez   CENIDET, México
Ana Ruiz   San Jorge University, Spain
Ana Carolina Olivera   Universidad Nacional de Cuyo, Argentina
Andrés Adolfo Navarro Newball   Pontificia Universidad Javeriana, Cali, Colombia
Andres Felipe Fuentes Vasquez   Pontificia Universidad Javeriana, Cali, Colombia
Ángel Zorita Lamadrid   Universidad de Valladolid, Spain
Angela Ferreira   Polytechnic Institute of Bragança, Portugal
Antonio Mauttone   Universidad de la República, Uruguay
Antonio Muñoz   University of Malaga, Spain
Armando Huicochea   Autonomous University of Morelos State, México
Belén Carro   Universidad de Valladolid, Spain
Bernabe Dorronsoro   University of Cadiz, Spain
Bouras Abdelkarim   Badji Mokhtar University, Algeria
Carlos Grande   Universidad Centroaméricana José Simeón
    Cañas, El Salvador
Carlos Meza Benavides   Anhalt University of Applied Sciences, Germany
Carlos Torres   CENIDET, México

Carmen Vasquez	Unexpo, Venezuela
Carolina Solis Maldonado	Universidad Veracruzana, México
César Varela	CENIDET, México
Christian Cintrano	Universidad de Málaga, Spain
Claudio Paz	UTN FRC, Argentina
Claudio Risso	Universidad de la República, Uruguay
Cleonilson Protasio	Federal University of Paraíba, Brazil
Cristina Sáez Blázquez	University of Salamanca, Spain
Daniel Morinigo-Sotelo	Universidad de Valladolid, Spain
Daniel Rossit	Universidad Nacional del Sur, Argentina
Daniel Stolfi	University of Luxembourg, Luxembourg
David Peña Morales	University of Cadiz, Spain
Deyslen Mariano	Instituto Tecnológico de Santo Domingo, Dominican Republic
Diana Sánchez-Partida	UPAEP, México
Diego Arcos-Aviles	Universidad de las Fuerzas Armadas ESPE, Ecuador
Diego Gonzalez-Aguilera	University of Salamanca, Spain
Diego Alberto Godoy	Universidad Gastón Dachary, Argentina
Diego Gabriel Rossit	Universidad Nacional del Sur and CONICET, Argentina
Edgardo Aníbal Belloni	Universidad Gastón Dachary, Argentina
Edith Gabriela Manchego Huaquipaco	Universidad Nacional de San Agustín de Arequipa, Perú
Eduardo Fernández	Universidad de la República, Uruguay
Elina Pacini	UNCuyo, Argentina
Emmanuel Millan	UNcuyo, Argentina
Enrique González	Universidad de Salamanca, Spain
Enrique Gabriel	Baquela, UTN, Argentina
Esteban Mocskos	UBA, Argentina
Fabian Castillo Peña	Universidad Libre, Cali, Colombia
Fermin Armenta	Centro de Enseñanza Técnica y Superior (CETYS Universidad), México
Fernando Velez Varela	Universidad Santiago de Cali, Colombia
Francisco Valbuena	Universidad de Valladolid, Spain
Franco Robledo	Universidad de la República, Uruguay
Gabriel Bayá	Universidad de la República, Uruguay
Gilberto Martinez	CIC-IPN, México
Gina Paola Maestre Gongora	Universidad Cooperativa de Colombia, Colombia
Harrison Oluwaseyi Ogunkalu	Niğde Ömer Halisdemir Üniversitesi, Turkey
Ignacio de Godos Crespo	Universidad de Valladolid, Spain
Ignacio Martín Nieto	Universidad de Salamanca, Spain

Ignacio Turias	Universidad de Cádiz, Spain
Irene Lebrusán	Harvard University, USA
Ivett Zavala Guillén	Centro de Investigación Científica y de Educación Superior de Ensenada, México
Jamal Toutouh	Massachusetts Institute of Technology, USA
Javier Rocher	Universitat Politècnica de València, Spain
Jennifer Kim	University of Mons, Belgium
Joao Coelho	Instituto Politécnico de Bragança, Portugal
Jonathan Muraña	Universidad de la República, Uruguay
Jorge Caramés	Grupo Igualatorio Bilbao, Spain
Jorge Mírez	Universidad Nacional de Ingeniería, Perú
Jorge Nájera	Centro de Investigaciones Energéticas, Medioambientales y Tecnológicas, Spain
Jorge Pérez Martínez	Universidad de Concepción, Chile
Jorge Mario Cortés-Mendoza	South Ural State University, Russia
Jose Aguerre	Universidad de la República, Uruguay
Jose Lizardi	Autonomous University of Mexico City, México
José Alberto Hernández	Universidad Autónoma del Estado de Morelos, México
José Ángel	Morell Martínez, UMA, Spain
Jose Antonio Martín-Jimenez	Universidad de Salamanca, España
José Antonio Ferrer	CIEMAT, Spain
José-Ramón Aira	Universidad Politécnica de Madrid, Spain
Juan Chavat	Universidad de la República, Uruguay
Juan Espinoza	Universidad de Cuenca, Ecuador
Juan Pavón	Universidad Complutense de Madrid, Spain
Juan Coca	Universidad de Valladolid, Spain
Juan Francisco Cabrera Sánchez	Universidad de Cádiz, Spain
Juan José Tarrio	CNEA, Argentina
Leonardo Cardinale	Instituto Tecnológico de Costa Rica, Costa Rica
Lilian Obregon	Universidad de Valladolid, Spain
Lorena Parra	Universitat Politècnica de València, Spain
Lucas Iacono	Know-Center GmbH, Austria
Lucas Mohimont	Université de Reims, France
Luis Garcia	Universidad de Concepción, Chile
Luis Hernandez Callejo	Universidad de Valladolid, Spain
Luis Marrone	UNLP, Argentina
Luis Tobon	Pontificia Universidad Javeriana, Cali, Colombia
Luis Bernardo Pulido-Gaytan	CICESE Research Center, México
Luis G. Montané Jiménez	Universidad Veracruzana, México
Luis Manuel Navas-Gracia	Universidad de Valladolid, Spain
Luis Omar Jamed Boza	Universidad Veracruzana, México

Rallou Taratori	University of Mons, Belgium
Ramiro Martins	Polytechnic Institute of Bragança, Portugal
Raul Luna	Universidad Veracruzana, México
Raúl Alberto López Meraz	Universidad Veracruzana, México
Renato Andara	Universidad Nacional Experimental Politécnica Antonio José de Sucre, Venezuela
Renzo Massobrio	Universidad de la República, Uruguay
Rhonmer Pérez	UNEXPO, Venezuela
Roberto Villafafila	Universitat Politècnica de Catalunya, Spain
Rodrigo Alonso-Suárez	Universidad de la República, Uruguay
Rodrigo Porteiro	UTE, Uruguay
Santiago Iturriaga	Universidad de la República, Uruguay
Sara Gallardo-Saavedra	Universidad de Valladolid, Spain
Saul Esquivel Garcia	CIATEQ, México
Sergio Nesmachnow	Universidad de la República, Uruguay
Sesil Koutra	University of Mons, Belgium
Silvia Soutullo	CIEMAT, Spain
Susana del Pozo	University of Salamanca, Spain
Teodoro Calonge	Universidad de Valladolid, Spain
Teresa Batista	Universidade de Évora, Portugal
Tiago Carneiro Pessoa	Inria, France
Vanessa Guimarães	CEFET/RJ, Brazil
Vicente Canals	Universidad de las Islas Baleares, Spain
Vicente Leite	Instituto Politécnico de Bragança, Portugal
Víctor Alonso Gómez	Universidad de Valladolid, Spain
Víctor Manuel Padrón Nápoles	Universidad Europea de Madrid, Spain
Yamila Soledad Grassi	Universidad Nacional del Sur and CONICET, Argentina
Yuri Molina	UFPB, Brazil
Zacharie De Greve	University of Mons, Belgium

Contents

Urban Informatics

Internet of Things, Smart Energy and Smart Grid

Computational Intelligence for Smart Cities

Methodology for Inspection of Defects in Photovoltaic Plants by Drone and Electroluminescence

Luis Hernández-Callejo$^{(\boxtimes)}$ ⓘ, Sara Gallardo-Saavedra ⓘ,
José Ignacio Morales-Aragonés ⓘ, Víctor Alonso-Gómez ⓘ,
Alberto Redondo Plaza ⓘ, and Diego Fernández Martínez ⓘ

University of Valladolid, Campus Universitario Duques de Soria, 42004 Soria, Spain
{luis.hernandez.callejo,victor.alonso.gomez}@uva.es,
ziguratt@coit.es

Abstract. The integration of photovoltaic systems is increasing in cities. Advanced maintenance methods should provide interesting results for maintenance companies. Of the inspection techniques, one of the most promising is that based on electroluminescence, although it has its drawbacks, such as the need to disconnect the string and photovoltaic modules. In this work, a new methodology for capturing electroluminescence images is presented for the detection of defects in photovoltaic modules, using a drone and a bidirectional inverter. The method is validated in an existing plant, and the results are satisfactory.

Keywords: Electroluminescence · Dron · Bidirectional inverter

1 Introduction

In the 21st century, the integration of renewable generation sources is a reality. Within renewable technologies, wind and photovoltaic systems are the most installed, and specifically in the last five years photovoltaic plants are the most interesting [1].

This increase in the installation of renewable plants will require changes in the electrical infrastructure. However, there are other areas that are going to change, and many of them will be in cities. These cities of the future (Smart Cities, SC) will need different control and management strategies from the current ones, and this will mean a paradigm shift in their design [2–4]. SC needs to integrate generation sources (mainly renewable) in order to meet its energy needs, and in this sense, photovoltaic technology is easily installable in its infrastructures [5, 6].

Regardless of the size of the photovoltaic plant (small and integrated in SC or large photovoltaic plant), photovoltaic systems need novel inspection techniques to keep their productive performance high [7]. Numerous techniques are used for this purpose, but the most important are those that detect failures in photovoltaic modules, and this is because this type of failure is the most common and the one that produces greater production losses [8].

S. Nesmachnow and L. Hernández Callejo (Eds.): ICSC-Cities 2021, CCIS 1555, pp. 3–14, 2022.
https://doi.org/10.1007/978-3-030-96753-6_1

Of the failure inspection techniques in photovoltaic modules, there are two of them above the others. Specifically, the inspection techniques with thermography [9–11] and electroluminescence [12–14] are the most used and promising.

The use of the drone for maintenance in photovoltaic plants is being used. The drone can do thermographic inspection with good results [15, 16], and the electroluminescence sensor is also shipped on drone [17]. Electroluminescence is very interesting, since many defects are detected, but it has a disadvantage, this technique is invasive, since it requires the disconnection of the photovoltaic module and its connection to an external source. However, lately work is being done on inspection techniques with electroluminescence, but without the need for disconnection, for which a bidirectional inverter is used [9, 14].

Therefore, it is clear that photovoltaic plants need maintenance. The photovoltaic systems integrated into the SC infrastructures will require advanced maintenance. The use of drones together with techniques such as electroluminescence are very interesting combinations. As already seen, electroluminescence has the disadvantage of the need to disconnect the photovoltaic modules for current injection. With all these conditions, this work presents a methodology for the inspection of defects in photovoltaic plants by drone and electroluminescence, for which a bidirectional inverter will be used (avoiding the disconnection of photovoltaic modules) together with the drone and an InGaAs camera. The document is as follows: Sect. 2 shows materials and methods; Sect. 3 shows the results; and Sect. 4 presents the conclusions.

2 Materials and Methods

In this section the materials that have been used for the investigation will be presented, and later the methods used to carry it out.

2.1 Materials

The experiments have been carried out in the facilities of the Duques de Soria University Campus of the University of Valladolid, in Soria (Spain). The experience has been performed in 11 PV modules connected in series (string) to a bidirectional inverter. The nominal characteristics of the modules are shown in Table 1 shows a real photograph of the installation previously described.

A specific power inverter with bidirectional power flow capability was placed in the pilot-site for this study. The power inverter is a neutral point clamped (NPC I-type) that has been recently developed to help in the maintenance of photovoltaic plants by means of electroluminescence image processing [14]. Figure 2 shows a classical converter control block scheme, electroluminescence control action is performed inside the high level controller layer (highlights in blue the blocks concerning EL functionality). Solar cells convert solar energy into electricity, however they also have the characteristic of being able to emit light if they are connected to an electrical current. This process, let's say inverse, is called electroluminescence (Fig. 1).

Finally, Fig. 3 shows the drone and the electroluminescence camera used. The camera is special, it is an InGaAs camera (Hamamatsu brand and C12741-03 model), specially designed to capture the light emission of the photovoltaic module when it is electrically excited. The drone used is a hexacopter drone.

Table 1. Main nominal data of photovoltaic (PV) modules.

Module	Model	Power (W)	Voc (V)	Vmpp (V)	Isc (A)	Impp (A)
1	Eoplly	175	44.35	36.26	5.45	4.83
2	Eoplly	175	44.35	36.26	5.45	4.83
3	Eoplly	175	44.35	36.26	5.45	4.83
4	Eoplly	175	44.35	36.26	5.45	4.83
5	Eoplly	175	44.35	36.26	5.45	4.83
6	Eoplly	175	44.35	36.26	5.45	4.83
7	Eoplly	175	44.35	36.26	5.45	4.83
8	Eoplly	175	44.35	36.26	5.45	4.83
9	Eoplly	175	44.35	36.26	5.45	4.83
10	EGNG	180	44.40	35.40	5.35	5.08
11	SKY Global	175	42.60	35.50	5.20	4.93

Fig. 1. Experimental installation, Campus of the University of Valladolid, in Soria (Spain).

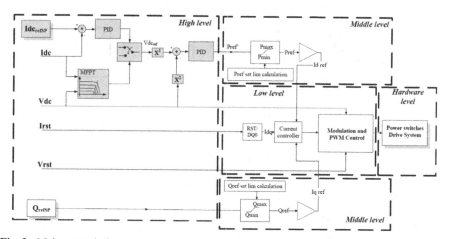

Fig. 2. Main control diagram of a photovoltaic inverter controller: in blue are marked the high-level control blocks related to the maximum power point tracking (MPPT) and electroluminescence (evaluation working modes. Experimental installation installed in Campus of the University of Valladolid, in Soria (Spain).

Fig. 3. Drone and InGaAs camera installed on gimbal.

2.2   Methods

The elements described in Sect. 2.1. must be integrated with each other. All the elements described are shown in Fig. 4, in order to later comment on their operation.

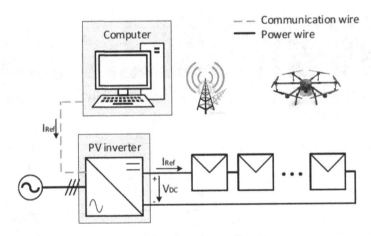

Fig. 4. Inspection process diagram.

Figure 5 shows the sequence of the process, which is related to the elements of Fig. 4, to later comment on the five steps that compose it.

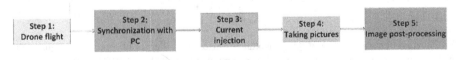

Process Sequence

Fig. 5. Sequence process of electroluminescence measurements performed.

Next, the five steps of the process will be described:

- **Step 1:** the drone with the camera (InGaAs) installed will be put into flight. The drone will have the flight prerecorded. In this case, the drone pilot will need to control the camera angle, but this process can be automated in another test.
- **Step 2:** with the drone in position to capture images (video in this case), the drone will send a signal to the PC in the field. The mission of this PC is to control the current (I_{ref}) to be injected into the string of the photovoltaic generator.
- **Step 3:** once the current reference is set in the bidirectional inverter control script, the converter changes its mode, and this device begins to inject the setpoint current into the string bus of the photovoltaic generator. This reference can be varied, and the value of the injected current will influence the luminosity emitted by the photovoltaic modules.
- **Step 4:** once the current injection is established, the PC sends a control command to the drone. At this time, and with the camera activated and in recording mode, the drone makes the programmed route, capturing the images of all the photovoltaic modules emitting light.
- **Step 5:** this step is the only one done with the drone on the ground. The images taken are recorded in the memory installed in the drone, so the post-processing must be carried out once the flight is finished. When performing the night flight, it is not necessary to apply a lock-in technique on the images, since these are of sufficient definition to identify the defects. Post-processing will consist of identifying the contour of the panels and correcting the angle of the image. The actual camera lens is not ideal and introduces some distortion to the image. To account for these non-idealities, it is necessary to add a distortion model to the perspective projection equation. Therefore, it is necessary to use a correction algorithm, and python or matlab has some optimized algorithms implemented.

3 Results and Analysis of Results

In this section the results of the experience will be presented, and an analysis of them will be made.

3.1 Results

As already mentioned, the bidirectional inverter is a fundamental element in this experiment. In addition, the possibility of regulating the current to be injected into the string of the photovoltaic generator has been discussed. This will allow this experiment to be carried out at different injected currents, and therefore at different light emissions from the photovoltaic modules. Figure 7 shows the transition from 5 A to 0.5 A in the injected current, as well as the voltage (V_{DC}) of the string. It is possible to see a good response stabilization of the bidirectional inverter. As is logical, a decrease in the injected current causes a decrease in the voltage in the string, since the current cuts the I–V curve of the photovoltaic module at a lower voltage (Fig. 6).

The flight data were: distance from the drone to the photovoltaic modules of 5 m, the flight in low light, wind speed 0.5 m/s. Below, in Fig. 7 several non-post-processed images

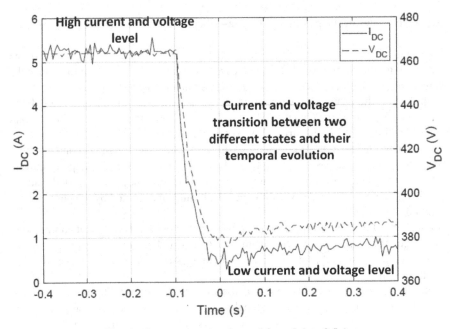

Fig. 6. Current set-point changed from 5 A to 0.5 A.

obtained in flight are shown. As can be seen, the images are of high quality, and this test has been carried out by injecting 5 A into the string of the photovoltaic generator. The figure represents two different image sequences, with different photovoltaic modules.

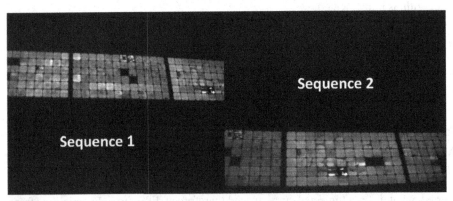

Fig. 7. Two different sequences of the flight of the InGaAs camera drone. Photovoltaic modules emitting light from 5 A of injected current.

As discussed above, in step 5 the contours of the photovoltaic modules are identified. In this way, it is possible to cut the contour of the photovoltaic module, and obtain a more optimal image than the views in Fig. 8. Figure 9 shows all the photovoltaic modules already cut, with interesting information.

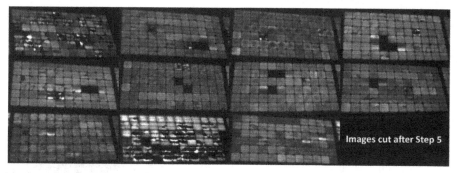

Fig. 8. Electroluminescence images of the 11 photovoltaic modules. Images taken with a drone, and with 5 A of injected current.

Another action in step 5 is the geometric correction of the images, mainly as a consequence of the fisheye in the image. Figure 9 shows the sequence of the geometric correction. The image shows the image enhancement, showing a rectangular image, without loss of information.

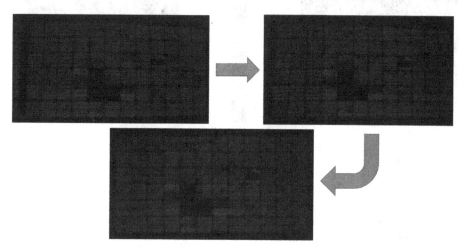

Fig. 9. Geometry correction process. Electroluminescence image taken by drone.

Once the image has been corrected, it is possible to increase or decrease the quality of the information by acting on the image histogram. In Fig. 10 the effect of acting on the histograms of the images is shown.

Finally, a last detection of the edges of the photovoltaic module is performed. With the geometrically corrected image, the edge detection algorithm is executed, and the results can be seen in Fig. 11. A projective transformation called homography has been used.

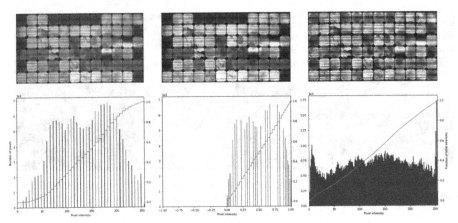

Fig. 10. Modification of the information displayed through the image histogram.

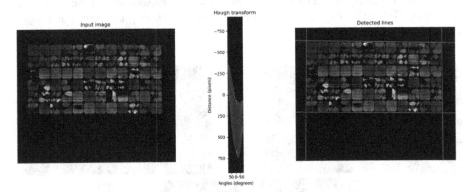

Fig. 11. Result of the edge detection algorithm.

3.2 Analysis of Results

As shown in the previous section, the bidirectional inverter is a critical element for electroluminescence imaging. This device has some interesting characteristics to be able to carry out the electroluminescence technique. The device presents a very interesting current control, allowing images to be made at different currents injected into the string, and thus being able to have images with different lighting. This device is essential for the electroluminescence technique, since the device avoids having to disconnect the string (or each photovoltaic module), and it is possible to take the images without disconnecting the photovoltaic modules.

Once the current is injected into the string, and synchronized with the drone, the drone can perform the scheduled flight, and capture all the images of the photovoltaic modules. These photovoltaic modules will be emitting light, which will depend on the amount of current injected. In the test carried out, the capture of electroluminescence images was carried out with a current injection of 5 A. On this occasion, as it is a night flight, the images obtained are of excellent quality, as can be seen in Fig. 8, so it is not necessary to apply lock-in techniques.

However, the amount of current injected is very important, as it is related to the amount of light emitted. The defects detected are related to the emissivity of the photovoltaic module. In this experience, electroluminescence imaging has been carried out at different injected currents, as can be seen in Fig. 12, where the electroluminescence image taken from the drone on the same photovoltaic modules, but at different injected currents, can be seen. Figure 12a) shows a photovoltaic module illuminated with different currents injected into the string (0.0 A, 0.5 A, 1.5 A, 3.5 A and 5.0 A). It is possible to appreciate the clear differences between them, and it is possible to affirm that the higher the injected current (in this case the Isc) the electroluminescence image obtained is of higher quality. Figure 10b) shows the same images as in Fig. 12a) but once processed, and it can be seen that the images obtained with a current injection of 3.5 A and 5.0 A are very similar.

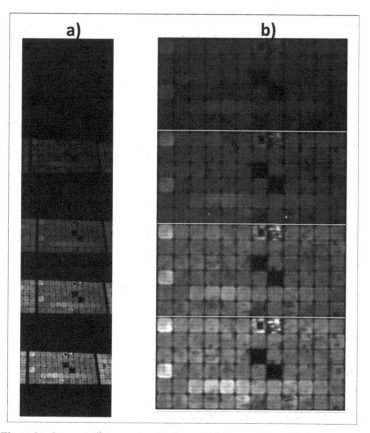

Fig. 12. Electroluminescence image taken by drone of the same photovoltaic module with different injected currents (0.0 A, 0.5 A, 1.5 A, 3.5 A and 5.0 A). a) uncorrected images; b) Corrected images.

Once the images are corrected, it is easy to detect the main defects of the measured photovoltaic modules. In the images shown in the results section, it is possible to see totally inactive cells (black cells in the image), or cells with a very high illumination density as a consequence of the inactivity of part of it.

Electroluminescence images by themselves serve to draw conclusions about the state of the photovoltaic module. And to corroborate this statement, Fig. 13 shows the electroluminescence images of the photovoltaic modules 4, 9 and 11, completed with the I–V curves of said photovoltaic modules. It is possible to observe in the I–V curves the clear deterioration of the photovoltaic module, from the point of view of its performance. All the photovoltaic modules shown present a clear degradation in their I–V curve, and this deterioration can be inferred from the electroluminescence images.

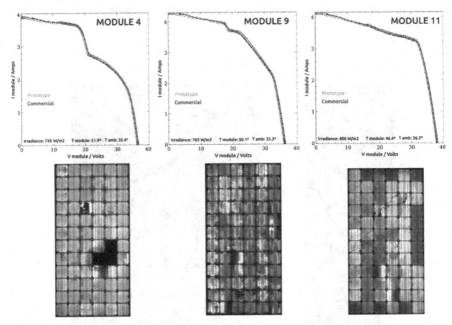

Fig. 13. Electroluminescence image and I–V curve of photovoltaic modules 4, 9 and 11.

4   Conclusions and Future Work

This work presents a new methodology for capturing electroluminescence images of photovoltaic modules, using drone, InGaAs camera and bidirectional inverter. The method has been validated in the photovoltaic plant located in Duques de Soria University Campus of the University of Valladolid, in Soria (Spain).

To begin with, the work has made clear the need for a bidirectional inverter. This new functionality (bidirectionality) allows taking electroluminescence images without the need to disconnect the string or the photovoltaic modules. It is possible to affirm that this device allows the technique to be non-invasive, and that it does not require human intervention to disconnect devices. In addition, this inverter gives the method a lot of versatility, since it allows electroluminescence to be made by injecting different amounts of current. In this work, images have been taken with 5 A current, but electroluminescence images have also been taken at lower currents.

The synchronization between the bidirectional inverter and the drone is essential. In this work, the results of electroluminescence images have been shown taking into account this synchronization.

Once the images have been taken, they have been found to be of sufficient quality to detect failures in the photovoltaic modules. However, the images have been subjected to classical algorithms to correct the effect of geometry. The results of this correction have been good, and there is no loss of quality in the image.

The results obtained from the electroluminescence images have been compared with the I–V curves obtained from the photovoltaic modules. It is possible to affirm that the images alone are used to make a decision regarding the state of the photovoltaic module.

These researchers will continue to work on new bi-directional inverters with complementary benefits. In addition, it is possible to investigate the possibility of locking in this method, but it will require greater rigor in synchronization. In addition, and from these electroluminescence images, the researchers will work on defect classification techniques based on artificial intelligence, and on photovoltaic module performance estimators.

The use of other drone models (for example DJI) is an interesting topic to address. The decision will depend on several issues, on the one hand, the drone must be able to raise and keep a camera stable (in this work a special and weighted camera has been used), and on the other hand, the flight time of the drone will also be critical., and this will depend on the size of the plant to be measured.

Acknowledgements. We would like to thank the CEDER by providing information for the development of this work. The authors thank the CYTED Thematic Network "CIUDADES INTELIGENTESTOTALMENTE INTEGRALES, EFICIENTES Y SOSTENIBLES(CITIES)" no 518RT0558.

This research was funded by the "Ministerio de Industria, Economía y Competitividad" grant number "RTC-2017-6712-3" with name "Desarrollo de herramientas Optimizadas de operaCión y manTenimientO pRedictivo de Plantas fotovoltaicas—DOCTOR-PV".

References

1. Korkeakoski, M.: Towards 100% Renewables by 2030: Transition Alternatives for a Sustainable Electricity Sector in Isla de la Juventud, Cuba. Energies 2021, vol. 14, p. 2862. https://doi.org/10.3390/EN14102862
2. Tanwar, S., Popat, A., Bhattacharya, P., Gupta, R., Kumar, N.: A taxonomy of energy optimization techniques for smart cities: architecture and future directions. Expert Syst e12703 (2021). https://doi.org/10.1111/EXSY.12703
3. Elberzhager, F., Mennig, P., Polst, S., Scherr, S., Stüpfert, P.: Towards a digital ecosystem for a smart city district: procedure, results, and lessons learned. In: Smart Cities 2021, vol. 4, pp. 686–716. https://doi.org/10.3390/SMARTCITIES4020035

4. James, P., Astoria, R., Castor, T., Hudspeth, C., Olstinske, D., Ward, J.: Smart cities: fundamental concepts. In: Augusto, J.C. (ed.) Handbook of Smart Cities, pp. 3–33. Springer, Cham (2021). https://doi.org/10.1007/978-3-030-69698-6_2

5. Dai, Y., Bai, Y.: Performance improvement for building integrated photovoltaics in practice: a review. Energies 14, 178 (2021). https://doi.org/10.3390/EN14010178

6. Mahian, O., Ghafarian, S., Sarrafha, H., Kasaeian, A., Yousefi, H., Yan, W.-M.: Phase change materials in solar photovoltaics applied in buildings: an overview. Sol. Energy 224, 569–592 (2021). https://doi.org/10.1016/J.SOLENER.2021.06.010

7. Hernández-Callejo, L., Gallardo-Saavedra, S., Alonso-Gómez, V.: A review of photovoltaic systems: design, operation and maintenance. Sol. Energy 188, 426–440 (2019). https://doi.org/10.1016/J.SOLENER.2019.06.017

8. Gallardo-Saavedra, S., Hernández-Callejo, L., Duque-Pérez, O.: Quantitative failure rates and modes analysis in photovoltaic plants. Energy 183, 825–836 (2019). https://doi.org/10.1016/J.ENERGY.2019.06.185

9. Gallardo-Saavedra, S., Hernández-Callejo, L., del Alonso-García, M.C., Muñoz-Cruzado-Alba, J.,Ballestín-Fuertes, J.: Infrared thermography for the detection and characterization of photovoltaic defects: comparison between illumination and dark conditions. Sensors 20, 4395 (2020). https://doi.org/10.3390/S20164395

10. Alfaro-Mejía, E., Loaiza-Correa, H., Franco-Mejía, E., Hernández-Callejo, L.: Segmentation of thermography image of solar cells and panels. In: Nesmachnow, S., Hernández Callejo, L. (eds.) ICSC-CITIES 2019. CCIS, vol. 1152, pp. 1–8. Springer, Cham (2020). https://doi.org/10.1007/978-3-030-38889-8_1

11. Dávila-Sacoto, M., Hernández-Callejo, L., Alonso-Gómez, V., Gallardo-Saavedra, S., González, L.G.: Detecting hot spots in photovoltaic panels using low-cost thermal cameras. In: Nesmachnow, S., Hernández Callejo, L. (eds.) ICSC-CITIES 2019. CCIS, vol. 1152, pp. 38–53. Springer, Cham (2020). https://doi.org/10.1007/978-3-030-38889-8_4

12. Pratt, L., Govender, D., Klein, R.: Defect detection and quantification in electroluminescence images of solar PV modules using U-net semantic segmentation. Renew Energy 178, 1211–1222 (2021). https://doi.org/10.1016/J.RENENE.2021.06.086

13. Otamendi, U., Martinez, I., Quartulli, M., Olaizola, I.G., Viles, E., Cambarau, W.: Segmentation of cell-level anomalies in electroluminescence images of photovoltaic modules. Sol. Energy 220, 914–926 (2021). https://doi.org/10.1016/J.SOLENER.2021.03.058

14. Ballestín-Fuertes, J., Muñoz-Cruzado-Alba, J., Sanz-Osorio, J.F., Hernández-Callejo, L., Alonso-Gómez, V., Morales-Aragones, J.I., et al.: Novel utility-scale photovoltaic plant electroluminescence maintenance technique by means of bidirectional power inverter controller. Appl. Sci. 10, 3084 (2020). https://doi.org/10.3390/APP10093084

15. Gallardo-Saavedra, S., Hernández-Callejo, L., Duque-Pérez, Ó.: Analysis and characterization of PV module defects by thermographic inspection. Rev. Fac. Ing. 93, 92–104 (2019). https://doi.org/10.17533/UDEA.REDIN.20190517

16. Gallardo-Saavedra, S., Hernandez-Callejo, L., Duque-Perez, O.: Image resolution influence in aerial thermographic inspections of photovoltaic plants. IEEE Trans. Ind. Inf. 14, 5678–5686 (2018). https://doi.org/10.1109/TII.2018.2865403

17. Dhimish, M., d'Alessandro, V., Daliento, S.: Investigating the impact of cracks on solar cells performance: analysis based on nonuniform and uniform crack distributions. IEEE Trans. Ind. Inf. (2021) https://doi.org/10.1109/TII.2021.3088721

VIA: A Virtual Informative Assistant for Smart Tourism

María Camila López[1] , David Hernández[1] ,
Andrés A. Navarro-Newball[1(✉)] , and Edmond C. Prakash[2]

[1] Pontificia Universidad Javeriana Cali, Cali, Colombia
{mclopez09,davidher28,anavarro}@javerianacali.edu.co
[2] Cardiff Metropolitan University, Cardiff, UK
eprakash@cardiffmet.ac.uk

Abstract. Tourism can be approached from the technological virtual continuum, calling it smart tourism which is related to cultural computing. To achieve that, we implemented an application for mobile devices to enrich the visit of locals and foreigners to the San Antonio neighbourhood in the city of Santiago de Cali, Colombia using concepts such as augmented reality, natural language processing and techniques such as speech-to-text, text-to-speech, skeletal animation and blend shapes. The main objective is to guide and inform about the neighbourhood in order to provide awareness of it as a heritage site. We developed the application following a software development cycle which included analysis, design, prototyping, implementation, and validation. Particularly, in validation, we performed unitary tests, functional tests and user tests. The resulting application was well received among participants in the test.

Keywords: Augmented reality · Natural language processing ·
Speech-to-text · Text-to-speech · Skeletal animation · Blend shapes ·
Smart tourism · Cultural computing

1 Introduction

The city of Santiago de Cali, Colombia in favour of standing out as a special district, is betting on increasing sports, culture, tourism, and business markets. To the west of the city is one of the most typical neighbourhoods of the Cali culture and that is part of the development plan, San Antonio. Its creation and consolidation are closely linked to the construction of the chapel of San Antonio (representative temple of the neighbourhood) carried out almost 300 years ago, more precisely in the year 1746. Hostels, dance academies, restaurants, theatres, and monuments, are some of the many things that have emerged over the years and that today represent the idiosyncrasy of the citizens of Cali. In this sense, our project focuses on recognising that the methods used to provide information regarding the different events and places in the neighbourhood show some limitations. For example, some of the information is in the hands of private individuals

© Springer Nature Switzerland AG 2022
S. Nesmachnow and L. Hernández Callejo (Eds.): ICSC-Cities 2021, CCIS 1555, pp. 15–30, 2022.
https://doi.org/10.1007/978-3-030-96753-6_2

and institutions; public media, such as posters, are unclear and scarce; and there is no bilingual information that is inclusive with international visitors. Therefore, we implemented an application to share and publicise the place through different designed and impactful ways using technology, in this case, with the use of augmented reality (AR) and natural language processing (NLP).

The architectural, anthropological, urban, and social heritage of the San Antonio neighbourhood is one of the fundamental pillars for locals and tourists to fall more and more in love with the city of Santiago de Cali, Colombia. Thus, all the history that characterises the neighbourhood should be known by all those who live among its streets daily, since it is a representative icon of the region. Recognising some of the oldest houses, keeping in mind events and fairs, differentiating the monuments, and distinguishing the hill where the church is located, would favour for the development of the place. Despite this, and after a field outing, it became clear that the way in which information about places and events in the neighbourhood that is provided is limited. There is no strategy to generate interest; the information is frequently outdated; the information posters are unclear or incomplete. In contrast, Boboc et al. [1] propose a system based on AR that shows an old church, now non-existent, in the place where it should have been located. Here, information is presented to visitors in a visual and interactive way, highlighting the importance of the place and its history. This suggests that the virtual continuum, which includes AR, mixed reality and virtual reality and its technologies, provide great information potential that could complement visits to the San Antonio neighbourhood.

Wei et al. [2] shows how interesting it was to expose the history of places, through comparative images with current and ancient facades. Perea-Tanaka et al. [3] expose interactive factors to attract the public's attention through AR. In addition, Sauter et al. [4] and Darwin et al. [5] provide their expertise with geolocation and how it contributes to certain functions such as using a map to locate users. Likewise, Wei et al. [6] and Cavallo et al. [7] present how AR can contribute to changing the behaviours in urban areas, generating greater tourism. Thus, our project recognises the importance of establishing actions to interact with an application by enhancing the use of AR. We propose an application for smart tourism, a Virtual Informative Assistant (VIA) that makes use of AR to provide information to locals and visitors to the San Antonio neighbourhood. To achieve this we: (1) identified, analysed and structured the information of the San Antonio neighbourhood that is used in a VIA; (2) developed an architecture for the VIA that allows to integrate the information obtained; (3) implemented the application of the VIA based on the proposed architecture and (5) evaluated the quality control and user experience of the implemented system. As Escobar and Margherita state [8], "Smart Tourism describes a plethora of advanced information and communication technologies applied in the tourism industry".

2   Analysis

To identify and define the places to be used in the VIA, a process was carried out in which the necessary information was obtained virtually and in person.

Initially, the San Antonio neighbourhood is recognised through tools such as TripAdvisor, Google Maps and Street View. Each of them offers different aspects to consider. For example, TripAdvisor, under its ideal of providing reviews of travel-related content, makes it possible to recognise the opinion of people who have visited the neighbourhood and its most representative places. While Google Maps and Street View allow to geographically locate and visually distinguish the neighbourhood in a way very close to reality. In this way, we selected different options of places in the San Antonio neighbourhood according to criteria such as opinions and valuation of locals and visitors, historical relevance reviewed on the web and location. Subsequently, we proceeded with a field outing and an approach to the owners that allowed to evaluate and confirm in person the choice made. The chosen places consist of a public place and two private places as follows. (1) St. Anthony's Church: it was built in 1786 and became public property in 1944. In addition, it was declared a national monument in 1997. (2) La Linterna (The Lantern): it is one of the oldest typographic printers in Colombia. Since 1938 this printing press has been providing its services in the San Antonio neighbourhood. (3) La Colina gathering place (The Hill): it is recognised as the oldest store in the city of Cali, it was created in 1942. Initially it was catalogued as a neighbourhood store and with the passage of time it became a gathering icon on the tourist route of the city.

When conducting a survey to a group of 32 people, it was evident that San Antonio is considered one of the most representative neighbourhoods in Cali with an acceptance score of 8.93 out of 10. Here, participants have had enriching experiences with family and friends. Gastronomy, architecture and a cosy and bohemian atmosphere stand out. Of the three places chosen to be part of the VIA, only the church is known by 85% of people, while La Linterna and La Colina are known only by 7% and 41% of respondents respectively, which is interesting since the latter places have an important history within the neighbourhood and the city, that many do not know. Some of the respondents highlighted their experiences in La colina as: "Good music, beer and food." However, there were also confusions such as: "it is fun to listen to the storytellers with their magnificent stories as well as to dance some Andean dances," referring to the storytellers located in the church. Regarding La Linterna only 2 out of 32 of the respondents said they knew about it by saying: "I know the traditional posters they make," and: "they print for saying something, the old-fashioned way. It once came out in the newspaper." In this way, it is considered of great importance to highlight them in the application so that tourist and local users know about them and their most notable aspects. We proposed the work flow in Fig. 1 accordingly.

3   Design

For the design section, the planning of the system architecture, the proposed data models, and the layout of the graphic interface of the VIA are presented.

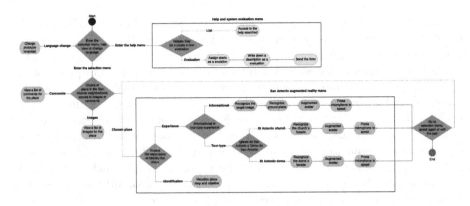

Fig. 1. Application flow.

3.1 Architecture

The architecture is a key piece in any technology project. In this case, we proposed to make use of an event-driven microservices architecture. This approach was chosen primarily because the system had a set of tools and services that communicated both locally and over the network. Therefore, using a low coupling and high cohesion architecture allowed the prototype to make use of memory and local processing, but also, make use of up to six different virtualised services on Microsoft Azure and Firebase servers. Here (Fig. 2), a client layer and a service layer are defined. In addition, these layers communicate by means of an event handler that is based on the occurrence of events for the generation of transitions and requests.

3.2 Data Model

Emphasising the architecture presented in Fig. 2 it is pertinent to say that we used three different types of databases. The first database works in an embedded way as a system of collecting visual objectives recognisable by the application. These objectives are stored in the database as sets of points recognisable by the camera at the time of deploying the system. In addition, it has an internal scheme in which it collects information about the images and areas, such as a recognition identifier, status, upload date and its augmentation level. The second schema used focuses on a knowledge database. This technology is implemented for the creation of a conversational layer with a virtual agent. Its approach is based on hosting a set of keys that are the possible questions from the users and, values that represent the possible answers of the agents. In short, a dictionary is proposed where all possible requests from users and responses from agents are defined. The third approach implemented is that of a schema-based non-relational database. This database hosts the data generated by users in sections of the VIA such as comments and the rating menu. In this sense, two schemes were proposed to model the information of the comments and the evaluations.

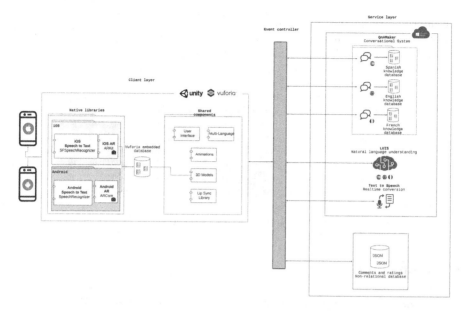

Fig. 2. Event-driven microservices architecture.

3.3 Prototyping

The graphical interface is a user's first point of contact with the application, and it directly influences usability and therefore the experience gained. To visually characterize the VIA, two phases were executed. In the first phase, we designed the complete flow of the application and how it was articulated with the requirements of this (Fig. 1). Also, we made an initial approach to the aesthetic design of the application. The second phase was carried out after the feedback in conjunction with users, therefore, the observations found were considered and final details were given to start with the implementation. It should be borne in mind that the VIA, being an application in AR, had two approaches to the design of its interface, which are the AR interface where a much more minimalist aspect is sought, and the interface of the application that provides relevant information to the user. Based on this, we initiated a design process with the help of the Figma tool. Figma is a design tool that allows creating interfaces and prototypes from vectors, therefore, it is modifiable in a short time. The main goal with the user interface design in this project was to provide a look that was intuitive, easy to use and provided a pleasant feeling in aesthetic terms for end users. For this, we followed the usability heuristics proposed by Jakob Nielsen [9] and the recommendations provided in the user evaluations. Five main interfaces were defined. Figure 3a shows the initial menu that allows the user to enter the help module and the places within San Antonio. Figure 3b shows the interface where the frequently asked questions and the assessment of user experience are listed, mainly for complaints and claims. Figure 3c shows the menu that allows

entering the places along with a slider that shows relevant information and pho-
tos corresponding to the places. Figures 3d and 3e are the interfaces associated
with the type of travelling and informative experience respectively.

Fig. 3. User interfaces of the VIA.

4   Implementation

A video of the resulting VIA application can be watched here. We used the
Unity engine due to the connectivity it brings to each of the technologies used
in the project, in addition to the knowledge and previous management of the
tool and the C# programming language. Likewise, this engine was chosen since
it supports the framework for the development of AR, Vuforia Engine. Its use
allowed, for example, if the application runs on a Google Pixel 2 XL to take
advantage of ARCore; while if the application is run on a device that does not
support ARCore, it will use Vuforia VISLAM if and only if the device has the
required sensors and has been calibrated by Vuforia. The same scenario applies
to iOS devices. If the prototype is deployed on an iPhone X, it automatically
leverages ARKit for all object and environmental recognition features. If this
same prototype runs on an older iOS device (which does not support ARKit but
has been calibrated by Vuforia) it will automatically use Vuforia VISLAM for
dependent tasks [10].

This means that all the AR technologies used in this research are accessible
through a wide set of devices with operating systems such as Android, iOS,
and Windows, making use of a priority model. The VIA made use of target
areas, target images and blueprint recognition for positioning avatars on real-life
horizontal planes. For the construction of the target areas, a respective point
cloud was mapped for one of the areas chosen as the basis of the research.
To achieve this, the possibilities lay in the use of laser scanning technology
such as Matterport, NavVis or Leica. However, this was implemented through
a three-dimensional imaging system called Vuforia Area Target Creator. The
areas created were the facade of the Church and the Dome of the San Antonio
neighbourhood in Cali, Colombia. In addition, these objectives allowed to locate
the avatars in real size according to the scanned facades. Likewise, the avatars
were created from a service for the parameterisation of each of its characteristics.

Among them, gender, skin and hair tones, accessories such as glasses, clothing such as t-shirts, trousers, and shoes. These avatars were created as humanoids with the ability to be animated (Fig. 4A). In addition, Blend shapes were used to create facial animations for lip sync simulation (Fig. 4B). This was carried out through the SALSA Lip Sync lip sync library [11], that provided the ability to combine facial animations according to the audio that is played by means of activation in an interval that is parameterised from zero to one.

Fig. 4. Use of animation. A) Skeleton for avatar animation. B) Facial animation using blendshapes. Pronouncing letter O (left) and letter T (right)

After a research process based on the verification of current technological capabilities, the team recognised the existence of native classes to convert speech into text in the operating systems. Both can be configured with any of the languages supported by both operating systems, which made it possible to continue an implementation based on multiple languages, with the vocal interaction (Spanish, English, French) of the users. To achieve the implementation of native classes in cross-type development, the Unity development platform allows the use of a layer in which plugin-type components can be defined for native communications with the project's target operating systems. Based on this, speech conversion was adapted and based on an open-source project documented on the GitHub platform [12]. Its implementation focuses on the capabilities of Android and iOS operating systems to convert speech into text and text into speech through their native libraries. In addition, it implements a direct communication bridge with Unity. Therefore, for the speech-to-text technique, native connection files were implemented in programming languages such as Java for Android and Objective-C for iOS, making use of the SpeechRecognizer and SFSpeechRecognizer libraries.

We had to focus the research on recognising how to carry out this type of interaction or voice control approach. We used artificial intelligence techniques to satisfactorily engage a user in a conversation or communication with the avatar. We proposed to reduce the problem of communication by voices, in a communication by text. With this, internally the system controls all the information as text inputs. Thus, the voice of the end users is captured and converted directly into text. Subsequently, when recognising what users said through the microphone, the next step focuses on studying the text to generate a response accordingly. To develop an application based on interactive and clear communication, we decided to make use of models for the recognition of the text and the understanding of requests or possible questions from users. These models were created through Microsoft Azure, exactly, through two cognitive cloud computing services, QnAMaker and Language Understanding (LUIS). This choice was made thanks to the keyword ranking and intent recognition capabilities of each of the tools. The models were trained from the server and through a user interface, which made it possible to use them through web services that allowed the generation of answers based on each of the questions asked by the end users of the application.

Because the prototype was built with a multicultural approach, on issues such as language, gender, and ethnicity of the avatars, it was also necessary to foray diversity into the speech of each of them. To achieve this, speech synthesis markup language (SSML) was used, which is an XML-based markup language that allowed to specify how input text is converted into synthesised speech from the Microsoft Azure text-to-speech cognitive service. Compared to plain text, SSML allowed us to adjust pitch, pronunciation, speech speed, volume, and other aspects of text-to-speech output. Normal punctuation marks, such as pause after a period or intonation when a sentence ends with a question mark, were handled automatically. A set of nine different types of voices were defined and associated with each avatar and the three languages of their domain. In addition, a method was developed to build the speech synthesis markup file at run time according to the avatar and the selected language in the system.

Emphasising the architecture developed for the VIA, we implemented an event handler. To do this, the approach used was based on the use of an event-driven finite state machine. The services used for the NLP were virtualised and accessed through the web using HTTP protocol through representational state transfer or REST requests. To achieve this, the virtualisation of each of the services was implemented through App Service, a Hosting service of Microsoft Azure and high compatibility with the technical features used in the project. The choice of this technology focused on its ability to host and execute in a dedicated and secure way of each of the services with the implementation of access tokens for its use. The communication was based on the sending and receipt of JSON type objects that were serialised and deserialised using the Newtonsoft JSON library.

5   Validation

In the validation process, all the activities related to quality tests are carried out. Therefore, the strategies used for the planning, execution and results are reflected together with their respective analysis and improvements within the functionalities that were considered pertinent. This, recognising that the environment in which the system had to be deployed required the timely classification of different types of tests, exactly three different categories.

First, we developed unitary tests before any other type of testing was performed. These were executed in each of the cycles in the testing phase as a first step. To carry out the development of these tests, the Unity Test Framework (UTF) provided by the tool used to develop the Unity application was used, so the integration and use occurs naturally and quickly [13]. The main module for which the system was tested was AR. Therefore, test scripts were used. Through these, the deployment of Vuforia's AR camera was tested. Even the test framework creates an isolated environment in which to carry out tests both at run time and editing and generates an acceptance result or not.

Second, the product tests were aimed at making sure of the correct functioning of the application. Here, the functional tests allowed to validate the existence of the functional requirements in the system and that they effectively complied with the proposal. In this case the tests were carried out manually. In contrast, non-functional testing verifies requirements based on software quality attributes such as performance, portability, and usability. Performance testing is necessary to identify bottlenecks that may arise with respect to CPU usage, memory, or other factors, leading to high response times and excessive device resource usage. The Unity development platform provides within its tools the Unity Profiler. Profiler collects and displays data about application performance in terms of CPU, memory, and renderability; identifying the relationship of its high or low performance with the source code, scenes, and configurations of the application [14]. In addition, it allows access to Android and iOS. For this reason this tool was used to carry out the profiling of the application in the operating systems used. Vuforia defines a set of frames per second objectives for the correct functioning of the applications according to the devices and operating systems. Based on this, if the experience has a duration of more than ten minutes, the target number of frames would be 30 Frames per Second (FPS) for both Android and iOS. According to Fig. 5 the number of frames per second is between 30 and 60 FPS, which demonstrates an expected operation based on what Vuforia proposed. In addition, when executing tasks with greater processing such as facial and body animation of avatars, the system demonstrated through the Unity Profiler to respond (communication with the CPU, not with the end user) in an average time not exceeding 30 ms. While in low processing tasks such as entering the selection menu, average response times of 17 ms were achieved. We concluded that, with respect to what Vuforia proposed, the characteristics found in this profiling follow the documented and expected standards for this type of application.

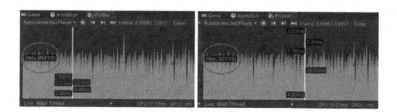

Fig. 5. Unity profiler in VIA. Lower limit in ms (left). Upper limit in ms (right)

Third, we performed user tests. We used the Think Aloud method to evaluate the first impression and the usability of the interface. We used informal summative evaluation for assessing user experience. With this approach [18], we were able to evaluate a smaller number of user participants and to present summary descriptive statistics. Considering that it was taken remotely and with only five people due to the COVID-19 pandemics; it was done using the WhatsApp messaging application as follows: (1) The participant was given a brief contextualisation of the project and the objective of the evaluation. (2) The link to the simulation of the prototype designed with Figma was shared. (3) After the users used the application, they sent the assessments regarding the interface and usability of the prototype openly, through text messages or voice notes. (4) All responses were gathered and analyzsd to finally highlight the specific elements that need to be modified.

After carrying out the evaluation to five people, their assessments were collected and analysed to specify what were those comments in common and make an improvement. We found that: (1) Three of the five people suggested that the interaction with the avatars should be enriched, since this was the element that most caught their attention. (2) Four of the five people considered that the interface contained many colours and elements that made it look saturated. (3) Three of the five people mentioned that they would like to be able to know about other users' experiences using the app.

While opinions on this method tend to be subjective and qualitative, they allowed the team to identify changes and improvements. The way of communication between users and the VIA was modified, allowing them to start a conversation with the avatar, going beyond the automatic reproduction of audio that was initially proposed. Taking into account the saturation at the interface level identified in the evaluation, we made adjustments based on the Nielsen heuristics. Here, the aesthetic characteristics of colour and proportion were adjusted to the application's screens so that they did not generate discomfort to the end user. Continuing with the findings, we proposed to add the options to submit comments to the application. Although the option of providing a review, complaint or claim through the help module had already been raised, the comments would allow to satisfy the exposed need to recognise the experiences of other users. It is worth clarifying that the system does not contain user creation or login, since the idea is to access easily and quickly the place the user (visitor) wants to know. The comments are made anonymously, and the visitor has the possibility of adding a reaction and the text of the comment, and so, be able to know the experiences of others to add value to the application.

Considering that the objective of the application is to provide tourists and foreigners with an experience of learning places, specifically those chosen within the San Antonio neighbourhood, this evaluation was carried out to account for the effectiveness of the VIA in terms of satisfaction and usability for end users. We carried out a usability test, which consisted of three main elements: Tasks, Facilitator, and Participant. This type of test allowed us to observe and analyse the user's behaviour in front of the learning process with the system and how it is positively or negatively affected through the user's facial and verbal expressions. This is intended to demonstrate the level of commitment that the user obtains in the time of initiation, transition, and progress [15]. Initiation behaviours are given by the first impression of the user, either observing others using it or when there is minimal interaction. Transition behaviours occur when the users finish performing some tasks and show their positive reaction to their experience and comfort with the response of the system. Progress behaviours are those that recognise a deep understanding of the system and possible future use. They are all part of a progressive set of reactions that contribute to demonstrating the acceptance of the application. Data collection was carried out in a joint test with visitors from the San Antonio neighbourhood, in the places of the Church of San Antonio and La Linterna. The evaluation took place in two moments, during the use of the application and after the use of the application. In this way, it was possible to evaluate the visitor's behaviour during the use of the application and subsequently their general appreciation of the system. We performed observation processes and questionnaires (Tables 3 and 4), to quantitatively measure the results of the test. During the use of the application, the facilitator oversaw guiding the users through the previously established tasks (Table 1). These tasks were read aloud to the participants as they progressed one by one, while each task was performed. The facilitator carried out an observation process following the plan established in Table 3, to convert the facial and verbal expressions evidenced by the user's behaviour into indicators (Table 2). On some occasions, the facilitator turned to the Think Aloud method to confirm interpretations of user behaviours. After the use of the software, we asked users to fill in a questionnaire (Table 4).

Based on the answers obtained in the questionnaire, we analysed the results obtained. As mentioned above, to carry out the evaluation, a usability test was used, in which the tasks allow to give a natural and orderly flow to the use of the application, in addition to covering at a general level all the functionalities and possible paths that it may have to obtain a complete analysis of the behaviour and acceptance by the end users. We proposed six tasks to be performed in the locations available in the VIA (Table 1). These tasks allowed to articulate the test objectively and precisely to be performed under realistic conditions of use. To perform the analysis of the results obtained in the test, we used an informal summative evaluation as exposed in Navarro-Newball et al. [16]. With this, it was possible to focus the measurement of the objectives based on indicators that show the acceptance and enjoyment by users when interacting with the application. To select these indicators the tests were made on real scenarios similar to Mekler et al. [17] and Navarro-Newball et al. [16], in addition to recommendations evidenced in [18]. An observation plan [16] was established to relate the indicators to the actions performed by the users while performing the tasks. These actions in turn were classified based on the different behavioural times evidenced by the test participants. Along with the strategy of the observation plan, a questionnaire was carried out adopting the recommendations of other questionnaire models, in this case the USE (usability, satisfaction and ease of use) [18]. To measure the results quantitatively by means of descriptive statistics, the questionnaire was evaluated on a differential semantic scale of 1 (little agreement) to 5 (completely agree).

To carry out the evaluation in the different places, we went to the San Antonio neighbourhood to have a scenario under real conditions. During application's usage, participants could ask the VIA several questions. The project was trained with questions related to the three places and with questions out of context or of a general nature through a Microsoft owned database. The "chit-chat" small talk datasets are available for five pre-built personalities in nine languages [19]. Among the questions the user could ask VIA about the three places were: tell me about this place; what do you know about this place? and; what is this place? Accuracy of avata's understanding of the questions seemed to be high and participants did not get any unanswered question, although further experiments could be done regarding this. Table 5 shows recorded scores of the semantic scale collected with the five participants, both in the observation plan (Table 3) made during the execution of tasks, and in the questionnaire (Table 4) resolved at the end of the test. Therefore, the values obtained were added and divided on the maximum score that could be achieved, considering the indicators that related to each task and question. In this way, we were able to show that the satisfaction (95%) and immersion (92%) was high. Users also provided positive feedback regarding the implementation of the application in the neighbourhood, highlighting how fun and useful it can be in the area, some mentioning that they did not know about La Colina and La Linterna. Linked to this is the fact that users intend to use the application in the future (88%), showing the viability of VIA. However, it would be worthwhile to continue working on the interface design to improve the ease of learning, since, although there were no drawbacks, as observed the indicator (86%) can be improved. This could be done through more test cycles.

Table 1. The tasks for the evaluation tests.

Task	Objective	Location
1. Enter to (San Antonio shurch/La Linterna)	Enter the place	Both
2. When was the San Antonio church built?	Obtain information about the church	Church
3. ¿Qué se realiza en la Imprenta La Linterna?	Obtain information about La Linterna	La Linterna
4. Watch the VIA dancing	Animate the VIA	Both
5. Where is (the church/La Colina) located?	Find address	Both
6. Send a comment about (the church/La Colina)	Send comment	Both
7. Change the VIA's language to English	Change the application's language	Both

Table 2. Usability and satisfaction indicators.

Indicator	Description
A. Satisfaction	I would recommend the app to someone else
	The app works the way the user wants it to work. It's fun to use
B. Better mood after using the app	The user feels satisfied and happy. Provides positive opinions
C. Easy to use	It's simple to use. The user uses the application intuitively.
D. Intention for future use	The user would use the app again
E. Frustration	The user was frustrated by not being able to use the application correctly
F. Immersion	The user concentrates on the application, learns to use it quickly

Table 3. Observation plan.

Action	Behaviour	Indicator
Performs the task	Initiation	C
Repeats task	Transition	D
Shows positive emotions	Transition	A
Recommends the application	Transition	A
Shows negative emotions	Transition	E
Quickly identify next steps	Progress	C
Engages with the app	Progress	F
Better mood after using the app	Progress	B

Table 4. Questionnaire for evaluation.

Question	Indicator
Did you enjoy the activity?	A
Did you enjoy the talk with the VIA?	F
Will you use the app again?	D
Would you recommend the app to a friend?	A
Do you think you could use the app without any instructions?	C
Do you think the app is easy to use?	C
Do you consider that the graphical Interface of the application is clear and adequate?	Usability

Table 5. Results of recorded scores from the observation plan during the tasks and the questionnaire.

Indicator	Observation plan	Questionnaire	Total	Maximum score	Result (%)
A	47	24	71	75	95
B	22	n/a	22	25	88
C	43	43	86	100	86
D	23	21	44	50	88
E	0	n/a	0	25	0
F	24	22	46	50	92
Usability	N/A	24	24	25	96

6 Conclusions and Further Work

Once the testing stage was finished we had evidence that the VIA application met the objectives. The presentation, animation, and voice of the three avatars proposed for the VIA application were well received (Table 5). To achieve this, we developed a VIA application that integrates technologies such as AR and NLP. Through these technologies, it was possible to communicate consciously and naturally about the three places chosen as the basis of the research in the San Antonio neighbourhood in Cali, Colombia, which promotes smart tourism based on new interaction technologies. Likewise, by approaching the research from the perspective of the end users, the implementation of three languages (Spanish, English, French) allowed the prototype to be used by both locals and foreigners. This validated the use of the VIA as a smart tourism and cultural computing application. In addition, the team in charge made use of environmental recognition technologies blending hardware and software, with which the facades of places such as the Church of San Antonio and the Dome of San Antonio (Open air theatre at the church) were recreated virtually. This, in order to improve the user experience when deploying the avatars in AR, doing so with a recognition of the existing real infrastructure. On the other hand, the graphical interface defined for the VIA was implemented under the suggestion of the Nielsen usability heuristics, generating an aesthetic and user-friendly interface. Finally, thanks to the combination of different techniques and technologies, it was possible to reach a functional application accepted by an archetype of end users.

Considering the activities carried out within this project and the entire development research process that emerged, it is considered important as future work to continue with the growth of the VIA, improving and adding functionalities that positively benefit the tourist and commercial development of the city of Santiago de Cali. Undoubtedly, the city has places that are worth adding within the proposed approach, both within the Barrio San Antonio and outside it (e.g.: Cristo Rey, Gato Tejada, La Tertulia museum). Therefore, it is considered interesting to continue with the research process by the hand of local entities that seek to highlight the history and heritage of the city, also providing necessary information to enrich the knowledge databases. In the same way, it is important to follow an exhaustive evaluation process with end users, to identify enhancements that can be added to VIA to captivate the attention of the public and improve the user experience. In addition to this, functionalities would be integrated, directly related to suggestions of commercial establishments, with the aim of providing visibility to small and large entrepreneurs in the region who also allow them to create a business model for the scalability and maintenance of the same application. Finally, it will be important to consider privacy issues and contemplate the possibility to expand the application to Windows and/or the Web. Finally, this sort of VIA becomes very relevant in current pandemics and post pandemics scenario. The VIA may be able to provide more autonomy to visitors, helping to avoid crowds of tourist flocking near a human guide, thus, contributing to smart tourism. Additionally, technologies such as VIA favour complementing, reintrepreting and reunderstanding history in a friendly manner, without the need of destroying the heritage sites. This becomes relevant in an era when many monuments that could be augmented in the virtual space worldwide, are being destroyed and vandalised, as it has recently happened with the Cali's foundation monument.

References

1. Boboc, R.G., Gîrbacia, F., Duguleană, M., Tavčar, A.: A handheld Augmented Reality to revive a demolished Reformed Church from Braşov. In: Proceedings of the Virtual Reality International Conference - Laval Virtual 2017 (VRIC 2017), Article 18, pp. 1–4, (2017). https://doi.org/10.1145/3110292.3110311
2. Wei, C., Chen, F., Chen, C., Lin, Y.: virtual and augmented reality to historical site reconstruction: a pilot study of East Taiwan old railway station. In: Proceedings of the 2018 International Conference on Artificial Intelligence and Virtual Reality, pp. 42–46 (2018). https://doi.org/10.1145/3293663.3293675
3. Perea-Tanaka, C.F., Moreno, I., Prakash, E.C., Navarro-Newball, A.A.: Towards tantalluc: interactive mobile augmented reality application for the Museo de América in Madrid. In: 10th Computing Colombian Conference, pp. 164–171 (2015). https://doi.org/10.1109/ColumbianCC.2015.7333427
4. Sauter, L., Rossetto, L., Schuldt, H.: Exploring cultural heritage in augmented reality with GoFind! In: IEEE International Conference on Artificial Intelligence and Virtual Reality, pp. 187–188 (2018). https://doi.org/10.1109/AIVR.2018.00041
5. Alulema, D., Simbaña, B., Vega, C., Morocho, D., Ibarra, A., Alulema, V.: Design of an augmented reality-based application for Quito's historic center. In: IEEE Biennial Congress of Argentina, pp. 1–5 (2018). https://doi.org/10.1109/ARGENCON.2018.8646296
6. Wei, X., Weng, D., Liu, Y., Wang, Y.: A tour guiding system of historical relics based on augmented reality. In: IEEE Virtual Reality, pp. 307–308 (2016). https://doi.org/10.1109/VR.2016.7504776
7. Cavallo, M., Rhodes, G.A., Forbes, A.G.: Riverwalk: incorporating historical photographs in public outdoor augmented reality experiences. In: IEEE International Symposium on Mixed and Augmented Reality, pp. 160–165 (2016). https://doi.org/10.1109/ISMAR-Adjunct.2016.0068

8. Escobar, S.D., Margherita, E.G.: Outcomes of smart tourism applications on-site for a sustainable tourism: evidence from empirical studies. In: Musleh Al-Sartawi, A.M.A. (ed.) The Big Data-Driven Digital Economy: Artificial and Computational Intelligence. SCI, vol. 974, pp. 271–283. Springer, Cham (2021). https://doi.org/10.1007/978-3-030-73057-4_21

9. Nielsen, J., Molich, R.: Heuristic evaluation of user interfaces. In: Proceedings of the ACM CHI 1990 Conference, Seattle, WA, 1–5 April, pp. 249–256 (1990)

10. Vuforia Fusion. https://library.vuforia.com/environments/vuforia-fusion

11. Crazy Minnow Studio: CMS. SALSA LipSync v2 suite. SALSA LipSync Suite - Online Documentation. https://crazyminnowstudio.com/docs/salsa-lip-sync/

12. j1mmyto9: Speech-And-Text-Unity-iOS-Android. GitHub. https://github.com/j1mmyto9/Speech-And-Text-Unity-iOS-Android

13. Unity Technologies: Unit testing. https://docs.unity3d.com/Manual/testing-editortestsrunner.html

14. Unity Technologies: Profiler overview. https://docs.unity3d.com/es/2021.1/Manual/Profiler.html

15. Barriault, C., Pearson, D.: Assessing exhibits for learning in science centers: a practical tool. Visit. Stud. 13(1), 90–106 (2010). https://doi.org/10.1080/10645571003618824

16. Navarro-Newball, A.A., et al.: Talking to Teo: video game supported speech therapy. Entertain. Comput. 5(4), 401–412 (2014). https://doi.org/10.1016/j.entcom.2014.10.005

17. Mekler, E.D., Bopp, J.A., Tuch, A.N., Opwis, K.: A systematic review of quantitative studies on the enjoyment of digital entertainment games. In: Proceedings of the SIGCHI Conference on Human Factors in Computing Systems, pp. 927–936 (2014). https://doi.org/10.1145/2556288.2557078

18. Hartson, R., Pyla, P.: The UX Book. Agile UX Design for a Quality User Experience. Morgan Kaufmann, Amsterdam (2019)

19. Microsoft: Personality Chat Datasets. https://github.com/microsoft/botframework-cli/blob/main/packages/qnamaker/docs/chit-chat-dataset.md

Photovoltaic Cells Defects Classification by Means of Artificial Intelligence and Electroluminescence Images

Héctor Felipe Mateo-Romero[1] , Álvaro Pérez-Romero[2] ,
Luis Hernández-Callejo[1(✉)] , Sara Gallardo-Saavedra[1] ,
Víctor Alonso-Gómez[1] , José Ignacio Morales-Aragonés[1] ,
Alberto Redondo Plaza[1] , and Diego Fernández Martínez[1]

[1] Universidad de Valladolid, Campus Universitario Duques de Soria, 42004 Soria, Spain
{luis.hernandez.callejo,sara.gallardo,
victor.alonso.gomez}@uva.es, ziguratt@coit.es
[2] Universidad de Cantabria, Av. de los Castros, s/n, 39005 Santander, Spain

Abstract. More than half of the total renewable addictions correspond to solar photovoltaic (PV) energy. In a context with such an important impact of this resource, being able to produce reliable and safety energy is extremely important and operation and maintenance (O&M) of PV sites must be increasingly intelligent and advanced. The use of Artificial Intelligence (AI) for the defects identification, location and classification is very interesting, as PV plants are increasing in size and quantity. Inspection techniques in PV systems are diverse, and within them, electroluminescence (EL) inspection and current-voltage (I-V) curves are one of the most important. In this sense, this work presents a classifier of defects at the PV cell level, based on AI, EL images and cell I-V curves. To achieve this, it has been necessary to develop an instrument to measure the I-V curve at the cell level, used to label each of the PV cells. In order to determine the classification of cell defects, CNNs will be used. Results obtained have been satisfactory, and improvement is expected from a greater number of samples taken.

Keywords: Photovoltaic cell defect · Classifier · Artificial Intelligence · Electroluminescence

1 Introduction

During the last years, global installation of renewable generation installations has significantly increased. In 2019, the last analyzed year in the Global Status Report [1], 201 GW of renewable power capacity were installed in the World, being 115 GW of Solar Photovoltaic (PV) capacity, which corresponds with more than 57% of the total renewable addictions.

In this context in which solar PV energy has such an important impact, being able to produce reliable and safety energy is extremely important. Ensuring energy production is a key factor in warranting plant profitability, and this has forced the design of increasingly

© Springer Nature Switzerland AG 2022
S. Nesmachnow and L. Hernández Callejo (Eds.): ICSC-Cities 2021, CCIS 1555, pp. 31–41, 2022.
https://doi.org/10.1007/978-3-030-96753-6_3

intelligent and advanced Operation and Maintenance (O&M) strategies. Traditionally, different inspection techniques have been used in PV sites with the objective of detecting anomalies that reduce the system efficiency and can generate safety issues, as Infrared thermography inspections (IRT) [2], electroluminescence (EL) [3–5] or current-voltage (I-V) curves capturing [5, 6]. The development of new equipment and methodologies for its application in PV plants are necessary, and in this sense, research and industry are evolving rapidly [7]. The increased plant size has promoted the use of drones for the image capturing [8, 9], however the amount of data to process is unapproachable, requiring important human efforts and being very expensive and time-consuming.

The use of Artificial Intelligence (AI) for the defects identification, location and classification is very interesting. AI is already being applied in PV solar plants. However, its main application has being long focused on energy production forecasting issues. Authors in [10] develop a solution that provides the electricity production based on historical and current available solar radiation data in real-time. Some authors present a taxonomy study, which is a process to divide and classify the different forecasting methods, and the authors also present the trends in AI applied to generation forecasting in solar PV plants [11]. The use of artificial neural networks (ANN) has been successful in the last decade, some authors use ANN together with climatic variables to forecast generation in PV solar plants [12], while others use Support Vector Machine (SVM) together with an optimization of the internal parameters of the model [13]. ANN have also been used for other tasks, such as for the detection of problems in energy production, as is the case of work [14], where the authors use radial basis function (RBF) to detect this type of failure in production. A similar goal is sought in [15], where this time an SVM-based model is employed for describing a failure diagnosis method that uses a linear relation between the solar radiation and the power generation graphs. This research studies the following failure types: inverter failures, communication errors, sensor failures, junction box errors and junction box fire. The model classifies string and inverter failures. However, in actual PV plants each inverter can cover thousands of modules, and therefore important failures information can be lost in the classification [16].

In general, the application of AI technologies based on data-driven mechanisms helps to construct automatic fault classifiers and improves the efficiency and accuracy of faulty diagnoses [17]. A convolutional network, based on the analysis of the difference in the I-V curves of PV arrays under different failure states, capable of identifying not only a single failure (e.g., short circuit, partial shading, and abnormal aging) but also hybrid failures [17]. Authors in [18], authors investigate the effect of data augmentation techniques to increase the performance of our proposed convolutional neural network (CNNs) to classify anomalies between up to eleven different classes, in PV modules through thermographic images in an unbalanced dataset. This work is performed at the PV module level.

This work presents a classifier of defects at the PV cell level, based on AI, EL images and cell I-V curves. To achieve this, it has been necessary to make an instrument to measure the I-V curve at the cell level, used to label each of the PV cells. In order to determine the classification of cell defects, CNNs will be used. The document is structured as follows: Sect. 2 presents the materials and methodology used, Sect. 3 shows the results and discussion and Sect. 4 deals the conclusions and future work.

2   Materials and Methodology

This section is intended to explain the materials used, as well as the followed methodology to validate the classifier.

2.1   Materials

For this work, it has been necessary to develop special equipment and material. Firstly, regarding the PV devices, individual PV cells have been used. In this case, researchers have made the necessary welds to connect the required equipment, as it can be seen in Fig. 1. One hundred PV cells have been used, which have subsequently been reused with artificial shadows, to have a greater number of measurements. Table 1 shows the basic electrical information of the PV cells used.

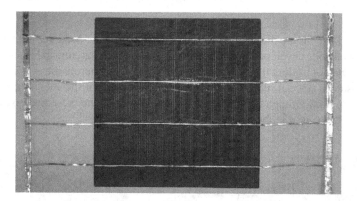

Fig. 1. PV cell sample with welds already made.

Table 1. Information of PV cells.

PV cell parameter	PV cell parameter value
I_{SC} (A)	7.5
V_{OC} (V)	0.6
P_{MP} (W)	4.67

Once the PV cells were prepared as detailed before, it is necessary to obtain their individual I-V curves. To do this, it has been required to excite the PV cells, for which a LED board composed of 42 LEDs has been used with the following characteristics: OSRAM brand, 850 nm, 1 A forward current, 630 mW of radiant flux at 1 A and 100 microseconds, with a maximum temperature of 145 °C. Figure 2 shows an image of the LED board. It has a diffuser screen to be able to homogenize the flow of light.

Fig. 2. LED plate with diffuser mounted on support to take measurements.

Once the PV cells are illuminated with the LED board, the I-V curves are taken from an ingenious device developed by the authors, based on the charging and discharging of capacitors, and controlling the sweep by means of a simple microprocessor. This device is very versatile, since it allows to make the I-V curve from the second quadrant to the fourth quadrant through the first quadrant. However, for the presented research, the interest is only focused in the first quadrant (Fig. 3).

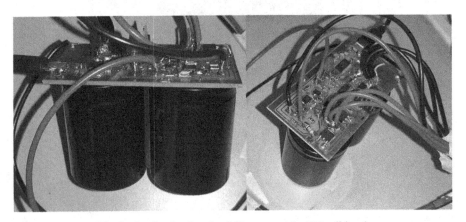

Fig. 3. Device for drawing I-V curves at the PV cell level.

On the other hand, to be able to do EL, it is necessary to connect the PV cell to an external power source and to obtain the corresponding image. In this case, it is no needed to illuminate the PV cell (by means of an LED board). To be able to make the capture, a special camera is necessary, specifically, it has been used an InGaAs camera, Hamamatsu brand and C12741-11 model (Fig. 4).

Fig. 4. InGaAs camera, Hamamatsu brand and C12741–11 model, for EL imaging.

Figure 5a) shows a PV cell exposed to artificial irradiance to obtain its I-V curve, and Fig. 5b) shows the same PV cell subjected to inverse voltage to obtain its EL image.

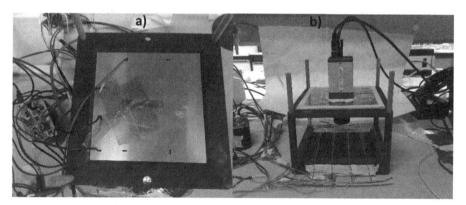

Fig. 5. a) Obtaining I-V curve of PV cell; b) Obtaining EL image of PV cell.

2.2 Methodology

As already mentioned, the data was obtained manually, since the I-V curve of each of the cells of the data set was required, as well as their EL images. Therefore, none of the datasets that were in free repositories could be used. To carry out the EL images, an EL camera has been used, using different shades and irradiances to increase the amount of data available in the final set. To obtain the I-V curve, the device built by the research team and previously presented has been used.

All images have had histogram adjustment done, making details and differences easier to see for the human eye, as well as for AI models. In order to be able to use the data of the I-V curve, the power values have been computed. Of all the values, only the highest value of each of the measurements will be taken into account. The power values will depend on the irradiance at which the measurement has been made, therefore, all measurements taken at the same irradiance will be processed. For this, the 5 highest power values will be chosen and the average will be made. In this way, authors will obtain a value that will represent the maximum power of a cell in good state. By choosing only the highest powers, the false information that the defective or shaded cells would provide will be ignored.

In order to have a greater number of samples, each of the measured cells has been subjected to partial shading, in order to repeat the measurements.

With the measurement of the absolute maximum power, authors will compute the relative power, calculating the proportion between the maximum power of each of the panels and the calculated power. This will give a continuous variable that will need to be divided into intervals if the problem is posed as a classification. The intervals should be decided in such a way that they allow the training to be carried out correctly and also the classes have a meaning in the context, that they are useful.

In Fig. 6 it can be seen the histogram of the random variable and of the chosen classes. Class 0: PV cells in good condition (relative power $> = 0.825$); Class 1: PV cells in questionable condition (relative power < 0.825 and $> = 0.725$); Class 2: PV cells in poor condition (relative power < 0.725).

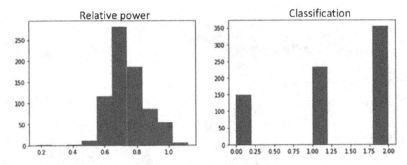

Fig. 6. Relative power and classification of PV cells once the I-V curves have been made.

Once the information is available (I-V curves and EL images), it is necessary to use AI-based models to be able to train this models and to make the classifier. To resolve the classifier issue, it was decided to use an ANN-based architecture, specifically a CNNs, since it is a network that works very well with images. This is evident in the scientific literature. Figure 7 shows the architecture used and the relevant hyper-parameters.

The structure was chosen following a systematic procedure of trial and error. Different configurations were tried until the best results were found, a deeper network only resulted on over-fitting and shallow networks performed worse.

The hyperparameters were optimized following a similar approach. Different learning rates (0.05, 0.005, 0.0005, 0.00005, 0.000005) were compared. The one which the best performance was found to be 0.00005. This same principle was followed when

	Hyper parameters	Value
CONV 64		
MAX POOL	Learning rate	0.00005
CONV 128	Epochs	200
CONV 128	Batch size	16
MAX POOL	Trigger function	ReLU
CONV 256	Output function	softmax
CONV 256	Dropout	Si
MAX POOL	Optimizer	Adam
DENSE 256	Función loss	Sparse categorical crossentropy
DROPOUT 0.6		
DENSE SOFTMAX	Metrics	accuracy

Fig. 7. Optimized architecture and hyper-parameters.

setting the activation function: Relu was compared with Elu, Selu and Leaky Relu. The optimizer was chosen after comparing Adam with Nadam.

Other important feature of the system was the use of Data-Augmentation. An online data generation was used in the network training in other to improve its performance. The images went through limited rotations of less than 5° and vertical or horizontal flips. The reason is that more intrusive modifications would not be real. Cells with big distortions would have a different IV curve. In each epoch new instances were generated choosing a new angle and flip.

Figure 8 shows the evolution of the accuracy and loss during the training and validation phases. In the accuracy graph, it can be seen how there is no difference between the train and validation sets, which implies that the network hardly experiences over fit. In the loss graph, an increase in over fit is observed from iteration 100, but at no point does it become considerable. The final network chosen will be that of iteration 195, which has a 90% in the validation set and a 0.5 in loss.

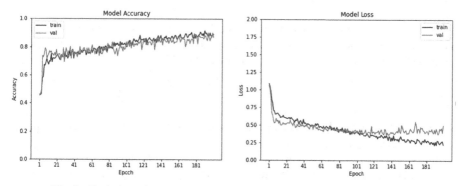

Fig. 8. Evolution of accuracy and loss, for the training and validation phases.

3 Results and Discussion

3.1 EL Imaging and I-V Curves

Figure 9 shows some EL images measured for this work. The images in the figure show the same PV cell, but with a different shade. The figure at the top left shows a PV cell without a shadow, but with a failure defect in the middle of it. The rest EL images, show the same PV cell with different added artificial shadows.

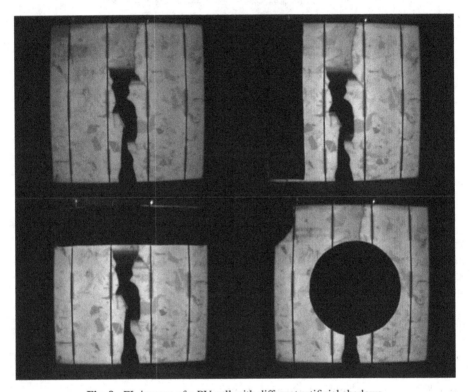

Fig. 9. EL images of a PV cell with different artificial shadows.

Figure 10 shows the measurements of the I-V curves of a specific PV cell. The different curves represent the I-V curve at different irradiances levels and/or with artificial shadows. The figure also shows the P-V curves of the PV cell.

3.2 CNNs

With the available data, the CNNs has been trained and its results have been obtained, after the validation phase.

In Fig. 11, it can be seen how the behavior in the non-training data set is similar to the validation one, reaching 87% precision, a very high behavior and very similar to

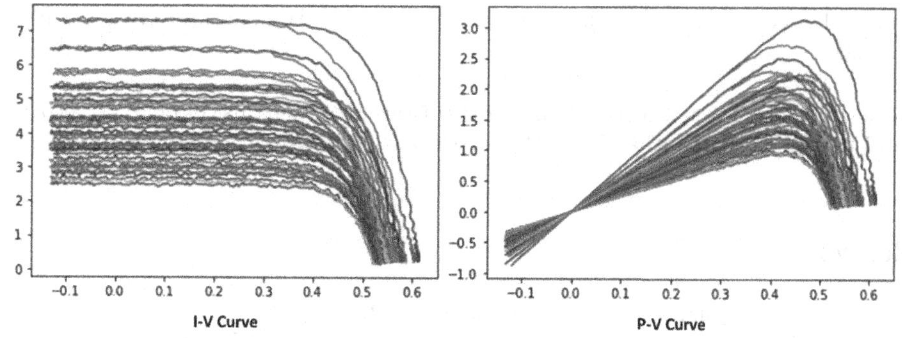

Fig. 10. I-V curves of a specific PV cell and P-V curves.

that obtained in the validation during the training phase. It can be seen how the CNNs perfectly distinguishes classes 0 and 2, with only one instance in which an error occurs, which indicates that the model differentiates PV cells in good condition from PV cells in poor condition. For class 1, its behavior can be improved, since it has more difficulties to classify this class well, although it still gives good results. The inclusion of data augmentation improved the performance of the model.

Validation set

Confusion matrix

```
[[20  0  0]
 [ 1 24  4]
 [ 0  4 38]]
```

Classification report

	precision	recall	f1-score	support
0	0.95	1.00	0.98	20
1	0.86	0.83	0.84	29
2	0.90	0.90	0.90	42
accuracy			0.90	91
macro avg	0.90	0.91	0.91	91
weighted avg	0.90	0.90	0.90	91

Final set

Confusion matrix

```
[[18  1  0]
 [ 1 26  1]
 [ 1  7 31]]
```

Classification report

	precision	recall	f1-score	support
0	0.90	0.95	0.92	19
1	0.76	0.93	0.84	28
2	0.97	0.79	0.87	39
accuracy			0.87	86
macro avg	0.88	0.89	0.88	86
weighted avg	0.89	0.87	0.87	86

Fig. 11. Results of the CNNs.

4 Conclusions and Future Work

The work has presented a classifier of defects in PV cells, based on AI and from EL images. For the perfect classification, it was necessary to use the I-V curve of each of the PV cells. For this, it has been necessary to make an instrument to measure the I-V curve at the cell level, which has served to label each of the PV cells. A CNNs has been used, and the results obtained have been satisfactory, and improvement is expected from a greater number of samples taken.

The researchers will expand the data set manually and using techniques to generate synthetic data as Generative Adversative Neural Networks (GANN), and will try another type of PV cell. In addition, the intention is to classify the defects of complete PV modules.

Acknowledgments. The authors thank the CYTED Thematic Network "INTELLIGENT CITIES FULLY INTEGRAL, EFFICIENT AND SUSTAINABLE (CITIES)" n° 518RT0558.

References

1. REN21 Secretariat: Renewables 2020 Global Status Report (2020)
2. Jordan, D.C., Silverman, T.J., Wohlgemuth, J.H., Kurtz, S.R., VanSant, K.T.: Photovoltaic failure and degradation modes. Prog. Photovolt. Res. Appl. **25**, 318–326 (2017). https://doi.org/10.1002/pip.2866
3. Kendig, D., Alers, G.B., Shakouri, A.: Characterization of defects in photovoltaics using thermoreflectance and electroluminescence imaging. In: Conference Record of the IEEE Photovoltaic Specialists Conference, pp. 1733–1736 (2010). https://doi.org/10.1109/PVSC.2010.5616126
4. Fuyuki, T., Kitiyanan, A.: Photographic diagnosis of crystalline silicon solar cells utilizing electroluminescence. Appl. Phys. Mater. Sci. Process. **96**, 189–196 (2009). https://doi.org/10.1007/s00339-008-4986-0
5. Gallardo-Saavedra, S., et al.: Nondestructive characterization of solar PV cells defects by means of electroluminescence, infrared thermography, I-V curves and visual tests: experimental study and comparison. Energy **205**, 1–13 (2020). https://doi.org/10.1016/j.energy.2020.117930
6. Blakesley, J.C., Castro, F.A., Koutsourakis, G., Laudani, A., Lozito, G.M., Riganti, F.: Towards non-destructive individual cell I-V characteristic curve extraction from photovoltaic module measurements. Sol. Energy. **202**, 342–357 (2020). https://doi.org/10.1016/j.solener.2020.03.082
7. Hernández-Callejo, L., Gallardo-Saavedra, S., Alonso-Gómez, V.: A review of photovoltaic systems: design, operation and maintenance. Sol. Energy. **188**, 426–440 (2019). https://doi.org/10.1016/j.solener.2019.06.017
8. Gallardo-Saavedra, S., Hernández-Callejo, L., Duque-Perez, O.: Technological review of the instrumentation used in aerial thermographic inspection of photovoltaic plants. Renew. Sustain. Energy Rev. **93**, 566–579 (2018). https://doi.org/10.1016/j.rser.2018.05.027
9. Gallardo-Saavedra, S., Hernandez-Callejo, L., Duque-Perez, O.: Image resolution influence in aerial thermographic inspections of photovoltaic plants. IEEE Trans. Ind. Inf. **14**, 5678–5686 (2018). https://doi.org/10.1109/TII.2018.2865403
10. Gligor, A., Dumitru, C.D., Grif, H.S.: Artificial intelligence solution for managing a photovoltaic energy production unit. Procedia Manuf. **22**, 626–633 (2018). https://doi.org/10.1016/j.promfg.2018.03.091
11. Wang, H., et al.: Taxonomy research of artificial intelligence for deterministic solar power forecasting. Energy Convers. Manag. **214**, 112909 (2020). https://doi.org/10.1016/j.enconman.2020.112909
12. Kayri, I., Gencoglu, M.T.: Predicting power production from a photovoltaic panel through artificial neural networks using atmospheric indicators. Neural Comput. Appl. **31**(8), 3573–3586 (2017). https://doi.org/10.1007/s00521-017-3271-6
13. Li, L.-L., Wen, S.-Y., Tseng, M.-L., Chiu, A.S.F.: Photovoltaic array prediction on short-term output power method in centralized power generation system. Ann. Oper. Res. **290**(1–2), 243–263 (2018). https://doi.org/10.1007/s10479-018-2879-y

14. Hussain, M., Dhimish, M., Titarenko, S., Mather, P.: Artificial neural network based photovoltaic fault detection algorithm integrating two bi-directional input parameters. Renew. Energy. **155**, 1272–1292 (2020). https://doi.org/10.1016/j.renene.2020.04.023
15. Cho, K.-H., Jo, H.-C., Kim, E.-S., Park, H.-A., Park, J.H.: Failure diagnosis method of photovoltaic generator using support vector machine. J. Electr. Eng. Technol. 1–12 (2020). https://doi.org/10.1007/s42835-020-00430-9
16. Pérez-Romero, Á., Mateo-Romero, H.F., Gallardo-Saavedra, S., Alonso-Gómez, V., del Alonso-García, M.C., Hernández-Callejo, L.: Evaluation of artificial intelligence-based models for classifying defective photovoltaic cells. Appl. Sci. **11**, 4226 (2021). https://doi.org/10.3390/app11094226
17. Gao, W., Wai, R.J.: A novel fault identification method for photovoltaic array via convolutional neural network and residual gated recurrent unit. IEEE Access. **8**, 159493–159510 (2020). https://doi.org/10.1109/ACCESS.2020.3020296
18. Fonseca Alves, R.H., de Deus Júnior, G.A., Marra, E.G., Lemos, R.P.: Automatic fault classification in photovoltaic modules using convolutional neural networks. Renew. Energy **179**, 502–516 (2021). https://doi.org/10.1016/j.renene.2021.07.070

Exact Approach for Electric Vehicle Charging Infrastructure Location: A Real Case Study in Málaga, Spain

Claudio Risso[1] , Christian Cintrano[2(✉)] , Jamal Toutouh[2] ,
and Sergio Nesmachnow[1]

[1] Universidad de la República, Montevideo, Uruguay
{crisso,sergion}@fing.edu.uy
[2] University of Málaga, Málaga, Spain
{cintrano,jamal}@lcc.uma.es

Abstract. This article presents an exact approach for solving the problem of locating electric vehicle charging stations in a city, whose goal is upon minimizing the distance citizens must span to charge their vehicles. Mixed integer programming formulations are presented for two variants of the problem: relaxed (i.e., without considering electrical constraints for the infrastructure) and full versions. The experimental evaluation is performed over a real-world case study defined in Málaga, Spain. Results show that the proposed approach can deal with the large number of variables (i.e., millions) of the problem, computing optimal solutions for all problem instances and variants addressed. The improvements in solutions quality over a previous metaheuristic approach applied to the same problem and application case are notorious.

Keywords: Electric vehicles · Infrastructure location · Sustainable mobility · Smart cities · Combinatorial optimization

1 Introduction

Sustainability has become a priority goal for society. Agreements and conventions, such as the Sustainable Development Goals, are shifting societies towards green-conscious ones. An important change is being experienced in road mobility because vehicles are shifting from inefficient combustion engines to more sustainable ones (i.e., hybrid or electric engines). Cars, scooters, and electric motorcycles are novel ways preferred by newer generations to move along the cities. Thus, electric vehicles (EV) have a great boom and socioeconomic impact [11].

Electric cars allow citizens to reduce gas emissions, if the electricity used to charge the cars is obtained from green sources. The number of kilometers that an electric car can drive without stopping is a decisive factor when deciding to opt for an electric car. Maximum kilometers would not be such a pressing problem if there were a good network of charging stations. Cities have not yet adapted to this new trend in transportation. Even though there are many plans to deploy networks of charging points for electric vehicles in the main cities of the world [9].

© Springer Nature Switzerland AG 2022
S. Nesmachnow and L. Hernández Callejo (Eds.): ICSC-Cities 2021, CCIS 1555, pp. 42–57, 2022.
https://doi.org/10.1007/978-3-030-96753-6_4

The selection of locations for these charging points has been studied by the Electric Vehicle Charging Stations Locations (EV-CSL) problem. The problem proposes determining the location of electric vehicle charging stations to optimize a quality of service metric, i.e., minimizing the sum of distances that citizens must walk to charge their vehicles. Our previous research addressed EV-CSL over a real scenario defined in Málaga city (Spain) [7]. A realistic instance was defined taking into account real information about the roads, the limitations of the power grid, and the location of the tentative charging point users. In turn, two metaheuristics were proposed to solve the problem.

This article present a new version of the EV-CSL problem model, to better capture realistic features in terms of energy supply constraints. In turn, an exact method based on ILP is applied to solve the problem. The main contributions of the research reported in this article include: *i)* Providing a new improved mathematical formulation of EV-CSL; *ii)* Proposing a new exact approach to address EV-CSL based on ILP; *iii)* Designing new realistic instances and variations of the problem to evaluate the proposed approach; *iv)* Reporting a comparison among the solutions provided in previous research and the results computed by our approach; *v)* Discussing the different solutions obtained in terms of the quality of service and the distribution of the charging points.

The article is organized as follows. Next section introduces the optimization problem addressed in this research and its mathematical formulation. Section 4 describes the main details of the proposed optimization approach. The experimental evaluation is reported in Sect. 5, including discussion of the obtained results and their applicability in the real case study in Málaga. Finally, Sect. 6 presents the conclusions and formulates the main lines for future work.

2   Infrastructure Location for Electric Vehicles Charging

The mathematical formulation of the EV-CSL problem is defined attending to the elements and considerations described in the following subsections.

2.1   Problem Data

An instance of the EV-CSL problem is determined by the following data:

- The set of potential charging points $S = \{s_1, s_2, \ldots, s_M\}$ comprises those physical locations considered suitable for installing recharging infrastructure. The formulation makes no distinction between points, other than its location and the set of power stations within the distribution grid capable of feeding each point. Particularly, no difference is considered regarding the number of customers that can be served in parallel at any given point.
- The maximum number of charging points to be deployed all over the city, M_s. For the optimization problem to be realistic, it is assumed that $M_s << M$.
- The set $C = \{c_1, c_2, \ldots, c_N\}$ comprises clusters of clients, grouped according on their geographical proximity. For each cluster $c \in C$, the number u_c of

clients is known. Since clusters are pre-calculated so that their members are not widely separated from each other, the average distance d_{cs} between cluster c clients and every potential charging point $s \in S$ is known in advance, and its variance is low regarding the average.

- There is a known bound D_c for the maximum distance that customers in cluster $c \in C$ are willing to walk to charge their vehicles. So, only points $s \in S$ where $d_{cs} \leq D_c$ are considered to serve customers of the cluster c.
- $E = \{e_1, e_2, \ldots, e_T\}$ is the set of power stations that might serve as source to feed charging points. For every pair $e \in E$, $s \in S$, the reference distance d_{es} over the power grid necessary to connect e with s is known in advance. This correspondence imposes viability among connections because of electric constraints, such as: tension drops, thermal or stability limits the grid must comply with. A maximum extent D_e is assumed between each power station $e \in E$ and those points $s \in S$ to be connected to it. Only those (e, s) pairs where $d_{es} \leq D_e$ are considered.
- A power-stations to charging-points assignment cannot lead to configurations that overload stations beyond their capacity. Every station $e \in E$ has a specific limit mp_e to the number of charging points it can feed.

2.2   Design Premisses and Control Variables

A feasible deployment of charging points must comply with a simple set of rules:

1. Every cluster of clients $c \in C$ must count an effective charging point $s \in S$ at a distance d_{cs} of at most D_c.
2. Every charging point to be installed must be fed from a unique power station $e \in E$, whose distance d_{es} is lower or equal to D_e.
3. The power-stations to charging-points assignment cannot press the number of charging points to be served by any station $e \in E$ beyond its limit mp_e.
4. The objective to optimize accounts the accumulated distance between clients and their nearest charging points available. Hence, though a cluster $c \in C$ could have more than one charging point within D_c range, only that at the nearest distance is considered to account in the QoS.
5. The number of charging-points is bound to a total limit M_s, so the election affects the whole and it must be globally coordinated.
6. Power limits at stations only concern with the number of charging points fed from them, not with the associated number of customers.

The main control variables of the problem regard with the selection of charging points to be installed. However, the formulation includes additional variables to capture other design concerns. The list of variables by kind is as follows:

- Boolean variables z_s indicate whether some charging point $s \in S$ is to be installed or not, so they are as many as $|S| = M$.
- Boolean variable x_{cs} is active if and only if those clients in the cluster $c \in C$ find their closest point of the charge at $s \in S$.

Constraint $d_{cs} \leq D_c$ must hold to comply with distance limits, what is achieved by solely considering x_{cs} variables where $d_{cs} \leq D_c$. Let $CS \subseteq C \times S$ be the a-priori computed set of *distance viable* clusters to charge-points assignments. Observe that the number $|CS|$ of x_{cs} variables could be as high as $M \times N$ ($|S| = M$, $|C| = N$) in the limit. The value depends of the maximum allowed distance D_c, the higher the limit, the greater $|CS|$.

Variables described so far only concern with the physical placement of charging points. Electric grid constraints require additional variables:

- Boolean variables y_{es} capture the fact that station $e \in E$ supplies power to charging point $s \in S$. Since the problem description also integrates distance limits amid these connections, (e, s) assignments fulfilling $d_{es} \leq D_e$ are prefiltered, whose outcome is referred to as $ES \subseteq E \times S$. The number $|ES|$ of y_{es} variables could be as high as $T \times M$ ($|E| = T$, $|S| = M$) in the limit. Unlike the previous CS set, the number $|ES|$ is fixed among instances to solve, since it is inherited by constraints coming from the power grid rather from some ultimately adjustable service goal, such as D_c.

Equations (1a)–(1g) expresses the mixed integer programming (MIP) for EV-CSL, i.e., finding the most efficient location for the electric vehicle charging infrastructure, in terms of the sum of distances between clusters and charging points.

$$\min_{x_{cs}, y_{es}, z_s} \sum_{cs \in CS} u_c d_{cs} \cdot x_{cs} \tag{1a}$$

subject to:

$$\sum_{cs \in CS} x_{cs} = 1, \qquad \forall c \in C \tag{1b}$$

$$z_s \geq x_{cs}, \qquad \forall cs \in CS \tag{1c}$$

$$\sum_{s \in S} z_s \leq M_s \tag{1d}$$

$$\sum_{es \in ES} y_{es} = z_s, \qquad \forall s \in S \tag{1e}$$

$$\sum_{es \in ES} y_{es} \leq mp_e, \qquad \forall e \in E \tag{1f}$$

$$x_{cs}, y_{es} \in \{0, 1\}, 0 \leq z_s \leq 1 \tag{1g}$$

The objective function (1a) directs the optimization towards the lowest per-customer combined distance between clusters and charging points. Given that the number of clients is fixed and it is assumed that they always recharge at the closest point available, the sum in Eq. (1a) is indeed a metric for the Quality of Service (QoS) of the infrastructure as presented earlier in this section.

Note that (1a) adds up to the distance that the whole of the customers should travel to recharge their vehicles. Without any other constraint, that number could be as low as zero when every $x_{cs} = 0$, which makes no sense, since no charge point is provisioned in that case. To prevent that, (1b) forces every cluster c to have one assigned station within D_c range, because CS only contains (c, s) pairs where $d_{cs} \leq D_c$ and there must be one and only one variable for which $x_{cs} = 1$. Whenever more than one station s is within D_c range, the optimization itself will choose that closest to c. Therefore, (1a) and (1b) combined guarantee that: i) every cluster c counts a charging point within D_c range; ii) each cluster is optimally assigned for a given set of charging points; and iii) after consolidated, that assignment achieves the lowest total distance for all clients combined.

Since installing a station accounts no cost, an optimal configuration would assign every cluster to the nearest station possible, what most certainly leads to configurations where the limit of stations M_s is exceeded. To prevent this violation, (1c) and (1d) are incorporated. Equations (1c) simply make a station $s \in S$ to be installed whether any cluster c is going to use it, since a variable $x_{cs} = 1$ is enough to force $z_s = 1$. Observe that although the integrality of z_s variables is intrinsic, it should not be explicitly imposed as it is with x_{cs} ones, which unlike z_s variables are declared as boolean in (1g).

The problem with variables and constraints defined so far only concerns with the physical placement of charging points, not with other limits imposed by the electric grid. Since it has less constraints, this subproblem clearly is a relaxation of the complete one, and its optimal solutions represent lower bounds of EV-CSL. Subtler is the fact that, since power station limits are set by the number of charge points assigned to them, not by the number of users, solutions to the previous relaxation might also be feasible in the complete problem, as long as the M_s limit is low when compared with mp_e values. This property is in fact exploded during the experimental evaluation, Sect. 5.

Power stations limits are incorporated into the problem, to get to the *full version*, as follows. Equations (1e) are equivalent to (1b), except that in this case, the assignment of a charging point $s \in S$ to a power-station $e \in E$ within D_e range (captured by variables in ES set) is triggered if and only if that point is to be installed (i.e. only if $z_s = 1$). Finally, Eqs. (1f) guarantee that no station $e \in E$ is assigned with a number of charging points higher than its limit mp_e.

3   Related Work

The optimal location of electric vehicle charging stations has been a relevant problem since the emergence of a renewed interest in electric transportation infrastructures, in the early 21st century.

Frade et al. [10] applied a maximal covering model to maximize the demand within a maximum desirable distance, assuming that coverage decays beyond that threshold distance. A MIP model was proposed, including a penalty term to prevent the installation of unnecessary supply points. The model was evaluated on four scenarios in Lisbon, Portugal, installing up to 324 supply points in 43 charging stations in a higher-demand scenario. Accurate covered demand results were computed, providing an acceptable level of service. Wagner et al. [17]

proposed a business intelligence model for EV-CSL to maximize demand coverage, based on potential trip destinations of vehicle owners, defined using urban data analysis [13]. An iterative method was proposed to find optimal locations using penalties to define ranks for points of interest and a MILP model solved in CPLEX. The proposed model achieved promising results on two case studies from Amsterdam and Brussels. Chen et al. [5] proposed a MILP formulation for locating charging stations minimizing the total walking distance according to parking patterns estimated using real urban data. The model was evaluated on a case study on 218 zones of Seattle, USA. Results achieved good accessibility: locating 20 charging station the walking distance was 1.1 km (average) and 3 km (maximum), whereas almost 80% of the demand was fulfilled.

Cavadas et al. [4] proposed a MIP model for EV-CSL to maximize the satisfied demand subject to a maximum budget constraint, considering the activity patterns of travelers. A multi-period formulation was introduced to model time intervals within a day. The model was evaluated in a small real scenario in Coimbra, Portugal, with just nine stations and four charging points each, to be installed on 129 candidate locations. Accurate solutions were computed, improving over the real configuration of EV charging stations installed in the city. Brandstätter et al. [2] proposed an ILP model for EV-CSL to maximize economic benefits in a car-sharing system, considering stochastic demands. The model was validated on medium-size synthetic scenarios and real world instances from Vienna (up to 693 potential locations). For Vienna, the exact approach was only able to solve instances for eight central districts of the city, whereas an heuristic method was applied for larger problem instances. Solutions confirmed the economic viability of implementing a electric car-sharing system.

Çalik and Fortz [3] proposed a MILP formulation for EV-CSL to maximize the profit of a public one-way electric cars system. The model and two relaxations were studied for 63 instances in New York, USA, with 85 potential locations for installing non-identical charging stations. The impact of cost changes in the number of stations was studied. Bian et al. [1] proposed a GIS-based approach for EV-CSL to maximize the profit. GIS was applied to determine the probability for users to charge their EV in different areas, using relevant traffic information. The model was evaluated in a small case study in Västerås, Sweden, with 268 square zones. Two scenarios were studied, adding three and ten new charging stations to 40 already installed in the city. When adding three stations, the best option was selecting fast chargers in commercial areas, whereas slow chargers installed in residential areas were better when including ten stations.

Lin et al. [12] proposed MILP model based on Geographic Information System (GIS) to optimally select the location and the size EVCS in urban scenarios. The MILP model is defined to maximize the economical profits of installing new charging stations, which are computed according to the charging demand based on the traffic flow data, charging profiles, and city land-use classification. In order to compute the charging demand, the authors generated an aggregated charging demand profile of the EVs based on the real-world travel data in National Household Travel Survey and charging behaviors. These daily charging behaviors, for each charging type of location, are represented by 24 hourly charging demands. GIS is employed to calculate the charging demand in different locations by taking into account traffic flow and land-use classifications (e.g., residential with villa, residential with apartment, working, etc.). In this study, it is assumed that a charging station will only serve the demands in specific given area. In turn, there is defined an acceptable walking distance from the charging station (parking lot) to the destination of the user. The researchers take into account the costs of a new station (which could include fast and slow chargers). Thus, the costs of a station consist of an aggregation of the economical costs of the equipment, installation, rent, maintenance and operation, and electricity consumption, which depend on the number and the type of chargers installed chargers. The optimization problem objective (the economical profits of deploying the new stations) is computed by subtracting the costs of locating the new charging station to the revenues of charging EVs. The proposed approach was evaluated over an area of 67 km^2 of Västerås, Sweden. Västerås had a population of 119 372 people, there were 44 192 personal cars, and the city had 324 plug-in EVs charging stations. The authors defined 532 tentative charging stations. The experimental analyses evaluated only the proposed method over four scenarios: installing three, five, ten, and 15 new charging stations. The results show that the proposed approach was able to provide charging station locations that provided competitive profits.

The EV-CSL problem and related variants have been also solved using metaheuristic approaches, due to the inherent complexity of specific variants using complex formulations or even simulations for solution evaluation.

In this line of work, this article contributes with an exact solution to EV-CSL, taking advantage of our expertise on location problems in the context of smart cities, including roadside infrastructure for vehicular networks [14], stations for public bicycles [6], bus stops [8], and waste bins [16], among other relevant problems. Our research demonstrates that a simple MILP formulation of EV-CSL can be solved with an exact method for medium-sized instances, and we solve a real-life scenario modeling the current reality in the city of Málaga.

4   The Proposed Optimization Approach

This section elaborates upon the developments implemented to solve variants of the EV-CSL. The previous approach to solve this problem relied on metaheuristics to find good-quality solutions for real-world instances [7]. Conversely, this work presents how exact methods have proven to be successful to solve the Mathematical Programming formulation for the previously studied instances, as well as over many others of such size.

A couple of tools were used along the development process. The optimization toolkit of MATLAB (release R2015a-8.5.0) was used in early stages of the work, mainly to validate the general formulation over a manually crafted test-set with relatively few variables. However, real-world instances solved in this article are far beyond capabilities of these tools. The number of x_{cs} variables could be as high as $M \times N$, which in some instances (e.g. $D_c = 8000$ m) reaches almost six and a half million integer variables.

To cope with the size of instances for the application case, `IBM(R) ILOG(R) CPLEX(R) Interactive Optimizer 12.6.3.0` was used as the optimization tool. The total time to optimal required by this solver to find solution was always below two hours. As we see later in this document, total times were quite below that value in general. It is worth mentioning that by optimal we mean: within the default GAP tolerance, which is set to the default value for the MIP solver (i.e. 0.01%). The GAP corresponds to the relative difference between the best integer solution found and the best upper bound estimated up to that moment, namely $(f(x) - bestBound)/f(x)$, where x is a feasible solution, $f(x)$ is its objective function value, and $bestBound$ is the higher lowest bound found for the optimum value. For the interface between the large instance data-sets and the solver, we developed a C++ program to read data and convert them to CPLEX LP-format. Afterwards, those LP files were launched in computing resources of the National Supercomputing Center, Uruguay (Cluster-UY) [15].

5   Experimental Validation

This section reports the experimental evaluation of the proposed exact approach for solving the EV-CSL problem over realistic instances in Málaga, Spain.

5.1   Methodology

The methodology applied in the experimental validation of the proposed exact methods is described next.

Analysis. Three relevant analysis are developed. First, the relaxed problem variant flexible (without including constraints defined by Eqs. (1e) and (1f)) is evaluated for a set of realistic instances, varying the maximum number of charging points to be deployed, M_s. Then, for the relaxed problem variant, results are compared with the corresponding previous EA applied to the problem [7]. Finally, the full (more realistic) problem variant, including the constraints that model the supply of the electrical grid (defined by Eqs. (1e) and (1f)) is studied.

Metrics. Relevant metrics are considered in the evaluation of the computed solutions. On the one hand, the objective function values account for the per-customer combined distance between clusters and their nearest charging point. On the other hand, other relevant QoS-related metrics are considered, such as the average and maximum distance a customer must travel for charging. In turn, the installation cost of the electric charging stations is also evaluated, according to a simplified cost model developed for the analysis. The cost model is based on real infrastructure installation costs (including the cost of the charger, civil infrastructure works, electrical installation, signaling, security, and legalization). A semi-rapid charger is considered, with a power of 22 kW and a cost of 10 500 €. In addition, the cost of the connection from the charging point to the corresponding electrical substation is added.

For the comparison with the previous EA for the problem, the GAP metric is used to evaluate the differences in the computed objective function values.

Problem Instances. Two set of instances are considered in the evaluation of the proposed exact approach for EV-CSL:

- For the evaluation of the exact approach on both the relaxed and full versions, a constant threshold distance of $D_c = 2500$ m is used, assumed as a reasonable distance citizens are willing to travel to charge their electric vehicles. Setting D_c fixes in turn the set of variables of the problem. The value of M_s varies from 20 to 80. Whenever Eqs. (1e) and (1f) are dismissed from the full version (Eqs. (1a)–(1g)), a relaxation is obtained, no matter what the dataset is. However, along the sequence of problem instances previously introduced and since D_c is fixed along them, as M_s increases, either version of the problem is in turn a relaxation of the previous problem instance. This is because the only difference between any instance and the following is on the right-hand side of Eq. (1d), which is exactly one unit larger than the previous. Hence, as M_s increases, the optimal objective can only decrease, and whatever solution for any prior instance previously tackled could be used as an initial feasible solution for the current, a property that whether used helps to improve the performance of the solver.
- For the comparison with results computed using the previous EA, instances reported in our previous work [7] are used. In these instances, both the values of M_s and D_c vary simultaneously, so no nesting exists among problems.

Regarding geographical information, both sets of instances were built considering real data for the city of Málaga. A total number of $M_s = 33.550$ potential locations for charging points are considered. In turn, 363 clusters and 14 electric substations are considered. Figure 1 presents the potential locations over the map of Málaga (green dots) and the electric substation location (blue squares).

Fig. 1. Potential locations for charging stations in Málaga (Color figure online)

Numerical Results. This section, discusses the results of the proposed exact approach for EV-CSL on the relaxed version and compares them against the results obtained by the previous EA [7]. Then, it presents the results provided by the proposed exact approach on the full version of the problem.

Tables 1 and 3 reports the results for the relaxed and full versions of the problem, Reported values are: the total distance between clusters and charging points (f_{BEST}), the economical cost of deploying that solution in euros (cost), and the actual distance in meters between the clusters and the charging points in terms of average (d_{AVG}) and maximum (d_{MAX}) for each M_s.

Table 1. Experimental results for the relaxed version of the problem.

M_s	f_{BEST}	Cost	d_{AVG}	d_{MAX}	M_s	f_{BEST}	$Cost$	d_{AVG}	d_{MAX}
20	515866608	3802015	1155.18	2497	51	246365755	8366825	777.61	2497
21	492189525	3913565	1139.56	2497	52	243013759	8486655	774.47	2497
22	470795972	4086410	1119.10	2497	53	239713988	8599355	763.06	2497
23	453698051	4296630	1062.30	2498	54	236423096	8604645	750.37	2492
24	437985284	4414850	1043.62	2498	55	233256211	8734480	739.11	2492
25	422884012	4704420	1013.72	2498	56	230153919	8838900	735.58	2492
26	408509548	4857025	998.26	2497	57	227101656	8911580	734.37	2492
27	394495141	4984790	978.34	2497	58	224085462	9037620	732.75	2492
28	382545839	5075295	960.75	2497	59	221071931	9164695	731.14	2492
29	370970640	5271485	942.30	2497	60	218127562	9367325	728.73	2492
30	361019674	5377515	931.24	2497	61	215241637	9436900	724.12	2492
31	351748722	5435935	922.01	2497	62	212386123	9498885	721.73	2492
32	344195535	5614875	916.74	2497	63	209542491	9601005	718.49	2492
33	337185494	5733670	910.92	2497	64	206798841	9665290	716.24	2492
34	330720516	5863620	906.91	2497	65	204076876	9873555	713.29	2492
35	324414266	6036350	898.78	2497	66	201380990	10037430	710.68	2492
36	318213955	6255310	880.72	2497	67	198701745	10148520	707.70	2492
37	312456675	6412285	864.77	2497	68	196042267	10657280	700.38	2492
38	306745623	6554770	858.26	2497	69	193486949	11233430	689.48	2492
39	301057871	6720830	853.57	2497	70	190941050	10886245	695.55	2492
40	295633585	7005800	840.68	2497	71	188385732	11462395	684.65	2492
41	290469709	7155415	830.72	2497	72	185844597	11668130	682.38	2492
42	285334212	7285825	822.28	2497	73	183382962	11842355	671.34	2492
43	280187531	7377250	817.70	2497	74	180841827	12048550	669.07	2492
44	275197190	7442455	811.21	2497	75	178437781	12159640	665.95	2492
45	270522493	7608515	806.30	2497	76	176095511	12220015	661.18	2492
46	265941206	7696490	804.07	2497	77	173834250	12423335	654.85	2486
47	261403566	7777335	801.43	2497	78	171624251	12515910	653.24	2486
48	257424493	7871750	800.53	2497	79	169445056	12624010	643.01	2486
49	253503768	7982150	794.28	2497	80	167282054	12693930	638.27	2486
50	249922088	8107385	784.61	2497					

Results in Table 1 show that as the number of charging points increases (M_s) the combined distance between clusters and charging points (f_{BEST}) decreases, as expected. d_{MAX} is slightly below 2500 m in all cases, so, optimal solutions tend to assign some clusters very close to the distance threshold.

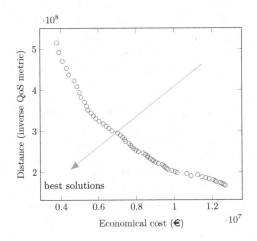

Fig. 2. Distance and the economical cost on the relaxed variation. (Color figure online)

The reduction in the calculated f_{BEST} values when increasing M_s implies that citizens generally travel shorter distances to charge their cars. Values of d_{AVG} and d_{MAX} in Table 1 show that the average distances decrease as the number of charging points increases. However, not all citizens benefit when adding only one charging point. For this reason, the maximum distance values do not improve in the same way as the average (it is always close to threshold distance of $D_c = 2500\,\text{m}$). This is illustrated in Fig. 3 that shows the distribution of the charging points through the real map of Málaga for different values of M_s. Even though the exact method distributes the charging points through the whole map as M_s increases, there are areas of the city that are not targeted because they have low population densities. This is mainly the objective to be optimized defined in Sect. 2 is the combined distance (see Eq. (1a)) that takes into account the population density of the clusters, and therefore, the method prioritizes the areas of the city with higher population densities.

Regarding the economical cost of deploying the solutions, Fig. 2 illustrates f_{BEST} values, i.e., the combined distance, given the economical cost as blue circles. This figure can be seen as a Pareto Front of an optimization problem in which the combined distance and the economical costs are two objectives to be minimized. Thus, the points close to the red row represent the solutions with the best trade-off between these two objectives. The figure shows that for solutions with fewer charging points (left side of the figure), a smaller economical investment gets a higher improvement in the QoS metric than when there are already a considerable number of stations (right side of the figure).

Even though the considered economical cost model takes into account the cost of the infrastructure of the charging point and the cost of wiring the charging

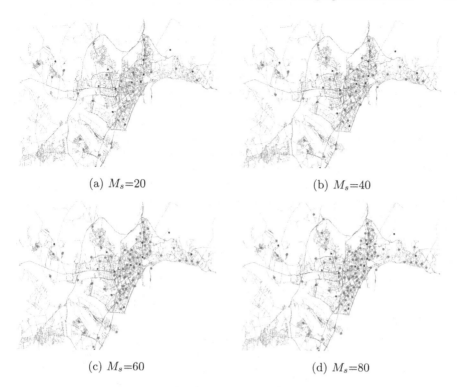

(a) M_s=20

(b) M_s=40

(c) M_s=60

(d) M_s=80

Fig. 3. Solutions computed by the proposed exact approach for the relaxed version of the problem over map of Málaga for different M_s.

point the cost behaves as a linear monotonic function increasing with respect to M_s because the cost of the infrastructure is significantly higher than the wiring cost and contributes much more to the cost of the proposed solution.

Results computed by the exact method are compared against the previous EA, for $M_s = \{10, 20, 30, 40, 50\}$ [7]. Table 2 reports the mean GAP between the exact solution and all computed solutions by the EA for the same M_s, and the best GAP, regarding the best EA solution. According to results in Table 2, the exact approach is better than the EA. The GAPs are always positive and they increase as M_s increases, takes advantage of installing more charging points.

Table 2. GAP between the proposed exact approach and the EA.

M_s	D_c (m)	#variables	Mean GAP	Best GAP
10	8.000	6.298.967	1.90%	0.30%
20	7.000	5.394.820	6.63%	4.02%
30	6.500	4.932.345	10.72%	7.96%
40	6.000	4.453.698	13.91%	11.16%
50	5.000	3.482.353	17.74%	14.45%

Exact solutions are the same for the full version and the relaxed version of the problem for M_s from 20 to 59, because they fulfill the constraints. However, solutions found for the greater of values of M_s get slightly higher f_{BEST}, i.e., less competitive QoS. This behavior is because when the number of charging points in the instance does not exceed a given threshold (i.e., $M_s < 60$), the exact approach is able to locate the charging points in any place (as in the relaxed version of the problem), without exceeding power station limits. However, as M_s grows the exact approach distributes in a different way the charging points, because solutions for the relaxed version of the problem are not feasible (they do not fulfill the power stations limit). Thus, the exact method in the full version locates the charging points in the way they are close to the high population areas but also the charging points are wired to different electric substations.

Table 3. Experimental results for the full version of the problem. Solutions when $M_s < 60$ always match those reported in Table 1.

M_s	f_{BEST}	Cost	d_{AVG}	d_{MAX}	M_s	f_{BEST}	Cost	d_{AVG}	d_{MAX}
60	218186006	9234270	726.53	2492	61	215329466	9441040	724.06	2492
62	212473952	9503025	721.67	2492	63	209630320	9605145	718.43	2492
64	206886670	9669430	716.18	2492	65	204164705	9878155	713.23	2492
66	201485460	9989245	710.24	2492	67	199062686	10149210	702.93	2492
68	196482690	10369665	696.94	2492	69	194149274	10388870	692.76	2492
70	191808940	10638765	690.08	2492	71	189547679	10842545	683.74	2486
72	187337680	10935120	682.14	2486	73	185174678	11005040	677.40	2486
74	183092960	11431690	671.67	2496	75	181210543	11561180	667.88	2496
76	179358901	11665255	665.65	2496	77	177549296	11855350	662.02	2496
78	175741776	11946085	660.05	2496	79	173953074	12183330	655.01	2496
80	172232296	12439895	649.31	2496					

Figure 4 shows the solutions deployed through the city for $M_s = 60$ and $M_s = 80$. These two solutions distribute more the charging points over the city in comparison with the solutions computed for the flexible version of the problem (which concentrate most of the charging points in the same Downtown locations).

Figure 5 plots (f_{BEST}) and economical cost results. Blue circles illustrate identical solutions for both versions of the problem, while gray squares represent different solutions. Whenever solutions in both versions do not match, that of the full version must be higher since the other is its relaxation. Those differences exist for $60 \leq M_s \leq 80$ only, but they are relatively negligible, and in fact, it is necessary to zoom into that range to notice any difference as is in Fig. 6.

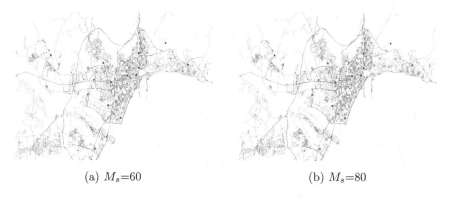

(a) M_s=60   (b) M_s=80

Fig. 4. Solutions computed by the exact approach for the full version of the problem over map of Málaga for different M_s.

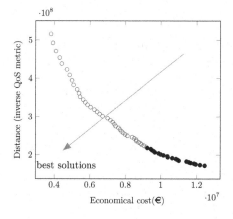

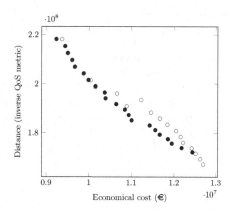

Fig. 5. Distance and the economical cost on restricted variation. (Color figure online)

Fig. 6. Solutions of both problem variations ($60 \leq M_s \leq 80$).

6 Conclusions and Future Work

Proposing efficient and effective networks of EV charging points has become a must in modern urban areas to allow easy adoption of sustainable mobility based on EVs. This article presented an exact optimization approach for solving a new variant of the EV-CSL problem defined on a real city, Málaga. This new variant is more realistic because it explicitly models the actual energy supply constraints and it takes them into account to compute the solutions.

Results of the experimental evaluation on a set of real-world instances of Málaga show that the proposed approach is competitive to address EV-CSL for the constrained and the flexible versions of the problem. The exact optimization approach based on ILP is able to automatically distribute the charging points along the city taking into account the real distribution of the tentative EV users, while optimizing the QoS of the whole charging points network.

Besides, the proposed exact approach has shown being more competitive than a GA proposed in previous research ta address EV-CSL. It is able to improve the QoS by 17,74% in instances with 50 charging points.

The main lines for future work are related to improve the realism of the model by considering general citizen's mobility behavior, the location of points of interest, and aspects related to the installation costs; to the definition of the EV-CSL problem by taking into account other objectives rather than QoS, such as installation costs; and to the definition of real instances over other cities.

Acknowledgments. This research was partially funded by ANII and PEDECIBA (Uruguay), by the Universidad de Málaga, and by MCIN/AEI/10.13039/501100011033 under grant number PID 2020-116727RB-I00 (HUmove).

References

1. Bian, C., Li, H., Wallin, F., Avelin, A., Lin, L., Yu, Z.: Finding the optimal location for public charging stations-a GIS-based MILP approach. Energy Procedia **158**, 6582–6588 (2019)
2. Brandstätter, G., Kahr, M., Leitner, M.: Determining optimal locations for charging stations of electric car-sharing systems under stochastic demand. Transp. Res. Part B Methodol. **104**, 17–35 (2017)
3. Çalık, H., Fortz, B.: Location of stations in a one-way electric car sharing system. In: 2017 IEEE Symposium on Computers and Communications (ISCC), pp. 134–139. IEEE (2017)
4. Cavadas, J., de Almeida Correia, G.H., Gouveia, J.: A MIP model for locating slow-charging stations for electric vehicles in urban areas accounting for driver tours. Transp. Res. E Logist. Transp. Rev. **75**, 188–201 (2015)
5. Chen, T.D., Kockelman, K.M., Khan, M.: Locating electric vehicle charging stations: parking-based assignment method for Seattle, Washington. Transp. Res. Rec. **2385**(1), 28–36 (2013)
6. Cintrano, C., Chicano, F., Alba, E.: Using metaheuristics for the location of bicycle stations. Expert Syst. Appl. **161**, 113684 (2020)
7. Cintrano, C., Toutouh, J., Alba, E.: Citizen centric optimal electric vehicle charging stations locations in a full city: case of Malaga. In: Alba, E., et al. (eds.) CAEPIA 2021. LNCS (LNAI), vol. 12882, pp. 247–257. Springer, Cham (2021). https://doi.org/10.1007/978-3-030-85713-4_24
8. Fabbiani, E., Nesmachnow, S., Toutouh, J., Tchernykh, A., Avetisyan, A., Radchenko, G.: Analysis of mobility patterns for public transportation and bus stops relocation. Program. Comput. Softw. **44**(6), 508–525 (2018)
9. Falchetta, G., Noussan, M.: Electric vehicle charging network in Europe: an accessibility and deployment trends analysis. Transp. Res. Part D Transp. Environ. **94**, 102813 (2021). https://doi.org/10.1016/j.trd.2021.102813. https://www.sciencedirect.com/science/article/pii/S1361920921001164
10. Frade, I., Ribeiro, A., Gonçalves, G., Antunes, A.P.: Optimal location of charging stations for electric vehicles in a neighborhood in Lisbon, Portugal. Transp. Res. Rec. **2252**(1), 91–98 (2011)

11. Kumar, R.R., Alok, K.: Adoption of electric vehicle: a literature review and prospects for sustainability. J. Clean. Prod. **253**, 119911 (2020). https://doi.org/10.1016/j.jclepro.2019.119911.   https://www.sciencedirect.com/science/article/pii/S095965261934781X
12. Lin, H., Bian, C., Li, H., Sun, Q., Wennersten, R.: Optimal siting and sizing of public charging stations in urban area. In: 2018 Joint International Conference on Energy, Ecology and Environment (ICEEE 2018) and International Conference on Electric and Intelligent Vehicles (ICEIV 2018), p. 7 (2018)
13. Massobrio, R., Nesmachnow, S.: Urban mobility data analysis for public transportation systems: a case study in Montevideo, Uruguay. Appl. Sci. **10**(16), 5400 (2020)
14. Massobrio, R., Toutouh, J., Nesmachnow, S., Alba, E.: Infrastructure deployment in vehicular communication networks using a parallel multiobjective evolutionary algorithm. Int. J. Intell. Syst. **32**(8), 801–829 (2017)
15. Nesmachnow, S., Iturriaga, S.: Cluster-UY: collaborative scientific high performance computing in Uruguay. In: Torres, M., Klapp, J. (eds.) ISUM 2019. CCIS, vol. 1151, pp. 188–202. Springer, Cham (2019). https://doi.org/10.1007/978-3-030-38043-4_16
16. Rossit, D.G., Toutouh, J., Nesmachnow, S.: Exact and heuristic approaches for multi-objective garbage accumulation points location in real scenarios. Waste Manage. **105**, 467–481 (2020)
17. Wagner, S., Götzinger, M., Neumann, D.: Optimal location of charging stations in smart cities: a points of interest based approach (2013)

A Multi-lens Approach to Smart City Planning: Philadelphia

Jennifer Kim(✉), Sesil Koutra, and Zacharie De Grève

Université de Mons, 7000 Mons, Belgium
`jenskim@alumni.princeton.edu`

Abstract. Smart city planning has become a popular concept in a time of increasing urbanization and its accompanying challenges, particularly in the face of climate change. Critiques say it is too generic to prove more useful beyond utilization as a buzzword in political discourse. Smart planning requires a cross-disciplinary and adaptable effort that combines and optimizes the range of quantitative and qualitative methodologies available to identify opportunities and actionable solutions while acknowledging the challenges and shortcomings of a given approach. In this paper, this theory of smart planning is applied to the case of Philadelphia, where a multi-perspective lens – specifically, from the viewpoints of mobility and quality of life – is used to develop an integrated and adaptive evaluation of the needs of the city along with practical solutions for implementation. We show that integrating interdisciplinary resources and perspectives can uncover alternative solutions which enrich planning development.

Keywords: Mobility · Philadelphia · Quality of life · Smart cities · Urban planning

1 Introduction

The idea of Smart Cities has rapidly grown since the start of the 21st century, first appearing in the early 2000s and being utilized in many papers and debates especially since 2013 [1]. The definition of what constitutes a smart city is still unresolved given that different stakeholders such as Giffinger [2], Caragliu [3], and Angelidou [4], have divergent ideas regarding what makes a city "smart." However, there are general characteristics which hold consistent, these being: 1) the role of technology, 2) the planning for sustainability, and 3) the role of governance in managing these for a policy that is beneficial to people [1–4]. The Centre of Regional Science at the Vienna University of Technology (CRS) identified six main areas which have become widely accepted as background for the framework upon which a city can be assessed for smartness: smart economy, mobility, environment, people, living, and governance [2]. One popular definition based on these axes says a city is smart "when investments in human and social capital and traditional (transport) and modern (ICT) communication infrastructure fuel sustainable economic growth and a high quality of life, with a wise management of natural resources, through participatory governance." [3].

S. Nesmachnow and L. Hernández Callejo (Eds.): ICSC-Cities 2021, CCIS 1555, pp. 58–73, 2022.
https://doi.org/10.1007/978-3-030-96753-6_5

This paper seeks to assess the opportunities and challenges for contributing to a "ideal plan" for a city and to develop proposals tackling these opportunities in an innovative manner using a multi-perspective, integrated, and adaptive approach. The City of Philadelphia is evaluated as a case study using this methodology to assess the needs of the city and to develop solutions that could be proposed for practical implementation. The methodology used may at first seem self-evident but is important to revise with an open mind that seeks opportunities for adaptations and syntheses for an ideal solution. Thus, the main contributions of this work are to show the value obtained by 1) synthesizing and finding relationships between seemingly disparate variables, data sources, and disciplines, 2) using a flexible and adaptive approach to optimize solution alternatives, and 3) applying this methodology to offer new perspectives on some urban planning challenges faced by Philadelphia.

The article is organized as follows: in the following section, the methodology adopted for approaching the planning project is discussed. Section 3 through 5 present the case study of Philadelphia through the phases described in Sect. 2. Section 6 discuss weaknesses of the methodology, and Sect. 7 presents the conclusions with some remarks and recommendations for future works.

2 Methodology and Materials

2.1 Methodology

The methodology adapted for a time-constrained evaluation of a city can be divided into three phases. First is selection of a research focus for the case study, exploring the motivation and background information for determining a location and the smart city pillars for comprehensive study. Given the smart city characteristics identified by the CRS [2], it is useful to select more than one to evaluate individually and also in relation to each other. Once these pillars are chosen, an extensive review is performed of the city's history and current situation with respect to the selected pillars of study, including recent statistics and planning documents developed by the city administration. This establishes a baseline from which challenges can be identified for further investigation. Case study constraints should also be defined in this phase.

Next, the identified challenges are evaluated to develop broad solutions for an "ideal city" from the lens of the selected perspectives. The proposals should be assessed both quantitatively and qualitatively for their impacts.

Following that is a refinement process to reevaluate the proposed solutions and process them into strategies and actions for implementation. Alternative scenarios are studied, and a "best approach" selected using varying methodologies of evaluation.

2.2 Materials

There are a plethora of tools and materials available for developing solutions for an "ideal city," to be selected depending on the area of interest and researcher's expertise. For this case study, the resources used include academic literature, open geospatial and survey-based data, articles and institutional reports, and planning documents.

3 Case Study Introduction: Philadelphia

3.1 Motivation and Research Focus

Given the long-term nature of infrastructure, planning a city by default requires consideration for sustainability from social, economic, and – increasingly – environmental perspectives. Following a preliminary review of the city's background, two issues of interest are selected for development using a multi-perspective approach.

The first is based on the phenomenon of the decrease in the city's population following publication of its first comprehensive city plan in 1960, from a peak of 2.1 million inhabitants in 1950 to 1.5 in 2010 [5]. Decline in population and neglected properties have become prominent characteristics of "unsavory" neighborhoods, giving rise to the question of whether these areas are thus due to the inherent qualities of their inhabitants or due to a systemic issue exacerbated by the built environment. Given that Philadelphia is still considered one of the most unsafe cities in the United States [6], it is of interest to explore how smart city solutions can improve safety and hence quality of life in the city. This assumes a correlation between safety and quality of life, which also bears further investigation.

The second issue centers upon transportation in Philadelphia. In 2020, Philadelphia was the second-most congested city in the United States, and the fifth most congested city in the world [7]. Although the city recently produced an extensive transit improvement plan and has been subject to discussions regarding new mobility solutions, there is a question of whether transportation issues can be cured just by improving transit, or whether there are more nuanced issues to examine in solution proposals.

The following two-pronged approach is adopted: examining how to plan a city smartly through the perspectives of quality of life and mobility. These two pillars may seem disparate and utilize different methodologies for analysis but are linked if only in the purest sense by the city resident for whose benefit the solutions are devised.

3.2 Case Study Constraints

Constraints must be identified at the beginning of the work which should be borne in mind throughout solution development, evaluation, and proposal:

– Data: availability, relevance, and quality of data may be limited.
– Scope: given a city's magnitude, the study scope should be limited to devise an applicable solution; thus, it is useful to focus on a single district or neighborhood.

3.3 Review of Extant Information

To develop a solution proposal, it is first necessary to understand the existing situation. This diagnosis can be performed by investigating the city history, contemporary facts and figures, reference plans, and literature review of the areas of interest. Integrating this information helps guide the development of a preliminary proposal.

The history of the selected location's urban development provides context leading to present-day characteristics. Recent plans present the planning efforts of the city while helping contemporize research efforts to actual developments in progress. This avoids redundancy in proposals developed through the study. Studying the academic information concerning the areas of interest related to the city helps the researcher better understand the complexities of the situation and contextualizes the interaction of the selected issues with social implications along with scientific investigations.

Historical Review. The City of Philadelphia was chartered in 1701 and became a key location for culture, science, and education. Until 1800, Philadelphia was the largest city in the United States and the second-largest English-speaking city worldwide [8].

By the early 20th century, Philadelphia was a railroad hub experiencing great transit growth in addition to the manufacturing, industrial, and financial growth from the century prior [9]. However, political corruption, disease, and violence caused waste and stagnation in infrastructure expenditures. This was exacerbated by the Great Depression, which hit the city hard, followed by suburbanization, as residences and businesses moved out from the city center to the Greater Philadelphia region [9].

In 1960, the first comprehensive plan for the city was developed by the Philadelphia City Planning Commission, which laid out a 20-year plan for the physical development of the city. At the time, the city plan had a population estimate of around 2.5 million residents by 1980, since between 1890 and 1950, the population had doubled in size from one million to two million inhabitants. However, instead of continuing the trend, Philadelphia's population would instead decline to 1.5 million by 2010 [5].

Entering the 21st century, Philadelphia's population has experienced some growth (+0.6%) between 2000 and 2010, according to the 2010 census [5]. However, as of 2013, the city still had the highest unemployment rate in the region, also 1.9% higher than the national rate of 6.5% [10]. Even though the population is no longer declining, Philadelphia has yet to return to the economic prowess it was known for in its past.

City Plans. The principal city plans examined are the comprehensive development plan [5] and transportation plan [11]. Other documents contributing information regarding Philadelphia's visions and goals include the city's plans for smart city planning [12], sustainability [13], road safety [14], and transit [15].

Academic Literature Review. The study undertaken ranges from exploring the design philosophies involved behind the 1960 Comprehensive Plan [16] to assessing the impact of urban revitalization plans through programs such as historic preservation and anchor institutions [17, 18]. Other literature also critiques the sustainability and smart planning efforts previously undertaken by the city, discussing strengths and drawbacks to Philadelphia's previous proposals for becoming "smart" [10, 19].

When measuring quality of life in a city, the determinant factors are difficult to identify, and usually only validated through subjective surveys and estimated correlations between select indicators and the mental/physical satisfaction of citizens. While some authors such as Cohen argue that incidents of crime do not have as strong of an impact upon quality of life as other factors [20], others find that exposure to high rates of crime can adversely impact short- and long-term health, which are associated with quality of life [21]. From an alternative lens, studies of crime and resulting costs to society find that programs designed to prevent crime reduce costs incurred by stakeholders on individual and systemic scales, impacting overall quality of life [22].

Publications on mobility in Philadelphia provide historical and social contexts for the present-day transportation system and current conditions. They emphasize the importance of the role that mobility plays in society with social, economic, and environmental impacts on both Philadelphia's residents and its physical setting. These papers range from explaining relationships between urban spatial form and mobility with the role of social issues such as racial segregation and discrimination in historic policies [23, 24] to recommendations for context-sensitive transport design [25] and strategies for reducing greenhouse gas emissions from transport [26].

3.4 Challenges and Areas for Development

Challenges. From the background research, several challenges can be identified. Predominantly, Philadelphia's physical infrastructure has been deteriorating in hand with its declining economy since the previous century. Its neighborhoods are also home to high rates of crime: 139% more violent crimes and 41% more property crimes compared to the national averages [27]. High crime rates also deter investors, both commercial and residential, creating a feedback loop resulting in locations left to degrade into conditions that may facilitate the occurrence of crime.

Deteriorating infrastructure is also a challenge for Philadelphia's transportation system. Lack of space and funding for new transportation infrastructure has resulted in reduced reliability of transit options and a declining public transport ridership [15]. The impact upon reliability is both a reason for and a result of growing congestion on the city's roadways with the corresponding increase in the number of single-occupancy vehicles. This negatively impacts economy, environment, and health.

Opportunities. Addressing the challenges of each pillar separately allows brainstorming of multiple opportunities. For example, to tackle the challenge of high crime rates, the authors select an urban planning lens, as design is not often considered as relevant to crime prevention yet is a potent tool for creating safer environments that deter crime occurrence [28]. Rather than examining individual motivation, environmental factors are assessed for correlations with crime occurrences including issues such as access for intervention, likelihood of passerby, and the likes.

From the mobility perspective, the authors choose to focus on congestion, which has social, environmental, and economic implications making it an ideal study in sustainability. Socially, relieving congestion has a safety impact and would also improve accessibility of transit for carless travelers. Reducing congestion decreases greenhouse gas emissions from vehicles that spend less time idling in traffic and through the increased use of transit. Economically, congestion management could add a revenue source for the city, and partnerships may boost economic growth.

4   Analysis and Initial Proposals

4.1   Quality of Life

Analysis. The analysis is primarily based on the census block groups defined by the U.S. Census Bureau. The data used is sourced from ESRI Living Atlas and from Philadelphia's open data portal, OpenDataPhilly. Population and economic data have been obtained from the U.S. Census Bureau and ESRI Living Atlas.

First, Incidents and Shootings from 2020 have been mapped in ArcGIS Pro [29] and Optimized Hot Spot Analysis performed over the data sets, using a fishnet grid data aggregation method over the census blocks. Figure 1 shows two main areas identified through this analysis, as indicated by the red zones.

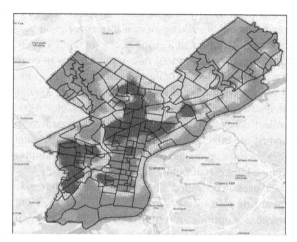

Fig. 1. Hotspot analysis of 2020 incidents. Data source: opendataphilly.org/dataset. Shapefiles downloaded April 14, 2021

Incidents are classified into Violent/Non-Violent and Opportunistic/Non-Opportunistic sets to determine whether patterns exist in motivations and/or nature of the crime. Hotspot analyses are performed over these and mapped against factors such as land use and demographic indicators. Positive correlations exist between crime and factors like vacant spaces, low household income, and high population density.

Google Earth Pro Street View [30] is used to examine neighborhoods of high crime rates; we observe that these areas are characterized by large, empty lots. These unused spaces are in disarray and may thus attract undesirable characters and their misdeeds.

Solutions. Defining a solution to address the problem of high crime rates in Philadelphia is complex due to the observed feedback cycle: neighborhoods with higher rates of crime are correlated to high poverty, low education, and low employment, but it is unclear which causes which.

Two possible solution approaches are considered: addressing crime motivations and addressing crime enablers. Looking at crime motivations evaluates which incidents are crimes of opportunity compared to personal grievances and helps understand which crimes might be addressable before the deed, and which are arbitrarily motivated by the human factor. Reducing crime enablers requires searching for specific scenarios or environments that are more conducive to crime occurrence, and how to suppress them. The practical implications of both approaches may be manifested in two ways: through environmental design, and through on-the-ground actions.

When evaluating the built environment, Crime Prevention Through Environmental Design (CPTED) is considered, which targets "designing safety and security into the environment of a specific area" [31]. This methodology first emerged in the 1960s following Jane Jacobs' theorization of concepts such as "eyes on the streets," the idea that urban design should locate people on public streets, thereby increasing the number of public witnesses which could deter potential offenders from committing crimes [32]. These implications are valuable not only for new developments but also for revitalization of an existing area. Studies investigating the relationship between safety and neighborhood vibrancy show that making more use of spaces in a neighborhood could significantly reduce the probability that a crime occurs in that location [33, 34].

To implement this concept in solution, one approach lies in enabling community ownership through a communal lens promoting actions such as 1) increasing community initiatives, 2) fostering formation of local-level leadership, 3) enabling community ownership via participatory actions like townhalls, surveys, etc., 4) developing "block properties" to be collectively used and maintained (such as gardens, playgrounds, and gathering areas), and 5) organizing communal activities like a cleanup day or "block party" cookouts. These actions are meant to foster sense of community and camaraderie and encourage communal upkeep of public and private properties.

A second approach uses an operational lens focusing on technical solutions, through services such as monitoring platforms or surveillance technologies which analyze locations of crime occurrences to optimize resource deployment to prevent or mitigate crime. Some actions promoted through this include 1) coordination and collaboration with neighboring municipal police divisions, 2) optimization of response routes, 3) predictive analysis using historic incidents to optimize patrols, 4) streetlight maintenance and surveillance camera installation in crime-prone areas, and 5) installation of smart cameras to detect weapons, incidents, flagged license plates, etc.

4.2 Mobility

Analysis. The analysis draws upon on traffic and congestion resources such as Texas A&M Transportation Institute, Google Maps, and the ESRI Living Atlas Portal. Neighborhood boundaries defined using PhillyOpenData's Philadelphia Neighborhood Boundary shapefile have been mapped with ESRI's World Traffic Service layer to identify areas of high congestion. The benefits of a congestion management solution are then analyzed using data from Texas A&M Transportation Institute.

First, congestion patterns can be identified by examining traffic patterns and average daily traffic within the city. The intent is to identify where and when congestion is most experienced to select an area best suited for implementing a pilot program with the proposed solution. This area is in and around the Center City neighborhood, a central location for many firms and a key commuter destination.

Solutions. Multiple strategies are studied for alleviating congestion: congestion pricing, lowering speed limits, restricting certain zones and times to public transit access, adding park & ride stations near key intersections and entry points to the city, and implementing electric shuttles between transit access locations and points of interest.

Since the part of the city experiencing the highest amount of congestion is the downtown, central area, downtown congestion pricing (DCP) is first explored for development. DCP is a strategy for reducing congestion by charging a payment for vehicles entering a city's downtown area.

A full in-depth analysis of the costs and benefits of implementing such a program is beyond the scope of this project; however, it is beneficial to identify the cost variables needed to be considered in an extensive feasibility analysis, as well as to develop high-level quantifications of the possible benefits.

The main costs include study and design, physical and systems infrastructure capital and integration, commercial costs, and operations and maintenance. The primary benefit of a DCP program is congestion reduction. The pricing mechanism should be designed to encourage drivers to take alternative modes of transportation or to enter the downtown part of the city during less crowded times of the day, thereby smoothing out traffic peaks and reducing the overall traffic delay resulting from congestion. The knock-on impact is a shift to modes of transport that have lower greenhouse gas emissions compared to a single occupancy vehicle.

Because crashes are more likely occur with higher speed variability [35], reducing congestion will also reduce stop-and-go motion with high variations of speed, thus effecting a decrease in car crashes. This not only increases safety, but also increases the total time that roads are clear, since accidents cause congestion when cars and emergency responders are blocking one or more lanes.

Reducing congestion should also improve trip times for travelers on all roadway transport modes. This produces cost savings in time and fuel, since time is money, in addition to the monetary cost per gallon of fuel. Based on studies in other cities where congestion pricing has been implemented, we estimate a 10% reduction in trips and 30% decrease in travel delays [36, 37]. Cost savings according to the value of time and from conservation of fuel wasted when idling in traffic are an estimated $1.1 billion annually. The reduction in travel delay will also have an environment impact of approximately 0.6 million-tons of annual CO_2-equivalent reduction in greenhouse gas emissions. These values are calculated using the assumptions in Table 1. In addition to these benefits, the program could also potentially procure revenues for investment in other initiatives like cycling, walking, and public transport.

Table 1. Congestion pricing benefits assumptions and sources

Indicator	Quantity	Source
Philadelphia annual VMT	11,132,500,000	Streetlight Data (2021)
Average fuel economy of passenger vehicle, miles/gallon	22	U.S. Environmental Protection Agency (EPA) (2018)
Average CO_2 emission rate for passenger vehicles, g CO_2/mile	404	EPA (2018)

(continued)

Table 1. (*continued*)

Indicator	Quantity	Source
Average tailpipe CO_2 emitted, g CO_2/gallon	8,887	EPA (2018)
Average price of gasoline, $/gallon	2.57	Texas A&M Transportation Institute (TTI) (2019)
Annual total delay, hours	194,655,000	TTI (2019)
Value of time, $/hour	18.12	TTI (2019)
Idling fuel use, gallons/hour	0.39	Calculated from U.S. Department of Energy (2015)

5   Revisions and Recommendations for Action

Quality of Life. The advantages and disadvantages of the two alternative scenarios previously proposed are evaluated in Table 2 below. "The Vibrant Block" refers to the communal approach; "The Policed State" refers to the technological method.

Table 2. Pros and cons of "The Vibrant Block" vs "The Policed State"

	The Policed State	The Vibrant Block
Pros	- More sensors allow quicker detection and deployment of resources to prevent or mitigate a situation - Data aids prediction of incident location and time of occurrence	- Fosters ownership behavior - Fosters relationships between community members, reducing likelihood of anonymous or unattended incidents - Supports economic development in underutilized spaces
Cons	- Unclear if increase in police force guarantees lower crime rates - Difficult to implement surveillance and responsive monitoring solutions on local scale - Subjective human factor complicates incident prediction	- Soft approach makes it difficult to quantify immediate impact - Difficult to assess scale of implementation - Requires community buy-in

"The Vibrant Block" is selected upon which to develop an action plan and strategy due to an interest in addressing design elements particularly following observation of the correlation between land use (or disuse) and crime occurrence shown in Fig. 2.

Actions and Strategies. The proposed action plan adapts the more recently developed Second Generation Crime Prevention Through Environmental Design (2nd Gen CPTED), which uses urban design to influence a potential offender's decision to commit a crime in a given space [32]. This approach centers on four main pillars: social cohesion, community culture, connectivity, and threshold capacity.

Fig. 2. Vacant lots per square mile (left), vacant lots per square mile overlaid with 2020 shootings hotspot analysis (right). Data source: OpenDataPhilly, US Census. Shapefiles downloaded April 14, 2021. Census data accessed May 14, 2021.

Social cohesion is the belief that communities form bonds by addressing problems together: proposed action elements associated with this pillar include 1) developing a local leadership committee, 2) organizing townhalls, listservs, etc., and 3) forming neighborhood watch groups. *Community culture* is the concept of creating a sense of ownership through interactions between residents as well as the built space. This can be fostered through 1) organization of neighborhood events like cleanup days or barbecues, and 2) cultivating shared spaces such as community gardens or art installations. *Connectivity* is important in and between neighborhoods due to the "permeability" of connected spaces, in which enacting measures in one space sometimes results in the criminal activities simply moving one street over, not actually mitigating the overall perpetration of crimes [38]. To address this, 1) neighborhood cluster leadership committees should be formed, and 2) inter-neighborhood activities will help improve network bonds. Lastly, *threshold capacity* is the concept of maximizing use of open spaces to reduce the physiotemporal opportunities for a crime to be committed. Some practical applications include 1) cleaning and transforming abandoned lots and buildings into communal spaces, and 2) diversifying uses for common public spaces. For example, vacant lots can be reimagined into a multi-functional space used for community-building, economy-boosting, health-improving initiatives.

A community-centric approach with design element considerations for the built environment creates an environment that is not only designed for, but also by, the community. To ensure this, community surveys would help determine which initiatives to prioritize. One major aspect of cultivating a sense of ownership and responsibility over a space is to motivate upkeep and order of the neighborhood. Areas with greater physical disorder tend to embolden criminals while (and perhaps because) residents are less protective of the common space and are hence less willing or able to intervene and prevent crime. An act as simple as "greening" a vacant lot can result in reduction of gun assaults and petty crimes, while also decreasing resident stress and improving health [34]. Proposed uses include spaces for picnic tables and playgrounds, an open space for multi-modal use, such as community activities, and spaces for mobile vendors like food trucks on various days throughout the week.

Mobility. Although downtown congestion pricing was initially the focus of the proposed solutions for resolving the issue of congestion in Philadelphia, other solutions should also be evaluated. Those programs already implemented or planned by the city are left out of the diagnosis to avoid redundancy, although it is helpful to keep them in mind for possible syntheses. The alternatives considered previously are assessed in comparison with the initial congestion pricing proposal and summarized in Fig. 3.

1. *Changing downtown speed limits:* Implement lower speed and/or variable speed limits near intersections downtown. Contrary to intuitive expectation that lowering speed limits results in slower trips (and more congestion), studies show that congestion causes slow speeds but slow speeds do not necessarily cause congestion, and in some cases actually improve traffic flow [39].
2. *Transit-only geo-temporal zones:* Define lanes along key transit routes dedicated exclusively for bus/transit use during peak travel periods. Implementing dedicated bus lanes during peak hours should improve travel times for buses and reliability of public transit options [40] while motivating drivers to shift to public transit.
3. *Expansion of Park & Rides:* Expand park-&-ride lots to key locations in suburbs and in the city with express routes to downtown. There is a dearth of parking lots providing good connections to the transit network. Designing lots as commercial centers may also help foster economic growth in areas near these access points.
4. *Micro-transit services:* Establish on-demand flexible or fixed route electric shuttle service between key transit stops and destinations of interest. Micro-transit services can help reduce traffic by 15%–30% [41] and can be implemented as a standalone solution or integrated with existing transit fleets running during off-schedule hours.

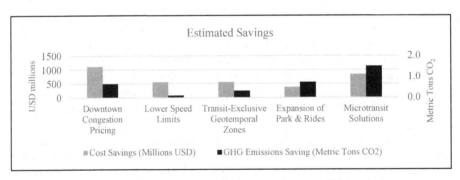

Fig. 3. Estimated benefits of time/fuel costs savings and GHG emissions.

To select the optimal solution, B-Box Software [42] is used to perform an analytic hierarchy process which evaluates the five alternatives discussed above, ranking them against and with respect to six different criteria. The criteria are defined and ranked using Saaty's scale [43] to assign intensities of importance and develop pairwise comparisons between alternatives with respect to the criteria, followed by establishing priorities of the criteria with respect to the objective as shown in Fig. 4 and Table 3. Based on the given inputs, micro-transit emerges as the alternative of choice.

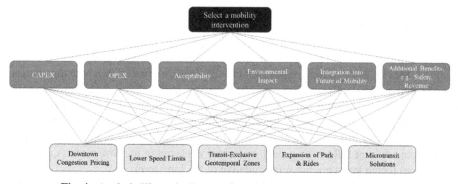

Fig. 4. Analytic Hierarchy Process for selecting a mobility intervention.

Table 3. AHP computation of final priorities and conclusion

	CAP-EX	OP-EX	Acceptability	Environmental impact	Future of mobility	Additional benefits	Total
Downtown congestion pricing	0.078	0.064	0.038	0.198	0.377	0.314	**0.150**
Lower speed limits	0.260	0.294	0.147	0.048	0.037	0.342	**0.183**
Transit-exclusive zones	0.481	0.409	0.075	0.325	0.104	0.047	**0.231**
Electric microtransit	0.128	0.157	0.370	0.325	0.393	0.086	**0.252**
Weight(s)	0.136	0.109	0.273	0.273	0.031	0.179	

Actions and Strategies. The proposed action plan is divided into three phases: planning, implementation, and follow-up. In the first phase, travel routes are assessed to determine which corridors would most benefit from micro-transit solutions. From these, one or two which run through the downtown area will be selected for an initial pilot. This phase will also consider on-demand options for non-fixed route services, i.e., if shuttles can deviate from usual routes to deliver passengers to alternative stops. Next, several options are assessed for implementing the solution: 1) form a public-private partnership with a micro-transit provider; 2) select an existing transit fleet to repurpose; 3) purchase new (ideally electric) vehicles for on-demand services. In addition, the platform for accessing the service must be developed and ideally integrated with existing services like that of the local transit operator. To follow-up, a marketing campaign will increase familiarity with the new service. Ridership and usage over the pilot period will be monitored and evaluated for continuity and scaling.

6 Weaknesses

The following are the most salient limitations identified in the case study.

First, **the city is a dynamic entity that changes continuously.** Even with limitations in accessibility, data collection continues to improve; however, it is critical to maintain organized, reliable, and updated information to ensure accuracy and relevancy of analyses. Philadelphia is a clear case demonstrating that a city is always changing and that it is crucial to remain up to date on information that serves as the foundation for planning. Philadelphia did not follow the growth trajectory expected in its 1960 plan; as a result, trends from recent years are not representative of the long term.

Second, **studies are restricted in time and expertise.** Researching, analyzing, developing, and evaluating an "ideal solution" for a city is a daunting endeavor. Even with restriction to just two of the six smart city pillars in this case study, it was difficult to narrow the scope to meet the time constraints of the project. Lack of expertise in the field also costs more time and effort spent collecting background information as well as limiting access to certain sector-specific resources.

Lastly, **robust quantitative data is necessary to support proposals.** The analyses of the demonstrated case study were highly simplified. Applying advanced statistical analyses and simulations would provide validation for the impact of proposed solutions. Proposals could be further strengthened with firsthand evidence like community surveys, which could be analyzed to assess scenarios and priorities of stakeholders.

7 Conclusions and Future Work

A key problem with traditional city planning is that most decisions are made in silos without accounting for the nuanced interactions between supposedly disparate variables. This work offers an integrated methodology to address this challenge, emphasizing the benefits of using a multi-perspective approach. The open-ended approach offers an innovative perspective that places seemingly disparate issues in the same room, enabling a more comprehensive evaluation of the city's needs.

It is seen through the evolution of hypotheses and solutions ultimately selected that the optimal solution is not always the first. For example, the initial expectation for addressing quality of life was to find a technological solution to mitigate crime, but additional research led to the conclusion that a human-centric approach is paramount. In the mobility case, while the study initially began with one value-adding solution, evaluating other criteria led to a different optimal solution. This demonstrates the importance of remaining open to new inputs which may influence initial hypotheses.

Future research lines include further exploration of the mathematical correlations between the different socio-economic and environmental factors and occurrences of crime, along with sensitivity analyses. Statistical analyses verifying the qualitative observations made in initial studies would further serve to support solution proposals.

References

1. Trindade, E.P., Hinnig, M.P.F., da Costa, E.M., Marques, J.S., Bastos, R.C., Yigitcanlar, T.: Sustainable development of smart cities: a systematic review of the literature. J. Open Innov. Technol. Market Complex. 3(1), 1–14 (2017). https://doi.org/10.1186/s40852-017-0063-2
2. Giffinger, R., Fertner, C., Kramar, H., Kalasek, R., Pichler-Milanović, N., Meijers, E.: Smart cities: ranking of European medium-sized cities. Centre of Regional Science (SRF), Vienna University of Technology (2007)
3. Caragliu, A., Del Bo, C., Nijkamp, P.: Smart cities in Europe. J. Urban Technol. 18, 65–82 (2011). https://doi.org/10.1080/10630732.2011.601117
4. Angelidou, M.: Smart cities: a conjuncture of four forces. Cities 47, 95–106 (2015). https://doi.org/10.1016/j.cities.2015.05.004
5. City of Philadelphia: Philadelphia2035: Citywide Vision (2011). https://drive.google.com/file/d/1gGEqfOR_WUWD3pgkc7TVyBHxzpvm4HLj/view
6. Samantha, D.: Philadelphia ranks among the least safe cities in the country (2019). www.thedp.com/article/2019/12/philadelphia-safety-report-wallet-hub
7. Pishue, B.: 2020 Global Traffic Scorecard. INRIX (2021)
8. Hein, C., Schubert, D.: Resilience and path dependence: a comparative study of the port cities of London, Hamburg, and Philadelphia. J. Urban Hist. 47, 389–419 (2021). https://doi.org/10.1177/0096144220925098
9. Weigley, R.F., Wainwright, N.B., Wolf, E. (eds.): Philadelphia: a 300 year history. W.W. Norton, New York (1982)
10. Wiig, A.: The empty rhetoric of the smart city: from digital inclusion to economic promotion in Philadelphia. Urban Geogr. 37, 535–553 (2016). https://doi.org/10.1080/02723638.2015.1065686
11. City of Philadelphia: CONNECT: Philadelphia's Strategic Transportation Plan (2018). http://www.phillyotis.com/wp-content/uploads/2018/11/Connect_9.8_11-09-18_sm.pdf
12. City of Philadelphia: SmartCityPHL Roadmap (2019). https://www.phila.gov/media/20190204121858/SmartCityPHL-Roadmap.pdf
13. City of Philadelphia: Greenworks: A Vision for a Sustainable Philadelphia (2016). https://www.phila.gov/media/20161101174249/2016-Greenworks-Vision_Office-of-Sustainability.pdf
14. City of Philadelphia: Vision Zero Action Plan 2025 (2020). https://visionzerophl.com/uploads/attachments/ckhnt3jvf042cx4d6x9nperbc-visionzeroactionplan2025-2020-11-17-print-compressed.pdf
15. City of Philadelphia: The Philadelphia Transit Plan: A Vision for 2045 (2021). www.phila.gov/media/20210222110702/OTIS-Philadelphia-Transit-Plan.pdf
16. Arkaraprasertkul, N.: Toward modernist urban design: Louis Kahn's plan for central Philadelphia. J. Urban Des. 13, 177–194 (2008). https://doi.org/10.1080/13574800801965676
17. Ryberg, S.R.: Historic preservation's urban renewal roots: preservation and planning in mid-century Philadelphia. J. Urban Hist. 39, 193–213 (2013). https://doi.org/10.1177/0096144212440177
18. Ehlenz, M.M.: Neighborhood revitalization and the anchor institution: assessing the impact of the University of Pennsylvania's West Philadelphia initiatives on university city. Urban Aff. Rev. 52, 714–750 (2016). https://doi.org/10.1177/1078087415601220
19. Moscovici, D., Dilworth, R., Mead, J., Zhao, S.: Can sustainability plans make sustainable cities? Sustain. Sci. Pract. Policy. 11, 32–43 (2015). https://doi.org/10.1080/15487733.2015.11908137
20. Cohen, M.A.: The effect of crime on life satisfaction. J. Leg. Stud. 37, S325–S353 (2008). https://doi.org/10.1086/588220

21. Office of Disease Prevention and Health Promotion: Crime and Violence. https://www.hea lthypeople.gov/2020/topics-objectives/topic/social-determinants-health/interventions-resour ces/crime-and-violence
22. McCollister, K.E., French, M.T., Fang, H.: The cost of crime to society: new crime-specific estimates for policy and program evaluation. Drug Alcohol Depend. **108**, 98–109 (2010). https://doi.org/10.1016/j.drugalcdep.2009.12.002
23. Sheller, M.: Racialized mobility transitions in Philadelphia: connecting urban sustainability and transport justice: racialized mobility transitions in Philadelphia. City Soc. **27**, 70–91 (2015). https://doi.org/10.1111/ciso.12049
24. Korb, A.B.: NOTE: SEPTA, Philadelphia, and Transportation Equity in America. Georget. J. Law Mod. Crit. Race Perspect. **3** (2011)
25. Casello, J.M., Wright, R.M., Vuchic, V.R.: Context-sensitive urban transportation design in West Philadelphia. Pennsylvania. Transp. Res. Rec. J. Transp. Res. Board. **1956**, 165–174 (2006). https://doi.org/10.1177/0361198106195600121
26. Al-Rijleh, M.-K., Alam, A., Foti, R., Gurian, P.L., Spatari, S., Hatzopoulou, M.: Strategies to achieve deep reductions in metropolitan transportation GHG emissions: the case of Philadelphia. Transp. Plan. Technol. **41**, 797–815 (2018). https://doi.org/10.1080/03081060.2018.152 6879
27. CityRating.com: Philadelphia Crime Rate Report (Pennsylvania). https://www.cityrating. com/crime-statistics/pennsylvania/philadelphia.html
28. Gaur, P.: How is urban planning an essential tool in crime prevention? (2019). https://www. re-thinkingthefuture.com/city-and-architecture/a3485-how-is-urban-planning-an-essentialtool-in-crime-prevention/
29. ArcGIS Pro. ESRI (2020)
30. Google Earth Pro. Google LLC (2021)
31. U.S. Department of Transportation: "Built Environment Strategies to Deter Crime." https:// www.transportation.gov/mission/health/built-environment-strategies-to-deter-crime
32. ICA: Primer in CPTED - What is CPTED? https://cpted.net/Primer-in-CPTED
33. Humphrey, C., Jensen, S.T., Small, D.S., Thurston, R.: Urban vibrancy and safety in Philadelphia. Environ. Plan. B Urban Anal. City Sci. **47**, 1573–1587 (2020). https://doi.org/10.1177/ 2399808319830403
34. Branas, C.C., Cheney, R.A., MacDonald, J.M., Tam, V.W., Jackson, T.D., Ten Have, T.R.: A difference-in-differences analysis of health, safety, and greening vacant urban space. Am. J. Epidemiol. **174**, 1296–1306 (2011). https://doi.org/10.1093/aje/kwr273
35. Marchesini, P., Weijermars, W.: The relationship between road safety and congestion on motorways. SWOV Institute for Road Safety Research (2010)
36. Peach, J.: 5 Cities with Congestion Pricing. https://www.smartcitiesdive.com/ex/sustainablec itiescollective/five-cities-congestion-pricing/28437/
37. Parks, H.: Investigating the Impact of Congestion Pricing Around the World. https://climatexchange.org/2019/05/29/investigating-the-impact-of-congestion-pricing-around-the-world/
38. Metropolitan Area Planning Council: Crime Prevention through Environmental Design. http:// cpted.mapc.org/index.html
39. Soriguera, F., Martínez, I., Sala, M., Menéndez, M.: Effects of low speed limits on freeway traffic flow. Transp. Res. Part C Emerg. Technol. **77**, 257–274 (2017). https://doi.org/10.1016/ j.trc.2017.01.024
40. National Association of City Transportation Officials: Dedicated Curbside/Offset Bus Lanes. https://nacto.org/publication/urban-street-design-guide/street-design-elements/ transit-streets/dedicated-curbside-offset-bus-lanes
41. Hazan, J., Lang, N., Wegscheider, A.K., Fassenot, B.: On-Demand Transit Can Unlock Urban Mobility. BCG Henderson Institute (2019)

42. B-Box. CalebABC Co., LTD (2009)
43. Forman, E.H., Gass, S.I.: The analytic hierarchy process—an exposition. Oper. Res. **49**, 469–486 (2001). https://doi.org/10.1287/opre.49.4.469.11231

Upgrading Urban Services Through BPL: Practical Applications for Smart Cities

Noelia Uribe-Pérez[1]([✉]) [iD], Igor Fernández[2] [iD], and David de la Vega[2] [iD]

[1] TECNALIA, Basque Research and Technology Alliance (BRTA), Parque Científico y Tecnológico de Bizkaia, C/ Astondo Bidea, Edificio 700, 48160 Derio-Bizkaia, Spain
noelia.uribe@tecnalia.com
[2] Department of Communications Engineering, UPV/EHU, University of the Basque Country (UPV/EHU), Pz. Torres Quevedo s/n, 48013 Bilbao, Spain
{igor.fernandez,david.delavega}@ehu.eus

Abstract. Current initiatives related to smart cities in LATAM reveal an increasing interest in the improvement of cities and the wellbeing of their citizens. In addition, specific working groups have been created for this purpose. In this sense, the communication technologies set the basis for gathering, transporting, and managing the large amount of data generated in cities to provide a wide range of services. Within the many alternatives available, BPL positions as a promising technology, since smart cities can greatly benefit of its higher data rates and low latency. In addition, since the medium is already deployed and most of the assets and sensors are connected to the same medium, the cost of the communication systems will be reduced in price and simplicity. The work presents four practical applications: smart buildings, urban lighting, energy assets management and broadband access, in which the possibilities and advantages of BPL are further addressed. Finally, some conclusions and key aspects relating BPL to the success of smart cities are identified.

Keywords: Smart city · Broadband Power Line Communications · Urban services · Communication technologies

1 Introduction

Latin America is the region with the highest concentration relative to urban population, but it is also one of the most lagging behind in when it comes to Smart Cities. However, there is notably increase in related initiatives, which shows that there is a growing interest in this field. Medellin, Buenos Aires, Mexico and Santiago are at the top of the list of smart cities in Latin America. Other cities such as Bogotá, São Paulo and Rio de Janeiro are also deploying initiatives in the field of smart cities, showing that these trends have come to stay. In addition, specific groups in relevant international groups, such as the SG20 Regional Group for Latin America (SG20RG-LATAM) at the International Telecommunication Union (ITU), has been created and is responsible for studies relating to Smart Cities and Communities and Internet of Things (IoT) and its applications [1].

S. Nesmachnow and L. Hernández Callejo (Eds.): ICSC-Cities 2021, CCIS 1555, pp. 74–85, 2022.
https://doi.org/10.1007/978-3-030-96753-6_6

When referring to technologies for Smart Cities, it is usual to associate them to wireless options. Recent trends related to IoT are usually conceived as wireless. But the reality is that there are still wired alternatives with very remarkable advantages that can play an interesting role in the Smart City context. One of them is the electric cable, nevertheless, the power wire, with more than 100.000 km deployed throughout Latin America, is an option to consider. Specially in those assets already connected to the grid (traffic lights, urban lighting, buildings, energy resources, …) a communication system can be easily deployed through Power Line Communication (PLC) devices without relying on external batteries. Specifically, this work addresses the potential of the broadband version of PLC – Broadband Power Line Communications (BPL) for smart cities applications in LATAM region. BPL technology allow high transfer data rate, being able to offer rates of up to hundreds of Mbps and significantly shorter response times of less than 50 ms, while using a communication media already deployed as well as robust and secure, hence leading to less installation costs when stablishing the communication system.

The remaining work in this documented is grouped as follows: Sect. 2 reviews the concept of smart city and particularly, within the LATAM region; Sect. 3 introduces the fundamentals of PLC and highlights the benefits of BPL; Sect. 4 describes the opportunities of BPL for the smart city and, finally, Sect. 5 summarizes the main conclusions of this work.

2   Smart Cities of XXI Century

Beyond the concept of "digitalization", Smart Cities are conceived as enablers of better-living for their citizens as well as increasing sustainability through technology-driven initiatives. The Inter-American Development Bank (IDB) understands that smart cities *"use connectivity, sensors distributed in the environment and computerized intelligent management systems to solve immediate problems, organize complex urban scenarios and create innovative responses to meet the needs of their citizens… [using] technologies to integrate and analyses an immense amount of data generated and captured from different sources that anticipate, mitigate and even prevent crisis situations.* In this sense, the communication infrastructure of the city set the basis for a whole set of applications and services.

2.1   Needs of Smart Cities in Terms of Communications

Digital technology can indeed make a city better. Energy efficiency can be improved through the street lighting control and the management of the energy resources. Citizens can be connected using mobile applications with cameras while receiving alerts and useful information as well as send data to the government. Safety can be improved in the streets and buildings through cameras and sensors. Also, the traffic can be benefited from the installation of cameras combined with motion sensors installed on the streets. Pollution can be controlled and effectively reduced with sensors and air quality monitoring systems. In the same line, smoke, toxic gases, and temperature sensors associated with ambient cameras and warning systems can prevent environmental disasters. At the core of these applications are a communication infrastructure, sensors, an integrated operation and control center and communication interfaces [2].

Focusing on the communication infrastructure, it is required that the smart city ensures not only the existence of broadband networks that can support digital applications, but also the availability of this connectivity throughout the city and to all citizens. This communication infrastructure can be a combination of different data network technologies using cable transmission, optical fiber, and wireless networks. In summary, communication technologies should allow the following [3]:

- Interconnection between very different devices.
- Hybrid communications systems, where wired and wireless systems must live together.
- Fast communications.
- Robustness in communications.
- Flexibility and scalability in infrastructure.
- Security in communications and devices

In addition, some important requirements that a city should consider when selecting a technology for their network foundation are listed as follows [4]:
- End-to-end solutions: the network should encompass wired and wireless indoor spaces and wireless outdoor and network backbone coverage and provide a service-delivery platform for functions such as identifying end users and the applications and resources they access.
- Standards-based: the network should support security standards, and con-sider the use of both licensed and unlicensed frequencies.
- Easy to deploy: the access points should be configured themselves for optimum performance, eliminating the need for personnel to configure each device manually.
- Highly reliable: the selected solution should be "self-healing" and automatically selects an alternate path through the network if a link fails and avoids congested areas.
- Unified, easy management: the communication system should enable the management of the wired and wireless outdoor networks and wireless in-door networks as one unified network.
- Scalable: the network should enable the city to build and expand outdoor coverage incrementally, without reconfiguring the installed base. Scalability of a mesh network is a function of the number of channels available, which is why the network should use different channels for access and backhaul
- Secure: the network should incorporate integrated security technologies to maintain the confidentiality of private information, protects against the spread of viruses, and provides different levels of access to municipal constituents.

2.2 Smart Cities in LATAM

According to [5], Latin America is the most urbanized region of the developing world. Two thirds of the Latin American population live in cities of 20,000 inhabitants or more and almost 80% in urban areas and is projected to increase up to 89% by 2050. However, it is also one of the most lagging regions when it comes to Smart Cities. Following the annually Smart City Index prepared by the Institute for Management Development, which ranks cities based on economic and technological data, the Latin American city that has advanced the most in this field is Medellin, which ranks 72nd in the world, followed by Buenos Aires (88th), Mexico (90th), Santiago (91st), Bogotá (92nd), São Paulo (100th) and Rio de Janeiro (102nd) from a list with a total of 109 cities listed and headed by Singapore [6].

Large cities such as Buenos Aires, Medellín or Rio de Janeiro are making budgetary efforts to modernize both their urban infrastructure and the services they provide to citizens, from smart traffic lights to improve mobility, and the installation of surveillance cameras to improve public safety [7]. Santiago is addressing air contamination and traffic congestion through different initiatives moving towards clean mobility (electric vehicles, bike sharing). Medellin has implemented an Intelligent Mobility System of Medellin (SIMM) that uses cameras, networked traffic lights and traffic lights with vehicle detection sensors to detect traffic violations and capture traffic information. Bogota has also moved towards sustainable mobility with the increase of the public transportation system while to connected horizontal and vertical signage, smart traffic lights, and monitoring cameras. Rio de Janeiro has implemented an integrated risk management system which includes connected weather radars and a rain gauge network installed in mobile phone towers. Itu has implemented a selective garbage collection system, able to identify need for repair or replacement of containers and the optimization of the routing of collection while reducing collection time and fuel expenses [6]. These are just a few examples of the initiatives which show a growing interest in the field of smart cities in Latin America.

3   Broadband Power Line Communications

3.1   Fundamentals of Power Line Communications

Power line communications (PLC) use the power lines typically employed for electricity transmission and distribution for the transmission of communication signals by adding a modulated carrier signal over the electricity signal at 50/60 Hz. According to the bandwidth of use, PLC can be classified into three main groups:

- Ultra-narrow band PLC (UNB-PLC): this technology operates in the fre-quency range from 30 Hz to 3 kHz. Its main drawback is that it provides low data rates (up to 100 bps) but for long distances (up to 150 km). Some typical and proprietary examples of this technology are ripple control sys-tems and TWACS [8].
- Narrow-band PLC (NB-PLC): operates in the frequency range up to 500 kHz, depending on the region and it can provide high reliability of data transmission up to several hundreds of Kbps and can reach up to hundreds of km. NB-PLC had experienced a remarkable rise for smart metering due to their good overall performance and efficiency, setting an inflection point in the rise of smart grids. Most deployed standards of NB-PLC are: PRIME (ITU-TG.9904), G3-PLC (ITU-T G.9903), IEEE 1901.2 and ITU-T G.hnem.

- Broadband PLC (BPL): this technology operates in the frequency band from 1.8 to 250 MHz, reaching data rates up to hundreds of Mbps for relatively short distances - up to few km. Traditionally, BB-PLC has been used for internet access and but it is currently experiencing a wide presence in smart metering, substation automation and control, and related applications within the smart grids due to the high available data rate, the secure & cybersecure as well as the robust transmission media that it provides.

The biggest advantage of PLC is that there is no alternative with such as an extensive infrastructure already deployed, leading to reduction of deployment costs while guaranteeing a secure communication at rationale speeds. In addition, PLC systems are robust and secure. In contrast to wireless alternatives, PLC allows an immediate establishment of communication during the installation process, does not need antenna tunning or adjustment of antenna direction required and the communication is also possible in difficult environments (e.g., metal-shielded cases, deep underground installations, etc.), where no other access technology can provide a solution [9].

On one hand, PLC presents some valuable advantages for smart city applications, as it has a wide potential coverage due to the electricity wires, making every line-powered device a potential target of value-added services through PLC. Moreover, the installation is already deployed, easy to manage, and stable. On the other hand, the greatest disadvantages of PLC are mainly related to the medium, due to existing disturbances, noises, and attenuations, and consequently, the global capacity of PLC in terms of bandwidth is less than other technologies [10].

3.2 The Role of BPL

Since the beginning of the 21st century, BPL technologies have been widely used within homes for internet communications, as an alternative or complement to WiFi networks. Currently, these technologies offer speeds of one megabit per second (Mbps). The success of NB-PLC in smart metering suggest a technological evolution towards higher bandwidths and lower latencies, in line with stricter requirements regarding real time management and cybersecurity. This has made BPL increasingly considered in monitoring and control applications within the smart grid in the recent years.

Added to the benefits to the power grid system, other smart services, such as the management of electric vehicles (EVs), energy resources, building automation, traffic and lighting control, disposal management, among others, all of them typical systems of smart cities, can be greatly improved with the higher data rates and low latency inherent to BPL, since they could be performed through BPL in real time while assuring cybersecurity and integrity of the data.

4   Opportunities of BPL for the Smart City

4.1   Smart Buildings

Smart Buildings are buildings which integrate and account for intelligence, enterprise, control, and materials and construction as an entire building system, with adaptability, not reactivity, at the core, in order to meet the drivers for building progression: energy and efficiency, longevity and comfort [11]. By means of available data from different sources, smart buildings become adaptable and resilient.

Smart buildings use technologies with automated controls, networked sensors and meters, advanced building automation, energy management in conjunction with information systems and data analytics software. Among the different applications within a smart building, Fig. 1 shows a visual summary of some of them [12]. The following can be highlighted:

- Building energy management: entails the management of loads as well as the generation sources, if included. Heating, ventilating, and air-conditioning (HVAC) systems, which represent a very notable percentage of the electricity consumption, specially in commercial buildings, shall be considered as energy assets as well. All the connected devices (computers, machinery, office appliances, lighting, etc.) are loads of the building, that define the load profile of the building. This load profile can be efficiently managed through an energy control center (CC) when combined with internal data from the building, generation, and storage systems, for instance; and with external data, such as the energy market. As generation sources, renewable energy, such as photovoltaics, and storage sources can be integrated into smart buildings to reduce retail electricity purchases, peak load demands in buildings while moving towards energy self-sufficiency [13]. EV charging stations can be included in the energy management, so that the energy control center of the building can identify the most appropriate time slot to recharge EV with the surplus renewable energy from the building.
- Building management system: this system can include applications such as building entrance control, capacity control, parking slots management and lighting control. These systems get the information from a network of sensors deployed all over the infrastructure: humidity, heat, and lighting sensors; presence detection; people counters, cameras, etc. These sensors get the information and send it through the proper transmission media towards the management control center. In advanced system, the communication can be bidirectional, and some orders can flow from the control center towards actuators installed in specific areas. For instance, if too many people are withing the same area, the center station can decide to decrease the temperature or activate the ventilations system, if necessary. Sometimes it is common to see a general building management system on which the rest of the subsystems/applications depend (energy, surveillance, ...) depending on the complexity of the system itself.
- Surveillance systems: the degree of sophistication of surveillance systems implies that it is getting increasingly common to see independent systems. Real time images in HD as well as video recording, including data processing (facial recognition) is becoming more and more common. Some government buildings and businesses with high security needs are including the systems, hence, high available bandwidth and secure communication networks are required.

The particularity of most of the services commented above is that they are connected somehow to the electricity wire of the building, either because they control energy resources (consumption, EV monitoring) or because they need electricity (lighting). In addition, secure communications and high bandwidth are also demanded (surveillance

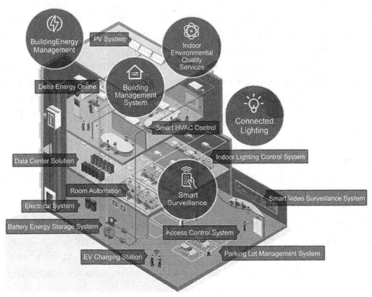

Fig. 1. Overview of services and applications in a smart building. (Source: DELTA Building Automation Solutions [12])

systems, control and monitoring). In these scenarios, BPL can serve as communication media with high bandwidth, robust and reliable, while providing an already installed infrastructure (the power wire of the building).

In line with the possibilities of BPL for smart buildings, there are some related initiatives: authors in [14] explore the efficacy of PLC as a sensor network backbone in a modern building by testing BPL modules. First results show a promising role for BPL as a viable physical and link layer for wired sensor networks. In the same line, in [15] two different BPL technologies are evaluated under different conditions of noise and attenuation, the results show a sufficient throughput on the application layer (18 Mbps in the worst case) for smart building applications. Finally, authors in [16] present the design of a BPL module suitable for installation in an electrical outlet to increase energy efficiency and power management or in local networks as a possible alternative to existing technologies.

4.2 Urban Lighting

Streetlights are one of the most important assets to maintain and control, providing safe roads, inviting public areas, and enhancing security in homes, businesses, and city centers. However, lighting is indeed very costly to operate, with a share of about 40% of the total amount of electricity spent in a city [17].

LED (Light Emitting Diode) has being an inflection point in the lighting field, specially regarding efficiency, improved options (color, intensity and direction of the light beam) and durability. When combined with a smart control on the lighting management system, new advantages emerge, such as the ability of the system for reducing energy consumption and decreasing costs with the possibility of being operated and monitored remotely.

In fact, outdoor lighting is projected to register approximately 20% growth rate through 2025 due to the increasing smart city development initiatives worldwide [18]. The smart lighting solutions are widely used across highways and roadways, bridges and tunnels, as well as public places to optimize the lighting, reduce energy consumption and provide safety. In addition, the need among the government authorities to optimize the use of energy is further increasing the adoption of smart lighting solutions.

Regarding technologies, wired technology captures the major share in the smart lighting market, accounting for more than 70% in 2018 [18], due to its robust nature coupled with high reliability and control, makes it an ideal solution for outdoor lighting applications. A further step in smart lighting can be seen in the infographic of Fig. 2 where the street light set the basis of the smart city platform. This approach presents the streetlight as a multidisciplinary asset with basic and advanced light applications as well as the inclusion of several sensors (noise, traffic, air quality), cameras and assets (EV charging, digital signaling), which can provide additional services such as traffic monitoring; surveillance and safety; EV charging station; parking control; environmental quality; Related experiences taking advantage of BPL for lighting can be found in the literature. For instance, in [20] a lighting solution based on BPL for the smart city is described, aiming at transforming outdoor lighting networks into high speed data networks for additional smart city services.

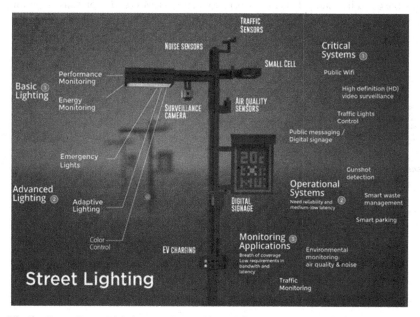

Fig. 2. Smart Street Lighting as a Smart City Platform (Source: SmartCityExpo [19]).

4.3   Energy Assets Management

In a smart city, the optimal management of the energy resources within the city is gaining importance, especially considering the current concern for the environment and increasingly stricter energy efficiency regulations. In this sense, two considerations can be done: first, the management of resources in terms of production of the energy in the cities and secondly, the elaboration of a comprehensive plan for generation, storage and distribution of the energy [21].

In the coming future, each home and building might have the chance not only to generate their own energy, but also it can have the plan to sell the produced energy.

In a smart city, there are, and there will be many assets related to energy somehow: starting with buildings and houses, through fleets of EVs to the city's own energy resources and prosumers. Hence, having a management system and a schedule for all these assets of the city could significantly cause a huge improvement in the context of the energy in the smart communities [22]. The data that should be collected from all the assets includes the generation capacity (from resources and prosumers), storage and a plan that determines how each source could distribute energy among all parts of the city. Therefore, an extensive, reliable, and robust communications network is required.

An example of a city smart energy management can be seen in Fig. 3, where the pilot of the smart city of Yokohama is represented. In this envision, the comprehensive energy management system (EMS) is established integrating ICT, energy resources (e.g., solar panel and EVs), and other smart infrastructure. The hierarchical bundling of EMS enables energy management at the level of individual EMS and demand-side management at the level of the overall system. This involves introducing HEMS (EMS for house) for homes, BEMS (EMS for building) for offices and commercial buildings, FEMS for factories (EMS for factory), and EV and charging stations for the transport sector [23].

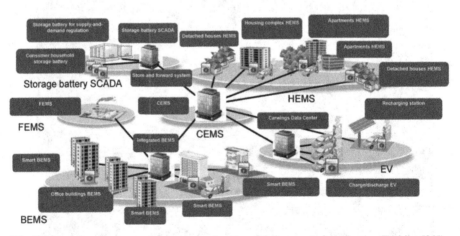

Fig. 3. Overview of an energy management system for the smart city. (Source: Toshiba [23]).

Considering that most of the energy assets will be connected to the power line, it seems natural to think of BPL as a powerful option for the management of resources. In this sense, related initiatives are taking advantage of the ubiquity of PLC in their cities. Smart City Mannheim, under the scope of the German government funded program 'E-Energy', was created to demonstrate how renewable energy can be optimally integrated into the grid as well as how the city can act as an energy store through the use of BPL [24].

4.4 Broadband Access

The Inter-American Development Bank (IDB) designed the Broadband Development Index (BDI), which allows to easily measure the current status and development of broadband in the region of Latin America and the Caribbean [25]. This index not only helps BDI to identify the barriers towards the development of the broadband access in member countries, but also is a measurement of the quality of life in a region.

According to the IDB, the benefits of the broadband access can be broadly classified in two groups:

- Quantifiable benefits: those derived both from investment in infrastructure and from the creation of public policies to promote demand and the use of services made possible by broadband. Within these we find three types of benefits: benefits that users themselves would obtain from the service (e.g. tariff reduction); increased productivity of companies as a result of the adoption and use of the services that broadband enables; and improvement in activities during the working day (efficiency in tasks, remote work, ...)
- Intangible benefits: externalities resulting from the impact of broadband in various sectors. Among them, the IDB includes the government spending reduction; greater transparency in government processes; improved communications at the country level; knowledge sharing; increase in literacy rates and educational levels; reduction of crime and violence, enabling telemedicine services, creation of new companies and new ways of relating on a personal and commercial level; improved productivity of companies and reduced environmental pollution, among others.

Based on the latest version of the index, it can be derived that the gap between the IDB region and the OECD is on average decreasing slightly. However, there is a very important gap in the development of digital infrastructure, which continues to be the main obstacle to the development of the digital ecosystem in the countries of the region.

In this sense, BPL can play an interesting role towards the broadband access. It has been historically employed for in-home internet access and considering the power grid extension, its network can be considered as a massive internet provider. Since the power grid extends to both urban and rural areas (particular in the latest, where often broadband access is less present), this advantage of the technology will be not limited only the urban areas.

5 Conclusions

This work presents the advantages of BPL for the smart cities through the practical application of four examples: smart buildings, urban lighting, energy assets managements and broadband access. In addition, related initiatives of BPL within the urban context are also described.

Through these applications it has been shown that BPL is a promising technology for the enforcement of smart cities since it provides real-time communications with low latency and guaranteeing cybersecurity while providing a robust and reliable communication backbone for the city. In addition, since the communication medium is already deployed and most of the assets are connected to the power grid, the commissioning of the system is reduced in time, costs and complexity.

Acknowledgments. This work has been partially funded by the Basque Government (Ref. KK-2020/00095 "BB-Grid project", and Ref. IT-1234-19).

References

1. ITU-T Regional Group for Latin America, SG20RG-LATAM. https://www.itu.int/en/ITU-T/studygroups/2017-2020/20/sg20rglatam/Pages/mandate.aspx
2. IDB. The Road toward Smart Cities: Migrating from Traditional City Management to the Smart City. https://publications.iadb.org/publications/english/document/The-Road-toward-Smart-Cities-Migrating-from-Traditional-City-Management-to-the-Smart-City.pdf
3. Hamaguchi, K., et al.: Telecommunications systems in smart cities. Hitachi Rev. **61**, 152–158 (2012)
4. Villa, N.: Wireless cities: a strategic roadmap. In: CISCO Whitepaper (2007). https://www.cisco.com/c/dam/en_us/about/ac79/docs/wp/Wireless_Roadmap_WP_0629a.pdf
5. Giannattasio, G.: America Latina, Ciudades Inteligentes. https://www.itu.int/en/ITU-T/webinars/20210920/Documents/Presentations/Gustavo%20Giannattasio.pdf
6. Institute for Management Development: "Smart City Index 2020". https://www.imd.org/smart-city-observatory/smart-city-index/
7. Cacace, J.: Digital Latam: Smart Cities - The Long Latin American Road. https://www.accesspartnership.com/smart-cities-the-long-latin-american-road/
8. Mak, S.T., Moore, T.G.: TWACS™, A new viable two-way automatic communication system for distribution networks. Part II: inbound communication. In: Proc. IEEE Trans. Power Apparatus and Syst. **PAS-103**(8), 2141–2147 (1984)
9. Landis+Gyr: Introducing the power of PLC. White paper. http://eu.landisgyr.com/hs-fs/hub/358550/file-673231343-pdf/Resources/LG_White_Paper_PLC.pdf
10. Uribe-Pérez, N., Angulo, I., De la Vega, D., Arzuaga, T., Fernández, I., Arrinda, A.: Smart grid applications for a practical implementation of IP over narrowband power line communications. Energies **10**, 1782 (2017)
11. Buckman, A.H., Mayfield, M., Beck, S.B.: What is a smart building? Smart and Sustainable Built Environment (2014)
12. DELTA Building Automation Solutions. https://www.deltaww.com/en-US/solutions/Building-Automation-Solutions/ALL/
13. Qi, J., et al.: Demand response and smart buildings: a survey of control, communication, and cyber-physical security. ACM Trans. Cyber Phys. Syst. **1**(4), 1–25 (2017)
14. Pannuto, P., Dutta, P.: Exploring Powerline Networking for the Smart Building (2011)
15. Mlýnek, P., Rusz, M., Benešl, L., Sláčik, J., Musil, P.: Possibilities of broadband power line communications for smart home and smart building applications. Sensors **21**, 240 (2021)

16. Rusz, M., Mlýnek, P.: Broadband power line module integrated into power plug for smart buildings. In: 2020 12th International Congress on Ultra Modern Telecommunications and Control Systems and Workshops (ICUMT), pp. 159–162 (2020)
17. Castro, M., Jara, A.J., Skarmeta, A.F.G.: Smart lighting solutions for smart cities. In: 2013 27th International Conference on Advanced Information Networking and Applications Workshops, pp. 1374–1379. IEEE (2013)
18. Global Market Insights: Smart Lighting Market Trends (2018). https://www.gminsights.com/industry-analysis/smart-lighting-market
19. Navigant Research: Smart Street Lighting as a Smart City Platform. https://www.pdxeng.ch/wp-content/uploads/2018/10/Smart-Street-Lighting.jpg
20. Martínez Vázquez, M.: G.hn technology for industrial and smart grid applications. ITU-T roadmap and homegrid forum certification update. In: IEEE International Symposium on Power Line Communications and its Applications (ISPLC) (2020)
21. Calvillo, C.F., SánchezMiralles, A., Villar, J.: Energy management and planning in smart cities. Renew. Sustain. Energy Rev. **55**, 273–287 (2016)
22. Azgomi, H., Jamshidi, M.: A Brief survey on Smart Community and Smart Transportation (2018)
23. Toshiba: News Release. Toshiba Announces Participation in Summer 2014 Yokohama Smart City Project Demonstration (2014). https://www.global.toshiba/ww/news/corporate/2014/07/pr1001.html
24. Moma – Smart City Mannheim Research Project. https://www.ppc-ag.com/projekte/moma-smart-city-mannheim/
25. IDB. Informe Anual del Índice de Desarrollo de la Banda Ancha en América Latina y el Caribe (2018). https://publications.iadb.org/publications/spanish/document/Informe_a nual_del_%C3%8Dndice_de_Desarrollo_de_la_Banda_Ancha_en_Am%C3%A9rica_Lat ina_y_el_Caribe_es.pdf

Visualization in Smart City Technologies

Teresa Cepero$^{(\boxtimes)}$ (ID), Luis G. Montané-Jiménez$^{(\boxtimes)}$ (ID),
Edgard Benítez-Guerrero (ID), and Carmen Mezura-Godoy (ID)

Facultad de Estadística e Informática, Universidad Veracruzana, Xalapa, Mexico
{lmontane,edbenitez,cmezura}@uv.mx

Abstract. Smart cities aim to use technology to connect people with information to make evidence-based decisions, use resources more efficiently, improve citizens' quality of life, and make cities more sustainable. Smart cities generate massive amounts of data due to a large number of embedded technology; although useful to achieve the city goals, these data are complex for people to manage. Data visualization is an efficient means to represent urban data and help people to understand the underlying information, uncover hidden patterns in data sets, and generate insights that support decision-making. This paper presents an overview of the usage of data visualization in smart city technologies, identifies the technologies used to visualize information, analyzes the visualization techniques, and offers an overview of the biggest challenges and future directions of visualization in smart cities systems.

Keywords: Visualization · Smart cities · Dashbaords · Literature review

1 Introduction

Most cities are introducing technology into their infrastructure to gather data from the urban environment and their citizens that helps understand the city's situation. Real-time data from sensors capture environmental conditions such as noise, water, and air quality, as well as the dynamics that take place within the city, such as vehicular traffic. In addition to machine-generated data, people, processes, paperwork, business and government transactions can be a data source [48]. For example, government records and population surveys produce data on the size and characteristics of the population, such as demographics, employment statistics, crime rates, and well-being [51].

The transition from raw data to information has been simplified through technological tools. In particular, smart city technologies help integrate and analyze data from various sources to develop a comprehensive vision of the city [15]. Smart city platforms integrate the information of the urban environment elements to optimize the efficiency of the city's processes, activities, and services by joining various elements and key actors in an intelligent system [47]. In the face of the challenge of efficiently monitoring and interpreting large amounts of

S. Nesmachnow and L. Hernández Callejo (Eds.): ICSC-Cities 2021, CCIS 1555, pp. 86–100, 2022.
https://doi.org/10.1007/978-3-030-96753-6_7

data, most smart city systems integrate visualizations to show the information in a visual and meaningful way to help users understand the information [28].

Smart city technologies enable the retrieve, analysis, and visualization of urban data in almost real-time [30]. However, data visualization in these environments represents a challenge, given the volume and diversity of the handled data. In recent years, there has been a technological and theoretical growth specialized in visualization in smart cities; however, the information is scattered. There have been reviews of the smart city literature [19,27,50], but these studies have focused on technology, data generation and analysis. Some studies [1,2,38,55] have addressed data visualization by reviewing some of the latest smart city projects; others have focused on visualizing a specific type of data or domain [43,63]. More analytical work is needed to integrate the dispersed knowledge of the field and provide an overview of the usage of visualization. In this paper, we present a literature review of visualization in smart city technologies that integrates and describes technological features, analyzes data visualization techniques, and offers an overview of the challenges in the field.

This document is organized as follows. Section 2 describes the methodology followed in the literature review. Section 3 presents the results of the study of data visualization in smart city technologies. Finally, in Sect. 4, the conclusions are presented.

2   Literature Review Methodology

This paper presents a structured literature review based on the guidelines proposed by Kitchenham [22]. The objectives of the study were to analyze the literature on visualization in smart city technologies, analyze the systems used to visualize information, review the visualization techniques most used to represent urban data, and offer an overview of the biggest challenges and future directions of visualization in smart city systems.

Based on the research objectives, the following keywords were defined as the most relevant for the research: information, data, visualization, decision support, urban data, and smart city. These keywords were used to create a search string connecting them and different synonyms of the words with the boolean operators "AND" and "OR".

- ("information" OR "data") AND ("visualization" OR "visualisation") AND ("decision support" OR "decision making") AND ("urban data" OR "smart city" OR "smart cities")

The papers were searched using the search string in five specialized online databases: ScienceDirect, IEEE Xplore Digital Library, SpringerLink, ACM Digital Library, and Wiley. The search was made for titles, keywords, abstracts, and the body of the documents, without any specified time range. Table 1 shows the results of the resource identification process, 2 343 papers were found in total.

In order to evaluate the relevance of the identified papers, we selected articles in English or Spanish focused on data visualization in smart cities. The selection

Table 1. Results of the resource identification process

Databases	Identified papers	1st selection	2nd selection
ScienceDirect	1242	40	15
IEEE Xplore Digital Library	37	9	7
SpringerLink	540	37	10
ACM Digital Library	314	37	17
Wiley	210	2	2
Total	**2343**	**125**	**51**

process was carried out in two stages. First, we selected a set of papers based on titles and abstracts. This first filtering of the documents helped establish which studies were relevant and reduced the documents to 125. Based on the content analysis of the selected papers, another filtering was carried out to select the studies that help identify advances in information visualization in smart city technologies. This second stage reduced the total number of documents to 51 (see Table 1). Later, in the data extraction stage, an analysis of the literature was carried out based on the selected articles.

Based on the literature review, we analyzed the advances in data visualization for decision-making in cities, the visualization technologies used, visualization techniques used in smart city systems, and the challenges in the field. The next section presents the results of the analysis of the literature review of visualization in smart city systems.

3   Data Visualization in Smart City Technologies

The smart city concept aims to use information and communication technologies (ICT) to improve the functioning of cities and the quality of life of their citizens [4]. These cities are highly instrumented and interconnected, allowing the collection of data on multiple phenomena -both natural and social- through the use of satellites, sensors, cameras, smartphones, personal devices, the web, and other data-acquisition systems, including social networks as networks of human sensors [20,39,58].

The data generated in a city contributes to creating useful content for stakeholders, including local governments, businesses, citizens, and city visitors [23]. In order to get value from data, data analysis is necessary to extract useful information from the collected data, and visualization is key to conveying the information to stakeholders in an efficient way. For example, instead of viewing Madrid weather station logs and a list of geographic coordinates of places with free internet, a citizen might prefer to consult a dashboard that shows the weather forecast on a line chart and a map with the places with free WiFi.

In smart cities, technology is used to collect and analyze large-scale data in real-time, from which visualizations can be generated to monitor the city and make better decisions based on evidence [38, 47]. Of the range of technologies used to make a city "smarter", the most used technologies for visualizing urban data are smart city platforms, city dashboards, and the graphical interfaces of smart city systems.

3.1   Smart City Platforms

A smart city platform is a software that systematically collects, integrates, and analyzes urban data from different sources. This definition conveys the general concept of the smart city platform; however, there is no universally accepted definition. Some authors like [7, 16, 37, 50] conceive the smart city platform as a middleware to build smart city applications. On the other hand, authors such as Ghosh [15] and Raj [44] define a smart city platform as software that collects and analyzes various data sources to generate information that promotes new knowledge that leads to better decision-making and optimized actions.

Smart city platforms provide information on the current situation in the city that is used to support short-term city management tasks. This short-term approach predominates in the literature and on the platforms available on the market (FIWOO, kaa, Thingsboard, and Ubidots) due to developments strongly oriented to real-time data sources, such as sensors and social networks. There are some attempts to analyze data from different time periods, such as Pettit's platform [40] that updates its information at different time intervals according to the updates of the data source, or the Zdravesk's platform [61] that collects data almost in real-time, in addition to monthly and annual information, such as economic indicators. However, so far, the main smart city development approach has been on real-time or near-real-time data [2].

The literature review shows that smart city platforms integrate and analyze data from various sources, and these platforms may or may not include data visualization. When the platform is designed as software that integrates and analyzes urban data to promote an understanding of the elements in a city [3, 8, 26, 54, 60, 61], the smart city platform includes a user interface that displays the analyzed information. On the other hand, when the platform is designed as middleware [7, 16, 37, 50], its architecture does not include a component to display the data -user interface-, but usually contemplates the connection to apps, dashboards, or other external systems to display the information.

3.2   City Dashboards

Another key smart city technology is the dashboard. A dashboard is a software characterized by having a predominantly visual interface that people use to monitor at a glance the most important information necessary to achieve one or more objectives [12]. The city dashboard or urban dashboard can have the mechanisms to collect, process, and analyze urban data [40], or access the information through services, such as a smart city platform. These integrate live data feeds from sensors, official and social media data into a single interface through data visualization [1].

The information contained in a dashboard varies in each city; however, the elements most commonly displayed in city dashboards are related to the following categories: transport, environment, statistics, economy, community, culture, and security [55]. Dashboards can present information from more than one category but not necessarily from all of them (see Fig. 1).

Based on a comprehensive analysis of city dashboards worldwide, Tong and Wu [55] summarize the six main characteristics of city Dashboards: recording, connectivity, sensing, interaction, adaptation, and integration. Recording refers to the process of saving all kinds of city data. Connectivity means creating seamless connectivity to the gathered data through all kinds of devices. Sensing refers to collecting data through sensors to perceive the city environment. Interaction refers to the way a user interacts with a system (and its data); this defines the content and structure of information presented; some ways of interaction are point selection, adding, zooming, and narrowing. Adaptation refers to the ability to personalize data products and services based on user needs. The integration enables integrating all kinds of information sources and services to display information on the dashboard [55].

City dashboards need data from the urban environment to display. There are multiple schemes (frameworks, indices, indicators, and rankings) of urban data to monitor and evaluate the performance of cities [52]. Most of these schemes are formed with a hierarchical structure of data, where each level is described by the results of the previous level. The hierarchical information structure of smart city schemes is commonly used for the analysis of urban data and its organization in dashboards. According to theese organization, the relevant features of the city are organized into sections. Each section is defined by a series of composite indicators, which contain information from simple indicators.

Sharifi [52] analyzed the characteristics of 34 smart city schemes. The results of this study indicate that schemes have been developed under three approaches: market-oriented (to assess the competitive capacity of cities); research-based (schemes focused on the valuation of the smart city with scientific solidity); and schemes focused on the development of a smart city and the improvement of governance (to improve the understanding of data on smart city governance). Regarding the target audience of the schemes, the analysis shows that the target audience in decreasing order of frequency is: city authorities, police and decision-makers, the public, investors, smart city developers, and academia [52].

Data visualization through city dashboards serve to create a communication channel between data and people. So local authorities and citizens can easily explore data and take advantage of city information and infrastructure [55]. Yet, there has been little research concerning the optimum design for city dashboards that takes account of users' expectations and skills [59]. Professional designers and developers can improve city dashboard design to help citizens and government departments to monitor the city and foster technology adoption.

3.3   Smart City Systems

Smart city systems and apps process and analyze urban data to generate information that leads to developing an awareness of the current situation and acting

Fig. 1. London dashboard

Fig. 2. Smart city platform for an automatic garbage collection system

based on it, taking optimized actions, and improving the provision of urban services [14,47]. Smart city systems have been proposed to address the challenges of different public services, such as traffic and transport control, air pollution monitoring, waste management, public safety, water resource decision-making, energy and emergency management.

Currently, there are different approaches to design visualization in smart city systems. Some proposals focus on the data and technology selected for the construction of the system; other authors focus on the activity; there are also user-centered proposals; while others proposals are designed from a comprehensive approach in which the above elements are considered.

Most of the smart city systems analyzed were developed under a technology-centered approach [13,21,25,31,45,57,60]. The systems designed under this approach developed visualizations based on the data or technology selected, without considering the user's information needs or the activities they seek to support. For example, Ming [31] used a network of carbon dioxide sensors to monitor air quality and presented the results of the sensor reading expressed in particles per million in a line chart; however, interpreting the number of carbon dioxide particles can be difficult for a non-specialist audience.

There are projects of smart city systems that start from the analysis of the activity to propose a system that makes processes more efficient. An example of this kind of development is Popa's platform for an automatic garbage collection system [42]. Popa designed a system capable of collecting, separating, and storing waste, with the ability to monitor containers and generate automatic alerts. The waste management system (see Fig. 2) includes a map with the location of the containers, tables, and icons that show the status of the containers.

On the other hand, there are projects with a user-centered approach that seek to generate systems that meet the needs of end-users [14,38]; for example, the criminal incident analysis system [14] developed to support police and federal agents. Based on the analysis of police officers' needs, Ghosh [14] determined the use of natural language processing to extract information about crimes from police reports; the results were presented through keywords to facilitate processing the reports. On the other hand, Pettit [38] proposed two systems to support water resource decision-making: a geo-visual analysis system designed to support urban researchers and another system to support local authorities.

There are projects with a comprehensive approach [9] that design smart city systems considering the available technology and data, the best practices to make activities more efficient, and users' information needs. With the aim of developing a next-generation parking management system, Dunne's projects [9] involve experts in transportation planning, computer science, urban planning, data analysis, and visualization in the design and development process.

In the last decade, research has focused on developing technologies that analyze urban data to optimize the monitoring of cities and improve the provision of services. A smart city platform is a software that systematically collects, integrates, and analyzes data generated in a city, which sometimes integrates data visualization. On the other hand, a city dashboard is a system that presents urban data visualizations to give an overview of the current situation in a city. Each city dashboard integrates different information according to the priorities of each city. Unlike city dashboards, smart city systems focus on a specific issue of a city, such as air quality monitoring, waste management, or monitoring of energy use in the city. The literature review of smart city systems [9,13,21,31,38,42,45,57] shows a wide use of data visualization to facilitate the monitoring of the data collected by sensors and different sources of information, detect patterns, and make decisions based on evidence.

3.4   Data Visualization Techniques

According to a study about smart city data, data can be classified as raw data -data collected from sensors, crowdsourcing, or city records- and enhanced data -data processed through analytics-. Data can also be classified according to their dynamism in static data related to the use of land, roads, and buildings; semi-dynamic related to cultural events, entertainment, and social networks; and dynamic, such as data collected by sensors used for weather and traffic [46]. Analyzing these data can be a difficult task for a person; visualization is an efficient mean to represent data and help people to understand the information [28].

The literature review shows that the use of traditional visualization techniques such as tables, bar charts, line charts, and scatterplots predominates in dashboard and smart city system interfaces, in addition to the wide use of maps to represent geospatial information. Table 2 presents the most common visualization techniques in smart city systems and their use.

Maps are the main technique used to represent data in smart city systems. According to a review of open data visualization by Eberhardt [10], the most commonly used map types are dot maps, pointer maps, route maps, choropleth maps, and heatmaps. These maps are used for a variety of purposes: for exploring the spatial dynamics of some attributes (dot maps and heatmaps), for easily locating elements and events in a city (maps with pointers), for understanding urban areas and comparing them (choropleth map), for analyzing transport routes and trajectories (route maps), among other uses. For all the advantages

Table 2. Visualization techniques used in smart city systems

Technique	Usage	Papers
Map	-Exploring the spatial dynamics of an attribute	[30,38]
	-Locate elements and events of interest in the city	[28,34,57]
	-Understand the areas of the city and compare them	[30]
	-Monitor environmental variables	[57]
	-Analyze routes and trajectories	[6,45,53]
	-View the location of public transportation	[40]
	-View the location of sensors	[42]
	-Analyze changes in space over time	[63]
Choropleth map	-Represent information from predefined regions with clear boundaries. It is useful for making comparisons	[17,24]
Flow map	-Show the movement of objects from one place to another	[6,17]
Heatmap	-Analysis of the relationship between geographic characteristics and another measurement	[6,28,38] [40]
	-Presentation of quantitative values of two dimensions through a matrix using a color code	[19,36]
Line chart	-Analyze the change in the values of different categories over time (time series)	[17,21,31,38] [19,36,60]
	-Analyze trends	[30,49]
Bar chart	-Compare (quantitative) values by category	[17,38,45]
	-Present data by category	[19,28,36]
Pie chart and	-Show the percentage distribution	[8,40]
Donut chart	-Show the constituent parts that make up a whole	[43,58]
	-Show data proportions	[19,36]
Table	-Show records	[21,38,45]
	-Organize, relate and compare elements	[40,42]
Stacked bar chart	-Show the composition of the data	[8,19,35,43]
Scatterplot	-Analyze the relationship between two variables	[6][10][19,43]
Buble chart	-Analyze the relationship between three variables	[10,19,43,45]
Histogram	-Analyze the frequency or distribution of a variable over time	[6,19,43]
Space time cube	-Analyze trajectories over time	[6,38,63]
3D model	-Model the dynamic environment of a city	[21]
	-Analysis of possible changes in the urban space	[9]
Gauge chart	-Display the current value of an indicator relative to the best and worst target value of the indicator	[30]
Treemap	-Show the hierarchical categories that make up a whole and their values	[10,36]
Strip plot	-Show events over time	[53]
Sankey diagram	-Illustrate the flow of relationships, such as input vs output	[35]
Sunburst chart	-Show the composition of the organizational structure	[58]
Spectrogram	-Overview of audio data	[49]

that maps offer to understand urban space, maps have been widely used to identify places of interest such as schools and restaurants; monitor the environment (water level, climate, air quality, etc.); and analyze public transport in the city.

Tables, bar charts, and line charts are other widely used visualization techniques in smart city systems. Tables are the second most used form of presentation of information. The tabular display is a popular data representation technique due to the possibility of presenting multiple attributes and containing quantitative and qualitative data. However, analyzing the information contained in a table can be time-consuming and difficult, especially if the table is large; that is why in many of the smart city interfaces, the table is used to show a summary of the information - with a manageable number of records - or as an alternative to access more information on demand.

Bar charts and line charts summarize large data sets in an easy-to-interpret way. A bar chart is useful for comparing values by category - such as energy consumption by sector - while a line chart analyzes the change in values over time and detects any possible trends. Line charts are commonly used to analyze the evolution of indicators over time and present the values collected from sensors. For example, McArdle [30] used a line chart to plot Dublin home prices, population growth, and unemployment rates. On the other hand, [17] and Kim [21] used a line chart to display the hourly energy consumption records.

In addition to the traditional visualizations, new techniques have been developed to present multiple dimensions or variables. In recent years, efforts have focused on visualizing massive data with spatial and temporal properties [6,13,24,33,62,63]. For example, Moustaka [32] developed a visualization based on the Human DNA helix to represent the relationship between the different dimensions of a smart city. Fortini [13] proposed the Urban Transit Fingerprint visualization, which consists of a graph with associated geographic information, where different transport routes are represented. And Obie [33] presented a visualization to represent space-time attributes through a radial graph (to represent time) on top of a map (to represent space) and the color to describe the third attribute. Although these representations are exciting, animation techniques remain the most used strategy to represent changes in space and time [6,63].

To select a visualization technique, it is necessary to analyze the needs of the users and their goals to determine the objective of the visualization [36]. To perform this analysis, Grainger [18] proposed a framework for visualization in non-scientific professional contexts that offers a set of guidelines for a user-centered visualization design. The framework [18] is oriented to support the design process and does not offer sufficient guidance for selecting a type of visualization. On the other hand, Protopsaltis [43] proposed a set of rules for the selection of charts based on the number of variables (one, two, or multiple) and the objective of the visualization, which can be to analyze relationships, evaluate a distribution, compare data, and study a comparison. For example, Protopsaltis [43] recommends using scatterplots to analyze the relationship between two variables and using bubble charts for three variables. However, these guidelines are limited to statistical charts (bar chart, line chart, histogram, among others).

The revised visualization techniques enable synthesizing, organizing, and presenting the information collected in a city in a visual and meaningful way. Although data visualization libraries and tools currently facilitate the integration of visual representations in smart city technologies, there are still challenges to overcome to achieve greater growth and acceptance of smart city systems.

3.5 Discussion and Future Challenges

There are challenges in the different stages of the visualization process (see Fig. 3), from collecting data to implementing the visualizations and interpreting it. According to Eberhardt [10], access to data can be challenging. Although smart cities are characterized by integrating technology to collect data in real-time, there is a lot of information on paper that cannot be accessed. This historical or static data could be useful to complement real-time data [52].

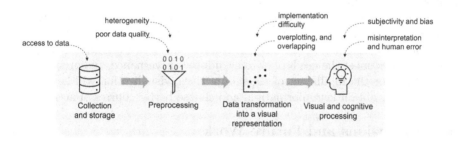

Fig. 3. Visualization challenges in smart city technologies.

In smart cities, there are different systems, services, and devices that generate and consume data [50]. Heterogeneity in data types and structures (unstructured, structured, and semi-structured) represents a challenge for cleaning, analyzing, and visualizing data [27,43,50]. In addition to heterogeneity, poor data quality is one of the most cited challenges in the literature [10,27,29]. If the data has not been cleaned, poor-quality data can lead to erroneous analysis and convey the wrong information through visualizations [29].

The large volume of data generated in a city can be difficult to display on a single screen due to space limitations and the perceptual capabilities of humans. Visualizing a large data set in a single chart can lead to data overloading, overplotting, and overlapping, making the visualization difficult to perceive and interpret [43]. Some possible solutions are reducing the size of points, making the points semi-transparent, binning the data into rectangles or hexagons, and showing a subset of points [5]. However, issues related to overplotting are still a common problem in big data visualization. That is why some researchers' efforts have focused on effectively visualizing big data.

Eberhard [10] and Matheus et al. [29] report a gap between data visualization initiatives and stakeholders. There is low development and adoption of smart city systems due to a lack of technical knowledge, skills, and experience [10,11,29]. In order to bring smart city technologies closer to the citizens and government actors without technical knowledge, current projects incorporate interactive visualizations that enable dynamic data queries by visual manipulation (visual analytics). Visual analytics is the science that aims to provide techniques and tools for data analysis through visual interfaces [41]. Visualization and visual analytics have been incorporated into most smart city systems since they allow efficient use of space and facilitate its use. However, implementing interactivity in visualizations can also be a challenge for developers of smart city systems [43].

Human intervention in the visualization process can involve some risks of subjectivity, bias, misinterpretation, and human error [29,43]. Although they are risks of human interaction, some of them can be caused by poor design and can be mitigated by creating effective visualization. In response to design and technology adoption challenges, studies of perceptual aspects and human-centered visualization design have increased in recent years.

The human-centered approach to smart city systems goes beyond visualization design. According to [56], the new generation of smart cities systems will be developed with a human-centered approach. These systems will serve to improve public services, meet the needs of citizens, improve governance, and promote sustainability. For the fulfillment of these objectives, visualization will help to see the problems, obtain key information, and choose better courses of action [56].

4   Conclusions and Future Work

This study presents a literature review of visualization in smart city technologies. This study analyzed visualization in smart city platforms, dashboards, and smart city systems and presented the most used visualization techniques and their use. The presented analysis of visualization techniques helps to see the options and may help designers and developers choose one method. The visualizations described are not infallible; a wrong visualization selection and poor design can lead to data misinterpretation and a bad user experience. To develop technological solutions that meet user needs and communicate information effectively and satisfactorily, we recommend iterative development -preferably user-centered- with evaluations at different stages of development to detect and correct possible design problems.

Visualization in smart cities is a growing area. Although some tools facilitate incorporating visualization in smart city systems, the visualization of massive data sets still requires more research, from strategies to visualize data effectively to the development of new algorithms and visualization methods for large-scale data. Analyzing the development of several smart city systems, we observed the lack of protocols for evaluating data visualization; some authors evaluate usability and others ease or difficulty of interpretation. That is why we consider the evaluation of visualizations an open issue. To facilitate the design of interactive visualizations in smart city systems, the analysis of city decision-makers' needs and the construction of a visualization framework are potential lines of research.

References

1. Barns, S.: Smart cities and urban data platforms: designing interfaces for smart governance. City Cult. Soc. **12**, 5–12 (2018)
2. Batty, M., Hudson-Smith, A., Hugel, S., Roumpani, F.: Visualising Data for Smart Cities, pp. 453–475. IGI Global, Hershey (2018)
3. Bocconi, S., Bozzon, A., Psyllidis, A., Titos Bolivar, C., Houben, G.J.: Social glass: a platform for urban analytics and decision-making through heterogeneous social data. In: Proceedings of the 24th International Conference on World Wide Web, pp. 175–178. WWW2015 Companion, Association for Computing Machinery, New York (2015)
4. Camero, A., Alba, E.: Smart city and information technology: a review. Cities **93**, 84–94 (2019)
5. Chang, W.: R Graphics Cookbook: Practical Recipes for Visualizing Data. O'Reilly Media, Farnham (2018)
6. Chen, W., Guo, F., Wang, F.Y.: A survey of traffic data visualization. IEEE Trans. Intell. Transp. Syst. **16**(6), 2970–2984 (2015)
7. Cheng, B., Longo, S., Cirillo, F., Bauer, M., Kovacs, E.: Building a big data platform for smart cities: experience and lessons from santander. In: 2015 IEEE International Congress on Big Data, pp. 592–599 (2015)
8. Chun, S.A., Lyons, K., Adam, N.R.: The smart city of Newark, NJ: data analytics platform for economic development and policy assessment. In: Anthopoulos, L. (ed.) Smart City Emergence, pp. 315–331. Elsevier, Amsterdam (2019)
9. Dunne, C., Skelton, C., Diamond, S., Meirelles, I., Martino, M.: Quantitative, qualitative, and historical urban data visualization tools for professionals and stakeholders. In: Streitz, N., Markopoulos, P. (eds.) Distributed, Ambient and Pervasive Interactions, pp. 405–416. Springer International Publishing, Cham (2016)
10. Eberhardt, A., Silveira, M.S.: Show me the data! A systematic mapping on open government data visualization. In: Proceedings of the 19th Annual International Conference on Digital Government Research: Governance in the Data Age. DGO 2018, Association for Computing Machinery, New York (2018)
11. Evertzen, W.H.N., Effing, R., Constantinides, E.: The internet of things as smart city enabler: the cases of Palo Aalto, Nice and Stockholm. In: Digital Transformation for a Sustainable Society in the 21st Century. pp. 293–304. Springer International Publishing, Cham (2019). https://doi.org/10.1007/978-3-030-29374-1
12. Few, S.: Dashboard Confusion Revisited. Perceptual Edge pp. 1–6 (2007)
13. Fortini, P.M.A., Davis, C.A.: Analysis, integration and visualization of urban data from multiple heterogeneous sources. In: Proceedings of the 1st ACM SIGSPATIAL Workshop on Advances on Resilient and Intelligent Cities, pp. 17–26. ARIC 2018, Association for Computing Machinery, New York (2018)
14. Ghosh, D., Chun, S.A., Shafiq, B., Adam, N.R.: Big data-based smart city platform: real-time crime analysis. In: Proceedings of the 17th International Digital Government Research Conference on Digital Government Research, pp. 58–66. Association for Computing Machinery, New York (2016)
15. Ghosh, P., Mahesh, T.: Smart city: concept and challenges. Int. J. Adv. Eng. Technol. Sci. **1**(1), 25–27 (2015)
16. González-Briones, A., Chamoso, P., Casado-Vara, R., Rivas, A., Omatu, S., Corchado, J.M.: Internet of Things Platform to Encourage Recycling in a Smart City, pp. 414–423. Elsevier, Amsterdam (2019)

17. Gouveia, J.P., Seixas, J., Giannakidis, G.: Smart city energy planning: integrating data and tools. In: Proceedings of the 25th International Conference Companion on World Wide Web, WWW 2016. pp. 345–350. International World Wide Web Conferences Steering Committee (2016)

18. Grainger, S., Mao, F., Buytaert, W.: Environmental data visualisation for non-scientific contexts: literature review and design framework. Environ. Model. Softw. **85**, 299–318 (2016)

19. Habibzadeh, H., Kaptan, C., Soyata, T., Kantarci, B., Boukerche, A.: Smart city system design: a comprehensive study of the application and data planes. ACM Comput. Surv. **52**(2) (2019)

20. Harrison, C., et al.: Foundations for smarter cities. IBM J. Res. Dev. **54**(4), 1–16 (2010)

21. Kim, S.A., Shin, D., Choe, Y., Seibert, T., Walz, S.P.: Integrated energy monitoring and visualization system for smart green city development: designing a spatial information integrated energy monitoring model in the context of massive data management on a web based platform. Autom. Constr. **22**, 51–59 (2012)

22. Kitchenham, B.: Procedures for performing systematic reviews. Tech. Rep. 0400011T.1, Keele University, Keele, July 2004

23. Lim, C., Kim, K.J., Maglio, P.P.: Smart cities with big data: reference models, challenges, and considerations. Cities **82**, 86–99 (2018)

24. Liono, J., Salim, F.D., Subastian, I.F.: Visualization oriented spatiotemporal urban data management and retrieval. In: Proceedings of the ACM First International Workshop on Understanding the City with Urban Informatics, pp. 21–26. UCUI 2015, Association for Computing Machinery, New York (2015)

25. Liu, X., Nielsen, P.S.: Air quality monitoring system and benchmarking. In: Bellatreche, L., Chakravarthy, S. (eds.) Big Data Analytics and Knowledge Discovery, pp. 459–470. Springer International Publishing, Cham (2017)

26. Lv, Z., Li, X., Wang, W., Zhang, B., Hu, J., Feng, S.: Government affairs service platform for smart city. Fut. Gener. Comput. Syst. **81**, 443–451 (2018)

27. Ma, M., Preum, S.M., Ahmed, M.Y., Tärneberg, W., Hendawi, A., Stankovic, J.A.: Data sets, modeling, and decision making in smart cities: a survey. ACM Trans. Cyber-Phys. Syst. **4**(2) (2019)

28. Marras, M., Manca, M., Boratto, L., Fenu, G., Laniado, D.: Barcelonanow: empowering citizens with interactive dashboards for urban data exploration. In: Companion Proceedings of the the Web Conference 2018, WWW 2018. pp. 219–222. International World Wide Web Conferences Steering Committee, Republic and Canton of Geneva, CHE (2018)

29. Matheus, R., Janssen, M., Maheshwari, D.: Data science empowering the public: data-driven dashboards for transparent and accountable decision-making in smart cities. Govt. Inf. Q. **37**(3), 101284 (2020)

30. McArdle, G., Kitchin, R.: The dublin dashboard: design and development of a real-time analytical urban dashboard. In: First International Conference on Smart Data and Smart Cities; ISPRS Annals Photogrammetry, Remote Sensing and Spatial Information Sciences, III-4/W1, pp. 19–25. September 2016

31. Ming, F.X., Habeeb, R.A.A., Md Nasaruddin, F.H.B., Gani, A.B.: Real-time carbon dioxide monitoring based on IoT & cloud technologies. In: Proceedings of the 8th International Conference on Software and Computer Applications, ICSCA 2019, pp. 517–521, Association for Computing Machinery, New York (2019)

32. Moustaka, V., Vakali, A., Anthopoulos, L.G.: Citydna: smart city dimensions' correlations for identifying urban profile. In: Proceedings of the 26th International Conference on World Wide Web Companion, WWW 2017, pp. 1167–1172. Companion, International World Wide Web Conferences Steering Committee, Republic and Canton of Geneva, CHE (2017)
33. Obie, H.O., Chua, C., Avazpour, I., Abdelrazek, M., Grundy, J., Bednarz, T.: Pedaviz: visualising hour-level pedestrian activity. In: Proceedings of the 11th International Symposium on Visual Information Communication and Interaction, VINCI 2018, pp. 9–16. ACM, New York (2018)
34. Panagiotou, N., et al.: Intelligent urban data monitoring for smart cities. In: Berendt, B., et al. (eds.) Machine Learning and Knowledge Discovery in Databases, pp. 177–192. Springer International Publishing, Cham (2016)
35. Pardo-García, N., Simoes, S.G., Dias, L., Sandgren, A., Suna, D., Krook-Riekkola, A.: Sustainable and resource efficient cities platform – SureCity holistic simulation and optimization for smart cities. J. Clean. Prod. **215**, 701–711 (2019)
36. Peddoju, S.K., Upadhyay, H.: Evaluation of iot data visualization tools and techniques. In: Anouncia, S.M., Gohel, H.A., Vairamuthu, S. (eds.) Data Visualization, pp. 115–139. Springer, Singapore (2020). https://doi.org/10.1007/978-981-15-2282-6_7
37. Petrolo, R., Loscri, V., Mitton, N.: Towards a smart city based on cloud of things, a survey on the smart city vision and paradigms. Trans. Emerg. Telecommun. Technol. **28**(1), 294–307 (2017)
38. Pettit, C., Widjaja, I., Russo, P., Sinnott, R., Stimson, R., Tomko, M.: Visualisation support for exploring urban space and place. In: ISPRS Annals of the Photogrammetry, Remote Sensing and Spatial Information Sciences. vol. 1, pp. 153–158 (2012)
39. Pettit, C., et al.: Planning support systems for smart cities. City Cult. Soc. **12**, 13–24 (2018)
40. Pettit, C., Lieske, S.N., Jamal, M.: CityDash: Visualising a Changing City Using Open Data, pp. 337–353. Springer International Publishing, Berlin (2017)
41. Pinto, A.L., Gonzales-Aguilar, A., Lima Dutra, M., Ribas Semeler, A., Denisczwicz, M., Closel, C.: The Visualization of Information of the Internet of Things, Chap. 5, pp. 117–137. John Wiley & Sons, Ltd., New York (2017)
42. Popa, C.L., Carutasu, G., Cotet, C.E., Carutasu, N.L., Dobrescu, T.: Smart city platform development for an automated waste collection system. Sustainability **9**(11), 2064 (2017)
43. Protopsaltis, A., Sarigiannidis, P., Margounakis, D., Lytos, A.: Data visualization in internet of things: tools, methodologies, and challenges. In: Proceedings of the 15th International Conference on Availability, Reliability and Security. ARES 2020, Association for Computing Machinery, New York (2020)
44. Raj, P., Kumar, S.A.P.: Big Data Analytics Processes and Platforms Facilitating Smart Cities, chap. 2, pp. 23–52. John Wiley & Sons, Ltd (2017)
45. Ram, S., Wang, Y., Currim, F., Dong, F., Dantas, E., Sabóia, L.A.: Smartbus: a web application for smart urban mobility and transportation. In: 25th International Conference on World Wide Web Companion. WWW 2016, pp. 363–368. Companion, International World Wide Web Conferences Steering Committee, Republic and Canton of Geneva, CHE (2016)
46. Rhazal, O.E., Tomader, M.: Study of smart city data: categories and quality challenges. In: Proceedings of the 4th International Conference on Smart City Applications. SCA 2019, Association for Computing Machinery, New York (2019)

47. Sachsenmeier, R., Marinescu, L., Oliveira, J., Silva, M., Verhijde, M.: Smart cities. In: Guide to Open Government, Chap. 3, pp. 4–18. Lifelong Learning Program (2015)
48. Saggi, M.K., Jain, S.: A survey towards an integration of big data analytics to big insights for value-creation. Inf. Process. Manag. **54**(5), 758–790 (2018). (Big) Data we trust: Value creation in knowledge organizations
49. Sanaei, S., Majidi, B., Akhtarkavan, E.: Deep multisensor dashboard for composition layer of web of things in the smart city. In: 2018 9th International Symposium on Telecommunications (IST), pp. 211–215 (2018)
50. Santana, E.F.Z., Chaves, A.P., Gerosa, M.A., Kon, F., Milojicic, D.S.: Software platforms for smart cities: concepts, requirements, challenges, and a unified reference architecture. ACM Comput. Surv. **50**(6) (2017)
51. Schunke, L.C., de Oliveira, L.P.L., Villamil, M.B.: Visualization and analysis of interacting occurrences in a smart city. In: 2014 IEEE Symposium on Computers and Communications (ISCC), pp. 1–7, June 2014
52. Sharifi, A.: A typology of smart city assessment tools and indicator sets. Sustain. Cities Soc. **53**, 101936 (2020)
53. Steptoe, M., Krüger, R., Garcia, R., Liang, X., Maciejewski, R.: A visual analytics framework for exploring theme park dynamics. ACM Trans. Interact. Intell. Syst. **8**(1) (2018)
54. Suciu, G., Necula, L., Usurelu, T., Rogojanu, I., Dițu, M., Vulpe, A.: IoT-based 3d visualisation platform for an efficient management of the smart city ecosystem. In: 2018 Global Wireless Summit (GWS), pp. 37–42 (2018)
55. Tong, X., Wu, Z.: Study of chinese city "portrait" based on data visualization: take city dashboard for example. In: Marcus, A., Wang, W. (eds.) DUXU 2018. LNCS, vol. 10919, pp. 353–364. Springer, Cham (2018). https://doi.org/10.1007/978-3-319-91803-7_26
56. Trencher, G.: Towards the smart city 2.0: empirical evidence of using smartness as a tool for tackling social challenges. Technol. Forecast. Soc. Change **142**, 117–128 (2019)
57. Trilles, S., Calia, A., Belmonte, Ó., Torres-Sospedra, J., Montoliu, R., Huerta, J.: Deployment of an open sensorized platform in a smart city context. Fut. Gener. Comput. Syst. **76**, 221–233 (2017)
58. Vila, R.A., Estevez, E., Fillottrani, P.R.: The design and use of dashboards for driving decision-making in the public sector. In: Proceedings of the 11th International Conference on Theory and Practice of Electronic Governance, ICEGOV 2018. pp. 382–388. ACM, New York (2018)
59. Young, G.W., Kitchin, R., Naji, J.: Building city dashboards for different types of users. J. Urban Technol. **28**, 1–21 (2020)
60. Zaldei, A., et al.: An integrated low-cost road traffic and air pollution monitoring platform to assess vehicles air quality impact in urban areas. In: 20th EURO Working Group on Transportation Meeting, EWGT. vol. 27, pp. 609–616 (2017)
61. Zdraveski, V., Mishev, K., Trajanov, D., Kocarev, L.: ISO-standardized smart city platform architecture and dashboard. IEEE Perv. Comput. **16**(2), 35–43 (2017)
62. Zhang, J., Chen, Z., Liu, Y., Du, M., Yang, W., Guo, L.: Space-time visualization analysis of bus passenger big data in Beijing. Cluster Comput. **21**(1), 813–825 (2018)
63. Zhong, C., Wang, T., Zeng, W., Müller Arisona, S.: Spatiotemporal Visualisation: A Survey and Outlook. In: Arisona, S.M., Aschwanden, G., Halatsch, J., Wonka, P. (eds.) Digital Urban Modeling and Simulation. CCIS, vol. 242, pp. 299–317. Springer, Heidelberg (2012). https://doi.org/10.1007/978-3-642-29758-8_16

A Case Study of Smart Industry in Uruguay: Grain Production Facility Optimization

Gabriel Bayá[1]([✉])[iD], Pablo Sartor[2][iD], Franco Robledo[1][iD], Eduardo Canale[1][iD], and Sergio Nesmachnow[1][iD]

[1] Universidad de la República, Montevideo, Uruguay
{gbaya,frobledo,canale,sergion}@fing.edu.uy
[2] Universidad de Montevideo, Montevideo, Uruguay
psartor@um.edu.uy

Abstract. This article presents a Mixed-Integer Linear Programming model for cost optimization in multi-product multi-line production scheduling. The proposed model applies discrete time windows and includes realistic constraints. The model is validated on a specific case study from a real Uruguayan grain production facility. Results of the evaluation indicate that the proposed model improves over the current ad-hoc heuristic planning, reducing up to 10.4% the overall production costs.

Keywords: Grain facility optimization · Smart industry · Mixed-Integer Linear Programming · Real case study

1 Introduction

Intelligent systems for decision making are a valuable asset in production, especially under the novel Industry 4.0 paradigm [13]. The integration of new technologies and intelligent methods into classical industrial processes offers the capability of designing innovative processes and even business models. In any case, technological advances also enhance the application of traditional techniques aimed at improving business performance through efficiency. In agriculture, computational tools have been widely applied for crop planning and production [14]. Efficient and accurate models and algorithms to manage resources are crucial for improving competitiveness and minimizing operation costs.

This article presents a Mixed-Integer Linear Programming (MILP) optimization model for a capacitated multi-product multi-line production scheduling process. The model incorporates several constraints, which are frequently found on real applications. The problem is restated by using discrete time windows.

A specific case study of the proposed problem is analyzed: the optimization of the generalized production costs in a real grain production facility in Uruguay. The case study involves the batch production scheduling of 17 products spanning 16 weeks, 2 production lines, limited storage capacity and restrictions regarding product switching times and limited lifetime. Results of the application of the

S. Nesmachnow and L. Hernández Callejo (Eds.): ICSC-Cities 2021, CCIS 1555, pp. 101–115, 2022.
https://doi.org/10.1007/978-3-030-96753-6_8

proposed model to the real case study demonstrate that significant improvements are obtained over an ad-hoc planning.

The article is organized as follows. Next section describes the proposed grain facility optimization problem and the MILP formulation. Section 3 presents the real case study. The experimental evaluation is reported in Sect. 4, including a comparison with the ad-hoc planning, based on several common-sense rules, applied before the model was conceived.

2   The Grain Facility Optimization Problem

This section describes the grain facility optimization problem and its mathematical formulation.

2.1   Problem Description

The problem concerns grain processing facilities, which must treat the seeds using resources such as machinery, workers, and storage capacity, in order to meet pre-planned delivery demands for each harvest. Several varieties of seeds are processed and delivered. Some of them expire a certain number of days after being processed, which imposes a restriction relating the production and withdrawal dates. Once the seeds are processed, they are stored in silos waiting to be withdrawn by clients, based on a planned list of withdrawals that were previously communicated in the planning phase. The production is carried out according to the withdrawals of the established products and the processing and storage capacities that the company has. To carry out the required processes on the seeds there are different production lines, which in turn have different processing capacities, commonly measured in tons per hour. These production lines must be supervised by operators during the period of time that they are operational. Since the machines are generally producing at maximum capacity, operator shifts are established and assigned to each of the lines. The number of shifts is set for every week, and remains the same within the same week. Every time a line ends the production of a certain product, it must be stopped and cleaned before proceeding with the processing of a different product. If the line stops after having met a certain demand and later returns to produce the same product, such cleaning is not necessary. The production process covers several weeks per year, and for each week a set of demanded products must be produced and withdrawn according to the previously specified conditions.

The problem models should minimize production costs, considering the number of production hours, the number of operator shifts and the amount of cleanings performed on the machines. In the same way, it must be ensured that the production is sufficient so the withdrawals can be fulfilled, the expiration periods of the products that expire are respected and the production not delivered immediately does not exceed the available storage facilities.

2.2   Problem Formulation

The mathematical formulation of the proposed grain facility optimization problem considers the following sets and parameters:

- V_I is the set of products that expire.
- V_T is the set of products that do not expire.
- V is the set of all products, $V = V_I \cup V_T$.
- L is the set of production lines.
- S_f is the number of weeks in which production is scheduled.
- M is the maximum number of withdrawals for each product.
- C is the total storage capacity in tons.
- τ is the shelf life (in weeks) of products that expire.
- N is the maximum number of shifts per week.
- H_f is the number of productive hours in a shift.
- π_l is productivity in tons/hour of the production line $l \in L$.
- L_l is the cleaning time in hours of line $l \in L$.
- R_v is number of batches of a product, when $v \in V_I$, if $v \in V_T \rightarrow R_v=1$.
- S_v^r is the week in which the r-th withdrawal of product $v \in V$ is located.
- δ_v^r is the demand for product $v \in V$ in its r-th withdrawal, $r = 1 \cdots M$.
- d_v^s is the demand for product $v \in V$ to withdraw in the week s.
- D_s working days for each week s (e.g., 5 days from Monday to Friday, 5.5 days from Monday to Saturday noon, etc.).

In turn, the considered decision variables are:

- $x_{v,l}^{s,r} \in \mathbb{R}^+$, the quantity of product $v \in V$ produced in the line $l \in L$ in the week s for the r-th withdrawal.
- $t_l^s \in \mathbb{Z}^+$, the number of shifts to put in line $l \in L$ in week s.

$$y_{v,l}^s = \begin{cases} 1 \text{ if and only if line } l \text{ is producing product } v \in V \text{ in the week } s \\ 0 \text{ otherwise} \end{cases}$$

$$p_{v,l}^s = \begin{cases} 1 \text{ if and only if product } v \in V \text{ is the first product to be produced in week } s \text{ in } l \in L \\ 0 \text{ otherwise} \end{cases}$$

$$u_{v,l}^s = \begin{cases} 1 \text{ if and only if product } v \in V \text{ is the last product to be produced in week } s \text{ in } l \in L \\ 0 \text{ otherwise} \end{cases}$$

$$w_{v,l}^s = \begin{cases} 1 \text{ if product } v \in V \text{ ends the week } s \text{ and starts the week } s+1 \text{ in line } l \in L \\ 0 \text{ otherwise} \end{cases}$$

$$c_l^s = \begin{cases} 1 \text{ if in the week } s, \text{ one cleaning of the line } l \in L \text{ is avoided} \\ 0 \text{ otherwise} \end{cases}$$

Considering the previously defined constants and variables, the mathematical formulation of the problem as a Mixed-Integer Linear Programming (MILP) problem is presented in Eq. 1–16.

$$\min P \sum_{l \in L} \sum_{s=1}^{S} t_l^s + Q \sum_{l \in L} \frac{1}{\pi_l} \sum_{v \in V} \sum_{r=1}^{R_v} x_{v,l}^{s,r} + R \sum_{l \in L} L_l \left(\sum_{s=1}^{S} \sum_{v \in V} y_{v,l}^s - \sum_{s=1}^{S-1} c_l^s \right) \quad (1)$$

$$\text{subject to} \sum_{z=S_v^r-\tau}^{S_v^r} \sum_{l \in L} x_{v,l}^{z,r} - \delta_v^r \geq 0, \forall v \in V_I, \quad r = 1 \cdots R_v \quad (2)$$

$$\sum_{z=1}^{S_v^r} \sum_{l \in L} x_{v,l}^{z,1} - \sum_{z=1}^{S_v^r} d_v^z \geq 0, \forall v \in V_T, \quad r = 1 \cdots M \quad (3)$$

$$\sum_{z=1}^{s} \sum_{v \in V} \sum_{l \in L} \sum_{r=1}^{R_v} x_{v,l}^{z,r} - \sum_{z=1}^{s} \sum_{v \in V} d_v^z \leq C \quad \forall s = 1 \cdots S \quad (4)$$

$$t_l^s \leq N \quad \forall l \in L, \quad \forall s = 1 \cdots S \quad (5)$$

$$d_v^s \cdot y_{v,l}^s - \sum_{r=1}^{R_v} x_{v,l}^{s,r} \geq 0 \quad \forall l \in L, \quad \forall v \in V, \quad \forall s = 1 \cdots S, \quad (6)$$

$$\sum_{r=1}^{R_v} x_{v,l}^{s,r} - y_{v,l}^s \geq 0 \quad \forall l \in L, \quad \forall v \in V, \quad \forall s = 1 \cdots S, \quad (7)$$

$$y_{v,l}^s - p_{v,l}^s \geq 0 \quad \forall l \in L, \quad \forall v \in V, \quad \forall s = 1 \cdots S, \quad (8)$$

$$\sum_{v \in V} p_{v,l}^s \leq 1 \quad \forall l \in L, \quad \forall s = 1 \cdots S, \quad (9)$$

$$y_{v,l}^s - u_{v,l}^s \geq 0 \quad \forall l \in L, \quad \forall v \in V, \quad \forall s = 1 \cdots S, \quad (10)$$

$$\sum_{v \in V} u_{v,l}^s \leq 1 \quad \forall l \in L, \quad \forall s = 1 \cdots S, \quad (11)$$

$$2w_{v,l}^s - u_{v,l}^s - p_{v,l}^{s+1} \leq 0 \quad \forall l \in L, \quad \forall v \in V, \quad \forall s = 1 \cdots S - 1, \quad (12)$$

$$c_l^s - \sum_{v \in V} w_{v,l}^s \leq 0 \quad \forall l \in L, \quad \forall s = 1 \cdots S - 1, \quad (13)$$

$$|V| p_{v,l}^s + |V| u_{v,l}^s + \sum_{v_1 \in V, v_1 \neq v} y_{v_1,l}^s \leq 2|V| \quad \forall l \in L, \quad \forall v \in V, \quad \forall s = 1 \cdots S, \quad (14)$$

$$\pi_l \left(D_s H_f t_l^s - L_l \sum_{v \in V} y_{v,l}^s - c_l^s \right) - \sum_{v \in V} \sum_{r=1}^{R_v} x_{v,l}^{s,r} \geq 0 \quad \forall l \in L, \quad \forall s = 1 \cdots S - 1, \quad (15)$$

$$\pi_l \left(D_S H_f t_l^S - L_l \sum_{v \in V} y_{v,l}^S \right) - \sum_{v \in V} \sum_{r=1}^{R_v} x_{v,l}^{S,r} \geq 0 \quad \forall l \in L, \quad (16)$$

The objective function (Eq. 1) proposes minimizing the overall cost of production. The cost is composed of three different terms, which model the costs associated to labor, production, and cleaning. The generalized cost is defined as a number that summarizes these three cost sources for each production cycle.

The first term of the objective function represents the labor cost, which is proportional to the total number of shifts (of operators) to be used in production, for all available machines. The second term represents the costs associated to the time during which the machines produce, other than labor (e.g., energy and amortization). The third term represents the costs incurred every time a line is cleaned, other than labor (e.g., supplies and energy; the latter has a different hourly consumption than in the second term). Parameters P, Q, and R are the unit conversion coefficients, which allows expressing the total cost (sum of all the terms of the objective function) in a single unit. The linear aggregation approach is appropriate since all costs are variable and directly proportional to the decision variables: labor cost is proportional to the number of shifts, energy, supplies and amortization costs are proportional to the operational hours and to the cleaning hours (at different rates).

Equations 1–16 formulate the constraints of the optimization problem. Equation 2 guarantees that there is sufficient production of inoculated products to be delivered, thus implying that production must be greater than demand. Since inoculated products have an expiration date, the model must ensure that the number of weeks elapsed since they were produced until they are delivered does not exceed parameter τ. Equation 3 ensures that the enough treated product are produced. As for Eq. 2, the production must be greater than the demand, but in this case the products can be produced at any moment of the production cycle. Equation 4 rules the storage capacity. The first term of the left side of the inequality is the production of week s and the second term correspond to the deliveries in that week. The difference between production and delivery must be positive, thus ensuring that the products can be stored without exceeding the total capacity C. Equation 5 limits the number of shifts for each of the production lines in each week.

Equations 6–11 rule the activation of binary variables $y_{v,l}^s$ $p_{v,l}^s$, $u_{v,l}^s$ y $w_{v,l}^s$, which act as auxiliary variables to calculate the number of cleanings avoided in the production lines. Equations 6 and 7 work together to activate the variable $y_{v,l}^s$ if and only if some quantity of a certain product v was produced on the line l in the week s. Equation 8 indicates that the necessary condition for the variable $p_{v,l}^s$ to be activated (v is the first product to be produced in the line l in the week v) is that some quantity of product v has been produced in the week s. Equation 9 guarantees the uniqueness of the first product produced in week s on line l, thus ensuring that the definition of the variable $p_{v,l}^s$ is consistent. Equations 10 and 11 are analogous to Eqs. 8 and 9, but applied to the last product produced in the week. To guarantee the existence of a last product v to be produced on the line l in week s, there must be a production of said product v and it is also guaranteed that this last product is unique. Equation 12 forces the variable $w_{v,l}^s$ to take the value 1 only if the product v crosses the weekly border, that is, if it is the last of the week s and the first of the week $s + 1$ for the production line l.

Equation 13 rules variable c_l^s, i.e., whether a cleaning is saved on production line l for week s. The sum of variables c_l^s has a negative sign in the objective function, therefore the model presses for this quantity to be the maximum possible. Equation 14 ensures that if a certain product v is the first and the last of the week s for a production line l, no other product is produced on line l in the same week.

Equation 15 expresses that the maximum production capacity of line l must be greater than that produced in the line for that week. The nominal production capacity of line l is subtracted from the necessary stop times and the cleanings saved are added, as a result of the correct sequencing of the products to be produced. Equation 16 is analogous, to cover the last week, where there are no savings in cleaning, since no more productions are to be scheduled.

2.3 Related Work

Several articles in the literature have proposed MIP models for solving grain production and/or delivering optimization problems.

Early works in the area applied MILP models for problems related to harvesting methods and machinery selection. Al-Soboh et al. [3] applied MILP for mixed cropping systems, computing an optimal spacing for planting navy bean. Ait Si Larbi et al. [1] proposed a MILP model for multi-stage optimization in agri-food supply chain, which outperformed a planning heuristic in a real case study in Algeria. Later, the authors [2] applied the AUML protocol specification to build an effective system for production and transportation. The proposed model was effective to compute accurate values of the optimized functions.

Bilgen and Ozkarahan [4] proposed a multi-period MILP model for minimizing costs of blending and shipping on the wheat supply chain. An hybrid deterministic/non-deterministic model was proposed by Granillo et al. [5] for minimizing the building cost of a distribution network farm. The model computed accurate solutions for the supply chain of barley in Mexico. Sanches et al. [10] applied a multi-period MIP model for the optimization of production scheduling of fruit beverages. The proposed approach computed accurate results under realistic assumptions for a case study in Brazil. Hosseini et al. [6] proposed a two-stage mixed-stochastic approach to deal with uncertainty on costs, demand, and supply in the wheat supply chain network. The proposed model outperformed a deterministic model in real case study in Iran.

León et al. [7] proposed a MILP formulation for minimizing the total cost of the bioethanol supply chain. Accurate results were computed to satisfy the demand in a case study considering corn and barley residues in México. The proposed MILP approach was robust and applicable to other similar problems.

Several articles related to food supply chain and logistics have applied MILP models for optimization. Soysal et al. [12] proposed a MILP model for beef industry, extended to minimize cost and greenhouse gas emissions in the transportation system. Mishra et al. [8] applied a nonlinear programming model to minimize refrigeration cost in the storage process of leafy greens. Shekarian et al. [11] proposed a MILP model for profit optimization in the soybean supply chain network, computing accurate results for a real case in Ontario.

3 Case Study: Production Optimization in a Grain Processing Facility

The case study considered in this article corresponds to the production planning of a company that processes and sells soybeans. The main details of the scenario are presented in this section.

3.1 Description of the Case Study

The company operates in Uruguay serving, among others, soy producers. Producers send orders for 17 different kinds of soybeans for the harvest, that must be processed and delivered according to a schedule that extends over a period of 19 weeks (the annual soybean harvest). The main problem that the company faces when the orders are received is the accurate planning of the production and preparing the deliveries in a timely manner.

The company has two production lines with 6.165 and 6.65 tons per hour respectively of processing capacity; both are able to produce any of the 17 products. Every time the machines finish processing a product, they must stop and be cleaned if a different product is to be processed next. The duration of stoppage and cleaning times of these production lines are 6 and 8 h respectively. The period of time the machines are stopped to be cleaned is a time in which the company stops producing and therefore reducing this downtime is of paramount importance for improving the efficiency. The adequate quantity to produce, as well as the correct sequencing of the products that must enter the two production lines, helps reducing stoppages with the corresponding savings in time and associated costs. This strategy often implies producing a larger quantity of grains than withdrawals in particular weeks, which must therefore be stored. For this purpose, the company has a storage capacity of 2.700 tons of grain. Using machinery efficiently and taking advantage of storage silos, the company must produce and store enough grain to cover the withdrawals required by its customers.

Processed products can be divided into two classes, inoculated and treated. This adds an additional control that the company must resolve. Products within the class named as *inoculated* (7 out of the 17 products) have an expiration time. Such products therefore cannot be produced and stored too far in advance, due to their upcoming expiration date. In the considered case study the expiration time is two weeks, which is a major constraint for planning. In turn, there is no expiration time for products within the *treated* class (10 out of the 17).

The supervision of the machinery during production as well as cleaning are carried out by shifts of operators, who work 7.5 effective hours in every shift. Due to worker management policies, given a week w and a specific line l, the same number of shifts (1, 2 or 3) are performed from Monday to Friday (and half of it on the corresponding Saturday); the number of shifts can be set to different values for every combination of week and line (w, l).

3.2   Conception of the Optimization Model

This subsection describes the process for conceiving the optimization model.

The company raised the need to improve the scheduling efficiency to the research group. The main goal of the company was exploring intelligent planning methodologies such as the ones applied in smart logistics to improve over the costs obtained applying an non-formalized planning, following a basic set of intuitive criteria (this planning is referred as Plan-1 hereafter).

After several interviews, a first simple model of the problem was created as a spreadsheet, whose cells stores numbers equivalent to the decision variables x and t of the mathematical formulation presented in Sect. 2. The spreadsheet was organized with rows representing the weeks and columns representing pairs (product, line) as amounts of tons to produce. The simple model in the spreadsheet allowed manually changing values in the mentioned cells and showing the corresponding use of lines and storage capacities, and also displaying alerts in case of violated constraints.

The production plan for year 2020 was computed using the described spreadsheet and a heuristic procedure that is described in Sect. 4.3. The resulting plan is referred as *ad-hoc* plan and its was significantly better than the one of Plan-1 (i.e., providing a reduction of approximately 20% on the necessary number of cleaning cycles). The ad-hoc heuristic schedule is used as a reference baseline to compare the results computed by the proposed MILP model, as described in the next section.

4   Experimental Evaluation

This section reports the experimental evaluation of the proposed approach for solving the real case study of production planning.

4.1   Evaluation Methodology

The proposed formulation was implemented using the AMPL modelling program language and solved with IBM CPLEX Solver ver. 20.1.0.0. The hardware used for running this model was an Intel Core i9-9900K CPU @ 3.60 GHz, 16 processors with 64 Gb. of RAM. Equipment OS is CentOS Linux release 7.7.1908. The default configuration of CPLEX was used for all parameters for all executions. A fixed effort stopping criterion is applied: CPLEX ends execution after reaching a predefined threshold on the execution time.

Two metrics were considered to evaluate the performance of the model: the execution time considered as threshold and the gap of the computed solution with respect to a certain lower bound calculated by the solver. The gap is related to the execution time, i.e., a inversely proportional relationship is observed, as increasing the total execution time of the model allows computing more accurate results. For the considered case study, several executions of the proposed model are performed considering as stopping criterion 1, 5, 30, 60, 120, 180, and 240 min, respectively.

4.2   Definition of the Problem Instance

The experimental evaluation of the proposed model was performed on a specific instance of the case study. The parameters that define the used instance are:

- $V_I = \{1 \cdots 7\}$; $V_T = \{8 \cdots 17\}$; $V = V_I \cup V_T$; $\tau = 2$

  The products defined as inoculated in this instance are those specified with an index between 1 and 7, whereas products defined as treated have an index between 8 and 17. The τ parameter specifies the shelf life of the inoculated products and it is set to 2 weeks.

- $L = \{1, 2\}$; $\pi_l = \{6.165, 6.5\}$; $L_l = \{6, 8\}$, with $l \in L$

  These parameters correspond to the set of machines available, their production capacity, and their cleaning times in hours respectively.

- $S_f = 19$; $C = 2700$; $N = 3$; $H_f = 7.5$; $D_s = 5.5 \forall s$

  The total number of weeks that the harvest lasts (parameter S_f) is set to 19 weeks, the storage capacity of processed grains (parameter C) is set to 2700 tons, the maximum number of operator shifts (parameter N) is set to 3, and the number of productive hours in a shift (parameter H_f) is set to 7.5. The number of working days for each week (parameter D_s) is set to 5 days (i.e., from Monday to Friday and a half day at Saturday).

- The maximum number of withdrawals for each product (parameter M) is set to 10.

- The number of batches corresponding to the inoculated products is $R_v = \{6, 7, 8, 4, 5, 2, 2\}$ with $v \in V_I$ and the treated products belonging to a single batch is $R_v = 1$ $\forall v \in V_T$.

Demands are established by customers. Table 1 reports the planned demand for products and the week in which these products are to be withdrawn. Values in the table are the main input to the model, corresponding to the parameter d_v^s that describes the quantity of product v to be withdrawn in week s. Products 1–7 are inoculated (i.e., the limited lifetime constraint applies to them), while 8–17 are treated. From Table 1 the last two parameters that define the problem instance are defined: the week in which the r-th withdrawal of product v is located (S_v^r) and the demand for product v in its r-th withdrawal (δ_v^r).

4.3   Baseline Solution for Comparison

This subsection describes the heuristic procedure followed by the operations manager to create the baseline ad-hoc production plan, used to compare the results computed by the proposed model.

The heuristic applies the following procedure:

1. Set 3 shifts for all weeks in both lines and 0 tons to produce in every (week, line) combination.

Table 1. Demand (d_v^s, in tons) of products (v) by week (s)

Week	Products																
	1	2	3	4	5	6	7	8	9	10	11	12	13	14	15	16	17
8										20	600	60				200	
9				80	140	100				60	600	120				200	
10			40	120	400	100		80		120	600	140	60	24		200	
11		160	200	120	600			80		120	400	40	140	24	60		40
12		240	400	120	360		120	200	120	40			200	60	80		120
13	36	240	440		300		120	200	40				140	60	60		80
14	60	160	440					400					20	48			40
15	80	160	280					400						24			
16	40	80	120											40			
17	100	40	80											80			
18	40																

2. Set the production of product p in week w, equal to the demand of p in w, always in the fastest line (several capacity overflow and/or storage overflow will appear).
3. Repeat while possible: choose a week in which there is overflow on capacity and move any product to the other line, provided that it does not imply a capacity overflow on the latter.
4. Repeat while possible: choose a week and a treated product (w, p) for which there is capacity overflow or storage overflow, and move its production to earlier weeks (seeking to soften the capacity-need peaks).
5. Repeat the previous step, over the inoculated products, anticipating production at most two weeks to respect the expiration dates constraint.
6. Reduce all shifts as possible, as long as the reduction does not cause new capacity overflow to appear.

Finally, a visual inspection is performed, searching for other movements of products between lines and weeks trying to reduce shifts and cleanings without introducing capacity overflows or storage overflows until no further evident improvements arise. Preparing the spreadsheet and executing the above described steps took approximately 16 h of human work (operations manager) and yielded a production plan that involved 319 shifts and 34 cleanings.

4.4 Numerical Results

Once the input parameters of the model have been specified, the solver is executed to find the solution for the proposed instance of the real case study. The solution found is described in Tables 2, 3 and 4, which report the week and the quantity of products to be processed, in order to obtain the best computed production plan that meets the demand requirements and adjusts to both the production capacities of the machinery and the storage volume of the facilities.

Table 2. Production schedule (in tons) by week for the considered case study

Week	Line	Product	Production (tons)	Hours	Cleans	Cleans saved	Stockpiled
3	2	9	320	48.12	1	0	320
3	2	11	175.43	26.38	0	1	175.43
4	2	11	548.62	82.5	0	1	724.05
5	2	11	274.31	41.25	0	1	998.36
6	2	11	822.94	123.75	0	1	1821.3
7	2	11	274.31	41.25	0	1	2095.61
8	1	12	254.72	41.25	0	1	254.72
8	2	11	104.39	15.7	1	0	2200
8	2	10	360	54.14	1	0	360
8	2	16	252.15	37.92	0	1	252.15
9	1	12	105.28	17.05	1	0	300
9	1	6	200	32.39	1	0	200
9	1	14	168	27.21	1	0	168
9	1	4	179.73	29.11	0	1	179.73
9	2	16	347.85	52.31	1	0	400
9	2	5	421.89	63.44	0	1	421.89
10	1	4	260.27	42.15	1	0	360
10	1	3	297.03	48.1	1	0	297.03
10	1	13	109.94	17.8	0	1	109.94
10	2	5	822.94	123.75	0	1	1104.83
11	1	13	450.06	72.88	1	0	500
11	1	15	200	32.39	1	0	200
11	1	17	40	6.48	0	1	40
11	2	5	555.17	83.48	1	0	1260
11	2	2	214.56	32.27	0	1	214.56
12	1	17	240	38.87	1	0	240
12	1	7	240	38.87	1	0	240
12	1	8	200	32.39	0	1	200
12	2	2	426.76	64.17	1	0	481.33
12	2	3	342.97	51.58	0	1	400
13	1	8	600	97.17	1	0	600
13	1	1	116	18.79	0	1	116
13	2	3	769.15	115.66	0	1	769.15
14	1	1	60.38	9.78	1	0	140.38
14	1	2	182.96	29.63	0	1	184.28
14	1	14	192	31.09	1	0	192
14	2	3	274.31	41.25	0	1	603.46
15	1	2	254.72	41.25	0	1	279
15	2	3	316.54	47.6	1	0	480
15	2	8	400	60.15	1	0	400
16	1	2	1.00	0.16	1	0	120.00
16	1	1	179.62	29.09	1	0	180

Table 2 presents the production schedule, reporting for each week, line, and product, the quantity to be produced, the hours the process will take, if a cleaning must be performed after the product has been processed and it can be avoided, and the stored stock of the product at the time of finalizing its production, subtracting the withdrawals for the week, if any.

An important point to take into account, which is reported in Table 2, is the correct sequencing for each production line of the products to be processed within the same week. Every time the column *cleans saved* takes the value 1, the product (which was the last processed in the week for the line) continues its production as the first product in the following week, therefore avoiding a cleaning of the machine.

Table 3. Production and cleanings for the considered case study

Line	Shifts	Production (tons)	Hours per line	Cleanings	Saved cleanings	Cleaning hours
1	20	4531.70	733.88	14	8	84
2	31	8024.30	1206.66	8	12	64
Total	51	12556	1940.54	22	20	148

Table 3 summarizes for each production line, the total number of operator shifts used, the production amount and production hours, the cleanings required and cleanings avoided by optimization, and the total hours of effective cleaning.

Table 4 reports for each week of the harvest the total products stored (production minus withdrawals) and the storage capacity available in the facility.

Table 4. Stored production and available capacity by week for the case study

Week	1	2	3	4	5	6	7	8	9	10
Stored production (tons)	0	0	495	1044	1318	2141	2415	2506	2629	2235
Available capacity	2700	2700	2205	1656	1382	559	285	194	71	465
Week	11	12	13	14	15	16	17	18	19	
Stored production (tons)	1711	1101	870	412	439	339	39	0	0	
Available capacity	989	1599	1830	2288	2261	2361	2661	2700	2700	

Figure 1 reports the results (value of the objective function and the percentage gap) of seven executions of the proposed model with different time limits.

The graph in Fig. 1 shows a decrease of the gap metric as the solver execution times increase. Convergence towards the global optimum is faster in the first minutes, becoming stagnant for execution times greater than two hours. The gap of 0.89% obtained after four hours of running the model can be taken as an excellent approximation to the global optimum.

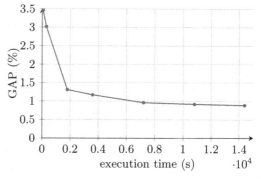

run	objective	GAP	time (s)
1	73839	3.46%	60
2	73700	3.02%	300
3	72740	1.31%	1800
4	72718	1.17%	3600
5	72625	0.96%	7200
6	72625	0.92%	10800
7	72625	0.89%	14400

Fig. 1. Numerical results and GAP evolution for the considered case study

Regarding the comparison with baseline method, Table 5 reports the values obtained by the existing heuristic method and the proposed method in CPLEX for three relevant metrics: number of shifts, number of cleanings needed, maximum storage used, and overall cost. Values of Δ reports the improvements (reductions) of the proposed method.

Table 5. Accuracy of the computed plans

	Heuristic	CPLEX	Δ	$\Delta\%$
Shifts	58	51	7	12.1%
Cleanings	34	22	12	35.3%
Maximum storage used	3666	2629	1037	28.3%
Overall cost	81070	72625	8445	10.4%

Results in Table 5 indicate that the proposed methods computed plans that reduced more than 12% the number of shifts, more than one third the number of cleanings, and more than 28% the maximum storage used. These results demonstrate the accuracy of the computed plans, which directly imply a better resource management, which is crucial for improving competitiveness and minimizing operation costs. Overall, the plan computed by the proposed model improved cost values 10.4% over the the heuristic planning and more than 30% over the original manual planning.

5 Conclusions and Future Work

The novel paradigm of Industry 4.0 has revitalized production in smart cities. Intelligent systems are now being applied for transforming traditional production processes into smart value chains. This way, Industry 4.0 developed new relationships in production systems, focused on improved interactions between manufacturers, suppliers and citizens, via efficient models and algorithms.

Inspired on the need to effectively plan production, organize deliveries, and manage storage in a seed sales and processing company, this article presented a mathematical model for the exact resolution of a typical production problem in the soybeans logistic chain. A MILP model was specified and implemented to optimize the overall production costs, including machine operating hours, number of assigned shifts, and stops for cleaning. The problem model includes several features from real-world production facilities, including multi-product, multi-line processing, machinery cleaning stops and storage of processed products. In turn, the formulation accounts for realistic constraints considering that demands can be met, all processed products can be stored if it is necessary, inoculated products are produced so that they do not expire before delivery and shifts do not exceed working hours.

The proposed model was implemented in AMPL and solved using CPLEX20.0.0.1 in a an Intel Core i9-9900K with 16 processors and 64 Gb of RAM to optimize a real case study of a Uruguayan grain processing facility for the year 2020 soybean harvest, which previously applied manual and an heuristic method to plan production and deliveries.

The results obtained in the experimental evaluation indicated that an orderly production plan is obtained, with efficient storage capacity, notably reducing the number of stops for cleaning as well as the supervisory shifts used. Overall, the proposed model computed plans that improved more than 10% and more than 30% regarding cost over the manual and the heuristic planning, respectively. Furthermore, the computed plans also improving storage occupancy and costs of machinery cleaning supplies.

The main lines of future work include additional realistic features in the optimization model. Regarding the discretization applied to determine productions, moving from planning weeks to planning days will allow for a more accurate production planning, further optimization of supervisor shift costs, and improved storage management. In addition, introducing a silo farm for raw grains, shared to store the processed grains, will certainly reflect the current reality of grain production companies. The proposed model should be adapted to take in consideration these new features and related new constraints. All these considerations will imply more complex models and a direct increment on the computing demands of the exact resolution approaches, then developing efficient optimization approaches using high performance computing techniques and the infrastructure of National Supercomputing Center [9] is also a promising line for future work.

References

1. Ait Si Larbi, E., Bekrar, A., Trentesaux, D., Bouziane, B.: Multi-stage optimization in supply chain: an industrial case study. In: 9th International Conference on Modeling, Optimization & Simulation (2010)
2. El Yasmine, A.S.L., Ghani, B.A., Trentesaux, D., Bouziane, B.: Supply Chain Management Using Multi-Agent Systems in the Agri-Food Industry. In: Borangiu, T., Trentesaux, D., Thomas, A. (eds.) Service Orientation in Holonic and Multi-Agent Manufacturing and Robotics. SCI, vol. 544, pp. 145–155. Springer, Cham (2014). https://doi.org/10.1007/978-3-319-04735-5_10

3. Al-Soboh, G., Srivastava, A., Burkhardt, T., Kelly, J.: A mixed-integer linear programming (MILP) machinery selection model for Navybean production systems. Trans. ASAE **29**(1), 81–84 (1986)
4. Bilgen, B., Ozkarahan, I.: A mixed-integer linear programming model for bulk grain blending and shipping. Int. J. Prod. Econ. **107**(2), 555–571 (2007)
5. Granillo-Macias, R., Hernandez, I.J.G., Martinez-Flores, J.L., Caballero-Morales, S.O., Olivarez-Benitez, E.: Hybrid model to design a distribution network in contract farming. DYNA **86**(208), 102–109 (2019)
6. Hosseini-Motlagh, S.-M., Samani, M.R.G., Abbasi Saadi, F.: Strategic optimization of wheat supply chain network under uncertainty: a real case study. Oper. Res. **21**(3), 1487–1527 (2019). https://doi.org/10.1007/s12351-019-00515-y
7. León-Olivares, E., Minor-Popocatl, H., Aguilar-Mejía, O., Sánchez-Partida, D.: Optimization of the supply chain in the production of ethanol from agricultural biomass using mixed-integer linear programming (MILP): a case study. Math. Probl. Eng. **2020**, 1–25 (2020)
8. Mishra, A., Buchanan, R., Schaffner, D., Pradhan, A.: Cost, quality, and safety: a nonlinear programming approach to optimize the temperature during supply chain of leafy greens. LWT Food Sci. Technol. **73**, 412–418 (2016)
9. Nesmachnow, S., Iturriaga, S.: Cluster-UY: collaborative scientific high performance computing in Uruguay. In: Supercomputing, pp. 188–202 (2019). https://doi.org/10.1007/978-3-030-38043-4_16
10. Sanches, M., Morabito, R., Oliveira, M.: Otimização da programação da produção de bebidas à base de frutas por meio de modelos de programação inteira mista. Gestão & Produção **24**(1), 64–77 (2016)
11. Shekarian, S., Amin, S.H., Shah, B., Tosarkani, B.M.: Design and optimisation of a soybean supply chain network under uncertainty. Int. J. Bus. Perform. Supply Chain Model. **11**(2), 176 (2020)
12. Soysal, M., Bloemhof-Ruwaard, J., van der Vorst, J.: Modelling food logistics networks with emission considerations: the case of an international beef supply chain. Int. J. Prod. Econ. **152**, 57–70 (2014)
13. Industry 4.0: Managing The Digital Transformation. SSAM, Springer, Cham (2018). https://doi.org/10.1007/978-3-319-57870-5_9
14. Woodruff, D., Voß, S.: Introduction to Computational Optimization Models for Production Planning in a Supply Chain. Springer-Verlag, Berlin (2006). https://doi.org/10.1007/978-3-540-24764-7

Smart Technologies for Monitoring Older Adults with Dementia

Jessica Beltrán[1,4(✉)], Omar A. Montoya-Valdivia[2],
Ricardo Bañuelos-De La Torre[2], Leonardo Melendez-Lineros[2],
Gabriel Parada-Picos[2], Cynthia B. Pérez[3], and Ciro Martínez-García-Moreno[1]

[1] Instituto Politécnico Nacional, México City, México
{jbeltranm,cmarting}@ipn.mx
[2] Universidad Autónoma de Baja California, Tijuana, México
{montoya.omar,ricardo.banuelos,leonardo.melendez,
gabriel.parada}@uabc.edu.mx
[3] Instituto Tecnológico de Sonora, Guaymas, México
cynthia.perez@itson.edu.mx
[4] Consejo Nacional de Ciencia y Tecnología, México City, México

Abstract. Nowadays, the elderly population has increased considerably as well as health problems related to old age, such as dementia. Consequently, there is a need for constant monitoring, assistance and support provided by caregivers in people's home causing high economic costs and a shortage of healthcare professionals. Informal caregivers, usually relatives, provide many caregiving services although they might suffer of stress and burden for being aware 24/7. This has motivated the development of systems based in new technologies such as Internet of Things, Cloud Services and Machine learning. In this work, we propose a system architecture based on these new technologies along with a dashboard prototype for monitoring older adults with dementia through a video, sound and map visualization. Hence, we obtained GPS, audio and video data for future behavior analysis in order to provide as well, notification services to caregivers to inform them about the status of people with dementia.

Keywords: Internet of Things · Aging in place · Smart monitoring · Dementia · Dashboard

1 Introduction

In cities, and generally worldwide, older adults population is on the rise since life expectancy has increased during the last decades. However, age-related health problems also have shown an increase, for instance, the number of people with dementia is expected to grow from 55 million to 139 million in 2050 [10].

People living with dementia (PwD) suffer a cognitive and a functional decline and are incrementally dependent on caregivers support. However, people with early dementia, like most older adults, choose aging in place as much as possible [7], which means they rather live in their own homes being independent instead

© Springer Nature Switzerland AG 2022
S. Nesmachnow and L. Hernández Callejo (Eds.): ICSC-Cities 2021, CCIS 1555, pp. 116–127, 2022.
https://doi.org/10.1007/978-3-030-96753-6_9

of living in geriatric residences [19]. Indeed, public policy makers encourage new smart cities technologies for healthy aging [4] due to shortage in healthcare professionals and health services costs [16].

However, there are various risks associated with PwD aging in place, such as wandering, being engaged in hazardous activities, insufficient food and fluid intake and many others as shown in [15]. Although people in early stages of dementia might not require 24/7 attendance, their caregivers, usually a relative, can leverage their stress and burden [3] with new technologies that allow the development of systems to aid aging in place [18]. These systems can be designed to support PwD and their caregivers, for instance, by detecting when a PwD is engaged in a potentially risky situation, and notify the carer if the person has fallen, missed food or medication or any other action towards delaying geriatric residence or hospital admissions [13].

An example of these technologies is Internet of Things (IoT) that makes it possible to use wearable or fixed sensing devices in PwD houses to capture relevant data from their context. These devices can be interconnected either for sharing or for data processing purposes. Additionally, recent advances in cloud services technologies, such as those provided by Amazon Web Services (AWS) or Google Cloud, allow gathering incoming data from heterogeneous sources. These data can be transformed, processed, stored and rules can be defined to enact actions to provide services to caregivers, such as to notify them when an event has occurred. Moreover, machine learning techniques can be applied over the collected data, weather within IoT devices or within the cloud services. These techniques could be used for detecting PwD's activities, behaviors and surrounding events.

While urgent situations can be notified via messaging, dynamic dashboards allow caregivers to visualize real time information about PwD. For example, the PwD's location to known if they are wandering, the activities performed by the PwD and even a tool to see inside PwD home [17]. All of these information is gathered with sensors such as GPS devices, microphones and cameras.

In this paper, we present a system architecture base on smart technologies along with a dashboard in an scenario to support caregivers of people with early dementia. This dashboard depicts information collected and processed with IoT devices and AWS. Moreover, machine learning techniques are applied to detect relevant sounds from the environment.

In the next section, we present related work, followed by the description of the architecture, the dashboard and conclusions.

2   Related Work

Since the availability of IoT devices, different approaches have been developed towards supporting PwD and their caregivers. Literature reviews summarize the trends, challenges and advances in this field. These reviews show that the growth of this approach started in 2000 showing a big increase from 2016 to nowadays [9]. Also, describe the emerging areas, such as robotic technology and integrated applications [14] and recommendations to design new approaches, such as using geo-fencing services, i.e. services triggered depending on a defined location, emergency support and the incorporation of user experience [12].

Apart from data collection and transmission, processing is important when developing systems to support PwD and their caregivers. It's possible for instance, to infer behaviors or behavior changes by analyzing sensor data provided by doors sensors [11] or smart glasses [5]. The prediction of behaviors or activities can be used to generate daily reports or to alert in case of emergencies. Moreover, visualizations have been proposed to display relevant information of PwD using dashboards. For example, to inform to caregivers about sleep patterns of PwDs [8] or other activities such as dietary consumption and step counting [20].

Among the different types of sensors that can be used, we are interested in analyzing audio since it can provide relevant information from PwD context; while providing user's privacy. With audio analysis it's possible to infer activities, disruptive behaviors [2], emotions, and to identify keywords and even have interaction with users through speech recognition [6]. Moreover, it has been found that levels or quality of audio can affect the mood or emotions of PwD and that we can even relate audio levels with socialization, which is also important for their mental health [1].

In this work, we describe the development of a prototype cloud architecture and a dashboard to support PwDs and their caregivers. We are interested in provide geo-fencing services to alert in case of wandering, since it has been found to be relevant for caregivers [12]. We are also interested in performing audio processing and display sound levels in a PwD's house, to know the audio quality and because it serves as a proxy to know what the PwD doing, for instance if sound levels are bigger than a threshold are found in the kitchen it can be inferred that the person is performing an activity there. With machine learning techniques it's also possible to identify audio events and inform emergency situations to caregivers or store the events for later reports. We also display the content of a camera in PwD's homes to provide caregivers with an extra tool in case they can't communicate or know the status of PwD, for instance if they suspect PwD fell. We also provide caregivers the ability to control the camera from distance using the dashboard to move it as they find convenient. Moreover, we storage the GPS locations and events detected for further behavior analysis that can be used to monitor the deterioration or to understand more about PwD. The cloud service used has the advantage of being elastic so more sensors could be easily added.

3   Proposed System Architecture

To collect data from PwD, we propose using the devices shown in Fig. 1. The cloud architecture is based in AWS and is composed by three modules: the GPS, the sound and the camera modules, see Fig. 2. The devices send data using the Message Queuing Telemetry Transport (MQTT), that is a publish-subscribe lightweight protocol commonly used in IoT.

Fig. 1. IoT devices. a) GPS Module in NodeMCU. b) RaspberryPi 4 with mini USB microphone. c) Raspberry Pi 4 camera module, with Sony Exmor IMX219 sensor mounted over a pan-tilt hat.

3.1   GPS Module

The purpose of the GPS Module is to gather location information from PwD and to inform the caregiver in case the PwD has exited a predefined area over a map, i.e. provide a geo-fencing service. All data is stored to be used in future work for behavior analysis. To capture location, we are using a basic GPS module in NodeMCU (see Fig. 1), set to send data every minute using the MQTT protocol. Additionally, the GPS current location of the PwD is displayed in the map section of the dashboard shown in Fig. 3.

The detailed description of the components of the GPS module of Fig. 2 are the following:

PwD represents the PwD GPS tracker device.

A0 MQTT protocol, the GPS tracker sends data with the location using this protocol. The device publishes payloads to the topic 'aws/gpsDevices'.

A1 Broker where A0's payloads arrive. From there, they are distributed to all AWS services subscribed to the 'aws/gpsDevices' topic. Since the Dashboard is subscribed to this topic it also receives the payload for visualization.

A2 IoT rule where the messages are distributed to both IoT Analytics and a Lambda function.

A3 Lambda function that computes if the PwD is inside or outside a predefined virtual area. If it detects that the PwD is exiting the area, an email to notify the caregiver is sent.

A4 Amazon Simple Email Service (SES) used to send notifications to caregivers.

A5 IoT Analytics where the data is processed, cleaned and stored.

A6 A Channel to pass the data to be analyzed.

A7 A Pipeline where the data is transformed.

A8 Lambda function that adds the timestamp to arriving payloads.

A9 A Datastore where all the messages from the IoT Analytics channel are stored.

A10 The Dataset where all the payloads from the GPS are stored. This can be used to query the Datastore (A9) to get historical information from the PwD.

A11 A Bucket where the Dataset is stored to allow client-applications to get the historical information.

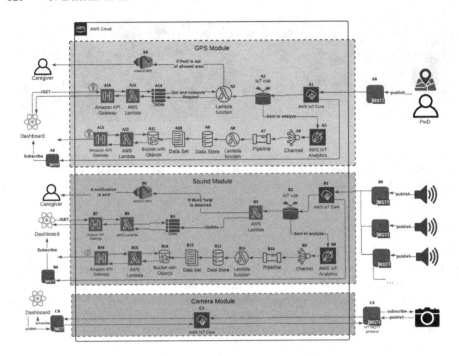

Fig. 2. Proposed system architecture. We used Lucidchart to create this figure (https://www.lucidchart.com/pages/es.).

A12 Lambda function that access the A11 Bucket to retrieve data for the Api Gateway.

A13 Endpoint where client-applications can request the historical information.

A14 DynamoDB table containing information about the PwD. This information comprises the location of the PwD, the caregiver email and the allowed area (described with a polygon).

A15 Lambda function that queries the DynamoDB table A14.

A16 Endpoint where the dashboard request the information to be displayed.

Caregiver is the person that will visualize the dashboard and receive notifications.

The flow of information in the GPS module is the following. First, from right to left according to the Fig. 2, the GPS device from the PwD publishes to the topic "aws/GpsDevices" through MQTT protocol a message with a Json payload including the *deviceId, latitude, longitude*. The message is received by the AWS IoT Core broker.

Afterwards, two Iot Rules are defined to distribute the message. In one rule, the message is sent to a lambda function (A3) that uses the library *robust-point-in-polygon*[1] and a function used to classify if the PwD is inside our outside the

---

[1] https://www.npmjs.com/package/@types/robust-point-in-polygon.

polygon area. This lambda function queries the DynamoDB Table (A14) that already includes the information of a polygon defining a virtual geo-fencing. This polygon is defined previously by the caregiver. If the PwD exits the polygon area, the Lambda function (A3) invokes Amazon SES to send an email to the caregiver. Afterwards, the lambda function updates the current location stored in the DynamoDB table of the PwD with the GPS data.

The other rule is to send the payload to IoT Analytics (A5) in order to create a Dataset with the PwD's GPS historical data. The pipeline to store the data goes from A6 to A11 and the services A12–A13 will be used in case we require to query the stored data. For instance, to apply machine learning algorithms.

In the other hand, from left to right we can see that the dashboard requests the data through an endpoint (A16) to get the current location of the PwD stored in the DynamoDB table to display it as a map as seen in Fig. 3.

3.2 Sound Module

This module is in charge of managing the information coming from microphones located in the PwD's house. In this case, we process the audio information before sending it to AWS which helps maintain user privacy. The results of audio processing are stored for further behavior analysis and also displayed to the caregiver. The dashboard shows in the upper right (see Fig. 3) the intensity of sounds in decibels of different rooms from the PwD house. A color map is used to show different decibels (dB) intensities (see Fig. 4). These sound intensities inform to caregiver in which room are activities been performed, for example, from the Fig. 3 the caregiver would interpret that the PwD is in the living room. Since the raw audio data is not sent, neither the current activities are informed, this setup allows to maintain PwD' privacy.

We used mini USB microphones (see Fig. 1) to capture audio with 16 kHz, 16-bits and a single channel. The microphones are connected to a RasperryPi 4 module where we compute the root mean square (rms) and then apply the next formula to compute the decibels: $dB = 20 \, log_{10}(\text{rms}) \pm \text{ref}$.

We trained Hidden Markov Models (HMM) using the *hmmlearn* library[2] over Mel Frequency Cepstral Coefficients (MFCC) obtained from the sounds using the *Python Speech Features* library[3] as mentioned in our previous work [6]. Since we are developing a prototype we tested only with few classes, but we planned to include more classes and to improve the F1Score results. Also, a reason to use in this case HMM is because it does not require large processing, compared to deep learning approaches, and it can be deployed within the Raspberry Pi devices. For future work, we will use Nvidia Nano devices to allow more processing. In any case, the AWS cloud architechture does not change since the payload would be the same.

If the sound intensity is larger than 20 dB, we use previously trained models to classify four different types of sound events, the words "ayuda" and "help"

---

[2] https://hmmlearn.readthedocs.io/en/latest/index.html.

[3] https://python-speech-features.readthedocs.io/en/latest/.

and the sounds of "coughing" and "unknown" (keyboard, yawn, singing, etc.). Each HMM model was trained using 10 recordings and tested with 5 different recordings, giving a 90% of F1Score. The purpose of classifying these keywords is to identify if the PwD is trying to ask for help, for example if he/she fell. Predefined keywords would send a notification to caregivers. In general, the detection of all sound events will be stored for future behavior analysis.

We formed a json payload to send it to AWS using *Paho MQTT client*[4]. This payload includes the *dB* and the *class* with the type of sound detected. The detailed description of the components of sound module of Fig. 2 are the following:

B0 MQTT protocol. The sound devices send information about their sound intensity and the event detected using this protocol, the device publishes to the topic 'aws/soundDevices.

B1 Is the broker where B0's payloads arrive and are distributed to all the devices that are subscribed to a 'aws/soundDevices topic. Since the dashboard is subscribed to this topic, it also receives the payload for visualization.

B2 Iot rule where the message is distributed to IoT Analytics and to a Lambda function.

B3 Lambda function that checks if the payload from B0 has an attribute 'tag' with the value 'help'. If it has it, it sends a notification to the caregiver using Amazon SES.

B4 DynamoDB table where data about the sound devices attached to the cloud are stored

B5 Amazon SES to send email notifications to the Caregiver.

B6 Lambda function that gets the data from the DynamoDB table B4

B7 An Endpoint where the dashboard requests the data from the sound devices stored in a DynamoDB table B4 using a lambda function B6.

B8 IoT Analytics where the data is processed, cleaned and stored.

B9 A Channel where the data passes through in order to get analyzed.

B10 A Pipeline where the data is transformed using activities.

B11 A Lambda function that adds the current time to the new payload from a device.

B12 A Datastore where all the messages from an IoT Analytics channel are stored.

B13 Dataset where all the payloads from the sound devices are stored. This Dataset queries the Datastore B12 to retrieve data. In this case the historical data is stored in order to do machine learning with it.

B14 A Bucket where the data of the Dataset is stored so that client-applications can get the historical data of any sound devices.

B15 Lambda function that access the B14 bucket to retrieve the data for the Api Gateway.

B16 An endpoint where the dashboard requests the required information about the sound devices.

The Dashboard is the same in all modules.

---

[4] https://www.eclipse.org/paho/index.php?page=clients/python/index.php.

The flow from the sound module is similar to the GPS module. The difference is that in this module a notification is sent in case that a keyword suggesting help has been detected and instead of location, the sound intensity levels are sent to the dashboard. The three dots in the sound module indicate that more sound devices could be added without changing the cloud's architecture.

3.3   Camera Module

The purpose of this module is to display the content of a camera inside the PwD's home. This camera is mainly turned off, due to privacy constraints, however, if the caregivers considers important to visualize video from within the PwD's house it can be turned on. Moreover, the caregiver can move the camera using the dashboard to explore different parts of a room. We used a Raspberry Pi 4 camera module, with Sony Exmor IMX219 Sensorlens to broadcast images of 640×480 pixels to the main dashboard every second (although the camera can reach over 4k resolution at 60 fps). We encode the image using the standard python library *base64* to send it to AWS using MQTT. The camera was mounted in a two degrees of freedom structure (pan-tilt HAT) that uses two servo motors to move it from -90 to $90\,°$ (see Fig. 1). These signals can be controlled with a python library called *pantilthat*[5]. To control the camera-movement we made a 5 button control on the main dashboard that sends (via MQTT) two variables that moves the structure with a $5\,°$ resolution.

The description of the Camera module from Fig. 2 is the following.

C0 MQTT protocol, the camera device sends an image every second, the device publishes to the topic 'aws/cameraView. The Dashboard publishes to the 'aws/cameraControls' topic using MQTT to remotely control the camera.
C1 Is the broker where C0's payloads arrive and are distributed to the Dahsboard, that is subscribed to a 'aws/cameraView' topic and to the camera that is suscribed to the 'aws/cameraControls' topic.

4   Dashboard

The proposed dashboard consists of multiple panels that show visualizations of the data being generated by heterogeneous sensors, see Fig. 3. Data queried from AWS Tables A14 and B4 is processed within the dashboard platform to provide updated and accurate visualizations of the PwD's current state. The dasbhoard shows the location of the PwD in case that wandering is suspected, sound levels in their home serve as a proxy of the activities that the PwD is performing and to monitor the sound quality and video comming from a camera located in the PwD's home in case the caregivers needs to see if she/he suspects risks or that the PwD fell. For the later case, the dashboard is interactive providing buttons to the caregiver to move the camera.

---

[5] https://github.com/pimoroni/pantilt-hat.

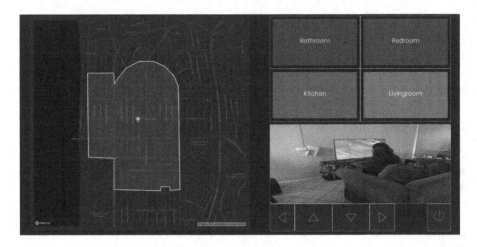

Fig. 3. Example of a visualization of the Dashboard. In the left, the map is shown along with a predefined area. In the upper right, the sound levels are shown and in the lower right, the video along with the camera controls are shown.

The dashboard is designed with simplicity in mind, and to provide to users important information without having to navigate menus. A dark scheme with contrasting colors is used, where the elements can be easily distinguished from each other. The dashboard is based on the React project, since it provides useful tools for bootstrapping a web app. The widespread support React also provides advantages in terms of the implementation of useful libraries and tools, such as Mapbox and MaterialUI. Considering the cases of a monitoring application, the dashboard has to be accessible from different devices, while being simple to use.

4.1 Map Visualizaton

We decided to implement the map visualization using *Mapbox GL JS*[6], a JavaScript library useful for rendering custom maps. The map panel focuses on the PwD's home location and the surrounding area, with indicators that show the current position of the GPS sensor, as well as a blue outline of the area geo-fenced. The caregiver can move, zoom in or out, and drag the map as needed.

The geolocation data from the sensors is rendered through the use of layers, which define the way data is represented on the map. This data is obtained from multiple types of sources. Given that we are working with JSON, we can format the data obtained from the endpoint into a *GeoJSON*[7] data type, since Mapbox supports it nicely. The GPS coordinates of the sensor are used to create a marker object that the user can click on to obtain additional information.

Currently, the GPS coordinates defining the geo-fenced polygon are predefined within a DynamoDB table inside the cloud architecture (A14 from Fig. 2).

---

[6] https://docs.mapbox.com/mapbox-gl-js/api/.

[7] https://geojson.org/.

However, in a future work, we will allow the caregiver to changes it. We chose polygons instead of squares since allow delimitate better on map streets, as shown in the defined area in Fig. 3.

4.2 Sound Visualization

Sound levels in each of the rooms can be monitored through the corresponding panel, showing the decibels reported by each sensor, with the intensity of the background color changing according to a predefined threshold (see Fig. 4). The number of panels can be adjusted depending on the amount of sensors used.

Fig. 4. Sound intensity levels colors

4.3 Video Visualization

A component containing the camera feed is used to observe a particular room. The React app uses the *aws-iot-device-sdk*[8] to subscribe to a IoT Core topic where the device that operates the camera continuously publishes images encoded using the base64 Python library. The use of the MQTT protocol allows for a streamlined flow of data from our distributed devices all the way to the dashboard application. Accounting for possible image quality fluctuations, the image component takes up a relatively small space. There are several buttons located below the camera feed. The user can turn the camera on or off by pressing the power button. A yellow icon indicates that the camera is powered on. The user can also control the camera angle with the arrow buttons.

5 Conclusions and Future Work

Our main contribution in this work is the implementation of a system oriented to support PwD and their caregivers. The adoption of this systems within smart cities brings social benefits since allows to reduce stress and burden of people with caregiving activities, it also provides them the opportunity to work and perform other activities besides caregiving. This system takes advantage of several available benefits from current technologies. For example, the ability to deploy a complete infrastructure to manage and process data using AWS. This infrastructure can be easily modified and scaled if new services or devices are added and it can manage data from heterogeneous sources. We implemented audio processing and machine learning algorithms over inexpensive computing devices, such as the Raspberry Pi module, to detect sound events that can be

---

[8] https://github.com/aws/aws-iot-device-sdk-js.

used to infer PwD's activities, this can be used for future behavior analysis and to provide monitoring elements to caregivers. We also implemented a geo-fencing notification services to inform caregivers if a PwD could be wandering and to notify if a help scream has been detected. Future directions include sessions with older adults with mild dementia and their primary caregivers to conduct a user-centered design approach and further evaluation of the user experience and effectiveness of the system. Another work in progress is to develop a wearable device for GPS data gathering. Additionally, we will work in including the detection of more sound classes and automatic image analysis to detect falls or other relevant events. Another future direction includes to develop a communication channel between the PwD and the caregiver, for example using voice assistant devices. Finally, we can take advantage of having stored data to analyze and find patterns and predictions about the PwD's behavior.

Acknowledgments. This work was partially supported by project 20210010 from the Secretaría de Investigación y Posgrado of the Instituto Politécnico Nacional in Mexico.

References

1. Aletta, F., et al.: Monitoring sound levels and soundscape quality in the living rooms of nursing homes: a case study in Flanders (Belgium). Appl. Sci. **7**(9), 874 (2017)
2. Beltrán, J., Navarro, R., Chávez, E., Favela, J., Soto-Mendoza, V., Ibarra, C.: Recognition of audible disruptive behavior from people with dementia. Pers. Ubiquitous Comput. **23**(1), 145–157 (2018). https://doi.org/10.1007/s00779-018-01188-8
3. Bossen, A.L., Kim, H., Williams, K.N., Steinhoff, A.E., Strieker, M.: Emerging roles for telemedicine and smart technologies in dementia care. Smart Homec. Technol. Telehealth **3**, 49 (2015)
4. Bryant, N., Spencer, N., King, A., Crooks, P., Deakin, J., Young, S.: IoT and smart city services to support independence and wellbeing of older people. In: 2017 25th International Conference on Software, Telecommunications and Computer Networks (SoftCOM), pp. 1–6. IEEE (2017)
5. Chen, W.L., Chen, L.B., Chang, W.J., Tang, J.J.: An IoT-based elderly behavioral difference warning system. In: 2018 IEEE International Conference on Applied System Invention (ICASI), pp. 308–309. IEEE (2018)
6. Cruz-Sandoval, D., et al.: Semi-automated data labeling for activity recognition in pervasive healthcare. Sensors **19**(14) (2019)
7. Grave, A., Robben, S., Oey, M., Ben Allouch, S., Mohammadi, M.: Requirement elicitation and prototype development of an intelligent environment to support people with early dementia. In: 2021 17th International Conference on Intelligent Environments (IE), pp. 1–8 (2021)
8. Hu, X., Abdulghani, A.M., Imran, M., Abbasi, Q.H.: Internet of things (IoT) for healthcare application: wearable sleep body position monitoring system using IoT platform. In: Proceedings of the 2020 International Conference on Computing, Networks and Internet of Things, pp. 76–81 (2020)
9. Morato, J., Sanchez-Cuadrado, S., Iglesias, A., Campillo, A., Fernández-Panadero, C.: Sustainable technologies for older adults. Sustainability **13**(15) (2021)

10. Organization, W.H.: Dementia (2021). https://www.who.int/news-room/fact-sheets/detail/dementia. Accessed 30 Sep 2021
11. Pandey, P., Litoriya, R.: An IoT assisted system for generating emergency alerts using routine analysis. Wirel. Pers. Commun. **112**, 607–630 (2020)
12. Ray, P.P., Dash, D., De, D.: A systematic review and implementation of IoT-based pervasive sensor-enabled tracking system for dementia patients A systematic review and implementation of IoT-based pervasive sensor-enabled tracking system for dementia patients. J. Med. Syst. **43**(9), 1–21 (2019)
13. Rostill, H., Nilforooshan, R., Morgan, A., Barnaghi, P., Ream, E., Chrysanthaki, T.: Technology integrated health management for dementia. Br. J. Commun. Nurs. **23**(10), 502–508 (2018)
14. Stavropoulos, T.G., Papastergiou, A., Mpaltadoros, L., Nikolopoulos, S., Kompatsiaris, I.: IoT wearable sensors and devices in elderly care: a literature review. Sensors **20**(10) (2020)
15. Thoma-Lürken, T., Bleijlevens, M.H., Lexis, M.A., de Witte, L.P., Hamers, J.P.: Facilitating aging in place: a qualitative study of practical problems preventing people with dementia from living at home. Geriat. Nurs. **39**(1), 29–38 (2018)
16. van Boekel, L.C., Wouters, E.J., Grimberg, B.M., van der Meer, N.J., Luijkx, K.G.: Perspectives of stakeholders on technology use in the care of community-living older adults with dementia: a systematic literature review. Healthcare **7**(2) (2019)
17. VandeWeerd, C., et al.: Homesense: design of an ambient home health and wellness monitoring platform for older adults. Health Technol. **10**(5), 1291–1309 (2020)
18. Wang, S., et al.: Technology to support aging in place: older adults' perspectives. Healthcare **7**(2) (2019)
19. Wiles, J.L., Leibing, A., Guberman, N., Reeve, J., Allen, R.E.S.: The meaning of "aging in place" to older people. Gerontol. **52**(3), 357–366 (2011)
20. Yoo, B., Muralidharan, S., Lee, C., Lee, J., Ko, H.: Klog-home: a holistic approach of in-situ monitoring in elderly-care home. In: 2019 IEEE International Conference on Computational Science and Engineering (CSE) and IEEE International Conference on Embedded and Ubiquitous Computing (EUC), pp. 390–396. IEEE (2019)

Urban Informatics

Prescriptive Analytics in Smart Cities: A Combinatorial Approach in Rescue Operations

Igor Morais$^{(\boxtimes)}$ (ID), Vanessa de Almeida Guimarães (ID),
Eduardo Bezerra da Silva (ID), and Pedro Henrique González (ID)

Federal Center for Technological Education of Rio de Janeiro, Rio de Janeiro, Brazil
{igor.morais,pegonzalez}@eic.cefet-rj.br,
{vanessa.guimaraes,eduardo.silva}@cefet-rj.br

Abstract. Rio de Janeiro has two of the biggest urban forests in Brazil. They receive many tourists every year and as they have such an extensive area, some people get lost. Rescue tasks have to mobilize firefighters, helicopters and many public resources. Seeking to reduce the public sector's cost, this paper presents an applied approach for monitoring visitors to reduce the time for these rescue tasks. In order to do that, sensors are displayed in a grid, taking into consideration limits of the technology and the area of the urban forest. Besides, an Unmanned Aerial Vehicle (UAV) is used to collect the data generated by the sensors and the UAV battery is also considered for making feasible solutions closer to the real scenario, as the urban forests usually have big areas. An integer programming formulation is proposed, along side with a metaheuristic. The proposed metaheuristic framework is used for finding solutions for the proposed optimization problem. Experiments show that the integer programming formulation failed to obtain feasible solution in the given timelimit, while the GRASP methodology was able obtained solution in at most, 20 s. After analysis, one may verify that this approach could be used as public policy to improve urban management in the context of smart and digital cities.

Keywords: Rescue operation · UAV · Combinatorial optimization

1 Introduction

The concept of smart cities is based on three pillars: urban governance, energy and transport management [6], with the main objective of improving the quality of life in urban spaces [11]. This concept came up with the challenge of improving the habitability of cities and the well-being of citizens [4]. Therefore, it involves agendas and policies aimed at dealing with natural resources and energy, transport and mobility, buildings, housing, government, economy and people [11].

In this sense, the smart cities project must deal with [2]: (i) the understanding of urban problems related to cities, transport and energy; (ii) coordination of urban technologies; (iii) the development of models and methods for the use

S. Nesmachnow and L. Hernández Callejo (Eds.): ICSC-Cities 2021, CCIS 1555, pp. 131–145, 2022.
https://doi.org/10.1007/978-3-030-96753-6_10

of urban data at spatial and temporal scales; (iv) the development and dissemination of new communication technologies; and, (v) proposition of new forms of urban governance.

Therefore, this work presents an application for the data mule routing problem, which consists of collecting data produced by sensors, which can monitor people in urban forests and reduce the time spent searching for missing people. Many searches are carried out every year for missing persons in the National Park of Tijuca, one of the largest Atlantic Forest parks in Brazil. Another important urban forest in Rio de Janeiro is the Pedra Branca State Park, the most extensive urban forest in Brazil. Both are studied in this article.

National Park of Tijuca receives approximately 2.5 million visitors every year, representing 3.5% of the territory of Rio de Janeiro [7]. In such a vast area with so many visitors, many of them usually go missing (approximately 0.01%). Thanks to this, public resources such as firefighters and helicopters must be allocated to a rescue task force to rescue them. This type of operation can have a high cost for the public sector. As a possible solution, wireless sensor networks can be used to monitor park users and reduce the cost of rescue task forces, although many sensors are needed to cover the entire park area. To reduce the task force's cost, an Unmanned Aerial Vehicle (UAV) can be used to collect sensor data and return it to a base station, which firefighters can analyze before the search begins. This problem can be seen from the perspective of smart cities, considering that parks are part of the quality of life in urban areas. In addition, the proposed application can assist the government in managing public resources that are directly related to governance in smart cities.

Many articles have used Wireless Sensor Networks (WSN) for disaster, military and environmental monitoring [3,10]. This type of network has been used due to its low cost, easy deployment and maintenance. In a multi-hop network, sensors can communicate with each other due to the communication range of the network sensors. Whenever networks are sparse, this type of connection is impossible [13] to be done. One way to gather data into a sparse WSN is to use an UAV, for this problem called data mule, due to its storage and computational capabilities improvements.

UAVs are used for problems like delivery in large cities and other routing applications. Many articles present the concept of data mules [13], and some of them show ways to use it to collect data at the intersection of these sensors, while other articles use data mules to improve the reach of *ad-hoc* networks. Sugihara [13] shows an approach to using wireless sensor networks, the multi-hop. These networks depend on all sensors having intersections so that communication is made peer-to-peer.

In Munhoz et al. [10], two meta-heuristics are used to solve the Data Mule Scheduling Problem: the GRASP with Random variable Neighborhood Descent (RVND) and the General Variable Neighborhood Search (GVNS). In Munhoz et al. [10], the problem analyzed was the time spent to collect data from all sensors. Finally, in Munhoz et al. [9], the authors proposed an integer programming formulation and a distributed heuristic to solve the Data Mule Routing Problem (DMRP). Furthermore, they proved that DMRP belongs to the NP-Hard class.

Considering the problem described, in this article, we propose the construction of an applied scenario to collect data on the position of visitors in the urban forest. The data mule is responsible for collecting the last location data of the urban forest visitors and guiding the firefighters in the rescue process. A mathematical formulation and a metaheuristic are proposed to find high quality routes to collect all the data in the sensors.

Following this Introduction, Sect. 2 describes the problem and presents a integer programming formulation. Besides the mathematical formulation, a GRASP metaheuristic is presented with its components in Sect. 3. Section 4 presents the description of the used instances and the computational experiments done. At last, Sect. 5 presents out conclusions and future work.

2   Data Mule Routing Problem with Limited Autonomy

An instance of Data Mule Routing Problem with Limited Autonomy (DMRP-wLA) can be mathematically represented as a complete graph $G(V \cup \{b\}, E)$, where V represents the set of sensors, b represents the base node from where the data mule leaves and where it returns and E are the set of edges that represent the possible paths between pairs of $v \in V' = V \cup \{b\}$. In addition, each $v \in V$ sensor has a radius attribute that represents the range of its communication. Let us define that two sensors can communicate if there is an intersection between the areas covered by their communication rays. For each edge $(i, j) \in E$, a distance d_{ij} is used to calculate the cost of the displacement between i and j and, consequently, the cost of the final route that the mule will take to go through. Also, one must define that the data mule has limited autonomy and, thanks to that, it can not collect the data from all sensors without recharging. Knowing the characteristics of a DMRP-wLA instance, considering the set of cycles C as the set of all cycles that have cost inferior to a battery limit. A C_i is a subset of cycles of C that passes through all sensors contained in $c_i \cup \{b\}$, where c_i, is one of the subcycles, you can define the DMRP-wLA mathematically as Eq. 1.

$$\text{DMRP-wLA} = \{C_i \subseteq C \mid \sum_{(i,j)} c_i d_{ij} \leq \sum_{(i,j)} c_j d_{ij}; \forall C_j \subset C, \text{ such that } C_i \cap C_j = b; \} \quad (1)$$

Once defined the problem and considering the definitions above one can represent the DMRP-wLA using a Integer Programming Formulation. To do that, besides the above defined elements, one must define the set $A = \{(i, j) \wedge (j, i)$ if either $(i, j) \in E$ or $(j, i) \in E\}$ and the decision variable x_{ij}^k which is responsible for representing the decision of whether or not the UAV goes from sensor i to sensor j during cycle k:

$$\text{min} \quad \sum_{k \in K} \sum_{(i,j) \in A} d_{ij} x_{ij}^k \tag{2}$$

$$\text{s.a.} \quad \sum_{k \in K} \sum_{j \in \bar{C}(i) \cup \{i\}} y_j^k \geq 1, \qquad \forall i \in V \setminus \{0\} \tag{3}$$

$$\sum_{k \in K} y_i^k \leq 1, \qquad \forall i \in V \tag{4}$$

$$\sum_{j \in V \setminus \{i\}} x_{ij}^k = y_i^k, \qquad \forall i \in V, \forall k \in K \tag{5}$$

$$\sum_{j \in V \setminus \{i\}} x_{ji}^k = y_i^k, \qquad \forall i \in V, \forall k \in K \tag{6}$$

$$\sum_{k \in K} y_0^k \geq 1, \tag{7}$$

$$\sum_{j \in V \setminus \{i\}} z_{ij}^k = \sum_{j \in V \setminus \{i\}} z_{ji}^k + y_i^k, \qquad \forall i \in V \setminus \{0\}, \forall k \in K \tag{8}$$

$$z_{ij}^k \leq \sum_{l \in V} y_l^k, \qquad \forall (i,j) \in A, \forall k \in K \tag{9}$$

$$z_{ij}^k \leq |V| x_{ij}^k, \qquad \forall (i,j) \in A, \forall k \in K \tag{10}$$

$$\sum_{j \in V \setminus \{0\}} z_{0j}^k = y_0^k, \qquad \forall i \in V, \forall k \in K \tag{11}$$

$$\sum_{j \in V \setminus \{0\}} z_{j0}^k = \sum_{l \in V} y_l^k, \qquad \forall k \in K \tag{12}$$

$$\sum_{(i,j) \in A} d_{ij} x_{ij}^k \leq C, \qquad \forall k \in K \tag{13}$$

$$x_{ij}^k \in \{0, 1\}, \qquad \forall (i,j) \in A, \forall k \in K \tag{14}$$

$$y_i^k \in \{0, 1\}, \qquad \forall i \in V, \forall k \in K \tag{15}$$

$$z_{ij}^k \in \mathbb{Z}^+, \qquad \forall (i,j) \in A, \forall k \in K \tag{16}$$

$$K = [0, ..., |N| - 1] \cap \mathbb{Z} \tag{17}$$

where, variables x, y, z represents respectively edges used, when a sensor is visited and flow in each arc. Constraints 3 and 4 ensures that sensors are covered, Constraints 5 and 6 guarantees that a sensor can only be visited in one trip. Constraint 7 represent that the base has to be visited in all trips. Constraints 8–12 are the flow constraints that avoid sub routes and at last Constraint 13 ensures that the battery constraint is respected.

Besides, it is possible to verify that the DMRP-wLA can be reduced to the Traveling Salesman Problem (TSP), implying that the DMRP-wLA is an NP-Hard problem. Considering its complexity and the size of real-world-based instances, it is suitable to consider that the proposed integer programming formulation is going to struggle to solve it, so the use of a metaheuristic approach to find high-quality solutions in an acceptable computational time can be an alternative way of dealing with its difficulties. For finding solutions to the problem, the proposed metaheuristic divides the problem into two core sub-problems: (i) determine which sensors to visit; (ii) and, then, in what order they are visited. In the next section, the details of the methodology used are presented.

3   Methodology

In this section, we present the proposed method for obtaining a high-quality solution. The constructive approach consists of constructing a feasible solution. The local search procedure searches in a neighborhood of solution space for a local optima that improve the constructive solution. The two are combined using a Greedy Randomized Adaptive Search Procedure metaheuristics.

3.1   Semi Greedy Adaptive Constructive

The DMRP-wLA consists of finding a set of cycles that minimizes the total cost and collects all data produced by the sensors, while respecting the UAV autonomy. The data from a sensor is collected by visiting it or by visiting some other sensor in its communication ray. One way of solving this problem could be dividing it into two sub-problems, first finding the minimum number of sensors that have to be visited and, then, finding the route that reduces the cost of visiting them. These two problems are defined as the Minimum Dominating Set and the Vehicle Routing Problem (VRP), as each of the multiple vehicles could be viewed as one exiting many times from a base station.

To generate diverse solutions, the two heuristics procedures used were semi greed. This means that in each heuristic, a candidate is chosen at random in a window of proximity to the greedy candidate [5]. These two procedures will be explained in the following two subsections.

3.2   Minimum Dominating Set

Given a graph G(V,E), the Minimum Dominating Set(MDS) is defined as finding the subset of vertices "$\bar{V}$" $\subset V$ with the minimum cardinality that has a subset of edges $\bar{E}$, that connects every vertex of V. For solving this problem, a heuristic procedure was developed. At first, the eigenvector centrality [8] was used and it consists in finding the biggest Eigenvalue of an adjacency matrix and its associated eigenvector, this one has a property that every value in it is bigger than 0 and it measures connectivity between the vertices. This one was chosen because, as shown in [8], it is the most stable centrality measure between other centralities explored.

For the constructive heuristic, a candidate list is generated containing the centrality measure for each vertex, following Eq. 18. This candidate list generates a window of possible candidates to be chosen at random. The maximization version of the Restricted Candidate List (RCL) ensures that each candidate visited has a reasonable amount of data from the other sensors.

$$RCL^{max} = \{i \in \mathcal{CL}_{mds} \setminus \mathcal{S} | h_{max} \ge h_i \ge h_{min} + \alpha(h_{max} - h_{min})\} \qquad (18)$$

The cost function h used for this problem is represented by the eigenvector centrality measure, the $\mathcal{S}$ is the solution that is being constructed, i is the candidate to be chosen from the candidate list CL. Also, α is a real number between zero and one, defining how greedy the choice will be. Algorithm 1 presents in detail how this whole process works.

Algorithm 1: Minimum Dominating Set

```
 1  Data: G,α
 2  begin
 3  │   S ← ∅;
 4  │   V̄ ← ∅;
 5  │   CL_mds ←EigenVectorCentrality(G);
 6  │   for v ∈ |V| do
 7  │   │   if |v_n eighbors| = 0 then
 8  │   │   │   S ← S ∪ v ;
 9  │   │   │   V̄ ← V̄ ∪ v ;
10  │   │   end
11  │   end
12  │   while |V̄| < |V| do
13  │   │   RCL^max ← GenerateRCL(CL_mds, α) ;
14  │   │   v ←rand(RCL^max) ;
15  │   │   S ← S ∪ v;
16  │   │   UpdateCandidateList(v);
17  │   │   UpdateVisited(V̄, v) ;
18  │   end
19  │   return S ;
20  end
21  f
```

The functions "UpdateCandidateList" and "UpdateVisited" are responsible respectively for removing from the CL the values visited in the neighborhood of the selected vertex and updates the vector $\bar{V}$, that contains the sensors visited in the neighborhood of the chosen candidate. The parameter G that the constructive receives is the graph that represents the network. This method generates the set that has to be visited to ensure that all data were collected. With this, the first phase for finding a solution is complete. Now it is necessary to find an order to visit the chosen sensor with the heuristics of the VRP.

3.3 Vehicle Routing Problem (VRP)

This phase can be viewed as a VRP, as the necessity to visit all sensors is defined as a dominating set without consuming more than the capacity for the battery. This constructive uses the nearest neighborhood constructive defined as one heuristic for collecting that gets the sensor with the minimum distance to a node and then calculates if it is possible to visit the next chosen candidate and return to the base. For this approach, the cost function h is defined as the distance to visit a node.

For this problem, an approach similar to the presented in Sect. 3.2, but the version used here is the minimization version because it is necessary to find a way of reducing the cost for the UAV travel. The differences are presented in Eq. 19.

$$RCL^{min} = \{i \in \mathcal{CL}_{vrp} \setminus \mathcal{S} | h_{min} \geq h_i \geq h_{max} - \alpha(h_{max} - h_{min})\} \qquad (19)$$

In Eq. 19, the cost function h concerns the distance o adding one sensor in a trip, while the other elements are the same as presented in Eq. 18. Using the defined equation to diversify solutions generated for the VRP and maintaining the battery restriction, a path is chosen using Algorithm 2.

Algorithm 2: Vehicle Routing Problem

---

1   **Data:** S,α,$max_{capacity}$
2   **begin**
3      $\mathcal{NS} \leftarrow \emptyset$;
4      $\mathcal{NS} \cup \mathcal{B}$;
5      $CL_{vrp} \leftarrow$ CreateCandidateList(S);
6      $capacity = 0$;
7      $cost = 0$;
8   **while** CL_{vrp} not $\emptyset$ **do**
9        $RCL^{min} \leftarrow$ GenerateRCLVRP(CL_{vrp}, α) ;
10        $v \leftarrow rand(RCL^{min})$;
11        $o \leftarrow$ last $\mathcal{NS}$ value ;
12   **if** $capacity + get\_distance(o, v) + get\_distance(v, \mathcal{B}) \leq max_{capacity}$ **then**
13          $\mathcal{NS} \cup v$;
14          $capacity \leftarrow get\_distance(o, v)$;
15          $CL_{vrp} \leftarrow CL_{vrp} \setminus v$;
16          $cost \leftarrow cost + get\_distance(o, v)$;
17   **end**
18   **else**
19          $\mathcal{NS} \cup \mathcal{B}$;
20          $cost \leftarrow cost + get\_distance(o, \mathcal{B})$;
21          $capacity \leftarrow 0$;
22   **end**
23   **end**
24   return $\mathcal{NS}, cost$;
25 **end**

The set $\mathcal{NS}$ represents the new solution created for the DMRP-wLA with its cost. The function GenerateRCLVRP calculates the distance between every candidate possible to visit. With the two constructive procedures executed, a complete solution is returned with its cost. For improving the solution quality, a local search procedure is defined in Subsect. 3.4.

3.4 Random Variable Neighborhood Descent (RVND)

Local search is a heuristic procedure that changes components from the candidate solution, searching in the solution space for improving a solution's quality based on a previously found solution. It consists of searching in the neighborhood definition for a change in a solution for improving the quality, guiding it to a local optimum. In this paper, two traditional neighborhoods were defined, using only existing neighborhoods for the VRP problem. The used neighborhoods are the 2-Opt and the shift inter-trips (inter-trips are defined as a trip before returning to the base). The local search is the uses best improvement policy that tests every solution in the neighborhood then executes the best movement.

The 2-Opt neighborhood structure, Fig. 1, consists of exploring the candidate solution, selecting two vertices and switching their position. As an example, the path for the trip on the left is using the arcs (2,3),(3,4),(4,5) and (5,6), and vertices 3 and 5 were chosen. The right trip represents the movement that uses the arcs (2,5),(5,4),(4,3) and (3,6) and explains the reversion made by the 2-Opt neighborhood.

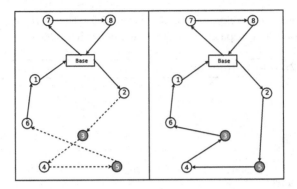

Fig. 1. Neighborhood structure 2opt

Neighborhood structure Shift, Fig. 2, consists of exploring the search space by selecting a vertex and search for a new position, testing its insertion between every two vertices in a cycle, in the same route, and placing it in the position that best improves the solution. For example, the selected vertex is 4, connected by the arcs (5,4) and (4,3). The vertex is reinserted between the arc (3,6), generating a new solution that contains arcs (5,3), (3,4) and (4,6).

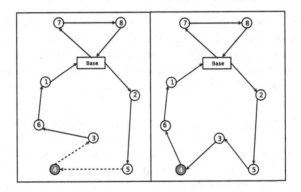

Fig. 2. Neighborhood structure shift

Random Variable Neighborhood Descent [12] is a local search process that combines more than one neighborhood structure, using the idea that it is hard to determine which order for the exploration of a neighborhood structure is better to explore. Having said that the order of exploration of the neighborhood is shuffled at the beginning of the local search phase, detailed in Algorithm 3.

This procedure first randomizes the two neighborhood structures and then explores the neighborhoods in the pre-defined order to improve the solution received as a parameter. The function f evaluates the cost of a solution. After this component, the constructive and the local search procedure are united in a metaheuristic described in the next section.

Algorithm 3: RVND for the DMRP-wLA

---

1 **Data:** S
2 **begin**
3 $\quad$ Shuffle($N^{2-opt(1)}$,$N^{Shift(2)}$);
4 $\quad$ $k \leftarrow 1, S^* \leftarrow S$;
5 $\quad$ **while** $k \leq 2$ **do**
6 $\quad\quad$ Find best $s' \in N^k(s)$;
7 $\quad\quad$ **if** $f(s') < f(s^*)$ **then**
8 $\quad\quad\quad$ $s^* \leftarrow s'$;
9 $\quad\quad\quad$ $k \leftarrow 1$;
10 $\quad\quad$ **else**
11 $\quad\quad\quad$ $k \leftarrow k+1$
12 $\quad$ **end**
13 $\quad$ **return** $s^*, cost$
14 **end**

3.5 Greedy Randomized Adaptive Search Procedure (GRASP)

In search of high-quality solutions, a GRASP that combines the constructive heuristics and local search procedure [5] is used. This proposed GRASP generates a solution with the semi-greedy adaptive constructive that unites the heuristic for the minimum dominating set and the VRP with the RVND local search procedure. The best solution found is chosen as the solution for the problem. Algorithm 4 describes in detail the proposed method.

Algorithm 4: GRASP-RVND

---

1 **Data:** α,max_{iter}
2 **begin**
3 $\quad$ $bestcost \leftarrow \infty$;
4 $\quad$ **for** i *from 1 to* max_{iter} **do**
5 $\quad\quad$ $s' \leftarrow$ MinimumDominatingSet($alpha$) ;
6 $\quad\quad$ $s' \leftarrow$ VehicleRoutingProblem(s',α,$max_{capacity}$) ;
7 $\quad\quad$ $s', cost \leftarrow$ RVND(s');
8 $\quad\quad$ **if** $cost < bestcost$) **then**
9 $\quad\quad\quad$ $s^* \leftarrow s'$;
10 $\quad\quad\quad$ $k \leftarrow 1$;
11 $\quad\quad$ **end**
12 $\quad$ **end**
13 **end**

---

4   Computational Experiments

This section describe the applied scenario and explore the proposed methodology results. The case instances are based on the two urban forests from Brazil: Tijuca's National Park and Pedra Branca State Park.

4.1   Instances Generation

The applied context consists of using sensors and a smartphone application that captures the last active location of the person while in the urban forest to reduce the rescue time whenever someone gets lost. This data would only be used when people are lost and firefighters need it to rescue the missing person.

For the applied scenario, five instances were created based on the limits defined on two urban forests from Rio de Janeiro. The first four instances are defined based on the Tijuca's National Park. The others consider the Pedra Branca State Park. Sensors placements are defined as a grid that intersects the polygon of the urban forest limits. All points are approximately 200 m of distance between each other, so they can intercept each other and communicate data. The distance between sensors is structured based on a real sensor distance radius of 110 m to connect sensors. Figure 3 presents the park limits.

Fig. 3. Urban forest and city limits, the one in left is the Pedra Branca State Park and in the right is National park of Tijuca

Instances were created using the urban forests' delimitation available at the National Register of Public Forests, which is used to manage and publicize the data about Forests in Brazil [1]. As one could notice, Tijuca's National Park is divided into four parts and was used to construct Tijuca instances. To cover all the area the possible positions would be like described in Figs. 4a, 4b, 4c, 4d, which show in more details the divisions and the sensors positioning. It is possible to notice that the urban forest has these divisions because some roads cross its area.

The operation base is set to be in the entry of the urban forest areas. There are four different bases for Tijuca's National Park, while for Pedra Branca State Park, there is only one. Three densities were used to build the instances (60%, 70% and 90%) considering the percentage of the urban forest's area covered by the sensors. To define this, a sensor list with all sensor's degree of centrality was used and, after sorted, the sensors with the lowest degree were removed. Figures 5a, 5b, 5c, 5d show an example of the removed sensors. One may notice that the sensors near the limits of the urban forest are removed since they have fewer connections.

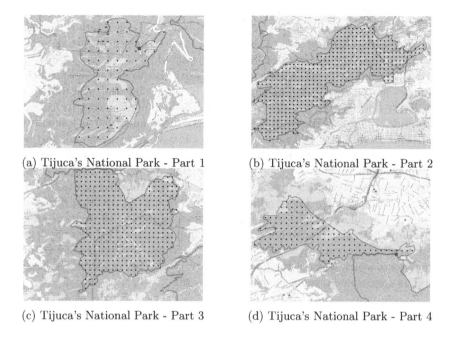

(a) Tijuca's National Park - Part 1   (b) Tijuca's National Park - Part 2

(c) Tijuca's National Park - Part 3   (d) Tijuca's National Park - Part 4

Fig. 4. Images with the total of sensors. (Black represent sensors and red the base) (Color figure online)

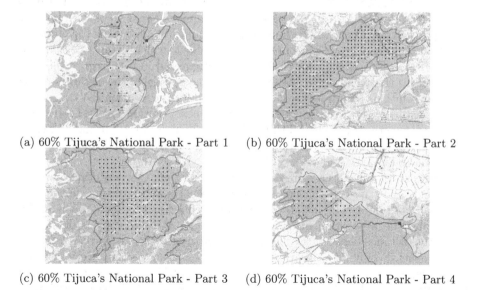

(a) 60% Tijuca's National Park - Part 1   (b) 60% Tijuca's National Park - Part 2

(c) 60% Tijuca's National Park - Part 3   (d) 60% Tijuca's National Park - Part 4

Fig. 5. Images of the reduction by 60% of sensors. (Black represent sensors and red the base) (Color figure online)

To create the instances, we considered that every sensor can multi-hop with its first neighbors and three levels of its neighborhood. To evaluate these neighborhoods, a Breadth-First Search (BFS) was used to create the neighborhood access and reduce the sensors that have to be visited.

From a practical point of view, the necessary infrastructure cost concerns to acquire the sensors, installing the sensors in the designated positions in the urban forest and the UAV. Sensors could be made using low-cost technologies like Arduino with a Wi-Fi shield, a data storage shield, and a battery shield that accepts two 18650 batteries, which can be associated in series in order to have a higher autonomy. Considering these specifications, the sensors would cost, at most, 70 US dollars. This data survey for the costs was done in August 2021 at Amazon.com. Deploying the sensor for all possible established positions would cost 338,660 US dollars. The studied scenarios considered covering 60%, 70%, 90% of the possible positions in the urban forest. However, to perform an economic analysis, the UAV price has to be taken into account. As the prices depend on ranges and autonomy, it would be necessary to evaluate with more detailed specifications, which was not the focus of this project. The computational experiments are executed considering these instances.

4.2   Computational results

The experiments were performed in a Intel Core i5 2.3 GHz with 16 GB of RAM machine and wer implemented in C++. Although in this paper we proposed a integer programming formulation, the straightforward used of Branch-and-Cut scheme from CPLEX Optimization Studio (without heuristics) failed to obtain feasible solutions in the given 1 h timelimit. Thanks to that, from now on, the discussed results will concern just the results obtained using the proposed GRASP. The main results are presented in Table 1, which details: (i) the best cost (BST), which is the sum of the distances covered in each trip of the best solution; (ii) the average cost (AVG), which is the average of the distances of the ten best solutions found; (iii) standard deviation for the solution (STD), related to the distance; (iv) average time to find the best solution (AVG_TIME); (v) standard deviation for time (STD_TIME); (vi) number of trips of the best solution (TRIPS); (vii) average number of trips (AVG_TRIPS); and (viii) standard deviation (STD_TRIPS).

The costs of solutions are presented in kilometers, the time to obtain solutions in seconds and trips are defined as collecting sensors and returning to the base with collected data. The instance names are defined as the name of the urban forest and the proportion of area covered. The UAV autonomy is defined as twice the distance between the base and the farthest sensor to be visited for the experiments. So, by adopting this autonomy, it guarantees that every instance has at least one feasible solution. Considering a 100% coverage, Pedra Branca State Park would have 3,448 sensors, while each of the four divisions of Tijuca's National Park would have, respectively, 68, 464, 401, 131 sensors.

As shown in Table 1 one may notice that the biggest time to obtain a solution is approximately 20 s which is not a problem as the routes are only used in

Table 1. Computational results

Instance	BST(KM)	AVG	STD	AVG_TIME	STD_TIME	TRIPS	AVG_TRIPS	STD_TRIPS
PedraBranca_0.6	1,522.64	1,556.72	17.40	10.709	1.009	68	69.90	10.90
PedraBranca_0.7	1,717.16	1,743.37	18.17	18.372	2.028	77	78.10	14.90
PedraBranca_0.9	2,008.55	2,069.09	30.75	20.125	1.258	81	83.60	26.40
Tijuca_1_0.6	3.77	4.39	350.24	0.005	0.001	1	1.80	1.60
Tijuca_1_0.7	5.37	5.58	140.98	0.006	0.000	2	2.00	0.00
Tijuca_1_0.9	6.36	6.66	343.81	0.007	0.000	2	2.10	0.90
Tijuca_2_0.6	103.68	114.77	5.35	0.072	0.004	11	11.90	2.90
Tijuca_2_0.7	122.06	130.71	3.54	0.099	0.008	13	13.70	2.10
Tijuca_2_0.9	158.75	166.46	4.25	0.197	0.014	16	16.70	2.10
Tijuca_3_0.6	57.21	65.94	3.90	0.060	0.002	9	10.10	2.90
Tijuca_3_0.7	75.21	79.97	2.49	0.079	0.005	11	12.00	2.00
Tijuca_3_0.9	96.94	103.87	3.83	0.122	0.009	14	14.70	2.10
Tijuca_4_0.6	33.64	34.93	1.63	0.012	0.001	5	5.10	0.90
Tijuca_4_0.7	34.77	38.77	2.51	0.016	0.002	5	5.60	2.40
Tijuca_4_0.9	44.00	50.32	2.85	0.026	0.005	6	7.00	2.00

the necessity of a rescue operation. Besides, the value is almost insignificant compared to the time a rescue operation team would take to search the whole area covered by the sensors. Note that the number of sensors is not the only factor influencing solution costs: considering 60% of coverage, the Tijuca 3 has twice as many sensors as Tijuca 1, but the cost of the best solutions is almost ten times bigger. So, if someone intends to work with this problem, it has to have in mind that the solution cost does not increase linearly considering the growth in the number of sensors.

Regarding the number of trips, Pedra Branca State Park is the most challenging urban forest to be monitored. It would be necessary to cover the area defined in the proposed scenarios from 68 trips (in the smaller instance) to 81 trips. As for Tijuca's National Park, the maximum number of required trips is 16. Besides, less than ten trips would be necessary for seven of the twelve instances related to Tijuca's National Park. However, the proposed approach would still be valuable in supporting the rescue tasks considering the size of the monitored areas and the difficult of access (due to its forests features). It is important to emphasize that, even in the instances with smaller coverage (as 60%), the proposed approach would help rescue tasks, giving insight into missing people instead of searching in the whole urban forest. In this case, the rescue team would consider the last information collected in the monitored part to reduce the search area. Therefore, it would only be necessary to perform the rescue search in the area near the last information collected.

From the operational point of view, considering a UAV that travels at a speed of 40 km/h, collecting all the data from sensors would take on average 10 h. However, each concluded trip gives insights about the person's location. If the last timestamp registered by the sensors are, for example, in the first trip, the UAV search could be interrupted. So, the time to identify the person's location might be inferior to 4 h. Therefore, this governance knowledge could be joined to the heuristics procedure to improve efficiency.

Besides, in a real case, the decision-maker would know the critical areas for people to get lost, and the order of the trips could be modified to attend first these critical areas. Thus, the search process would be improved. In addition, other types of drones with higher speeds could be used instead of a UAV, reducing, even more, the rescue operation time.

In the end, we emphasize that the proposed decision-making tool needs interaction with the public agent to propose better solutions. Therefore, it would be helpful in the smart cities design since it deals with two issues pointed by [2]: the coordination of urban technologies and the development of models and methods for using urban data across spatial and temporal scales.

5   Conclusions and Future Works

This paper proposed an integer programming formulation and a GRASP metaheuristic that could be used as a decision-making tool to support the rescue search in urban forests. This support system would provide the last known person's location or, at least, restrict the search area in a reasonable computational time.

Although the integer programming formulation failed to obtain a feasible solution in the given timelimite, the proposed GRASP was able to obtain solutions within 20 s. In these solutions, the time to collect the data was lesser than 4 h. Besides, using data sensors to get information about missing people in urban forests would improve the efficiency (less public resource would be consumed in these hard rescue tasks) and the effectiveness of the rescues (the person would wait less time to be rescued). The proposed approach could also obtain information regarding areas that have to be closed or noticed as risk areas, generating more knowledge to be used in public policies and minimizing the risk of someone or some group getting lost.

We identified that the number of sensors is not the only factor that influences in the results. Therefore, it should be performed experiments with different base positions in order to evaluate this change in costs. The financial analysis of implementing this system could also be evaluated.

As future works, one may search for more insights of solution quality. Exact methods can be used to find how close the obtained solutions of the proposed method are to the optimal solution. With this would be possible to propose other heuristics procedures to find better solutions for instances of different structures and types. That would reduce the costs associated with creating this infrastructure and the rescue task for the public sector.

Acknowledgement. The authors thank the CYTED Thematic Network "Ciudades Inteligentes Totalmente Integrales, Eficientes y Sostenibles (CITIES)" no 518RT0558.

References

1. Cadastro Nacional de Florestas Públicas - Atualização 2019 (2019). http:// www.florestal.gov.br/cadastro-nacional-de-florestas-publicas/127-informacoes-florestais/cadastro-nacional-de-florestas-publicas-cnfp/1894-cadastro-nacional-de-florestas-publicas-atualizacao-2019. Accessed 10 Sep 2020
2. Batty, M., et al.: Smart cities of the future. Euro. Phys. J. **214**(1), 481–518 (2012). https://doi.org/10.1140/epjst/e2012-01703-3
3. Erdelj, M., Król, M., Natalizio, E.: Wireless sensor networks and multi-UAV systems for natural disaster management. Comput. Netw. **124**, 72–86 (2017)
4. Ferraris, A., Santoro, G., Papa, A.: The cities of the future: Hybrid alliances for open innovation projects. Futures **103**, 51–60 (2018). https://doi.org/10.1016/j.futures.2018.03.012
5. Gendreau, M., Potvin, J.Y.: Handbook of Metaheuristics, 2nd edn. Springer Publishing Company, Boston (2010). https://doi.org/10.1007/b101874
6. Hammad, A.W., Akbarnezhad, A., Haddad, A., Vazquez, E.G.: Sustainable zoning, land-use allocation and facility location optimisation in smart cities. Energies **12**(7) (2019). https://doi.org/10.3390/en12071318
7. Institute, C.M.: Relatório Anual Tijuca 2017 (2019) http://parquenacionaldatijuca.rio/files/report_anual_2017.pdf. Accessed 10 Sep 2020
8. Meghanathan, N.: On the use of centrality measures to determine connected dominating sets for mobile ad hoc networks. Int. J. Ad Hoc Ubiquitous Comput. **26**(4), 205–221 (2017). https://doi.org/10.1504/IJAHUC.2017.087886
9. Munhoz, P.L.A., et al.: Locality sensitive algotrithms for data mule routing problem. In: Du, D.-Z., Li, L., Sun, X., Zhang, J. (eds.) AAIM 2019. LNCS, vol. 11640, pp. 236–248. Springer, Cham (2019). https://doi.org/10.1007/978-3-030-27195-4_22
10. Munhoz, P.L.A., González, P.H., dos Santos Souza, U., Ochi, L.S., Michelon, P., Drummond, L.M.d.A.: General variable neighborhood search for the data mule scheduling problem. Electr. Notes Discrete Math. **66**, 71–78 (2018)
11. Neirotti, P., De Marco, A., Cagliano, A.C., Mangano, G., Scorrano, F.: Current trends in smart city initiatives: Some stylised facts. Cities **38**, 25–36 (2014). https://doi.org/10.1016/j.cities.2013.12.010, http://www.sciencedirect.com/science/article/pii/S0264275113001935
12. Silva, M.M., Subramanian, A., Ochi, L.S.: An iterated local search heuristic for the split delivery vehicle routing problem. Comput. Oper. Res. **53**, 234–249 (2015). https://doi.org/10.1016/j.cor.2014.08.005, http://www.sciencedirect.com/science/article/pii/S0305054814002159
13. Sugihara, R., Gupta, R.K.: Path planning of data mules in sensor networks. ACM Trans. Sensor Netw. **8**(1), 1:1–1:27 (2011)

Energy-Aware Smart Home Planning: A Real Case Study in Montevideo, Uruguay

Diego G. Rossit[1,2(✉)] and Sergio Nesmachnow[3]

[1] Department of Engineering, Universidad Nacional del Sur, Bahía Blanca, Argentina
diego.rossit@uns.edu.ar
[2] INMABB UNS-CONICET, Bahía Blanca, Argentina
[3] Universidad de la República, Montevideo, Uruguay

Abstract. This article presents an approach for energy-aware smart home planning via direct control and planning of residential electric appliances for smart cities. Energy-aware planning is a crucial concept for achieving a better utilization of resources and improving the quality of life in modern cities. In this line of work, this article proposes a stochastic optimization approach to plan the utilization of domestic appliances considering stochastic user preferences. A specific case study is addressed, considering residential households in Montevideo, Uruguay. The case study is modeled using built using real data from existing appliances and a data analysis approach for modeling user preferences. The proposed approach is able to compute accurate plannings in the experimental evaluation performed. The developed approach contributes to energy efficiency and sustainability in modern smart cities.

Keywords: Energy efficiency · Smart planning · Smart cities

1 Introduction

Energy utilization has largely increased in modern cities, and it is expected to continue growing for years to come [8]. For instance, in 2019, the residential sector accounted for more than 27% of the total energy consumption in the European Union [3] and more than 21% in the USA [27]. The share of energy consumption was even larger for households in 2020, due to the COVID-19 pandemic. Thus, energy-aware planning is a crucial concept for achieving a better utilization of resources and improving the quality of life in modern smart cities.

An effective planning of residential energy consumption certainly contributes towards sustainability and the highly demanding environmental standards required by sustainable development approaches, to reduce both the incurred monetary costs and the carbon footprint of electric grid systems [6]. A crucial feature of smart residential energy planning is the ability of re-shaping the energy demand by users to provide cost-effective and rational energy consumption. In this regard, demand response strategies are one of the most important components of the modern smart grid paradigm for electric systems [14]. These

© Springer Nature Switzerland AG 2022
S. Nesmachnow and L. Hernández Callejo (Eds.): ICSC-Cities 2021, CCIS 1555, pp. 146–161, 2022.
https://doi.org/10.1007/978-3-030-96753-6_11

mechanisms are highly regarded as valuable strategies in the transition process of energy utilization towards a decarbonized economy, highlighting the importance of users as relevant agents in the energy market.

Effective energy management strategies must be complemented with easy-to-understand and easy-to-use computer-assisted applications, to properly involve citizens and organizations, and encourage then to be part of the improved energy utilization model. On the one hand, electricity companies should be able to implement effective demand response actions, properly evaluated in advance to reduce the negative impacts on users comfort [21]. On the other hand, citizens should have available useful applications for monitoring, managing, and evaluating the energy consumption at household level [15]. Smart computer-aid tools that help to take better decisions in energy planning are an important component of the smart electric grid, facilitating citizen engagement towards environment preservation and a better use of the energy resources in smart cities [19].

In this line of work, this article presents an energy-aware smart home planning strategy to determine proper schedules for the use of deferrable electrical appliances, i.e., those appliances that can be controlled by the user and deferred to be switched on in different time-slots on the scheduling horizon without a critical result in the comfort of users, in residential buildings. The planning strategy, which is based on an stochastic optimization model, simultaneously considers the cost of the electricity bill and the Quality of Service (QoS) offered to the users and is specially tailored for addressing this problem in the Uruguayan households. For this aim, the novel dataset ECD-UY [1] about the consumption of different households in Uruguay is used for retrieving information related to Uruguayans electric consumption patterns. The stochastic optimization model considers uncertainty on the users preferences by performing simulations of many probable scenarios based on historical data of the households and the computational experimentation is performed over scenarios of both individual households and community buildings. The obtained results demonstrate that the proposed planning strategy is able to compute accurate schedules, accounting for different trade-offs between the cost of the electricity bill and the Quality of Service (QoS) offered to the users. This way, the proposed approach is able to provide users different suggestions for planning the utilization of domestic appliances.

Thus, the main contributions of the research reported in this article are a planning strategy for scheduling deferrable appliances considering the electricity cost and the QoS provided to users which comprehends a mixed-integer programming formulation and a stochastic resolution algorithm and a computational experimentation based on case studies built using real data from residential electricity consumption for several appliances in the city on Montevideo, Uruguay.

The article is organized as follows. Next section introduces the energy-aware planning problem considered in the article, its mathematical formulation and a review of relevant related works. The proposed optimization model for the planning strategy is described in Sect. 3. The computational experimentation of the proposed approach performed over case studies in Montevideo, Uruguay, is reported in Sect. 5. Finally, Sect. 6 presents the conclusions and the main lines for future work.

2   Problem Description and Related Work

This section presents an overview of the household energy planning problem that is addressed in this work and reviews the most relevant related works.

2.1   Problem Description

The household energy planning problem addressed in this article is modeled considering the following elements:

Sets:

- a set of users $U = \left(u_1 \ldots u_{|U|}\right)$, each user represents a household;
- a set of time slots $T = \left(t_1 \ldots t_{|T|}\right)$ in the planning period;
- sets of domestic appliances $L^u = \left(l_1^u \ldots l_{|L|}^u\right)$ for each user u;

Parameters:

- a parameter D_l^u that indicates the average time of utilization for user u of appliance $l \in L^u$;
- a parameter C_t that indicates the cost of the power in time slot t in the ToU pricing system;
- a parameter P_l^u that indicates the power consumed by appliance l;
- a parameter n_l^u that indicates the number of times per day that each appliance is used by each user;
- a binary parameter UP_{lt}^u that is 1 if user u prefers to use the appliance $l \in L^u$ at time slot t, 0 in other case;
- a parameter E^u that indicates the maximum power contracted by user u;
- a parameter E^{joint} that indicates the maximum power that the (whole) set of users U are allowed to consume, which is used in building-like instances;
- a penalty cost ρ applied when surpass the maximum (electric) power contracted in building-like instances;

Variables:

- a binary variable x_{lt}^u that is 1 if user u has appliance $l \in L^u$ turn on at time slot t and 0 if the appliance is turn off;
- a binary variable δ_{lt}^u that indicates if the appliance $l \in L^u$ of user u is turn on from time slot t up to a period of time that its at least equal to D_l^u;
- a binary variable ψ_t that indicates if users are using more power than the maximum power contracted E^{joint} in building-like instances.
- a binary variable Ψ_t that indicates if users are using more power than 130% of the maximum power contracted E^{joint} in building-like instances.
- a non-negative continuous variable e_t that measures the excess of power used over the contracted power in building-like instances.

The problem aims at scheduling the usage of household appliances considering the maximization of users satisfaction and the minimization of the total cost of the power consumed, at the same time.

Two different situations in the electric market of Uruguay are analyzed: i) when users are considered standalone units for the electric system, and ii) when users conform a unique building -and, thus, represent a large consumer for the electric system-. In the case of buildings, the overall power usage by the building can surpass the contracted power but a penalization cost is applied. In the case of standalone users, each user has to strictly respect the individual contracted power. If the power used by the user is larger than the contracted power, the user is disconnected from the supply by the electric protections. This variation affects the corresponding mathematical model. The model for buildings is outlined in Eqs. (1)–(6).

$$\max F = \sum_{u \in U} \sum_{l \in L^u} \sum_{\substack{t_1 \in T \\ t \le |T| - D_l^u}} \left(\delta_{lt_1}^u \left(\sum_{\substack{t_2 \in T \\ t_1 \le t_2 < t_1 + D_l^u}} U P_{lt_2}^u \right) \right) \tag{1}$$

$$\min G = \sum_{t \in T} \left(\sum_{u \in U} \sum_{l \in L^u} x_{lt}^u P_l^u C_t + e_t \rho \left(2\psi_t + 2\Psi_t \right) \right) \tag{2}$$

subject to

$$\delta_{lt}^u \le 1 - \frac{D_l^u - \left(\sum_{\substack{t_2 \in T \\ t \le t_1 < t + D_l^u}} x_{lt_1}^u \right)}{D_l^u}, \forall\ u \in U, l \in L^u, t \in T \tag{3}$$

$$\sum_{t \in T} \delta_{lt}^u = n_l^u, \forall\ u \in U, l \in L^u \tag{4}$$

$$\psi_t \ge \frac{\sum_{\substack{u \in U \\ l \in L^u}} P_l^u x_{lt}^u - E^{joint}}{\sum_{\substack{u \in U \\ l \in L^u}} P_l^u}, \forall\ t \in T \tag{5}$$

$$\Psi_t \ge \frac{\sum_{\substack{u \in U \\ l \in L^u}} P_l^u x_{lt}^u - 1.3 E^{joint}}{\sum_{\substack{u \in U \\ l \in L^u}} P_l^u}, \forall\ t \in T \tag{6}$$

$$e_t \ge \sum_{\substack{u \in U \\ l \in L^u}} P_l^u x_{lt}^u - E_{joint}, \forall\ t \in T \tag{7}$$

$$e \ge 0; \psi, \Psi, \delta, x \in \mathbb{B}$$

Regarding the objective functions of the problem, Eq. (1) maximizes the users satisfaction according to the time in which each appliance is used and their preferences. In turn, Eq. (2) aims at minimizing the energy expense budget, which include the charge for power consumption and the penalization for exceeding the maximum power contracted.

Several constraints are specified in the proposed model. Equation (3) enforces δ_{lt}^u to be one when the length of time an appliance will be on is equal or larger than the required by the user. Equation (4) enforces that each appliance is turn on the number of times per day required by the user. Equation (5) enforces ψ_t to be one if the users exceed the maximum power contracted. Equation (6) enforces Ψ_t to be one if the users exceed the maximum power contracted for more than 30%. Equation (7) measures the excess power used at each time interval.

The mathematical model for a set of standalone users replaces Eqs. (5)–(7) by Eq. (8), which establishes that each user cannot surpass the maximum power contracted.

$$\sum_{l \in L^u} P_l^u x_{lt}^u \leq E^u, \ \forall \ u \in U, t \in T \tag{8}$$

2.2 An Smart Home Energy Planning Strategy for the Uruguayan Households

The proposed problem model was conceived to capture the reality of the Uruguayan residential electricity market, by including specific constraints to model different aggregations of users and contracted power. In turn, specific details of real scenarios and real electricity tariffs are considered, taking into account the relevance of modeling real scenarios for smart home energy planning. The main motivation lays in the fact that different countries have different characteristics of electricity consumption and users behavior.

In addition, the cost of the electricity for the residential sector has a large dispersion through all countries around the world. According to the statistics provided by the U.S. Energy Information Administration, the average value in the world is 0.137 USD per kWh, but in December 2020 German households were charged 0.37 USD per kWh. In South America, electricity cost values have an average of 0.18 USD per kWh, but Uruguay has the most expensive prices, 0.204 USD per kWh. These different prices generate different user behaviors, according to the economic realities of each household. Cost is one of the major factors that influence energy consumption in households, significantly larger than non-financial benefits offered to users [22].

Furthermore, the type of tariffs also influences on the users behavior. Historically, almost all residential users have been subject to fixed (i.e., time-invariant) electricity prices, e.g., 95% in the US [27]. But the emergence of the modern smart grid paradigm has provided users a different alternative for managing electric devices, and more households have chosen to participate in time-varying pricing programs. The behavior of these users is changing for adapting to the new tariffs. All these matters must be taken into account when studying smart home planning strategies, which also must fulfill the regulations of each country.

Finally, the type of domestic appliances must match those most used in the country. In Uruguay, heating and air conditioning account for a significant share of electricity consumption (around 40%), following a global trend in developed countries. In Uruguay however, water heater is the appliance with the largest electricity consumption overall (almost 45% of the total consumption in households). A specific characteristic of the aforementioned appliances is that they have a seasonal electricity-intensive use, with a larger consumption in winter. Other appliances like fridge, washing machine, electric oven, electronic devices, etc., have a similar year-round electricity consumption.

All the aforementioned considerations have been taken into account in this research to build real scenarios, using real data gathered from Uruguayan homes in a pilot plan developed using smart meters. After processing the collected information, real instances of the problem were defined by properly defining the appliances, electricity prices, contracted power, and computing the user preference function based on statistical analysis of real data. The created scenarios and problem instances are specific contributions of the reported research.

2.3   Related Work

The household energy planning problem has been addressed in several works of the related literature [13]. Considered a NP-hard optimization problem already in its deterministic version [11], this work focuses on the complex stochastic version of the household energy planning problem [12].

Some other works have addressed stochastic version of this problem, by including uncertainty in different parameters. Chen et al. [2] considered uncertainties in the power consumed by the appliances and the renewable solar energy gathered by a photovoltaic array. A three-stages resolution process was proposed: i) a deterministic linear programming optimization model considering mean values for the appliances consumption and maximum solar power generation is solved, ii) they improved the obtained solution with Monte Carlo simulation considering different energy consumption rates of appliances, and iii) an online adjustment system is implement to adapt the previous (offline) solution to the actual reality. Hemmati and Saboori [5] proposed a particle swarm optimization algorithm to deal with uncertainty of photovoltaic panels in a similar problem. Assuming that the energy generated in the panels has a Gaussian probabilistic distribution, a Monte Carlo simulation was used to evaluate the stochastic function and obtain a sample of the generation values. Our previous works [25] considered an stochastic approach based on Monte Carlo simulation and discrete optimization to maximize the user preferences and minimize the cost of energy in households. Different instances were considered using REDD dataset [10]. Imanloozadeh et al. [7] proposed a model for scheduling appliances in a household located in an extreme desert environment while considering uncertainties in usage of deferrable appliances, electric vehicles discharge, illumination system and hot water heating. Different heuristics were applied to solve the problem and the best results were obtained by a grey wolf optimization algorithm. Waseem et al. [28] proposed a complex model that includes households appliances scheduling incorporating uncertainty in sudden absence of distributed energy resources and power failures. The problem model aimed at optimizing electricity cost, end-users comfort, and peak to average consumption ratio.

3 The Proposed Optimization Approach for the Stochastic Household Energy Planning Problem

This section describes the proposed resolution approach.

Stochastic Approach. The Sample Average Approximation (SAA) method is applied to deal with stochastic users preferences. In a stochastic optimization problem, the expected value of the objective function is optimized. For considering stochastic UP, Eq. (1) is replaced by the expected value of the function F as it is expressed in Eq. (9), in which **UP** is the random vector of the stochastic users preferences and $\mathbf{\Delta}$ is the vector of decision variables δ.

$$e = \mathbb{E}_{\mathbf{P}}\left[F\left(\mathbf{\Delta}, \mathbf{UP}\right)\right]. \tag{9}$$

Optimizing Eq. (9) requires computing all the possible realizations of vector **UP** with its corresponding probability of occurrence. Considering that there are $|T|^{\sum_{u \in U}|L^u|}$ realizations of this vector, simpler approaches have been proposed in the literature, such as the SAA [26] which is applied in this work. In this approach the expected value (Eq. (9)), is approximated with an independently and identically distributed (i.i.d.) random sample. Thus, Eq. (10) is an estimator of the expected value of Eq. (9), in which the set of values $UP^1, ..., UP^N$, is an i.i.d. random sample of N realizations of the stochastic vector parameter **UP**.

$$\hat{e} = \frac{1}{N}\sum_{j=1}^{N} F\left(\mathbf{\Delta}, \mathbf{UP^j}\right) \tag{10}$$

The optimization problem obtained when Eq. (10) is used instead of Eq. (9), is the sample average approximation optimization problem (hereafter SAA) and can be solved deterministically with commercial solvers. Since the solution of the SAA problem depends on the realizations **UP** that are included in the random sample, the larger the size of the sample (N), the smaller is the difference between Eq. (9) and its estimator Eq. (10). Particularly, when $N \to \infty$, $\hat{e} \to e$. An important feature of this approach is that different samples of size N (i.e., different set of realizations of the stochastic vector parameter **UP**) allow shaping different forms of Eq. (10). Therefore, all algorithms based on sample average usually solve the SAA problem several times with different samples and after that select the most promising solution as the final solution. In this case, to select the final solution we use the procedure proposed by Norkin et al. [18]. Let $\hat{s}_N^1, \hat{s}_N^2, ..., \hat{s}_N^M$ be the solutions (values of decision values) when solving M SAA optimization problems each one with a different sample of size N. Then, an independent sample of size N' with $N' >> N$ is built to evaluate the M solutions using this sample and the solution with the best value problem is selected. This method takes advantage from the fact that although using the large sample size N' for the optimization phase is very time consuming (specially in NP-hard problems as the one addressed in this paper), using it for just for evaluation of the objective function is achievable in reasonable computing time [9].

Biobjective Optimization. A weighted sum is applied to simultaneously optimize the objectives of user satisfaction and electricity cost . This approach has been successfully applied to related household energy planning problems [16].

A joint function is opitmized, in which the two objectives are normalized by the ideal and nadir values of the objectives, and weighted by the parameters α and β, in the unique expression reported in Eq. (11).

$$\max H = \alpha \frac{F - F^{ideal}}{F^{ideal} - F^{nadir}} - \beta \frac{G - G^{ideal}}{G^{nadir} - G^{ideal}} \tag{11}$$

The ideal and nadir values are approximated by single-objective optimization of each objective, i.e., the payoff table. Since the nadir value can be underestimated [23], the ideal and nadir values of the payoff table are used in the weighted sum formula along with a biased combination of weights. Two different problems are solved, using $\alpha \gg \beta > 0$ and using $\beta \gg \alpha > 0$. Finally, the ideal and nadir values are obtained from the solutions of the last two multiobjective problems.

4   Real Scenarios for Smart Home Planning: Case Studies in Montevideo, Uruguay

This section describes the methodology for designing real scenarios of the household energy planning problem addressed in this article.

4.1   Motivation and Overall Description

The evaluation of effective smart home planning strategies must be performed on realistic problem scenarios and instances.

Many related works have evaluated previously proposed methods over synthetic or non-realistic problem instances, in which several assumptions were formulated for users behavior, dissaggregated energy consumption, or even energy prices and tariff schemes. This practice hinders a proper evaluation of the applicability of the proposed strategies in practice.

The specific methodology applied in this article for the evaluation of smart home planning strategies is directly focused on considering real information from residential users, dissaggregated energy consumption, and energy rate/tariff plans, as described in the next subsection.

4.2   Data Sources

Data for the generated scenarios were gathered in a previous research effort (project 'Computational intelligence for detecting residential energy consumption patterns') that built the ECD-UY dataset [1]. The considered data include:

– *Residential users.* The ECD-UY dataset includes information about electricity consumption records of nine different households, recorded during a period of three weeks in 2019 in Montevideo, Uruguay. Five of those households were considered for the evaluation. Relevant information for those households includes the total electricity consumption, the contracted power, and the dissaggregated energy consumption (described on the next item).

- *Dissagregated energy consumption.* For each household, real electricity consumption of relevant domestic appliances were considered, including fridge, air conditioner, dehumidifier, electric air heater, electric oven, electric water heater, microwave, tumble dryer, and washing machine. Overall, water heater is the appliance that demands the largest energy consumption in Uruguayan households. The considered set of appliances accounts for more than 80% (in average) of the total electricity consumption in the considered households. Other minor electric devices were not considered in the analysis since they do nos contribute significantly to energy consumption.
- *Energy tariffs.* Real energy tariffs and plans from the Uruguayan Electricity Company (UTE) are considered. The company provides two smart plans that are based on Time-of-Use pricing systems to encourage users to displace appliances usage from peak hours to relatively cheaper of–peak hours (www. ute.com.uy).

4.3   Modeling User Preferences

A specific model was proposed based on data analysis for modeling user preferences and defining the stochastic vector parameter **UP**.

Noticeable differences in the electricity consumption of appliances are observed in weekends, mainly because the different lifestyle of users in weekends, which tend to stay at home more hours than in working weekdays [20], and the different ToU tariff that the electricity companies applies. Therefore, instances were divided among weekdays and weekends [16,17,24]

Historical information retrieved from the dataset about the power consumption of the selected appliances on each household was analyzed. This task involved cleaning the data from comparatively very small power consumption that are related to stand-by operation mode of each appliance, for example, small screen leds. After this, for each combination of user and appliance, a probability of usage for each time slot was estimated (p_{lt}^u). With this probability, M instances were constructed for each sample size N as is described in Sect. 5.2.

The parameter of the power consumption P_l^u was calculated as the median of all the values of power that were consumed by the appliance. Before calculating the median, a filter to discard outlier values of power consumption that can be due to atypical conditions or malfunctioning was applied. The filter discards the values that were outside of the range $[median - 8MAD; median + 8MAD]$ where MAD is the median absolute deviation used a robust measure of dispersion. A similar procedure was applied to calculate the duration of time of utilization of each appliance (D_l^u) as the median of all the durations and the times per day that each appliance is turn on (n_l^u).

5   Computational Experimentation

This section reports the validation of the proposed optimization approach for smart home electricity planning.

5.1   Validation Scenarios

The validation of the proposed approach is based of real data of the city of Montevideo. Five households of the ECD-UY dataset [1] were retrieved. Table 1 reports the electric appliances considered in the five households.

Table 1. Electric appliances considered in each household.

Household	Appliances
170001	Electric air heater, electric oven, electric water heater, fridge, microwave, and washing machine
170004	Electric water heater, fridge, microwave, tumble dryer and washing machine
170005	Electric water heater, fridge, microwave,and washing machine
170006	Air conditioner 1, air conditioner 2, and electric water heater
170007	Electric air heater, and washing machine

The ToU tariff systems that are used in this work were retrieved from UTE. As aforementioned, the company offers two ToU tariff systems: the Double Hour Residential Rate (hereafter double tariff system) and the Triple Hour Residential Rate (hereafter triple tariff system). The Double Hour Residential Rate tariff considers two categories of hours: the peak hours and the off-peak hours. For better customizing the system, UTE allows that each user selects the peak hours. These hours must be a four-hours consecutive hours between 5pm and 11pm. The Triple Hour Residential Rate considers three categories of hours. These are, from the most expensive to the cheapest, the peak hours, the plain hours and the valley hours. Similarly to the double tariff system, the peak hours can be selected by the user regarding they are four consecutive hours between 5 PM and 11 PM. The valley hours are between midnight and 7am and the rest of the hours are considered valley hours.

The five households were considered in four different scenarios: using the double tariff system, using the triple tariff system, and, finally, using a mix of both systems in a building-like fashion. Thus, considering weekdays and weekends profiles the instances are:

- the five households using double tariff system in weekdays (d.wd) and weekends (d.we).
- the five households using triple tariff system in weekdays (t.wd) and weekends (t.we).
- three households using double tariff system and two homes using triple tariff system in a building-like fashion in weekdays (b.wd) and weekends (b.we).

5.2   Methodology

After preliminary calibration experiments, three sample sizes were chosen $N = 1000$, 10000, and 100000. The number of independent samples of each size (M)

was set to 100. The evaluation sample size (N') was set to 10000000. Five weight vectors (α, β) were used for exploring different trade-off combinations between the problem objectives: (0.909,0.01), (0.25, 0.75), (0.5, 0.5), (0.75, 0.25), and (0.01, 0.909). The SAA problems were solved with ILOG CPLEX Optimization Studio version 20.1 through Pyomo as modelling language [4].

Experimentation was divided in two parts: computation of random realizations of vector **UP** and optimization considering the generated samples. The separation aims at studying the impact of the random samples of vector **UP** in the overall efficiency of SAA. Then, for each instance and size N, a set of 100 (M) independent realizations of vector **UP** were generated.

5.3   Experimental Results

Table 2 reports the execution times of the generation of independent samples of the scenario. The execution times indicate that the average time increases linearly with the sample size N e.g., as shown for instances with double tariff system. This result is connected to the trade-off between having a large sample size N, which is computationally expensive but provides a better estimation of the real expected value, or a smaller sample size N, which is lees time-consuming but provides a worse approximation of the real expected value.

Table 2. Computing times for generating the realizations of vector **UP**.

Instance	N	Time (s)		Instance	N	Time (s)	
		avg.	std.			avg.	std.
d.wd	1000	8.0847	0.1381	d.we	1000	8.0678	0.1097
	10000	81.9886	0.0870		10000	82.4326	0.1279
	100000	821.8834	1.1814		100000	821.8033	1.6480

Table 3 reports the experimental results of SAA in validation experiments. For each instance, the sample size N, the combination of weights (α, β), and five relevant metrics are reported:

– the average and standard deviation of the execution time;
– the average and standard deviation of the users satisfaction function F evaluated over N';
– the average and standard deviation of the cost function G evaluated over N';
– the values of F and G of the best solution, i.e., the solution that has the minimal value of function H, as defined in Eq. (11);
– the deviation of the solution to the ideal vector Σ, computed using the L^2 distance norm, according to Eq. (12).

$$\Sigma = \sqrt{\sum_{o \in O} \left(\frac{value - best_o}{best_o} \cdot 100\% \right)^2} \tag{12}$$

Table 3. Results of the SAA.

N	(α,β)	time (s)	$F(H^{N'}_{best})$	$G(H^{N'}_{best})$	Σ	time (s)	$F(H^{N'}_{best})$	$G(H^{N'}_{best})$	Σ
Double tariff system instances									
		Weekday (d.wd)				Weekend (d.wd)			
1000	(0.99,0.01)	0.1131	5.4423	17351.2209	34.63%	0.1069	5.0784	12145.3422	5.67%
	(0.01,0.99)	11.1970	5.2366	12888.6759	4.46%	10.2117	5.0783	11494.3428	0.19%
	(0.50,0.50)	0.6365	5.2760	13454.9187	5.77%	0.5805	5.0785	11907.8682	3.60%
	(0.75,0.25)	0.2705	5.4520	15449.8332	19.88%	0.2702	5.0786	12131.9154	5.55%
	(0.25,0.75)	2.6556	5.2363	12983.3649	4.52%	2.6105	5.0785	11781.4158	2.51%
10000	(0.99,0.01)	0.1255	5.4824	16497.0978	28.00%	0.1200	5.0706	11949.2508	3.96%
	(0.01,0.99)	12.8881	5.2662	12888.6759	3.92%	12.6046	5.0680	11513.7816	0.17%
	(0.50,0.50)	0.9855	5.4807	14922.8241	15.78%	1.0742	5.0702	11785.3236	2.53%
	(0.75,0.25)	0.3444	5.4823	15003.9861	16.41%	0.3120	5.0704	11846.0448	3.06%
	(0.25,0.75)	3.6069	5.3246	13147.1661	3.49%	3.4554	5.0702	11741.1354	2.15%
100000	(0.99,0.01)	0.1524	5.4824	16695.0423	29.53%	0.1411	5.0705	11824.5018	2.87%
	(0.01,0.99)	14.0165	5.2663	12888.6759	3.92%	14.4370	5.0710	11494.3428	0.05%
	(0.50,0.50)	2.7312	5.4812	14882.2431	15.47%	2.6138	5.0710	11682.6186	1.64%
	(0.75,0.25)	0.5974	5.4824	14963.4051	16.10%	0.6177	5.0713	11922.2970	3.72%
	(0.25,0.75)	4.9002	5.3243	13120.1121	3.38%	5.2922	5.0698	11594.3424	0.87%
Triple tariff system instances									
		Weekday (t.wd)				Weekend (t.wd)			
1000	(0.99,0.01)	0.1176	5.4408	14653.6178	116.99%	0.0983	7.2459	12562.4901	108.45%
	(0.01,0.99)	6.7751	4.8329	6753.0488	11.73%	5.7147	5.7662	6028.7598	20.45%
	(0.50,0.50)	0.6827	5.2832	9488.7445	40.66%	0.7872	6.9618	6921.9294	15.37%
	(0.75,0.25)	0.2820	5.4507	12749.1934	88.79%	0.2853	7.0990	8742.6267	45.11%
	(0.25,0.75)	1.3912	5.0483	7116.8405	9.48%	1.8756	6.9028	6701.5782	12.17%
10000	(0.99,0.01)	0.1324	5.4820	15957.4220	136.30%	0.1120	7.2677	12687.4428	110.52%
	(0.01,0.99)	7.1755	4.8433	6753.0488	11.54%	5.9961	5.8158	6030.3285	19.77%
	(0.50,0.50)	1.2873	5.3228	9268.1675	37.35%	1.5423	6.9630	6741.1074	12.49%
	(0.75,0.25)	0.4755	5.4812	12302.0264	82.17%	0.7575	7.2271	9192.6075	52.53%
	(0.25,0.75)	2.5086	5.0592	7032.9137	8.66%	2.7973	6.9623	6724.3662	12.23%
100000	(0.99,0.01)	0.1624	5.4819	15154.8956	124.42%	0.1428	7.2679	12465.7851	106.84%
	(0.01,0.99)	7.9994	4.8437	6753.0487	11.54%	6.0057	5.8164	6030.3285	19.76%
	(0.50,0.50)	2.1318	5.3236	9158.1686	35.72%	2.7583	6.9631	6731.4012	12.34%
	(0.75,0.25)	0.8098	5.4805	11825.5112	75.11%	1.5354	7.2673	9236.5179	53.26%
	(0.25,0.75)	4.0831	5.0592	7011.6512	8.51%	3.6560	6.9536	6708.0816	12.02%
Building-like instances									
		Weekday (b.wd)				Weekend (b.wd)			
1000	(0.99,0.01)	0.1852	5.4415	15573.6492	57.17%	0.1691	7.2166	11231.0796	34.28%
	(0.01,0.99)	23.0971	5.2353	9908.8092	4.35%	25.1296	5.9513	8364.0303	18.05%
	(0.50,0.50)	6.3228	5.3736	12506.7870	26.28%	6.3418	6.2954	8367.1677	13.31%
	(0.75,0.25)	1.6910	5.4423	14981.6673	51.20%	1.5304	6.9626	8751.6237	6.20%
	(0.25,0.75)	16.7783	5.2561	10395.6621	6.32%	16.3588	6.3058	8367.1677	13.17%
10000	(0.99,0.01)	0.2602	5.4820	16280.9307	64.31%	0.2573	7.2662	10839.6924	29.60%
	(0.01,0.99)	28.7164	5.2663	9908.8092	3.79%	29.2907	5.9532	8364.0303	18.02%
	(0.50,0.50)	9.6899	5.4813	12686.0631	28.03%	9.6318	6.5224	8445.7521	10.23%
	(0.75,0.25)	2.0274	5.4827	14050.4841	41.80%	1.9017	7.0697	8819.7003	6.06%
	(0.25,0.75)	16.3678	5.3246	10242.3396	4.33%	15.2221	6.3064	8367.1677	13.16%
100000	(0.99,0.01)	0.3001	5.4822	16385.9607	65.37%	0.2743	7.2676	10516.6188	25.74%
	(0.01,0.99)	28.3730	5.2660	9908.8092	3.79%	30.8415	5.9529	8364.0303	18.03%
	(0.50,0.50)	12.2024	5.4812	12533.7021	26.49%	13.2396	6.5221	8445.7521	10.24%
	(0.75,0.25)	4.2573	5.4811	12727.4946	28.45%	4.1211	7.0715	8819.7003	6.05%
	(0.25,0.75)	17.4095	5.3246	10235.2521	4.27%	19.0460	6.3065	8367.1677	13.16%

Results in Table 3 indicate that the proposed approach is able to solve the instances in relatively short computing times. The instances that prioritize the cost over the user satisfaction, i.e., with a combination of weights (0.01,0.99) and (0.25,0.75), are more difficult to solve and require larger computing times. Additionally, the average resolution time for building-like instances is significantly larger than for the other instances, since more integer variables are integrated in the MIP formulation with the penalization variables.

Results show that the triple tariff system allows reducing the cost of the energy consumed for similar level of preferences. For example, in Fig. 1, the solutions of the triple tariff system dominates in terms of cost and/or user satisfaction the solutions of the double tariff system, specially in the weekend.

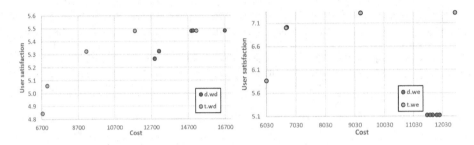

Fig. 1. Comparison of the best solutions for instances with double and triple tariff system with sample size $N = 10000$.

Table 4 compares the results of representative SAA solutions with a business as usual (BaU) strategy. The BaU strategy proposes assigning ON times to each appliance without planning considering only user satisfaction. These plannings have good user preference values, but inefficient costs. The SAA representative solutions that are compared are the best compromising solution of SAA, i.e., the one with the smallest Σ, and the solution biased to the user satisfaction, i.e., with a weight vector (0.99,0.01). Table 4 reports the percentage relative improvement of the SAA solution over the BaU solution for each objective.

Table 4. Comparison of SAA with BaU solutions.

	d.wd		t.wd		b.wd	
	F	G	F	G	F	G
Compromising	−2.89%	35.35%	−7.72%	62.84%	−3.95%	48.16%
Best preferences	0.00%	18.71%	−0.01%	15.44%	−0.01%	14.27%
	d.we		t.we		b.we	
	F	G	F	G	F	G
Compromising	−30.25%	18.91%	−4.33%	59.20%	−2.69%	40.65%
Best preferences	−30.11%	14.47%	0.00%	24.17%	0.00%	29.23%

Results indicate that, except for instance $d.we$, the compromising solution of the SAA are only slightly worse in terms of user satisfaction than the BaU solutions, less than 5% in all cases (Table 4). Regarding $d.we$, BaU solutions are about 30% better than SAA solution. In terms of cost, as expected, compromising solutions are substantially better than BaU solutions (up to 62%). In the case of the solutions of SAA biased to user satisfaction, i.e., those that have a large value of α, BaU solutions are almost equally competitive in terms of respecting user preferences but with higher electricity costs (up to 29%). The exception is $d.we$ in which the SAA solution is around 30% worse than BaU in terms of user satisfaction.

6 Conclusions and Future Work

This article addressed the problem of scheduling deferrable appliances in smart homes considering stochastic user preferences for appliances, focused on a specific case study on Uruguayan households. For solving the problem, a new MIP mathematical formulation of is presented, and a resolution approach based on exact solver and Monte Carlo simulation is proposed.

Results obtained in the computational experimentation on a set of real-world instances show that the proposed method is competitive to address the household planning problem, computing solutions that are similar in terms of user satisfaction to the business as usual strategy, but with smaller electricity costs.

The main lines for future work are related to the enlargement of the computational experimentation taking further advantage of the extensive database that has been published about households of Montevideo, including the use of electricity for water heating, and the application of other resolution approaches that explicitly consider the multiobjective nature of the problem, such as evolutionary algorithms.

References

1. Chavat, J., Nesmachnow, S., Graneri, J., Alvez, G.: ECD-UY: detailed household electricity consumption dataset of Uruguay. Sci. Data (in press 2021)
2. Chen, X., Wei, T., Hu, S.: Uncertainty-aware household appliance scheduling considering dynamic electricity pricing in smart home. IEEE Trans. Smart Grid 4(2), 932–941 (2013)
3. Eurostat: Energy consumption in households 2021. https://ec.europa.eu/eurostat. Accessed Sept 2021
4. Hart, W., et al.: Pyomo-Optimization Modeling in Python, vol. 67. Springer, Cham (2017). https://doi.org/10.1007/978-3-319-58821-6
5. Hemmati, R., Saboori, H.: Stochastic optimal battery storage sizing and scheduling in home energy management systems equipped with solar photovoltaic panels. Energy Build. 152, 290–300 (2017)
6. Hu, Z., Li, C., Cao, Y., Fang, B., He, L., Zhang, M.: How smart grid contributes to energy sustainability. Energy Procedia 61, 858–861 (2014)

7. Imanloozadeh, A., Nazififard, M., Sadat, S.: A new stochastic optimal smart residential energy hub management system for desert environment. Int. J. Energy Res. **45**, 18957–18980 (2021)
8. International Energy Agency. World Energy Outlook 2021. www.iea.org/topics/world-energy-outlook. Accessed Sept 2021
9. Kleywegt, A., Shapiro, A., Homem-de Mello, T.: The sample average approximation method for stochastic discrete optimization. SIAM J. Optim. **12**(2), 479–502 (2002)
10. Kolter, J., Johnson, M.: REDD: a public data set for energy disaggregation research. In: Workshop on Data Mining Applications in Sustainability, San Diego (2011)
11. Koutsopoulos, I., Tassiulas, L.: Control and optimization meet the smart power grid: scheduling of power demands for optimal energy management. In: Proceedings of the 2nd International Conference on Energy-Efficient Computing and Networking, pp. 41–50 (2011)
12. Liang, H., Zhuang, W.: Stochastic modeling and optimization in a microgrid: a survey. Energies **7**(4), 2027–2050 (2014)
13. Lu, X., Zhou, K., Zhang, X., Yang, S.: A systematic review of supply and demand side optimal load scheduling in a smart grid environment. J. Clean. Prod. **203**, 757–768 (2018)
14. Momoh, J.: Smart Grid: Fundamentals of Design and Analysis. Wiley, Hoboken (2012)
15. Nesmachnow, S., Baña, S., Massobrio, R.: A distributed platform for big data analysis in smart cities: combining intelligent transportation systems and socioeconomic data for Montevideo, Uruguay. EAI Endor. Trans. Smart Cities **2**(5), 153478 (2017)
16. Nesmachnow, S., Colacurcio, G., Rossit, D., Toutouh, J., Luna, F.: Optimizing household energy planning in smart cities: a multiobjective approach. Revista Facultad de Ingeniería Universidad de Antioquia **101**, 8–19 (2021)
17. Nesmachnow, S., Rossit, D., Toutouh, J., Luna, F.: An explicit evolutionary approach for multiobjective energy consumption planning considering user preferences in smart homes. Int. J. Ind. Eng. Comput. **12**(4), 365–380 (2021)
18. Norkin, V., Pflug, G., Ruszczyński, A.: A branch and bound method for stochastic global optimization. Math. Program. **83**, 425–450 (1998)
19. Orsi, E., Nesmachnow, S.: Smart home energy planning using IoT and the cloud. In: IEEE URUCON (2017)
20. Paatero, J., Lund, P.: A model for generating household electricity load profiles. Int. J. Energy Res. **30**(5), 273–290 (2006)
21. Porteiro, R., Chavat, J., Nesmachnow, S.: A thermal discomfort index for demand response control in residential water heaters. Appl. Sci. **11** (2021)
22. Rademaekers, K., et al.: Study on energy prices, costs and subsidies and their impact on industry and households. Tech. Rep. Final report, EU publications (2018)
23. Rossit, D., Toutouh, J., Nesmachnow, S.: Exact and heuristic approaches for multiobjective garbage accumulation points location in real scenarios. Waste Manag. **105**, 467–481 (2020)
24. Rossit, D., Nesmachnow, S., Toutouh, J., Luna, F.: A simulation-optimization approach for the household energy planning problem considering uncertainty in users preferences. In: International Conference of Production Research-Americas. pp. 253–267. Springer (2020)

25. Rossit, D.G., Nesmachnow, S., Toutouh, J., Luna, F.: Scheduling deferrable electric appliances in smart homes: a bi-objective stochastic optimization approach. Math. Biosci. Eng. **19**(1), 34–65 (2022)
26. Shapiro, A.: Monte Carlo simulation approach to stochastic programming. In: Proceeding of the 2001 Winter Simulation Conference. IEEE, Arlington (2001)
27. U.S. Energy Information Administration. Annual Energy Outlook 2021. https:// www.eia.gov/aeo. Accessed Sept 2021
28. Waseem, M., Lin, Z., Liu, S., Zhang, Z., Aziz, T., Khan, D.: Fuzzy compromised solution-based novel home appliances scheduling and demand response with optimal dispatch of distributed energy resources. Appl. Energy **290**, 116761 (2021)

A Machine Learning Approach for Detecting Traffic Incidents from Video Cameras

Guillermo Gabrielli[1]([⊠]), Ignacio Ferreira[1], Pablo Dalchiele[1],
Andrei Tchernykh[2,3] [iD], and Sergio Nesmachnow[4] [iD]

[1] Universidad de la República, Montevideo, Uruguay
{guillermo.gabrielli,ignacio.ferreira,pablo.dalchiele}@fing.edu.uy
[2] CICESE, Ensenada, Mexico
chernykh@cicese.mx
[3] Institute for System Programming of the Russian Academy of Sciences,
Moscow, Russia
[4] Universidad de la República, Montevideo, Uruguay
sergion@fing.edu.uy

Abstract. In the area of vehicular traffic analysis, many cities have surveillance devices (cameras) installed in different junctions as well as along roads, to obtain information on how vehicles behave in a certain area. To help in the process of preventing accidents, this article proposes a computer vision pipeline for detecting different types of dangerous/risky driving behavior. The pipeline includes object detection, tracking, speed normalization, and the application of computational intelligence, among other relevant features for pattern detection and traffic behavior analysis. The developed models are applied on videos from traffic cameras from eight different sites in the metropolitan area of the city of Montevideo. Three different algorithms were developed for detecting dangerous incidents in traffic in real time. Accurate results are reported for the case studies addressed in the experimental validation, reaching precision values up to 0.82 and recall values up to 0.91.

Keywords: Vehicular traffic · Road safety · Image processing · Computer vision · Artificial intelligence · Machine learning · Neural networks · Intelligent transport systems

1 Introduction

Nowadays, most modern cities have traffic surveillance cameras installed in different locations, to monitor traffic and gather information on how vehicles and pedestrian behave in specific areas [13]. Road safety is an important concept for the development of smart cities, since it allows citizens to live in a safe environment, reducing traffic jams and relevant social costs related to road accidents and pollution [16,17]. It also contributes to the safety of the most vulnerable

S. Nesmachnow and L. Hernández Callejo (Eds.): ICSC-Cities 2021, CCIS 1555, pp. 162–177, 2022.
https://doi.org/10.1007/978-3-030-96753-6_12

road users. In turn, road safety is also a key concept for the design and implementation of sustainable transportation systems [9] and for the Transit Oriented Development paradigm [10].

Traffic surveillance is of capital importance to properly manage and operate complex transportation systems with high traffic density. Automatic systems capable of providing assistance for traffic monitoring and analysis allow human operators to focus on relevant issues, instead of constantly observing many videos from different sources [12]. Automatic systems also allow to significantly reduce problems related to global attention degradation and errors due to boredom and/or fatigue [6]. Thus, automatic intelligent systems provide operators and regulators the capability of responding to diverse traffic issues and situations.

Vehicle counting and reckless driving detection are very important for Intelligent Transportation Systems [20,22]. The application of image processing and computer vision for developing detection algorithms has led to better results than traditional traffic surveillance methods, usually based on sensors [21]. Several recent studies have highlighted the importance of the subject and proposed smart methods for detecting traffic accidents or damaged vehicles that can indicate the occurrence of traffic incidents [15]. The detection of traffic incidents by automatic smart methods can save lives and improve traffic safety.

This article proposes a system to automatically detect usual traffic-related situations in metropolitan areas, from videos taken by road surveillance cameras. A flexible methodology is proposed, able to operate without human supervision. Computational intelligence and machine learning techniques are applied for detecting traffic incidents. Based on traffic camera videos, the system is capable of detecting reckless driving behavior in real time, taking advantage of high performance computing and Graphic Processing Units (GPU).

The proposed automatic system is based on a modular design consisting of a pipeline that includes object detection algorithms, tracking methods, labeling, image processing, and computing relevant metrics of the detected vehicles, pedestrians, and traffic infrastructure. Convolutional neural networks (CNN) are applied for object detection and learning patterns associated with reckless driving and pedestrian behavior. The system is targeted to execute on commodity hardware, to allow scaling to a large number of cameras without heavy expenses on hardware. The system is able to process video in real-time.

The developed system is validated and evaluated on a real case study using a dataset gathered from recordings of eight traffic cameras from the metropolitan area of the city of Montevideo, Uruguay. Selected areas were monitored in the city, to properly validate the reckless driving patterns and situations implemented in the system. Urban data analysis [14] is applied for the analysis of relevant data sources for the validation of the proposed system. Results of the evaluation demonstrate the effectiveness of the proposed system, according to standard metrics for detection and learning. Precision values up to 0.82 and recall values up to 0.91 were computed for the different problem instances solved.

The main contributions of this article are: the developed system, useful for traffic monitoring in modern smart cities; the pipeline applying image processing and computational intelligence for the detection of reckless driving behavior; ancillary applications for traffic image processing and labeling; and the evaluation of the proposed system on a real case study using real traffic data.

The article is organized as follows. Next section introduces the problem of automatic detection of traffic incidents and a review of the main related work. The proposed system for automatic traffic incidents detection is described in Sect. 3. The evaluation of the developed system for relevant case studies in Montevideo, Uruguay is reported in Sect. 4. Finally, Sect. 5 presents the conclusions and the main lines for future work.

2   Automatic Detection of Traffic Incidents

This section presents an overview of the problem of automatic detection of traffic incidents and a review of relevant related works on the subjects of object detection and tracking and their application to automatic traffic monitoring.

2.1   Problem Description

The problem consists in identifying traffic incidents in smart cities, as outlined by Ristvej et al. [16]. A Smart City Transport System should include a safe layer that incorporates the use of technology, planning, traffic rules and supervision to allow reducing traffic accidents, and improving transportation safety.

Automatic detection of traffic incidents is essential to improve the productivity of the users and operators of the Smart City Transport System because it lessens their workload, allowing them to focus on reviewing the incidents and reasoning about the causes of them. As explained in Chavat et al. [6], current detection systems are based on operational centers that manually analyse the traffic incidents thus the importance of the development of a system that addresses the issue in an automated fashion.

In order to approach the automatic detection of traffic incidents, it is crucial to have a reliable way to detect vehicles and other objects of interest. Background subtraction have been used in the past to detect vehicles at low complexity, however it is vulnerable to false detections from illumination changes, e.g. from shadows and vehicle highlights, as well as from movement of unrelated objects like trees, while offering poor results when the object color does not significantly differ from the background. Handling different perspectives, due to differences on camera height, angle with respect to the horizon and camera parameters like focal length, often would require running multiple models to cover different views of the object. In the last years there has been considerable interest in deep learning methods, which use large scale models with multiple layers to learn from the data how to solve a given task without human intervention. For dealing with images and video, particularly for object detection and classification, CNNs provide a useful approach. CNNs are translation invariant and while not inherently rotational and scale invariant, given sufficient scene variation during training, they are robust to changes in camera perspective and object size.

Furthermore, inference speed for CNN-based detectors is largely independent of the number of classes to detect and particularly of the number of objects in the image, which is a desirable property to achieve consistent speed for real-time processing.

2.2 Related Work

A number of articles have presented automated systems applying image processing and computational intelligence for traffic analysis and incidents detection. Related works are reviewed next.

Regarding vehicle detection and classification, Zhou et al. [24] studied the application of the You Only Look Once (YOLO) and Alexnet CNN architectures for classification and feature extraction. YOLO obtained similar precision than a multi-scale Deformable Parts Model in a public dataset, whereas Alexnet using Support Vector Machines (SVM) outperformed Principal Component Analysis. Dey et al. [7] implemented a CNN on a System-On-a-Programmable-Chip for the analysis and categorization of traffic. The prediction accuracy of the CNN was improved by including a combination of transfer learning with re-training. Arinaldi et al. [2] applied Mixture of Gaussian (MoG) and Faster Recurrent CNN (FR-CNN) for collecting traffic statistics. The evaluation on a public dataset from MIT and real Indonesian road videos showed that FR-CNN was the best method for detection and classification of vehicles, because MoG did not performed well the separation of overlapping vehicles. Chauhan et al. [5] applied CNN for real-time traffic analysis using a YOLO network, pre-trained on the MS-COCO dataset and annotations. A mean average precision of 65–75% was reported for real scenarios from Delhi, India. Results highly depended on the camera position and the type of vehicle. These results provide a reference baseline for the accuracy of YOLO models improved with annotated data. Khazukov et al. [11] proposed a system to measure traffic parameters such as vehicle counts and average speed. Vehicles are detected using YOLOv3 object detector and tracked using the SORT tracker [3], cameras are calibrated to eliminate distortion. Inverse Haversine method is used to calculate traveled distance and speed from coordinates. 6000 images containing 430,000 vehicles were collected from several cameras in the cities of Chelyabinsk and Tyumen (Russia), 80% was used for training and 20% for validation. Object detection mAP was 85% while Mean counting error was 5.5%. For speed estimation maximum error was 1.5 km/h while mean error was 0.57 km/h. Source code is available for a partial implementation using a tiny version of the model.

Regarding incidents detection, Uy et al. [18] applied genetic algorithms for detecting vehicles obstructing pedestrian crossings and ANN for recognizing the license plate number of offenders. Accurate results were reported (91.6% on 47 test images), but the methods were not highly robust against different vehicle positions respect to the camera. Ravindran et al. [15] proposed a supervised learning algorithm using SVM trained with histogram of gradients and grey level co-ocurrence matrix on several parts of cars (wheels, headlights and hood), to detect damaged cars and infer the occurrence of an accident. This work reported results of 80% precision, 83.75% recall and 81.83% accuracy. Zheng et al. [23]

applied a CNN for traffic accidents severity prediction. The model was able to properly represent relevant features and found deep correlations between accident data, improving over previous models in the evaluation performed. Agrawal et al. [1] proposed a system for automatic detection of traffic accidents. Key frame detection is used to detect important frames, then vehicles are detected and the distance between vehicles is used to detect possible collision situations. Key frames are processed through a ResNet50 model to obtain features vectors. Then, K-means clustering is applied on the feature vectors to obtain five clusters per video, the centroids of each cluster are used to build a bag of visual words representation of the video, which is fed to a linear SVM classifier to output whether the video contains a collision or not. In the evaluation performed on a small set of 32 videos, the system achieved an average accuracy of 94.14%, outperforming similar works in the area.

Previous articles from our research group proposed different automatic systems applied to pattern detection in smart cities. Chavat et al. [6] applied computational intelligence for detecting harmful pedestrian movement patterns. The proposed system processed several video sources in real time by using a pipes and filters architecture for two main tasks: features extraction by object detection and tracking, and harmful patterns detection. The experimental evaluation was performed on PETS09-S2L1 videos from the Multiple Object Tracking Challenge (MOTChallenge) benchmark and real surveillance videos. The proposed system was competitive with MOTChallenge benchmark results, yet simpler than other proposed software methods. Winter et al. [20] developed a system for collecting and analyzing traffic data applying computational intelligence, using the modern object detection library Detectron2, by Facebook Research. A loosely-coupled pipeline architecture was applied for frame processing. The system was validated on videos from Montevideo, Uruguay, on daylight, nightlight, and different video qualities. The system obtained MOTA values up to 0.89 for tracking, average precision values of 0.90 and average recall of 0.97 for daylight scenarios.

3   The Proposed System for Automatic Traffic Incidents Detection

This section describes an overview of the developed pipeline for detecting events, and a brief description of each of its parts.

3.1   System Architecture

The design of the proposed system is based on a modular architecture to implement an image processing and computational intelligence pipeline [6]. This design decision provides flexibility and extensibility to the developed system.

Figure 1 presents a diagram of the system architecture. The pipeline uses tagged information from a set of cameras. The information includes street lanes, intersections, and traffic lights tagged on every camera image. An initial geographic calibration is required to normalize the speed of vehicles. The object detector uses the frames of video to detect the vehicles, which are then feed to the object tracker module. The object detector used is YOLO version 3 algorithm (YOLOv3), whereas SORT [3] is used for object tracking, given its good performance and low complexity. The traffic light state module takes the video frames, as well as the tagged information, to generate a state (green, yellow, red or unknown) for each traffic light present in the screen, for each timestamp. By using the tracking information and the data tagged for the camera, the object history model is able to get information about the behavior of each vehicle (street movement, speed estimation, location, class, etc.). After building the object history data and the traffic light state is detected, these two elements are feed to each event detector, which outputs at each timestamp, all vehicles fulfilling the condition of each specific event detected.

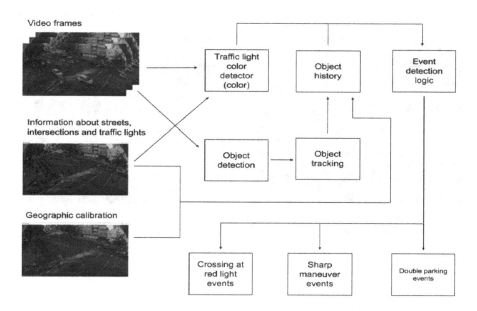

Fig. 1. System pipeline architecture.

3.2   Tagging Tools

Two ancillary tools were developed for assisting in the task of labeling data: a tool for labeling road infrastructure (lanes, lane groups, traffic lights, and intersections) and a tool for mapping screen coordinates (pixels) to real geographic coordinates (longitude and latitude). These ancillary tools are described next.

Road Infrastructure Labeling Tool. This tool consists of a user interface (UI) that takes a frame of a camera and allows the user to draw the different elements of the road infrastructure (e.g., lanes, traffic lights, intersections, etc.) and a second UI for creating several aggregations, e.g., by assigning traffic lights to lanes, lanes to lane groups, etc. The road infrastructure labeling tool is shown on Fig. 2. The aim of this tool is to ease the process of tagging the roads, lane groups, intersections and traffic lights in each camera using a simple UI.

Geographic Coordinates Tagging Tool. This tool has as inputs a polygon with four points selected in Google Earth and a frame for the reference camera from the same location. The tool allows to tag each screen point to its matching geographical coordinate point. It is able to ease the process of getting this matching, which is necessary to calculate vehicle speeds accurately. The geolocation mapping and tagging tool is shown on Fig. 2.

(a) UI to draw lanes, traffic lights, inter-sections and lane groups. (b) UI to translate screen coordinates to geographic coordinates.

Fig. 2. Tagging tools.

3.3   Object Detection

Object detection is performed using YOLOv3, which applies a convolutional neural network (CNN) to achieve real-time detection when running on GPU. In this article, with the goal of running on commodity hardware. The tiny variant with three yolo detection layers is used, with a five fold reduction in inference time and six fold reduction in number of operations, compared to the full YOLOv3 model. This YOLO variant, presented in Fig. 3, consist of 31 layers, 15 of which are part of the Darknet backbone (feature extractor).

YOLOv3 is a single-shot detector, i.e. the entire image is processed on a single step by the CNN, detecting bounding boxes and class probabilities at the same time. This approach avoids the overhead from running multiple steps and individual processing for each bounding box, which was required by previous works such as R-CNN [8]. Furthermore, information for a bounding box detection can be obtained from the entire image rather than only from its neighborhood. These features are processed on three scales, 1/32, 1/16, and 1/8 of the original size, to detect large to small objects (a two yolo layer model would skip the 1/8 scale). The last layer (yolo) for each scale predicts a 3D tensor by encoding bounding box, objectness (a detection certainty estimation, from 0 to 1), and the probabilities of each class. Then, the non max suppression step filters the bounding boxes, and outputs the one with maximum objectness for each set of overlapping bounding boxes of the same class (according to a threshold).

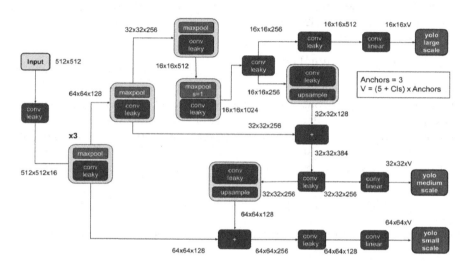

Fig. 3. YOLOv3 Tiny-3l architecture for 512 × 512 resolution.

3.4 Object Tracking

For tracking objects, the SORT method proposed by Bewley et al. [3] was used. SORT is a framework to track previously detected objects, at very low complexity. The tracker uses Kalman filters to predict future bounding boxes from past ones, matching predictions to detections from the new frame using the Hungarian algorithm. Every detection is either given the identity that maximizes the Intersection over Union (IoU) metric or a new identity if no association is found.

3.5 Object History

Based on tagged information and detections, the object history tracks several different types of elements from an object in time. The elements tracked for each frame for each vehicle include:

- Positions for detected bounding boxes and geographic locations corresponding to each bounding box position (center).
- Estimated speeds.
- Current lane and lane group.
- Bounding box classes detected.

Speed calculation is performed using perspective transform. A set of four annotated points is used to create a perspective transformation matrix to translate image coordinates into geographic coordinates for any point of the image at ground level, resulting in a homography. A coordinate reference system (CRS) transformation is used to convert from WSG84 coordinates in degrees to the local CRS system (EPSG:32721) in meters using the PyProj library.

3.6   Traffic Light Color Detector

Traffic light color is detected by finding ellipse (i.e., projected circle) shaped blobs within appropriate (Hue, Saturation, Value) ranges and maintaining a maximum aspect ratio. For each traffic light, either a color is emitted or 'undetermined' when it cannot be ascertained. In the latter case, an alternative traffic light can be used to infer the applicable color in certain cases, either a redundant traffic light or the one in the intersecting street.

3.7   Event Detection Logic

This section presents a general description of the implemented event detectors.

Crossing at Red Light. The event happens when a vehicle or pedestrian crosses the street while the traffic light is red. The event detection is performed slightly different according to the location on the image: detection for vehicles only happens while the vehicle is within an intersection, while detection for pedestrians must run both inside the street and within intersections. There are two subsystems according to the object location, detection for vehicle runs only on crossings while detection for pedestrians runs on both crossings and streets. As a first step, objects with speed below a certain threshold are excluded, to avoid detecting vehicles waiting at the red light or eager pedestrians waiting on the street.

To select the pedestrians who are crossing the street, only pedestrians whose trajectory makes an angle to the lane direction exceeding a threshold are considered (a value of 40° was determined in preliminary experiments). In case the pedestrian is on an intersection, the nearest lane is used. Lane direction is computed by obtaining oriented bounding boxes and selecting the axis for each lane which maximizes the concatenated length for all of the lanes in a street.

Sharp Maneuver. The procedure to detect if a vehicle is performing a sharp maneuver is as follows. First, the speed of the vehicle is computed, to determine if it exceeds the experimentally determined limit of 40 Km/h. Then, a low-pass filter is applied to smooth the noisy vehicle trajectory and two average movement vectors are calculated, using the first 15 and last 15 positions of the vehicle. If the angle between those vectors is between an (experimentally determined) range of 15 and 70°,-based on the histogram of turning angles of vehicles shown in Fig. 4, then the vehicle is considered to be likely doing a sharp maneuver. Finally, the object history is used to determine if the vehicle changed lane group, in which case it is turning the corner, thus not doing a sharp maneuver. Otherwise, it is considered to be doing a sharp maneuver (Fig. 5).

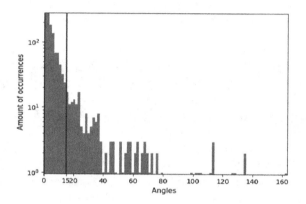

Fig. 4. Histogram of vehicles turning angles.

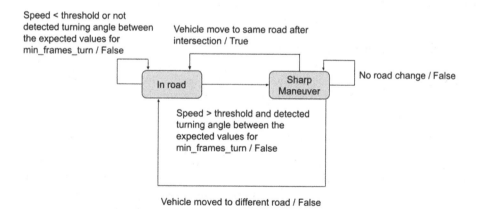

Fig. 5. State diagram for detecting sharp maneuver events.

Double Parking. Double parking occurs when a vehicle parks in a lane that is adjacent to the parking lane (the lane that borders the sidewalk), blocking the flow of traffic.

To detect a double parking, first the vehicles whose bounding box is smaller than the fifth percentile of bounding box sizes of its class are excluded. Then, if any of the representative points of the vehicle, shown in Fig. 6, intersects a double parking, the vehicle is considered as being in a double parking. Next, the average speed is checked and if it is less than a minimum the vehicle is considered to be stopped. Finally, the ratio of detections on the parking lane over the total number of detections is computed. If this ratio is over a predefined threshold, the vehicle is considered properly parked. If not, the traffic light that grants way to the vehicle is checked and if it has been green the vehicle is considered to be likely double parked and a counter is increased. To discard spurious detections, the event is triggered once the counter exceeds a parameter.

(a) Vehicle with representative point at 0.1. (b) Vehicle with representative point at 0.25.

Fig. 6. Examples of vehicles with representative points with respect to the bottom of their bounding box.

4   Experimental Evaluation

This section presents the validation of the proposed system in the events to be detected, the evaluation of the trained object detectors is also presented.

4.1   Evaluation Methodology and Metrics

Object Detection. The evaluation dataset was generated using videos provided by the Mobility Management Center of Montevideo City Council. The videos were obtained from 8 different fixed cameras and one pivoting camera from the metropolitan area of Montevideo. Two subsets were used: the training dataset and the validation dataset.

The training set contained 7200 frames from the eight real cameras plus all images (6471 frames) in VisDrone2019-DET, whereas the validation set contained 2100 frames. The objects were tagged using interpolation in the CVAT object detection tagging tool. Pseudo labeling was also used in the training process to improve the results. The teacher model was not used in the final solution, because it hinders the operation in real time. Cameras used in the training set were excluded from the object detection validation set. mean Average Precision (mAP) was used as the main metric For the evaluation of the object detectors. Precision, Recall and F-Score were also computed.

Event Detection. Usual metrics in literature were not suitable for evaluating the events in the given conditions, since they focus either only in the spatial dimension or only in the time dimension. Thus, approaches that evaluate events taking into account jointly the spatial and time dimension were reviewed, to develop a comprehensive metric. The analysis revealed that using IoU for detecting a match in two dimensions was the best approach. A threshold IoU value of 0.25 was used in the spatial dimension to match the vehicle to the ground truth, based on Bochinski et al. [4]. For the time dimension, Ward et al. [19] proposed using per frame event detections and then calculating Precision, Recall and F-score based on these detections. The proposed method for evaluating events combines both of these approaches into an evaluation metric for event detection.

4.2 Validation Scenarios

CVAT was used to generate the metadata to tag the events to be evaluated. For the sharp maneuvers event, both real time scenarios and synthetically generated ones were used, since few occurrences of the event were found in the studied videos. For the sharp maneuvers event, false positive tests were also added to have a better approximation of the number of false positives in a real video. Eleven tagged events were considered for sharp maneuvers and double parking and 78 for crossing at red light for both, vehicles and pedestrians. The scenarios were generated using different cameras to provide generalization. All videos are in MP4 format, with resolution 1280 × 720. Figure 7 presents sample images of the considered scenarios for the sharp maneuver and double parking events. In turn, Table 1 summarizes the main properties of the analyzed videos.

Table 1. Main properties of the validation scenarios.

Event type	Camera id	Test type	Start time	End time
Double parking	BVAR_RODO	Real	00:12	00:27
Double parking	21_BVAR	Real	00:54	01:50
Sharp maneuver	21_BVAR	Synthetic	01:06	01:20
Sharp maneuver	21_BVAR	False positives	02:00	03:00

(a) Example of double parking test for camera BVAR_RODO.

(b) Example of double parking test for camera 21_BVAR.

(c) Synthetic test for sharp maneuver event detection. Vehicle ground truth location tagged, event detected shown with red circle.

(d) False positives test for sharp maneuver event detection for camera 21_BVAR.

Fig. 7. Testing video scenarios.

4.3 Experimental Results

Object Detection. Table 2 reports the mAP results obtained on the validation of YoloV3 tiny object detection models with two and three yolo layers.

Results in Table 2 indicate that the 3l auto model computed significantly better mAP values than the other two models. The mean AP for the 3l model improved 7.79% over the 2l model, both trained using pseudo labeling, thanks to better small object detection. Pseudo labeling significantly improved mAP (by 13.65%) for the 3l model.

Event Detection. Table 3 reports the results obtained for events detection. The parameters of the detectors were tuned to maximize the Recall, trying to not miss events, but without penalizing Precision much. The rationale behind this decision is that it is preferable to detect a false positive, which can be discarded by a human operator, than missing a reckless driving that may cause an accident.

Results in Table 3 show different values of Precision and Recall for the studied events. The low precision for crossing at red light event may be related to differences on camera lighting and the small size of traffic lights. For double parking event, precision was limited by false positives caused by imprecision on the assignment of traffic lights to lanes in complex intersections. The best results

Table 2. AP for the most relevant classes and mAP for the tiny models: 2l auto (two yolo layers), 3ln and 3l auto (three yolo layers).

Class	Tiny model		
	2l auto	3ln	3l auto
AP car	50.68%	63.29%	**69.67%**
AP bus	53.00%	30.72%	**50.82%**
AP truck	12.57%	**20.97%**	19.24%
AP van	38.43%	16.27%	**46.11%**
mAP vehicles	38.67%	32.81%	**46.46%**

Table 3. Precision, Recall and F-score for the studied events

Event	Precision	Recall	F-Score
Sharp maneuver	0.82	0.82	0.82
Crossing at red light	0.42	0.63	0.51
Double parking	0.59	0.91	0.72

were computed for the sharp maneuver event, for which precision and recall were balanced and accurate. In this case, recall results can be improved by using a low pass filter that requires less previous data.

5   Conclusions and Future Work

This article presented a system for detecting traffic incidents, applying computational intelligence and machine learning techniques. Based on traffic camera videos, the proposed system is capable of detecting in real time different types of reckless behavior carried out by drivers.

The developed system was conceived to be an efficient and flexible solution for traffic monitoring, by applying conceptually simple computational intelligence methods to be executed on commodity hardware. Accurate results were obtained for the sharp maneuver event (precision and recall values 0.82). In turn, for the double parking event, a 0.91 recall value was computed, and a reasonable precision (0.59). The experimental evaluation suggests that the proposed system is a viable solution for detecting reckless driving behavior, able to execute in real time, to be applied for traffic monitoring in the metropolitan area of Montevideo.

The main lines for future work are related to improve the processing speed and the accuracy of the proposed system. Multi-threading processing can be enhanced to improve computational efficiency, whereas applying batch inference and recent advances in object detection models can lead to better accuracy on events detection. Finally, developing an automated procedure for tagging information would diminish the calibration time per camera.

References

1. Agrawal, A.K., et al.: Automatic traffic accident detection system using resnet and SVM. In: 2020 Fifth International Conference on Research in Computational Intelligence and Communication Networks, pp. 71–76 (2020)
2. Arinaldi, A., Pradana, J., Gurusinga, A.: Detection and classification of vehicles for traffic video analytics. Procedia Comput. Sci. **144**, 259–268 (2018)
3. Bewley, A., Ge, Z., Ott, L., Ramos, F., Upcroft, B.: Simple online and realtime tracking. In: 2016 IEEE International Conference on Image Processing (2016)
4. Bochinski, E., Eiselein, V., Sikora, T.: High-speed tracking-by-detection without using image information. In: 2017 14th IEEE International Conference on Advanced Video and Signal Based Surveillance, pp. 1–6 (2017)
5. Chauhan, M., Singh, A., Khemka, M., Prateek, A., Sen, R.: Embedded CNN based vehicle classification and counting in non-laned road traffic. In: 10th International Conference on Information and Communication Technologies and Development (2019)
6. Chavat, J., Nesmachnow, S., Tchernykh, A., Shepelev, V.: Active safety system for urban environments with detecting harmful pedestrian movement patterns using computational intelligence. Appl. Sci. **10**(24), 9021 (2020)
7. Dey, S., Kalliatakis, G., Saha, S., Kumar Singh, A., Ehsan, S., McDonald, K.: MAT-CNN-SOPC: Motionless analysis of traffic using convolutional neural networks on system-on-a-programmable-chip. In: NASA/ESA Conference on Adaptive Hardware and Systems (2018)
8. Girshick, R., Donahue, J., Darrell, T., Malik, J.: Rich feature hierarchies for accurate object detection and semantic segmentation. In: 2014 IEEE Conference on Computer Vision and Pattern Recognition, pp. 580–587 (2014)
9. Hipogrosso, S., Nesmachnow, S.: Sustainable mobility in the public transportation of montevideo, uruguay. In: Smart Cities, pp. 93–108. Springer, New York (2020). https://doi.org/10.1007/978-3-030-38889-8_8
10. Hipogrosso, S., Nesmachnow, S.: A practical approach for sustainable transitoriented development in montevideo, uruguay. In: Smart Cities, pp. 93–108 (2021)
11. Khazukov, K., et al.: Real-time monitoring of traffic parameters. J. Big Data **7**(1), 1–20 (2020). https://doi.org/10.1186/s40537-020-00358-x
12. Kruegle, H.: CCTV Surveillance, Second Edition: Video Practices and Technology. Butterworth-Heinemann, Newton, MA, USA (2006)
13. La Vigne, N., Lowry, S., Markman, J., Dwyer, A.: Evaluating the Use of Public Surveillance Cameras for Crime Control and Prevention. Technical report, Urban Institute, Justice Policy Center (2011)
14. Massobrio, R., Nesmachnow, S.: Urban mobility data analysis for public transportation systems: a case study in montevideo. Uruguay. Appl. Sci. **10**(16), 5400 (2020)
15. Ravindran, V., Viswanathan, L., Rangaswamy, S.: A novel approach to automatic road-accident detection using machine vision techniques. Int. J. Adv. Comput. Sci. Appl. **7** (2016). https://doi.org/10.14569/IJACSA.2016.071130
16. Ristvej, J., Lacinák, M., Ondrejka, R.: On smart city and safe city concepts. Mobile Netw. Appl. **25**(3), 836–845 (2020)
17. Toh, C., Sanguesa, J., Cano, J., Martinez, F.: Advances in smart roads for future smart cities. Proc. Royal Soc. A: Math. Phys. Eng. Sci. **476**(2233) (2020)
18. Uy, A., et al.: Automated traffic violation apprehension system using genetic algorithm and artificial neural network. In: IEEE Region 10 Technical Conference, pp. 2094–2099 (2016)

19. Ward, J., Lukowicz, P., Gellersen, H.: Performance metrics for activity recognition. ACM TIST **2**, 6 (2011)
20. Winter, H., Serra, J., Nesmachnow, S., Tchernykh, A., Shepelev, V.: Computational intelligence for analysis of traffic data. In: Smart Cities, pp. 167–182 (2021)
21. Yang, H., Qu, S.: Real-time vehicle detection and counting in complex traffic scenes using background subtraction model with low-rank decomposition. IET Intel. Transp. Syst. **12**, 75–85 (2018)
22. Yang, Z., Pun-Cheng, L.: Vehicle detection in intelligent transportation systems and its applications under varying environments: a review. Image Vis. Comput. **69**, 143–154 (2018)
23. Zheng, M., et al.: Traffic accident's severity prediction: a deep-learning approach-based CNN network. IEEE Access **7**, 39897–39910 (2019)
24. Zhou, Y., Nejati, H., Do, T., Cheung, N., Cheah, L.: Image-based vehicle analysis using deep neural network: a systematic study. In: IEEE International Conference on Digital Signal Processing, pp. 276–280 (2016)

A Covid-19 Vaccination Tracking and Control Platform in Santiago de Cali

Andres Felipe Fuentes[1]([⊠])(ID), Diego Fernando Botero[2]([⊠])(ID),
and Cristhian Torres Ramirez[3]([⊠])(ID)

[1] Pontificia Universidad Javeriana Cali, Cali, Colombia
`affuentes@javerianacali.edu.co`
[2] GRIEPIS - Universidad Libre Cali, Cali, Colombia
`diego.boteroh@unilibre.edu.co`
[3] Universidad Santiago de Cali, Cali, Colombia
`cristhian.torres00@usc.edu.co`

Abstract. The monitoring and control of epidemics is one of the most relevant topics in the field of smart health within smart cities. Smart health take advantage of a new generation of information technologies, such as big data, mobile internet, cloud computing and artificial intelligence, in order to transform the traditional medical system in a comprehensive way, making healthcare more efficient and personalized. From electronic Health records (EHR), diverse information about the epidemiological situation in institutions that provide health services can be extracted. This document describes the development of a platform to carry out the control and monitoring of vaccination process against Covid-19, which is based on cloud data storage technologies and make use of a existing platform designed for the registration of EHR emphasizing on data collection for structuring of epidemiological control strategies. The main goal is to identify and characterize patients who meet the prioritization criteria for Covid-19 vaccination according to stages defined by the Colombia Ministry of Health, execute the geocoding processes and identification of health conditions according to their previous EHR records, in order to accomplish an efficient and intelligent execution, monitoring and control of vaccination that impacts the epidemiological risk mitigation process. At the end of the document is described the use of the developed platform for the monitoring and control of the Covid-19 vaccination process in a Basic Health Services Unit called Medicips, which provides health services to approximately 90,000 people in the city of Santiago de Cali, Colombia.

Keywords: Smart health services · Electronic health records (EHRs) · Covid-19 · Epidemic control · BigData · Geocoding

1 Introduction

New trends in information and communication technologies (ICT) are used by smart city models to mitigate problems that affect the quality of life in the

© Springer Nature Switzerland AG 2022
S. Nesmachnow and L. Hernández Callejo (Eds.): ICSC-Cities 2021, CCIS 1555, pp. 178–191, 2022.
https://doi.org/10.1007/978-3-030-96753-6_13

population such as pollution, traffic, climate change, public health, epidemics, among others [1,2]. In regard to public health problems and epidemiology the use of ICTs provide the structural basis for the development of smart health services.

Smart health services, as part of the development of citizen-centered smart city services, must seek to offer efficiency, effectiveness, opportunity and availability in order to improve the quality of life of citizens. To achieve this objective is necessary to understand the interactions that arise between the different aspects of a population, analyzing the social determinants of health in which people lives, works, studies and interacts with the community [3]. It is here where technologies such as big data, mobile internet, cloud computing and artificial intelligence begin to be incorporated, through which data can be collected and transformed into useful information for resource planning, efficient provision of services, making of decisions adjusted to the needs in real time [4].

Within the framework of public health, vaccination schemes focus on breaking the chain of transmission of a virus, vaccinating as many people as possible, but these people should be prioritized in such a way that brings effectiveness interruption of the chain of transmission of the disease, taking into account the limitation of resources and availability of doses [5]. At this point, smart health services are used to support the vaccine supply model to a specific population within a territory, taking into account the quantities of doses, the dispersion of the population and the prevalent risk of this population determined for the EHR records analysis.

Applications like the previous one demand a technological platform that allows the interconnection of different data sources, as well as the identification and characterization of the population. This paper analyzes briefly some of the main components of smart health services applied to public health for a better understanding, including assisting diagnosis and treatment, health management, disease prevention and risk monitoring, epidemic Control [6].

Once the different components of smart health services have been analyzed, a platform based on some open source components and cloud services is proposed, which contains various of the functionalities that smart health systems must provide for the monitoring and control, in this case, applied to the Covid-19 vaccination process.

The presented platform works in real time and takes data from a previous EHR system implemented in a Big Data as a Service (BDaaS) [7] known as Big-Query which is a fully-managed, serverless data warehouse that enables scalable analysis over petabytes of data and is used for storage of EHR records. The presented platform uses BigQuery as well for data analysis. In addition, the platform includes in its development open source software such as javascript, Nodejs environments and MySQL database as well as cellular communications for mobile access to the platform and Google Maps API for the geocoding system.

At the end of the document, the results obtained through the developed platform are presented. To obtain the results, the platform was tested in a basic unit for the provision of health services called Medicips, located in Cali, Colombia, which was selected by the Colombian Ministry of Health as one of the entities in charge of the process of Covid-19 vaccination in the city of Cali and from which the previous EHRs were obtained. These results show an approach to the use of new ICT technologies applied to health platforms that involve an epidemiological control component, providing mechanisms for planning, monitoring and control of public health processes, within the framework of smart cities.

2 Related Work

Through different perspectives, several researchers have presented formal definitions of a smart city. In [8], it is defined as the need for a connection between the physical, social, business and information and communication technology (ICT) infrastructure to improve the intelligence of the urban area. In [9], it is defined as a modern city, which must get advance from ICT to improve the life quality and the condition of urban services for citizens. These two definitions shows that a smart city deals with a smart urban environment enhanced with ICT technologies in order to improve the daily life in communities [10].

In [6], the concept of smart healthcare is introduced in which a new generation of information technologies are used, such as the Internet of Things (IoT), big data, cloud computing and artificial intelligence, transforming the traditional healthcare delivery systems in a comprehensive way, making medical care more efficient, convenient and personalized.

In [11], an overview of smart health is provided where the use of mobile technologies and ICT brings opportunities for existing information health systems taking advantage of the ubiquity of mobile devices which provides immediacy, availability and capabilities of monitoring in dispersed territories.

Already in the application of the smart healthcare concept, in [12] a framework is proposed whereby enables various smart health services aimed at epidemic control and ways of implementing them, using EHR records.

On the other hand, works such as [13] exposes an overview of how the smart city infrastructure supports strategic healthcare through the use of mobile and environmental sensors combined with machine learning, considering the challenges that will be faced as that healthcare providers take advantage of these opportunities.

In the reviewed papers, definitions of smart cities are introduced which incorporates different aspects such as smart people, smart government, smart transport, smart health, etc., with a focus on taking advantage of data management technologies (that is, IoT, Big Data and Cloud Computing, etc.) to establish a deep connection between each component and each aspect of a city [14].

3 Smart Health Services

Smart Health Services are applicable to different branches of health such the clinical treatment, clinical research, family health, studying of social determinants of health among others. For the purpose of this work, services that are considered directly related to the monitoring and control of public health diseases are analyzed, without pretending that they are the only ones. This analysis identifies the importance of incorporating key technologies such as IoT, cloud computing, big data, Machine Learning, 5G, and artificial intelligence, as well as the participation of all entities involved in the provision of both private and public health services as well as the community itself.

In order to understand an Smart Health Services, it can be expressed in several applications such as (1) Assisting diagnosis and treatment, (2) Health management, (3) Disease prevention and risk monitoring and (4) Epidemic control component [15].

Assisting Diagnosis and Treatment. Medical diagnostic and treatment processes can take great advantage of technologies that apply intelligent algorithms to reduce diagnostic errors and personalize disease treatments. It is possible to use data from the EHR system to feed intelligent systems that previously trained can provide the healthcare professionals with guidance for making decisions about the patient and issue alerts about possible treatments and diagnoses.

Health Management. The health management of the disease becomes important with the increase of chronic diseases since it allows the decentralization of health services through smartphones, portable smart devices, smart homes and technologies such as 4G and 5G networks [16]. This empower a more precise monitoring of patients with chronic diseases by analyzing individual behavior facing their illnesses, performing preventive health maintenance and providing more economical solutions for the monitoring of chronic diseases [17].

Disease Prevention and Risk Monitoring. Customarily, the patient disease risk prediction is based on the collection of patient data according to the clinical guidelines defined by the health authorities, comparing these data with the guidelines and issuing a concept. This mechanism takes time and does not provide an accurate diagnosis to the patient. Predicting disease risk with smart healthcare is dynamic and personalized. The new disease risk prediction model collects data through mobile devices and smart applications, uploads it to the cloud using a network, and analyzes the results hinge on machine learning based algorithms witch feed back predicted results to users in real time [6].

Epidemic Control. A special area within smart health is dedicated to epidemic control. The existence of electronic data about health status claims of people, as well as knowledge of the social determinants of health on a specific territory improve the processes of detection and control of epidemics. Data about locations and activities of people can be introduced to machine learning algorithms and the results could be used to anticipate potentially new cases during an epidemic, effectively identify high-risk sites, and successfully manage an epidemic [12]. These methods are also useful for the identification and monitoring of other public health risks such as environmental pollution [11].

4   Architecture of the Platform

Thus, considering the different models used by the applications previously exposed as service components in smart health and the way in which information and communication technologies (ICT) are incorporated, in Fig. 1 is depicted a basic architecture used for the development of a Covid-19 Vaccination Tracking and Control platform, the main objective of this work. The architecture is based on two layers, a *Backend Layer* with access to a EHR data warehouse and a *Frontend Layer* for access and data visualization by end users.

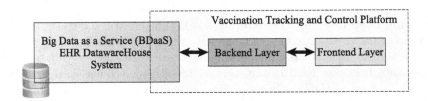

Fig. 1. Layered architecture used for the development of a Covid-19 Vaccination Tracking and Control platform

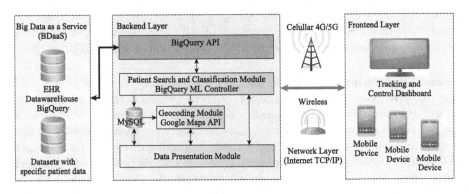

Fig. 2. Covid-19 Vaccination Tracking and Control platform including used technologies

Figure 2 depicts a diagram with a more detailed view of the components of the Covid-19 Vaccination Tracking and Control platform. The proposed architecture starts from an EHR data warehouse based on a BDaaS platform (previusly developed) which provides the electronic health record data of a set of patients. From this information a new dataset with specific patient data is created selecting the necessary information for segmentation and classification of each patient according to Covid-19 vaccination phases [18]. The new dataset is set on the

BDaaS BigQuery which provides the ability to interactively store, process and query massive datasets recorded [19].

In order the Covid-19 Vaccination Tracking and Control platform interacts with the EHR data warehouse an API was designed using the Google BigQuery API [20]. The API developed is part of the *Backend Layer* of the system. Similarly, a module for controlling the extraction, transformation and load process from BigQuery is developed, this module send to BigQuery the queries for the search and classification of patients according to the prioritization characteristics for vaccination defined by the health authorities.

Once the queries are executed on Bigquery, the results are stored on a Bigquery dataset, then through the API developed a summarie of the results are extracted to the backlayer and the data is processed according to the *Frontend Layer* requirements in the data presentation module which is part of the backlayer. The data presentation module generate the views used in the tracking and control dashboard shown in the *Frontend Layer* where health professionals who make up the coordinating team of the vaccination process located in the health center, can follow and make decisions about the vaccination process.

The tracking and control dashboard presents the indicators defined for the process, additionally in the dashboard the geolocation of the prioritized patients is presented whose information is obtained from the geocoding module which performs the addresses conversion of each patient into geographic coordinates and then carry out the geolocation on the map of the territory. The geocoding module is developed on the backlayer and is based on the Google Maps API [21].

In addition, the vaccination process requires a team of health professionals who commute to the homes of prioritized patients that will be vaccinated. Taking into account the above, the geolocation of each patient together with their prioritization allows establishing a route for the team commuting, who using mobile devices connected to a 4G network for access the frontlayer which display a responsive interface adapted for small screens devices, where they can follow the location of each patient on a map and record each visit made. The information registered by each team can be followed in real time by the coordinating team of the process located in the health center.

The description of the technologies chosen for the development of the architecture proposed in Fig. 2 are described below, indicating the advantages they offer regarding to smart health.

Big Data as a Service (BDaaS). Big data impose significant challenges to the traditional infrastructure, due to the characteristics of volume, velocity and variety of data. One of the challenges of designing big data infrastructure is the requirement to support many different data types. Currently, Big Data as a Service includes Storage-as-a-Service and Computing-as-a-Service, to store and process the massive data [7].

There are different BDaaS such as Google BigQuery, Amazon RedShift, Apache Drill among others. In this work BigQuery was used, since it started from an EHR data warehouse developed previously.

BigQuery is a Google Cloud product that can be used as a data warehouse, also offering support for interactive SQL queries through a graphical interface. This product implements the main features of Dremel technology, used internally by Google for tasks such as spam analysis or bug reporting for various Google products. Big Query shares with Dremel the performance, the internal structure, composed of data ordered by columns (column-oriented storage) and the division of queries on servers through a tree-shaped structure [22].

BigQuery includes BigQuery ML which lets create and execute machine learning models in BigQuery using standard SQL queries. BigQuery ML increases development speed by eliminating the need to export data to another schema to apply Machine Learning algorithms [23,24]. BigQuery ML supports the following types of models: Linear regression for forecasting, Binary logistic regression for classification, Multiclass logistic regression for classification, k-means clustering for data segmentation, Matrix Factorization for creating product recommendation systems, Time series for performing time-series forecasts, and others.

Access to Big Query can be done through a web client, an API or a third-party software. This work uses the API for Node.js framework.

Google BigQuery offers storage for up to 10 GB and 1 TB of data processed per query for free.

Geocoding System. Geocoding is a process for converting a text address into geographic coordinates. This process includes access the text address database, processing the text address and returning geographic coordinates along with described data back to the user [25].

There is geocoding services like TAPDM geocoder, ArcGIS Online, Google Maps API, Bing Maps API, MapQuest Maps.

This work uses The Google Maps API. This API allows using the Google Maps Platform service, which offer various services which can be included in web or mobile applications. For the proposed platform, the Google Maps API for javascript was used, which allows access to:

1. Geocoding, convert coordinates into addresses and addresses into coordinates.
2. Maps SDKs, Allow use of maps for the web and mobile and is possible add marks in order to show position into a geographic area shown in the map (Geolocation).
3. Directions, provide directions for multiple transportation modes, featuring real-time traffic information.

BackEnd Technologies. Additionally, for the development of the proposed *Backend Layer*, an integration of different technologies was carried out.

These technologies include the development of Representational State Transfer (REST) services, which is an interface between systems that uses the HTTP protocol to obtain data or generate operations on that data in various possible formats, such as XML and JSON [26]. REST services are useful for consuming subroutines, functions and procedures of systems exposed through an API.

The algorithms and programming logic were developed in Node.js which is an open source, cross-platform runtime environment for the server layer based on the JavaScript programming language. Node.js is oriented to the development of dynamic applications with access to information stored in databases. In Node.js, REST services can be developed by establishing subscription mechanisms to receive data from external applications and store it in a database, using its capabilities to connect with database engines such as MongoDB or MySQL [27]. Node.js in conjunction with HTML, Javascript and CSS can also be useful for the development of web pages in order to display data and information to the end user, as well as the design of forms to collect information.

4.1 Smart Health Service for Covid-19 Vaccination Tracking and Control System Development

According to the design of Fig. 2, both the *Backend Layer* and the *Frontend Layer* compose the architecture for the development of the Covid-19 Vaccination Tracking and Control Platform in Santiago de Cali, which is developed by integrating technologies previously exposed, bringing the design of the platform closer to the concepts analyzed in the smart health services section.

Backend Layer. The *Backend Layer* integrates the patient search and classification module, the EHR Datawarehouse API connection, a geocoding module, as well as the data presentation module.

Patient Search and Classification Module. This module is developed in Nodejs, mainly contains functions that execute the extraction, transformation and loading processes from BigQuery datasets. This module controls the data extraction queries from the EHR data warehouse creating datasets with specific patient data to be used by the BigQuery feature called BigQuery ML used to execute machine learning models such k-means clustering [23]. Additionally, this module records summaries of the results of the queries executed in BigQuery in a relational database (MySQL) where they are available to the other modules of the *Backend Layer* such as the geocoding module and the data presentation module. Additionally, this module controls the updating of the data of the vaccinated patients registered by the vaccination teams from the *Frontend layer*.

API Connection. For the API developed for the connection with the EHR Datawarehouse, a REST service was developed in Nodejs, which sends the requests from the patient search and classification controller module to the EHR Datawarehouse in BigQuery. Once the clustering models are executed in the EHR Datawarehouse, the results contain patient sets which are registered in a new dataset in BigQuery. These datasets are processed by machine learning algorithms and the results are interpreted and exposed to be consumed by the

Backend Layer to make it available for the geocoding and data presentation modules.

Geocoding Module. The geocoding module processes the addresses of each patient through Google geocoding API. The API returns geocoding information represented in latitude and longitude corresponding to the location of each patient [21]. This data is stored in the MySQL database in order to be available to the other layers. Google Geocoding API allows the processing of 25,000 requests per user per day at no cost.

Presentation Module. Based on the information of the clustering, classification and prioritization of patients obtained form BigQuery process and the geocoding of each address, information is available to be sent to the monitoring and control dashboard. For this, the data presentation module managed the data for visualization in the dashboard in the *Frontend Layer*.

Frontend Layer. The *Frontend Layer* is developed using the HTML, CSS and Javascript languages and is composed of two basic modules, the dashboard module and the vaccination process registration module.

Dashboard Module. This module presents the summary data of the vaccination process. In this module is depicted the geolocation of prioritized patients using the Google Maps API which allows to locate marks on a interactive map of a territory that indicate the location of patients. Additionally, the lists of prioritized and classified patients can be seen, as well as performance indicators and compliance with vaccination goals and vaccination team tracking. This module can be accessed by the user through a web browser.

Registration Module. Is used by the vaccination teams to visualize the patients prioritized for vaccination, locate them in a interactive map in order to be able to commute to the place where they are and thus vaccinate the patient. This module can be used as an app from a mobile device connected to a cellular network (4G/5G) and allows to view the geolocation of each patient and allows to register the status of the vaccine application process of each patient (application of first dose, second dose, not vaccinated, the patient was not found), via the completion of a form. These records can be observed in real time in the dashboard module.

5   Platform Implementation

In order to test the Covid-19 Vaccination Tracking and Control Platform in Santiago de Cali, the platform was implemented in the Medicips Basic Health Services Unit, which is an institution that provides basic health services to approximately 90,000 people and has the authorization of the Ministry of Health of Colombia to carry out vaccination processes for Covid-19 in the population assigned for the provision of health services. The EHR information for the Medicips population is located in the BigQuery-based EHR data warehouse. The implementation was developed in several steps:

First step, the classification of the population is carried out according to the stages of the vaccination plan of the Ministry of Health of Colombia [18], for which the following characteristics of the first three stages were taken.

1. Stage 1 (Population 80 years of age or older)
2. Stage 2 (Population between 60 and 79 years of age)
3. Stage 3 (Population between 50 and 59 years old and people between 16 and 59 years old with comorbidities or hypertensive diseases: Diabetes, Renal insufficiency, HIV, Cancer, Tuberculosis, COPD, ASMA, Obesity, on the waiting list for transplantation of vital organs or Post-transplantation vital organs)

In Table 1 the basic classification by age and the number of users by classification are shown.

Table 1. Population classification by age ranges

Age ranges	Population quantity
Population 80 years of age or older	3,003
Population between 60 and 79 years of age	14,046
Population between 50 and 59 years old	11,675

In order to approximate the distribution of the population and its relationship with the diagnoses of chronic diseases, necessary for the classification of stage 3, the BigQuery ML k-means Clustering model was used, identifying diagnoses associated with the patients, grouping the population by: age, age group, gender and ICD-10 group [28]. The grouping was performed on a set of 219,540 EHR records, belonging to Medicips patients older than 16 years.

Table 2. Population clustering in relation to age ranges and diagnoses

Cluster	EHR count	Age avg.	I10 group hypertension	E10 group mellitus diabetes
1	59,282	60	16.26%	1.49%
2	40,346	27	0%	0%
3	55,351	72	39.74%	1.52%
4	64,561	45	2.96%	0.1%

Table 2 shows the clustering results with k-means, using four (4) clusters and Euclidean distance. It is observed that cluster #3 has an average of 72 years and contains patients with diagnoses of Hypertension and Diabetes, as well as cluster #1, whose average age is 60 years. Cluster #2, which has an average age of 27, does not contain patients with chronic diseases. With the previous results, the population can be prioritized, taking into account that vaccinating patients between 60 and 79 years old covers a high percentage of patients with chronic diseases related to hypertension and diabetes, allowing optimization of costs and logistical resources.

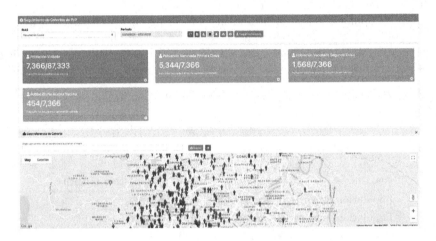

Fig. 3. Dashboard for Covid-19 Vaccination Tracking and Control platform in Santiago de Cali

Previously defined the clusters, proceed with a second step, where the lists of the patients that belong to each of the clusters are obtained. These lists are processed through the geocoding module, obtaining the geolocation of each one.

Further, in a third step the clustered patient lists are taken to build basic indicators which are deployed in the *Frontend Layer* and displayed in the control and tracking dashboard and in the app-type interface accessed by the vaccination teams.

Figure 3 shows dashboard for Covid-19 Vaccination Tracking and Control in Santiago de Cali which is deployed through the implemented platform. Figure 4 shows the access to the app from a mobile device. Across this interface, prioritized patients and their location can be accessed using geolocation on Google Maps. Additionally, the interface includes a functionality to calculate the route from a specific location to the position of a patient, which allows finding an optimal commuting route for the vaccination teams. Moreover, through the app interface the status of the vaccination process of each patient can be recorded, which will be showed in the indicators and data displayed on the monitoring and control dashboard.

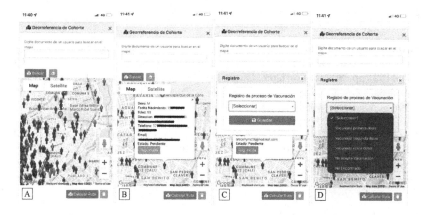

Fig. 4. *Frontend layer.* User interface used by vaccination teams in a mobile device to record the individual vaccination process of each patient. (A) Map, (B) Patient information, (C) (D) Register of vaccination process.

6   Concluding Remarks

This paper proposes a platform for the Monitoring and Control of Covid-19 Vaccination in Santiago de Cali, which was implemented in order to support the vaccination process of the population of a basic health unit. As a result, this allowed the application of smart health features, making possible the classification and prioritization of the population providing a better understanding of the inherent attributes of health from the application of Machine Learning algorithms in an EHR data warehouse.

The proposed platform shows the usage of information and communication technologies applied to health services, including smart characteristics, providing elements in decision-making adjusted to the real demands of a population, helping to improve health services, reduce inequity and enhance prevention strategies that impact the life quality.

Furthermore, from the proposed platform, it is possible to develop the implementation of the monitoring and control for other types of health services such as chronic diseases, social determinants of health, disease transmission, among others. Including sources of information from other areas of smart cities such as pollution data analysis, air quality, solar radiation, waste management, public security, public transport and alternative mobility among others, which can be used to feed the epidemiological data of a territory and its population, generating impact mechanisms about to the smart management of public health, including the participation of private entities, the government of cities and his population.

Acknowledgement. The authors would like to acknowledge the cooperation of the research group *GrIEpiS: Grupo de Investigación en Epidemiología y Servicios* and the basic unit of healthcare *Medicips Cali.*

References

1. Fuentes, A.F., Tamura, E.: LoRa-based IoT data monitoring and collecting platform. In: Nesmachnow, S., Hernández Callejo, L. (eds.) ICSC-CITIES 2019. CCIS, vol. 1152, pp. 80–92. Springer, Cham (2020). https://doi.org/10.1007/978-3-030-38889-8_7

2. Fuentes Vasquez, A.F., Tamura, E.: From SDL modeling to WSN simulation for IoT solutions. In: Figueroa-García, J.C., Villegas, J.G., Orozco-Arroyave, J.R., Maya Duque, P.A. (eds.) WEA 2018. CCIS, vol. 916, pp. 147–160. Springer, Cham (2018). https://doi.org/10.1007/978-3-030-00353-1_13

3. Jiménez, C.E., Falcone, F., Solanas, A., Puyosa, H., Zoughbi, S., González, F.: Smart government: opportunities and challenges in smart cities development. In: Civil and Environmental Engineering: Concepts, Methodologies, Tools, and Applications, pp. 1454–1472 (2016)

4. Gómez, L.F.C., Libreros, Á.M.C., Sánchez, R.A.A., Henao, D.F.B., Vásquez, A.F.F., Ramos, J.H.B.: Epidemiología y servicios en salud. Ediciones de la U (2021)

5. Jadidi, M.M., Moslemi, P., Jamshidiha, S., Masroori, I., Mohammadi, A., Pourahmadi, V.: Targeted vaccination for COVID-19 using mobile communication networks. In: 2020 11th International Conference on Information and Knowledge Technology (IKT), pp. 93–97. IEEE (2020)

6. Tian, S., Yang, W., Grange, J.M.L., Wang, P., Huang, W., Ye, Z.: Smart healthcare: making medical care more intelligent. Glob. Health J. 3(3), 62–65 (2019)

7. Zheng, Z., Zhu, J., Lyu, M.R.: Service-generated big data and big data-as-a-service: an overview. In: 2013 IEEE International Congress on Big Data, pp. 403–410. IEEE (2013)

8. Harrison, C., et al.: Foundations for smarter cities. IBM J. Res. Dev. 54(4), 1–16 (2010)

9. Kondepudi, S.N., et al.: Smart sustainable cities analysis of definitions. The ITU-T focus group for smart sustainable cities (2014)

10. Silva, B.N., Khan, M., Han, K.: Towards sustainable smart cities: a review of trends, architectures, components, and open challenges in smart cities. Sustain. Cities Soc. 38, 697–713 (2018)

11. Al-Azzam, M., Alazzam, M.B.: Smart city and smart-health framework, challenges and opportunities. Int. J. Adv. Comput. Sci. Appl. 10(2), 171–176 (2019)

12. Avdić, A.R., Marovac, U.M., Janković, D.S.: Smart health services for epidemic control. In: 2020 55th International Scientific Conference on Information, Communication and Energy Systems and Technologies (ICEST), pp. 46–49. IEEE (2020)

13. Cook, D.J., Duncan, G., Sprint, G., Fritz, R.L.: Using smart city technology to make healthcare smarter. Proc. IEEE 106(4), 708–722 (2018)

14. Kirimtat, A., Krejcar, O., Kertesz, A., Tasgetiren, M.F.: Future trends and current state of smart city concepts: a survey. IEEE Access 8, 86448–86467 (2020)

15. Hejazi, H., Rajab, H., Cinkler, T., Lengyel, L.: Survey of platforms for massive IoT. In: 2018 IEEE International Conference on Future IoT Technologies (Future IoT), pp. 1–8. IEEE (2018)

16. Andreu-Perez, J., Leff, D.R., Ip, H.M.D., Yang, G.-Z.: From wearable sensors to smart implants-toward pervasive and personalized healthcare. IEEE Trans. Biomed. Eng. 62(12), 2750–2762 (2015)

17. Liu, L., Stroulia, E., Nikolaidis, I., Miguel-Cruz, A., Rincon, A.R.: Smart homes and home health monitoring technologies for older adults: a systematic review. Int. J. Med. Inform. 91, 44–59 (2016)

18. Ministerio de Salud de Colombia. www.minsalud.gov.co/salud/publica/vacunac ion/paginas/mivacuna.aspx
19. Fernandes, S., Bernardino, J.: What is bigquery? In: Proceedings of the 19th International Database Engineering & Applications Symposium, pp. 202–203 (2015)
20. Pereira, C.R.: Building APIs with Node.js. Springer, Heidelberg (2016). https:// doi.org/10.1007/978-1-4842-2442-7
21. Zhu, Y.: Introducing Google chart tools and Google maps API in data visualization courses. IEEE Comput. Graph. Appl. **32**(6), 6–9 (2012)
22. Sato, K.: An inside look at Google bigquery. White paper (2012). https://cloud. google.com/files/BigQueryTechnicalWP.pdf
23. Mucchetti, M.: BigQuery ML. In: BigQuery for Data Warehousing, pp. 419–468. Springer, Berkeley (2020). https://doi.org/10.1007/978-1-4842-6186-6_19
24. Tigani, J., Naidu, S.: Google BigQuery Analytics. Wiley, Hoboken (2014)
25. Goldberg, D.W., Wilson, J.P., Knoblock, C.A.: From text to geographic coordinates: the current state of geocoding. URISA J. **19**(1), 33–46 (2007)
26. Cheng, B., Zhao, S., Qian, J., Zhai, Z., Chen, J.: Lightweight service mashup middleware with rest style architecture for IoT applications. IEEE Trans. Netw. Serv. Manag. **15**(3), 1063–1075 (2018)
27. Laksono, D.: Testing spatial data deliverance in SQL and NoSQL database using NodeJS fullstack web app. In: 2018 4th International Conference on Science and Technology (ICST), pp. 1–5. IEEE (2018)
28. Martín-Vegue, A.R., Vázquez-Barquero, J.L., Herrera Castanedo, S.: CIE-10 (I): Introducción, historia y estructura general. Papeles Medicos **11**(1), 24–35 (2002)

Travel Time Estimation in Public Transportation Using Bus Location Data

Renzo Massobrio$^{(\boxtimes)}$ and Sergio Nesmachnow

Universidad de la República, Montevideo, Uruguay
{renzom,sergion}@fing.edu.uy

Abstract. The user experience of passengers using public transportation is highly sensitive to travel time. In this regard, travel time is a key input to assess the quality of service offered by a public transportation system and to compute performance and service-level metrics. Moreover, travel time is needed to evaluate the accessibility to different opportunities in the city (e.g., employment, commercial activities, education) that can be reached using public transportation. This article presents a data analysis approach to estimate in-vehicle travel time in public transportation systems. Vehicle location data, bus stops locations, bus lines routes, and timetables from the public transportation system in Montevideo, Uruguay, are considered in the case study used to evaluate the proposed approach. Results are compared against scheduled timetables and are used to compute several performance indicators of the public transportation system of the city.

Keywords: Travel time · Public transportation · Data analysis · GPS data

1 Introduction

In urban scenarios, citizens are required to travel in order to engage in the social and economic activities of their city [3]. In this context, public transportation plays a major role, since it is the most efficient and socially-fair mean of transportation [7]. Understanding the accessibility of citizens to the public transportation service of a city is paramount in order to identify inequalities among the population and implement policies that aim at improving the quality of service offered to passengers. Several indicators may be considered to measure the accessibility offered by a transportation system, among them, travel time strikes as the most intuitive one, since it is tightly related to the perception of passengers of the quality of service of a transportation system [17].

Public transportation systems operate on predefined routes and depend on schedules that vary throughout the day. Additionally, travel speeds vary greatly due to traffic congestion, passenger demand, and road infrastructure. Thus, assuming constant speed of vehicles along routes usually results in significant

S. Nesmachnow and L. Hernández Callejo (Eds.): ICSC-Cities 2021, CCIS 1555, pp. 192–206, 2022.
https://doi.org/10.1007/978-3-030-96753-6_14

travel time differences between the estimations of the model and the actual reality. A comprehensive model for travel time estimation in public transportation networks needs to account for all these factors.

This article presents a model to estimate in-vehicle travel times in public transportation systems. The proposed model applies a data analysis approach [12] incorporating real vehicle location data from on-board GPS units as well as open data regarding the public transportation lines and bus stops. The public transportation system in Montevideo, Uruguay, is used as a case study. For the studied scenario, the difference between the estimated travel times and those available in the public timetables are reported. Furthermore, relevant metrics to assess the quality of service of public transportation systems are computed. Results indicate that the proposed approach is suitable to accurately estimate in-vehicle travel times in the city. The applied methodology is also useful to detect situations that prevent users from having a good quality of experience when using the public transportation system, which should be the focus of further studies by the city administration.

The remainder of the paper is organized as follows. Section 2 gives an overview of the topic and the context for this study. Section 3 reviews works in the related literature. Section 4 outlines the proposed methodology for travel time estimation. The application to the case study is presented in Sect. 5 and the conclusions and future work are presented in Sect. 6.

2   Characterizing Travel Times of the Public Transportation System

In the context of the research project that studies the territorial, universal, and sustainable accessibility in Montevideo, Uruguay, one of the most relevant tasks is the characterization and analysis of the public transportation system. In this regard, accessibility and quality of service provided by the public transportation system is a very important issue that can significantly affect vulnerable groups in society. A proper analysis of public transportation allows conceiving and applying sustainable mobility strategies (e.g., including electric mobility options and other alternatives for non-polluting means of transportation).

For studying accessibility, it is crucial to compute relevant indicators that allow determining the impact and availability of different means of transportation. Travel time using the public transportation system is a relevant indicator that assess how long it takes [a citizen] to make a trip using the public transportation system, and it is also considered as an indicator of mobility, defined as "the ease of traveling between locations within a community" [2]. The travel time metric is not only valuable as a subjective indicator, i.e., related to the user-experience of passengers of the public transportation system, but is also meaningful to determine the quality of service of any given bus route or the system as a whole. Furthermore, travel time also allows computing comparative indicators, such as the additional travel time required over an automobile making the same trip, as defined by the Transportation Research Board [1], and other metrics of route directness. Travel time is also useful to determine the reliability of the public transportation system, defined as "the ability of the transit system to adhere to schedule or maintain regular headways and consistent travel times" [18].

In order to quantify the provision of the public transportation system, the problem studied in this article consists in estimating in-vehicle travel times at each stop along the routes of the bus lines in the system. Travel times can be estimated from the (fixed) schedules established by the city administration for the different bus lines in the city, providing a static view of mobility and accessibility. Complementing this approach, this article proposes using real GPS data of the buses from the Metropolitan Transport System of Montevideo and open data providing information about the existing infrastructure for public transportation in the city (e.g., bus stops, bus lines). These sources of data allow characterizing the mobility offered by the transportation system and its accessibility, to complement the use of fixed information that may not accurately reflect reality.

3   Related Works

Lei and Church presented a short review on measuring the accessibility in public transportation systems [11]. The survey showed that several authors focus on the physical aspects of a system (e.g., distance to a bus stop) instead of focusing on the travel time between pairs of locations. Furthermore, previous works which do focus on travel times usually make assumptions which significantly impact the accuracy of their estimations, e.g., constant transfer and waiting times, average speed of vehicles, or not considering bus schedules at all. The authors propose an extended GIS data structure to account for the temporal dimension of public transportation systems which is applied to the public transportation system in Santa Barbara, California.

Salonen and Toivonen presented a comparison of different travel time measures [17]. The work covers both travel times using private vehicles and public transportation. Regarding the latter, three models are outlined and applied to a case study in the capital region of Finland: a simple model which does not include vehicle schedule information at all, an intermediate model which uses schedules only to estimate the average waiting time, and an advanced model which queries a government API with up-to-date schedules and uses its routing engine as a black-box to compute travel times. The proposed models identified travel time disparities accross modes (i.e., private vs. public transportation), with a lower effect in areas near the city center.

Previous works have addressed the public transportation system in Montevideo, Uruguay, which is used as a case study in this article. Massobrio and Nesmachnow proposed an urban data analysis approach to understand mobility in the city using different sources of urban data [12]. Origin-destination matrices, which describe mobility, were built using ticket sales data. Other studies have measured the quality of service offered by the public transportation service in Montevideo, by analyzing punctuality based on GPS bus location data [13,14].

Hernández et al. studied accessibility to employment opportunities in Montevideo, Uruguay [8]. For this purpose, the authors built a travel time matrix using the scheduled timetables for bus lines in the city. The methodology proposed by the authors models the public transport network as a graph, to compute travel times between different zones in the city. This model allows configuring the maximum walkable distance and the maximum number of transfers within the route. The computed travel time matrix was validated against a government web application and the results from a household mobility survey.

According to the review, few previous works have applied a systematic procedure to estimate travel times of public transportation in Montevideo, Uruguay. The model proposed in this article combines several sources of information including bus location data from on-board GPS units. Thus, the proposed approach extends the static approaches that only consider fixed timetables data when computing in-vehicle travel time by incorporating real data that reflect the reality of the buses operating throughout the network.

4 Methodology

This section outlines the methodology applied for data processing and analysis.

4.1 Data Sources

One week of bus GPS location data were obtained, corresponding to buses operating from Monday 5th to Sunday 11th of August 2019. Records in the bus location dataset correspond to measures registered with the on-board GPS unit in each bus, which are sampled every 20–30 s. Each record in the dataset includes a bus line identifier, a unique trip identifier (to discriminate different trips of the same bus line), the scheduled departure time for the trip, GPS coordinates, and a timestamp. For this study, we aimed to compute travel times during the morning peak, so we considered only trips with scheduled departures on working days between 7.00 am and 9.00 am (inclusive) as reported in [12]. Some trips had corrupted records, with timestamps spreading for very long periods. For this purpose, we discarded all trips that lasted more than four hours, as they are not representative of bus line lengths in the city and they are very likely outliers. After this filtering, the bus location dataset held more than 2.8 million records, corresponding to 8224 trips of 258 different bus lines.

Bus stop location data were also used for the analysis. Open data from the local government were processed to obtain, for each bus line, the ordered set of bus stops it visits, with their locations. Another source of open data used for the analysis were the timetables for each bus line. Records hold the scheduled departure of each trip and the expected arrival time at each bus stop. The same filter was applied to consider only trips within the morning peak. Open data were obtained in July 2021, thus, some discrepancies appear when combining it with bus location data from 2019. For instance, some bus lines and bus stops were modified, schedules were updated, etc. We deal with these issues throughout the data analysis process described next.

4.2 Data Processing

Each trip in the dataset is processed independently to compute in-vehicle travel times. The result of this processing is an ordered list of the time it takes from the first bus stop in the journey to each of the bus stops corresponding to the bus line of the trip. Vehicle location using GPS is prone to errors from a variety of sources, so several methodologies have been proposed to cope with this phenomena [10]. To address this issue we created a buffer on bus stops of 25 m an all directions and discarded all measures falling outside these buffers. When processing the records of a given trip, the timestamp assigned to each bus stop is set as the timestamp of the earliest record that falls within the bus stop buffer. This applies to all bus stops except the first one in the journey, where the latest timestamp is selected, as buses usually turn on their GPS device before departing, thus multiple records fall within the first stop. In some cases, drivers forget to update the on-board machine at the end of the trip. As a consequence, the trip identification is kept for more than one trip (e.g., inbound and outbound consecutive trips of the same line). This issue was mitigated by adding a validity check ensuring that the time between consecutive measures assigned to stops needs to be smaller than 30 min. Additionally, integrity checks are made to ensure that timestamps and bus stop identifiers are increasing monotonically and the bus line and trip identifier is unchanged. If any assertion does not hold, the process of that trip is interrupted.

As a result of the previous processing, the proposed method computes travel times (measured from the first stop of the bus line) for each of the bus stops with a valid nearby GPS record. However, some of the bus stops of the bus line being processed may still have no travel time information. For bus stops located between other bus stops that already have assigned travel times, we interpolate the values based on the distance between the stops along the bus route. For bus stops at the start or end of the bus line with no travel time assigned, we extrapolate using the travel times offered in the timetable for that bus line.

4.3 Metrics

After computing the travel times between bus stops for every line in the public transportation system, a set of relevant metrics are considered in the analysis. These metrics focus on evaluating different features of the public transportation system. The studied metrics include:

- *Difference between scheduled and real travel time*: This metric evaluates the gap between the scheduled time and the actual travel time computed from GPS records. It is a very relevant metric to assess the punctuality of buses when arriving at each stop. The ideal value for this metric is zero, for a perfectly synchronized bus system.
- *Operational speed* (OS): This metric evaluates the average speed of buses when operating a route. Operational speed is defined as the length of a bus route divided by the average travel time required to perform a trip from the

beginning to the end of the route. Larger values of the operational speed indicate a more efficient transportation system. Related to this metric, in a recent article, Deng and Yang [4] introduced an holistic metric to evaluate the dispersion of the operational times for all bus lines in a public transportation system, i.e., dispersion OS (dOS). This metric is defined by $dOS = \max(OS_l) - OS_l$.

- *On-time arrival rate* (OTAR): This metric evaluates the number of trips performed without a significant delay, considering a predefined delay threshold (the *buffer time*). OTAR is defined as the ratio of buses arriving on time at the final stop over the total number of bus trips performed. The buffer time coefficient accounts for any unexpected delay during the trip. It is computed as the ratio of the difference between the 95th percentile travel time and the average travel time, and the average travel time [6].

- *Additional travel time over automobile* (ATToA): This metric evaluates the directness of a bus route, by comparing the travel time required for performing a trip on the public transportation system over the time required using private transportation (automobile) that makes the same trip. Smaller values of this metric means a more direct route; thus, a most efficient transportation system [1].

5   Results and Discussion

This section reports and discusses the main results and finding of the proposed analysis of the public transportation system in Montevideo, Uruguay.

5.1   Analysis of GPS Records

Figure 1 shows an example of the data processing methodology to assign GPS records to bus stops to compute in-vehicle travel times. The example corresponds to the final stops of bus line 306 from Parque Roosevelt (located in the east side of the city, in the border with Canelones department) to Casabó (a neighborhood in the west of Montevideo). Blue dots correspond to GPS measures and gray circles correspond to the buffered stops for the bus line. Bus stops with at least one GPS measure in their vicinity (i.e., at least one blue dot within the gray area) are assigned the timestamp of the earliest of those GPS measures. Bus stops with no GPS measures in their vicinity are assigned a timestamp by interpolating the timestamps of the previous and next bus stops with matching GPS records and taking into account the distance between those stops along the route of the bus. This case is shown in yellow in the figure. Finally, the last four stops (shown in orange in the figure) have no matching GPS records. This happens on some trips when the driver turns off the on-board GPS unit prematurely, thus the end of the trip is not recorded. In this case, the travel time to reach each bus stop is extrapolated using the information available in the timetable for the bus line and the latest GPS timestamp assigned to a bus stop of the line.

As a result of the data processing, travel time estimations for 8 195 trips corresponding to 257 different bus lines were obtained. Overall, travel times of

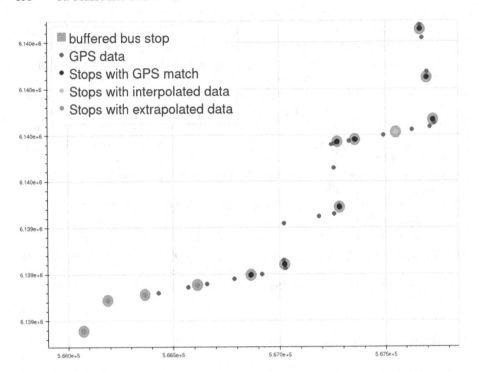

Fig. 1. Example of travel time assignment to bus stops at the end of line 306 from Parque Roosevelt to Casabó

trips at each bus stop were estimated directly in 67.9% of the cases, when there was a matching GPS measure of the trip at the bus stop. In turn, 21.6% of travel times were interpolated based on nearby GPS measures and 10.5% were extrapolated using data from the available timetables.

5.2   Differences Between Scheduled and Real Travel Times

The in-vehicle travel times estimated using bus location data can be compared against the scheduled timetables of the corresponding bus lines, to assess deviations from the scheduled times that may exist due to passenger demand, traffic congestion, and other external factors.

Figure 2 presents histograms of the difference between the (estimated) real travel time and the scheduled travel time that appears on the timetable. Histogram in Fig. 2a corresponds to each independent trip in the studied dataset, whereas results in Fig. 2b correspond to the median difference in travel time of each bus line. Values greater than zero correspond to trips/lines where the total travel time was larger than the scheduled time whereas negative values indicate that the travel time was shorter than that indicated by the schedule.

Results show that most trips adhere to their scheduled total travel time, with an average difference of half a minute with regards to the timetable.

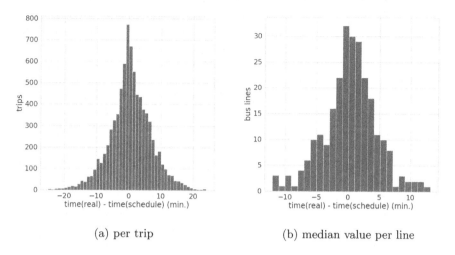

(a) per trip   (b) median value per line

Fig. 2. Histogram of difference between (estimated) real travel times and scheduled travel times

When looking at the 25th and 75th percentiles, the differences are of 3 an 4.4 min, respectively. These differences, while small, might affect passengers that may miss the bus and need to wait for a full headway for the next bus of the line and is specially significant for travelers transferring between different bus lines. Extreme values of trips arriving 30 min before the scheduled time and 37 min after the scheduled time were found, which might be useful to detect special events taking place along the route of those bus lines. When looking at the median differences of trips grouped by bus lines (Fig. 2b) it can be observed that, while most lines are consistent to their scheduled total travel time, some bus lines have significant differences with their schedules. On one extreme, line 137 from Paso de la Arena arrives to its destination in Plaza de los Treinta y Tres 12 min (in median) before its scheduled time. In contrast, line L1, a short local line that connects Paso de la Arena with Pajas Blancas arrives (in median) 13 min after its scheduled time.

Besides looking at overall differences in travel times among the trips and bus lines in the system, travel times of specific trips can be analyzed. Figure 3 shows the difference between the estimated travel time and the scheduled travel time at each bus stop of a trip of bus line 185, a bus line that travels through several neighborhoods of Montevideo going from Casabó to Pocitos. The same information is displayed in Fig. 4 using the bus stop location and the street map of the city. Each bus stop in the figure is colored according to the absolute difference between the estimated travel time to reach the bus stop and the scheduled time.

In the studied example, the trip of line 185 is, on average over all stops, 12 min ahead of its schedule. The difference increases along the route, reaching

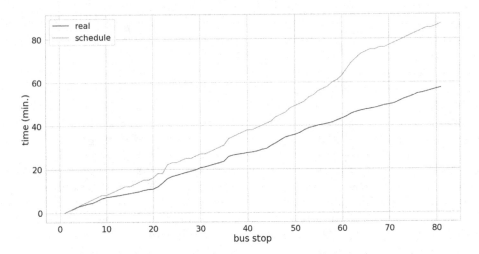

Fig. 3. Real (estimated) vs. scheduled travel time of a trip of bus line 185 from Casabó to Pocitos

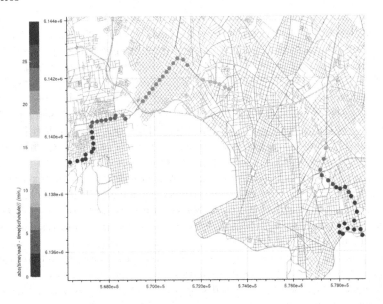

Fig. 4. Difference of estimated and scheduled travel times of a trip of bus line 185 from Casabó to Pocitos

its maximum at the last stop, where the bus arrives nearly 30 min ahead of its schedule. The average headway of this bus line for the morning peak considered is 5 min. Thus, in this case, a severe case of bus bunching occurs, which is detrimental to the quality of service and reliability offered to citizens.

5.3 Operational Speed

Several indicators can be computed using the estimated travel times as input. Among these, the operational speed is very useful to transport operators and authorities. Figure 5 outlines the results of computing the operational speed for all trips in the studied dataset. Descriptive statistics are outlined in Fig. 5(a) and a boxplot of the operational speed is presented in Fig. 5(b). Results are expressed in km/h.

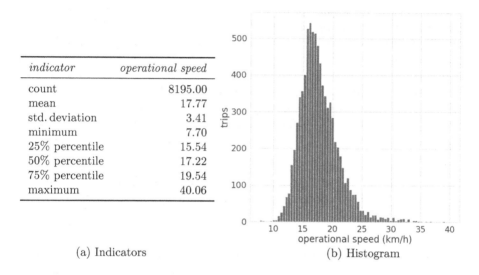

indicator	operational speed
count	8195.00
mean	17.77
std. deviation	3.41
minimum	7.70
25% percentile	15.54
50% percentile	17.22
75% percentile	19.54
maximum	40.06

(a) Indicators   (b) Histogram

Fig. 5. Descriptive statistics of operational speed

Results in Fig. 5 show that the average operational speed for all trips in the studied dataset is 17.77 km/h. This result is consistent with performance indicators published by local authorities corresponding to the year 2018 (www.montevideo.gub.uy/observatorio-de-movilidad, October 2021). The largest operational speed (40 km/h) is achieved by a trip of line L13, which operates on the outskirts of the city. The slowest operational speed (7.7 km/h) corresponds to a trip of line L31, a short local line. This particular trip took almost 17 min to complete the nearly 2 km of the bus line. Short local lines have the higher dispersion regarding operational speed. The median of operational speed (17.22 km/h) corresponds to a trip of line 105 from Parque Roosevelt (in the east of the city) to Plaza Independencia in the city center. This is a very long bus line, with a total route length of over 21 kms. In this specific trip, the total length of the route was covered in nearly one hour and fifteen minutes.

In turn, the dispersion of the operational speed (dOS) is outlined in Fig. 6. Descriptive statistics are reported in Fig. 6(a) and the distribution of results is shown in the histogram of Fig. 6(b).

indicator	dOS
count	8195.00
mean	22.29
std. deviation	3.41
minimum	0.00
25% percentile	20.52
50% percentile	22.84
75% percentile	24.52
maximum	32.36

(a) Indicators

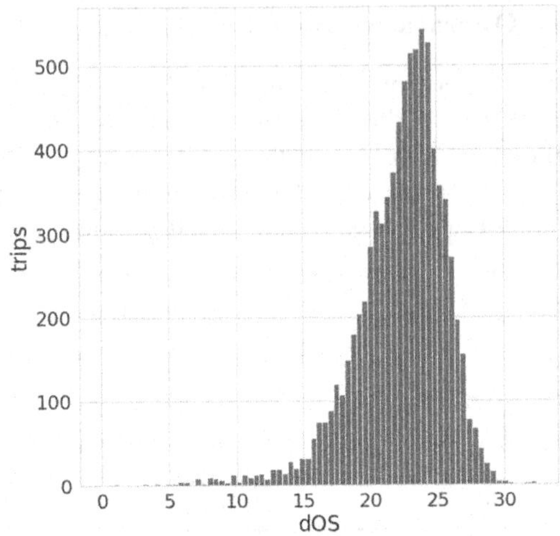

(b) Histogram

Fig. 6. Descriptive statistics of OS dispersion

The dOS metric results indicate that most lines have a large dispersion of OS values, with a mean of 22.29 km/h. This result is mainly conditioned by the extreme values of the OS metric for short local lines, which account for both the maximum and minimum values of OS, as reported in the previous analysis.

5.4 On-Time Arrival Rate

The calculation of the OTAR metric requires computing the buffer time, i.e. the coefficient that defines the acceptable delay threshold for completing a trip, with respect to the scheduled time. Table 1 outlines descriptive statistics for the buffer coefficients of the bus lines of the studied scenario. According to the computed results, the average value for acceptable delay is 11%.

Table 1. Descriptive statistics of buffer coefficients for on-time arrival rate

Indicator	Buffer coefficient
Count	257.00
Mean	0.11
Std. deviation	0.06
Minimum	0.00
25% percentile	0.08
50% percentile	0.11
75% percentile	0.15
Maximum	0.38

After determining the buffer coefficients, the OTAR metric was computed for each of the bus lines in the considered scenario. Results are shown in the histogram in Fig. 7.

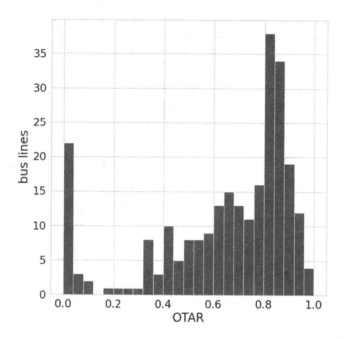

Fig. 7. Histogram of on-time arrival rate for bus lines

Results in Fig. 7 indicate that the average OTAR among all bus lines in the studied scenario is 0.64, with a standard deviation of 0.27. The histogram allows identifying a large number of bus lines with an OTAR value of 0.0. In these cases, none of the trips of a given bus line completed their journey within their scheduled time (even considering the time tolerance). In these extreme cases, authorities should review the predefined schedules and modify them to reflect the real operation times. These results confirm the usefulness of the proposed approach to detect anomalous situations in the public transportation system.

5.5 Additional Travel Time over Automobile (ATToA)

The heatmap in Fig. 8 reports the values of the ATToA metric for bus line 185. Bus line 185 has a higher-than-average operational speed, considering all bus lines in the city. The analysis is representative of those performed for other 'fast' bus lines in the city. Results correspond to the ATToA values computed from/to 17 (regularly spaced) stops along the route. Travel times in automobile were computed using the API provided by Google Maps.

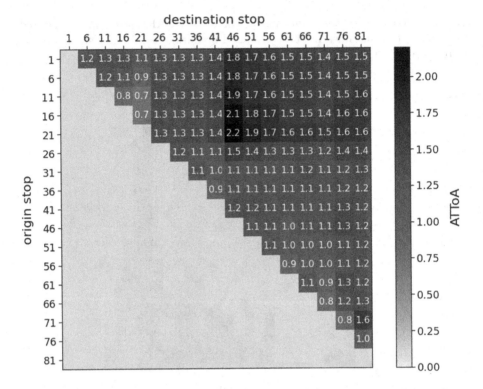

Fig. 8. Additional travel time over automobile (ATToA) of a trip of bus line 185 from Casabó to Pocitos

Results in Fig. 8 allow observing an almost regular pattern: the bus is very (time-wise) efficient for traveling between nearby stops, as demonstrated by ATToA values lower than 1.0, meaning that bus is faster than automobile in those cases. Values slightly increase for longer trips, up to reasonable 1.5× to 1.6× additional time factors. The only exceptions are for bus stop #46, for which the ATToA values are closer to 2.0 (and a worst value of 2.2 was computed for a trip with origin on stop #21). Two main reasons explain this result: between stops #21 and #46 the bus route has a big detour, which impacts on route directness, whereas the fastest way is traveling using automobile via a direct avenue (Bv. Artigas). Furthermore, bus stop #46 is located after a long red light that allows buses to turn left towards Bv. Artigas. Despite the reported delay, the bus line manages to recover a normal operational speed, as ATToA values after bus stop #46 reduce to a reasonable 1.6× additional time factor.

Overall, reported ATToA values are similar to the ones reported for other bus networks in similar cities (e.g., Stockholm, Sweden and Amsterdam, the Netherlands), and lower than values reported for larger cities such as São Paulo, Brazil and Sydney, Australia, for which average values up to 2.6× longer than driving a car have been reported [17].

6   Conclusions and Future Work

This article presented a data analysis approach to estimate in-vehicle travel time in public transportation systems, using GPS bus location data and several other sources of open data regarding the system infrastructure. The public transportation system in Montevideo, Uruguay, was used as a case study. A specific data analysis methodology is presented and then applied to one week of GPS bus location data comprised of over 2.8 million records corresponding to the morning peak hours. Estimated travel times were obtained for over 8 000 trips, corresponding to 257 different bus lines. These travel times were used as input to compute several relevant metrics, focused on evaluating different features of the public transportation system, including: i) differences against scheduled timetables, ii) operational speed, iii) on-time arrival rate, and iv) additional travel time over automobile. Computed metrics are a useful input for operators to evaluate the reliability of the transportation system and are relevant to policy-makers aiming to improve the quality of service offered to citizens.

The main lines of future work focus on improving the analysis and applying the computed results to solve relevant problems regarding public transportation in the case study considered. Regarding the first line, the data analysis process could be further improved by considering data from different peak and non-peak hours, as well as weekends, and by processing larger amounts of historical data. For the latter, parallel computing strategies should be devised to deal with the increased computational burden. Regarding the application of the computed travel times and indicators, several relevant lines are planned for future work, including bus timetable synchronization [15, 16], bus network redesign [5], sustainable mobility plans [9], and assessing accessibility using public transportation to different opportunities in the city. For this last application, a specific line of work is to extend the model presented in our previous work [8], which only used scheduled timetables, and incorporate the estimated (real) in-vehicle travel times to further refine the accessibility metric.

Acknowledgments. The research was partly funded by ANII (Uruguay), under grant ANII_FSDA_1_2018_1_154502 "Territorial, universal, and sustainable accessibility: characterization of the intermodal transportation system of Montevideo". The work of R. Massobrio and S. Nesmachnow was partly funded by ANII and PEDECIBA, Uruguay.

References

1. Benn, H.: Bus route evaluation standards a synthesis of transit practice. Technical Report TCRP Synthesis 10, Transportation Research Board (1995)
2. Bhat, C., Guo, J., Sen, S., Weston, L.: Measuring access to public transportation services: Review of customer-oriented transit performance measures and methods of transit submarket identification. Technical Report 0–5178-1, Center for Transportation Research, The University of Texas at Austin (2005)

3. Cardozo, O.D., Rey, C.E.: La vulnerabilidad en la movilidad urbana: aportes teóricos y metodológicos. In: Foschiatti, A. (ed.) Aportes conceptuales y empíricos de la vulnerabilidad global, pp. 398–423. Editorial Universitaria de la Universidad Nacional del Nordeste (2007)
4. Deng, Y., Yan, Y.: Evaluating route and frequency design of bus lines based on data envelopment analysis with network epsilon-based measures. J. Adv. Transp. **2019**, 1–12 (2019)
5. Fabbiani, E., Nesmachnow, S., Toutouh, J., Tchernykh, A., Avetisyan, A., Radchenko, G.I.: Analysis of mobility patterns for public transportation and bus stops relocation. Program. Comput. Softw. **44**(6), 508–525 (2018)
6. Federal Highway Administration: Travel time reliability: making it there on time, all the time. Technical Report HOP-06-070, U.S. Department of Transportation (2005)
7. Grava, S.: Urban Transportation Systems. McGraw-Hill Professional (2000)
8. Hernández, D., Hansz, M., Massobrio, R.: Job accessibility through public transport and unemployment in Latin America: the case of Montevideo (Uruguay). J. Transp. Geogr. **85**, 102742 (2020)
9. Hipogrosso, S., Nesmachnow, S.: Analysis of sustainable public transportation and mobility recommendations for montevideo and parque rodó neighborhood. Smart Cities **3**(2), 479–510 (2020)
10. Jagadeesh, G.R., Srikanthan, T., Zhang, X.D.: A map matching method for GPS based real-time vehicle location. J. Navig. **57**(3), 429–440 (2004)
11. Lei, T.L., Church, R.L.: Mapping transit-based access: integrating GIS, routes and schedules. Int. J. Geograp. Inf. Sci. **24**(2), 283–304 (2010)
12. Massobrio, R., Nesmachnow, S.: Urban mobility data analysis for public transportation systems: a case study in montevideo. Uruguay. Appl. Sci. **10**(16), 1–20 (2020)
13. Massobrio, R., Nesmachnow, S., Tchernykh, A., Avetisyan, A., Radchenko, G.: Towards a cloud computing paradigm for big data analysis in smart cities. Program.Comput. Softw. **44**(3), 181–189 (2018)
14. Massobrio, R., Pías, A., Vázquez, N., Nesmachnow, S.: Map-reduce for processing GPS data from public transport in montevideo, Uruguay. In: Simposio Argentino de Grandes Datos, vol. 45, pp. 41–54. Jornadas Argentinas de Informática (2016)
15. Nesmachnow, S., Muraña, J., Goñi, G., Massobrio, R., Tchernykh, A.: Evolutionary approach for bus synchronization. In: High Performance Computing, pp. 320–336. Springer International Publishing (2020). https://doi.org/10.1007/978-3-030-41005-6_22
16. Nesmachnow, S., Risso, C.: Exact and evolutionary algorithms for synchronization of public transportation timetables considering extended transfer zones. Appl. Sci. **11**(15), 7138 (2021)
17. Salonen, M., Toivonen, T.: Modelling travel time in urban networks: comparable measures for private car and public transport. J. Transp. Geogr. **31**, 143–153 (2013)
18. Turnquist, M., Blume, S.: Evaluating potential effectiveness of headway control strategies for transit systems. Transp. Res. Rec. **746**, 25–29 (1980)

Open-Source Big Data Platform for Real-Time Geolocation in Smart Cities

Pedro Moreno-Bernal[1]([✉]) [iD], Carlos Alan Cervantes-Salazar[1],
Sergio Nesmachnow[2] [iD], Juan Manuel Hurtado-Ramírez[3] [iD],
and José Alberto Hernández-Aguilar[1] [iD]

[1] Universidad Autónoma del Estado de Morelos, Cuernavaca, Morelos, Mexico
{pmoreno,jose_hernandez}@uaem.mx
[2] Universidad de la República, Montevideo, Uruguay
sergion@fing.edu.uy
[3] Instituto de Biotecnología, Universidad Nacional Autónoma de México,
Cuernavaca, Morelos, Mexico
jmanuel@ibt.unam.mx

Abstract. Nowadays, big data analytic tools and Internet of Things applications boost productivity in Intelligent Transportation Systems in the context of smart cities. Each day, location mobility data are generated continuously from Global Positioning System devices in a high temporal granularity. This article introduces a framework for public transportation mobility analysis. The proposed big data platform uses open source components for real-time geolocation tracking processing. The platform collects location information over Message Queue Telemetry Transport protocol to Apache Kafka, and then information is processed using Apache Storm, which guarantees fault tolerance, horizontal scalability, and low latency. Experimental evaluation is performed for a case study considering 10357 taxi tours (17 million GPS timestamps) using problem instances of different sizes. Results demonstrate that the proposed open-source big data platform is capable of processing a significantly large number of GPS timestamps of tested instances in reasonable execution times.

Keywords: Big data · Internet of Things · Real-time geolocation tracking

1 Introduction

Today, the Big Data revolution is advancing, and the Internet of Things (IoT) is driving it as an essential part of a transformative era of technology changes under the paradigm of smart cities [11]. As part of technological changes, urban mobility needs to provide intelligent mobility services that anticipate future changes and participate in decision-making. Mobility in high-density cities is complex for traffic, the different transportation modes, and the multiple origins and destinations [19]. In recent years, traffic congestion and pollution have

S. Nesmachnow and L. Hernández Callejo (Eds.): ICSC-Cities 2021, CCIS 1555, pp. 207–222, 2022.
https://doi.org/10.1007/978-3-030-96753-6_15

become a severe problem for the most significant cities. Cities are complex and dynamic and have associated problems related to high densities and mobility activities [13]. Traffic congestion is a severe problem that causes significant economic losses and impacts the quality of life of citizens. Hence, it is necessary to build intelligent traffic management systems by urban mobility tracking for achieving urban transportation efficiency and safety. For this reason, transportation systems require effective mobility techniques to reduce traffic incidents and congestion. In addition, transportation systems must ensure travel safety and efficiency, avoid negative impacts on the local economy, reduce environmental pollution, movement tracking, and impact the quality of people's lives, converging into Intelligent Transportation Systems (ITS). ITS are mobility systems that use technological advances, methods, and applications of the Information and Communication Technologies (ICT) field, with high technology and mobility data. ICT gather a wide range of data from sensors, infrastructure, and geolocation of mobility devices to operate and manage scientifically [1]. Also, ICT efficiently transfer the collected data to a data center to share and exchange information between connected devices [21]. Geolocation data are generated continuously from IoT devices, and these data streams are of high temporal granularity [13]. Every day, the amount of mobility data grows at an exponential rate.

Big data integrate high technologies and large amounts of data from ICT to develop new digital systems and applications in real-time to analyze, simulate, and process mobility data. Big data techniques require effective analytics, storage technologies, and distributed processing computer tools for exploiting large amounts of data on the cloud. Analyzing and processing large amounts of data has led organizations to develop distributed solution platforms to maximize the benefits of the value of large volumes data. Big data must be able to process data from Terabytes to Zettabytes at a high-velocity rate and near-real-time to explore and exploit the power of big data [20]. In real-time analytics, large volumes of data are continuously sending by mobile devices, and they are receiving on the cloud by online services for its process, analysis, and storage. Big data tools use models of batch, stream, and iterative methods for processing large-scale data. The model selected depends on the kind of problem to solve.

This article proposes a framework for gathering and processing large volumes of real-time geolocation data in the context of ITS. The proposed framework applies distributed computing and big data processing for real-time analysis by open source tools such as Message Queue Telemetry Transport (MQTT), Apache Kafka, and Apache Storm. Furthermore, a specific application of the proposed framework is presented for real-time vehicle tracking using geolocation data. The proposed framework provides fault tolerance, horizontal scalability, and low latency through the open-source tools used. Experimental evaluation is performed using three different size problem instances of tour trajectories of 10357 taxis, including 17 million GPS timestamps. Results demonstrate that the proposed big data platform can process a significantly large number of GPS timestamps in the considered scenarios in reasonable execution times.

The rest of the article is structured as follows. Section 2 describes the urban mobility problem in the smart cities context. Section 3 describes the proposed platform for real-time processing big data approach, including a brief description of the big data technologies used. Section 4 provides details of the experimental evaluation of the proposed platform, including describing different size problem instances of tour trajectories of 10357 taxis and the discussion of the results. Finally, Sect. 5 presents the conclusions and formulate the main lines for future work.

2   Transportation Geolocation Problem

This section describes the importance of geolocation data and how real-time vehicle tracking is essential in the context of smart cities and ITS. Also, the section reviews the related works about big data processing problems for geolocation mobility systems applying computational intelligence and distributed computing.

2.1   Transport Geolocation

Transport services companies such as taxis and delivery companies need to track their assets to ensure their vehicles are using appropriately. Vehicle tracking is essential to locate any asset if it is stolen or if it needs to relocate the original path. Therefore, geospatial interaction is an essential element for transportation mobility. Real-time geospatial data help to track vehicle movements to provide information about the infrastructure environment [13]. Therefore, an intelligent transportation application based on geolocation information becomes essential for efficient and safe urban transportation.

In addition, ITS must provide reliable information for drivers about their driving environment. Information of vehicles and roads help to improve driving conditions for safety, efficiency, comfortable and cleaner urban mobility. Therefore, reliable information must be collected about vehicles, location, infrastructure, road conditions, among others. Data collected allows optimized routes for safe mobility considering the capacity of the road network infrastructure. This information helps to attend to incidents and hazards by a better mobility response. Also, ITS provide better services for the different transport modes decreasing any negative economic impact. ITS interoperability require large amounts of mobility data, particularly geographical locations about vehicle mobility, to ensure the ITS functionality for public and private decision-making. Other benefits to tracking a vehicle are maintenance schedule control by kilometers, quick location of the vehicle, data collection for estimate future operational cost, improved up-time, and vehicle utilization [19].

2.2   Real-Time Geolocation Data Processing

ICT, sensor technologies, and digital devices use wireless sensor networks to collect real-time geospatial data automatically [2]. Wireless sensor networks produce large amounts of real-time geolocation data. In addition, real-time traffic monitoring uses sensors mounted on road lampposts, under pavement, on vehicles (geolocation by GPS), bridges, toll booths, traffic light poles, among others, to collect location, speed, moving directions, and weather data to estimate traffic-flow conditions in an urban mobility context. Urban mobility data in the context of smart cities provide the creation of new rules, regulations, and methods to control the traffic vehicle density growth. Also, urban mobility data permit the expansion and construction of new routes, roads, and mobility infrastructure to solve existing problems impacting significantly on the local economy.

ITS integrate big data technologies, computational intelligence techniques, and transport systems engineering to improve transportation mobility services. ITS must gather large volumes of data in real-time by IoT devices and mobile sensor networks in vehicles and road network infrastructure [15]. Also, Big data tools for ITS require adequate analysis data, storage techniques, and parallel/distributed processing tools for efficient and accurate data processing (real-time or offline). These technologies provide tools to address issues to be tackled in the context of storage technologies, batch-processing/analysis, or real-time processing/analysis [3]. Specific frameworks for real-time data analysis in Teradata scale and parallel/distributed processing in big data are Apache Storm [9] and Apache Kafka [10]. Both frameworks are characterized by fault tolerance and scalability for real-time streaming data processing. Also, these frameworks support different streaming stages such as collection, transportation, and process. Other frameworks related with similar capabilities with a functional development approach are Apache Spark and Apache Hive. Data processing is the main goal to compute relevant metrics for efficient transportation services [15].

This work focuses on distributed big data processing platforms using open source tools for real-time geolocation tracking. The goal is to track vehicles based on urban mobility for ITS in the smart cities paradigm.

2.3   Related Works

Research in smart cities uses big data technologies and IoT to support ITS for planning urban mobility. Many ITS applications use big data analytics tools for real-time data processing. Current works are proposing different architectures and platforms to collect, process, store, and analyze urban mobility data in the context of smart cities. A brief review of related works is presented next.

Wang et al. [22] proposed a real-time streaming data processing system using Apache Storm for road traffic monitoring. The system was evaluated on problem instances built with data of one-day trajectories of 7648 taxis. Every taxi sends a GPS timestamp at intervals of 3 to 5 min. The taxi trajectories represent a data set of 18 million GPS locations. The experimental analysis was made in a cluster with five PCs with processor 2-core 2.4 GHz, 1 GB of RAM, and Ubuntu operating system. Experimental results showed that the proposed system guaranteed correctness and low latency. Also, the article demonstrated a practical traffic estimation in cases where traffic trajectory data streams exhibit non-homogeneous sparseness in real-time.

Ding et al. [4] proposed a collaborative approach for the travel-time calculation of vehicles in typical business transportation problems. The approach combines spatio-temporal parallelism for real-time data and Bayes prior rules for historical data mining. The performance was evaluated on Apache Storm and Hadoop MapReduce. Apache Storm cluster was implemented on five computers with 4-Cores, 4 GB of RAM, 1.2 TB storage, and Centos 6 operating system. Also, the Hadoop cluster was implemented on five computers with the same characteristics. The system was evaluated considering real-data of vehicles collected from October 2012 to January 2013, about of 100 GB of data generated from 1000 monitors on the trunk roads at Beijing. The proposed approach maintained milliseconds latencies on a high streaming processing, showing nearly linear scalability with a predictive accuracy above 80%.

Zhou et al. [26] developed an efficient streaming mass spatio-temporal data access based on Apache Storm (ESDAS) for achieving real-time streaming vehicle data. Problems instances were made using Taiyuan BD bus network data. Experimental results showed that ESDAS speed insertion is approximately three times higher than the MongoDB platform.

Nesmachnow et al. [15] described a platform for Big Data analysis using a Map-Reduce approach in Hadoop in the context of smart cities. The problem instance data included different time intervals and GPS locations from buses of the transport system of Montevideo, Uruguay. The file sizes of the evaluated datasets are 10 GB, 20 GB, 30 GB, and 60 GB. The experimental analysis focused on evaluating the computational efficiency of the parallel/distributed Map-Reduce model and the correctness of the system over several scenarios using accurate GPS data collected in 2015 in Montevideo. The experimental evaluation was performed over the cloud infrastructure of Cluster FING, the high-performance computing facility at Universidad de la República, Uruguay [16]. The experimental results indicated that the solution approach scales appropriately when processing a large volume of data with a speedup of 22.16 times and computational efficiency of 0.92 using 24 computing resources compared to its sequential version.

Laska et al. [12] proposed a scalable architecture for real-time spatio-temporal stream data processing. The integration of IoT stream data used GeoMQTT to publish timestamp messages in Apache Kafka. The stream processing was made by Apache Storm. A dynamic amount of vehicle data were performed by the map matching algorithm on the proposed architecture. The dataset evaluated consists of 10357 taxi trajectories collected from 2 February to 8 February 2008. The dataset points were about 17 million, representing a distance of nine million kilometers. Experimental evaluation was performed using nine virtual machines with 2 GB of RAM on a Hypervisor with 64 cores. The experimental results showed a stable latency in milliseconds for instances that do not exceed a ratio of 100 trajectory points per second.

Fan-Hsun et al. [6] proposed a real-time traffic prediction model by analyzing large-scale streams data of road density, traffic events, and rainfall volume. The proposed approach applied the Support Vector Machine and fuzzy theory to evaluate the traffic level on-road sections. The big data platform for the collection, analysis, and processing was Apache Storm. The problem instances were created using open data from Police Broadcasting Service social media, Taiwan Area National Freeway Bureaus, and the Central Weather Bureau in Taiwan. Experimental evaluation was performed on virtual machines on a computer with an AMD Opteron processor, 16 GB of RAM, a GigaByte Ethernet Controller, and a Xen Server 6.2 operating system. Experimental results showed that the proposed model improves the prediction accuracy by 25.6% than the prediction method based on the weighted exponential moving average method.

Massobrio and Nesmachnow [14] proposed an urban data analysis study for the public transportation system in Montevideo in ITS and smart cities. The study analyzed the GPS bus location dataset and smart card ticket sales. Several insights were obtained from data analysis, like the number of passengers traveling by the same smart card, frequency of use of the smart cards, and the number of bus transfers. Also, the ticket sales analysis revealed three peak hours during working days. Besides, the work proposed a methodology for built origin-destination matrices by trip changing to estimate the destinations. The implemented algorithm correctly estimated the destination for 81.62% of urban mobility trips of the studied dataset from 2016 with a Spearman correlation coefficient of 0.895.

The related works allow identifying several proposals using big data platforms for ITS applications processing and analysis in the context of smart cities. This work contributes with a real-time processing platform for distributed big data frameworks on vehicle tracking applications. The proposed platform considers gathering data by an IoT GPS device for real-time processing until its storage. The benefits of the proposed platform for real-time GPS data include: providing helpful information about geolocation on a specific time interval and storing distances information processed for future purposes. Next, big data platforms and IoT protocols to provide mobility services in real-time are described.

3   The Proposed Distributed Big Data Platform

This section describes the proposed open-source big data platform for real-time geolocation tracking. In addition, the frameworks, protocols, design, and distributed architecture are described.

3.1   Data Gathering

MQTT is a client/server broker-based transport protocol for publishing and subscribes messages over the Transmission Control Protocol/Internet Protocol (TCP/IP). It is lightweight, open, simple, and it supports IoT Machine-to-Machine (M2M) communication. Recent MQTT specification has been standardized by the OASIS consortium and ISO/IEC 20922. Many IoT applications, such as autonomous/connected cars, smart cities, and cloud-connected industrial machines use MQTT to connect with cloud computing. The implementation of

MQTT brokers supports different scenarios, including distributed computing, to achieve high scalability and to provide high availability. MQTT by IoT technologies allows gathering data from smart-city devices. IoT acquires data through technologies such as RFID, WIFI, WSN, 5G, and satellite communication [13]. Generally, sensing technologies are used to gathering mobility information. Sensor technologies are classified into two categories: On-site and On-board. On-site technologies are sensors installed directly in the road infrastructure. On-board (or off-roadway) technologies collect information from vehicles/passengers to send it to a road device or the cloud for analysis [3].

3.2 Data Collection

Real-time mobility information is collected by streaming, using physical sensing or mobile devices from remote technologies. Mobility information is generated from different sources such as GPS devices, mobile devices, IoT sensors, and social networks. Many collected mobility data have low spatial precision due to the acquisition device. Also, many applications require data in periods (time) for mobility tracking. However, mobility collected data can be sparse and noisy in the location accurate [23]. Therefore, the information must be classified and organized according to the application requirements; for example, ITS need to collect data in time intervals on different dates for route planning or scheduling [15]. For these reasons, considerable information must be stored using structured and unstructured data to be processed by computational intelligence algorithms. Streaming platforms, such as Apache Kafka, have been proposed for collecting large volumes of data by high-throughput message brokers. Kafka is an open-source platform for distributed event streaming, high-performance data pipelines, streaming analytics, data integration, and mission-critical applications.

3.3 Data Processing

Processing of large volume of data on a single computer usually has limitations due to the computer resources, such as memory and CPU [13]. Nevertheless, the analysis of vast volumes of data in real-time requires many processing elements. Therefore, parallel and distributed systems are necessary to process large volumes of data. Parallel/distributed systems include a high-speed communication network and a distributed storage system as a part of the system.

Big data processing operates over data by applying batch or real-time stream data entry depending on the scenario. The batch processing work with collected data over some time, while the real-time processing work with collected data in a short time. Therefore, the real-time big data analysis must provide fault tolerance and scalability with a functional development approach, such as Apache Storm provides. Storm is a general propose parallel/distributed platform that provides flexibility, scalability, and real-time stream processing.

3.4 Data Storing

Real-time mobility services in the context of the smart city need to handle and store a huge amount of data for analysis [26]. Structured (SQL) and unstructured (NoSQL) solutions provide scalability and data acquisition capabilities in an easier programming way. High availability is needed to dispose of information at any time. Cloud computing storage provides high availability, data replication, and load balancing on demand.

3.5 The Proposed Platform for Real-Time Geolocation Data Processing

The design and architecture are divided into four stages. The first stage uses a GPS timestamp corresponding to location coordinates of a vehicle in movement. The timestamp contains four data: vehicle ID, date and time, latitude and longitude coordinates. Data are gathered from an IoT device that sends timestamps every time interval to an MQTT server. The IoT device components used in the platform design are an Arduino MEGA board and a GSM/SIM808 module. The second stage classifies information by topics using Kafka. The third stage computes the timestamps using a Storm topology. In this stage, timestamp strings are split by commas. Each part of the timestamp is sent to another process for processing. In the last stage, data persistence storing GPS timestamps directly on a database for future analysis. Figure 1 shows the architecture of the proposed open-source big data platform for real-time geolocation tracking.

The proposed open-source big data platform for real-time geolocation tracking is implemented using MQTT, Kafka, Storm, and MySQL. An IoT device makes data gathering through an Arduino MEGA board and a GSM/SIM808 module. MQTT broker is available by a Mosquitto server on a cloud host with a public IP. The broker filters incoming messages from the IoT device client into the topic gpsmqtt. In addition, a Zookeeper server is installed to coordinate the process communication between the cluster nodes. The communication between Mosquitto and Kafka uses the Kafka connect plugin of Confluent for sending and receiving data from the MQTT broker. Then, a Kafka partition with a replication factor one is created on the Kafka broker to collect data in the topic mqttgps. Once MQTT and Kafka brokers are working, Storm topology is deployed on the Storm cluster.

Storm works on local mode and a cluster mode (i.e., master-slave model). Storm processes are coordinated through the Zookeeper service. Storm cluster has a master node called Nimbus and at least one worker node (Supervisor). Input data is sent by the Spout element that transforms the data into tuples (data streams). The Bolt element execute operators or functions over the tuples. The topology defines the data streams flow between Spouts and Bolts by a directed acyclic graph. The topology is used to deploy the computational parallel model on the Storm cluster.

Figure 2 shows the spout/bolt workflow in the proposed topology. Blue arrows represent the spout phase, and green arrows represent the bolt phase. Each GPS

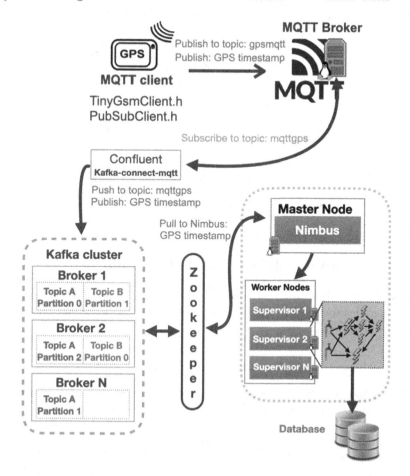

Fig. 1. Scheme of the platform for big data processing in real-time

timestamp is gathering by kafkaSpout component from a Kafka topic, and the data stream (tuple) is sending to different bolts (SplitBolt and MySQLBolt). Thus, each bolt performs a different task. First, SplitBolt receives a tuple that stores it on a string variable. After that, the string is split by commas, and two new tuples are sent to the CountBolt. Then, CountBolt classifies incoming tuples to accumulate the trajectories distances. Once the counting operation finishes, a new tuple with a distance value is sent by a new tuple to the ReportBolt and it stores processed distances on memory to show them on a final report. On the other hand, MySQLBolt performs the data persistence, storing the GPS timestamp directly on a MySQL database.

The proposed open-source big data platform collects, processes, and stores mobility location data every n seconds. Besides, Kafka and Storm setup guarantee fault tolerance, scalability, and low latency. The following section analyzes the experimental results of the proposed platform for three case studies.

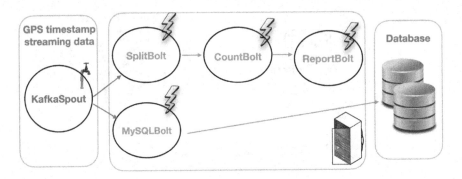

Fig. 2. Spout/bolt Storm topology for real-time geolocation tracking (Color figure online)

4   Experimental Validation and Discussion

This section describes the experimental evaluation of the proposed platform and the problem instances are described. Finally, the computational efficiency results are reported and discussed.

4.1   Development and Execution Platform

The Storm topology was implemented in the Java programming language, and the distribution of jobs works independently depending on the topology distribution (Fig. 2). Every spout/bolt component was assigned at least one executor (thread), and each executor was assigned one task (spout/bolt instance).

The experimental evaluation was performed using an Intel i7-8700 (6 cores, 12 threads) processor at 3.2 GHz, 32 GB of RAM, and the Ubuntu 20.04 Linux operating system.

4.2   Problem Instances and Data

The problem instances considered in each case of study are described next. GPS timestamps from the T-Drive trajectories benchmark [25] are used to define different scenarios. Three scenarios were defined with 3500, 7500, and 10357 GPS trajectories of 10357 taxi routes collected during February 2 to 8, 2008, within Beijing. The data format in a file contains many lines with the following fields, separated by a comma: idTaxi, date-time, latitude, longitude.

The interval of time between two consecutive GPS timestamps is 10 min. Each file name in the dataset corresponds to the taxi ID, and contains the trajectory of the taxi. GPS timestamp data are sent from the file to the Mosquitto topic through a bash script to perform the experimental evaluation of big data processing. Problem instance #1 includes 3500 trajectory files. Problem instance #2 includes 7500 trajectory files containing, and problem instance #3 includes the whole 10357 trajectory files containing.

4.3 Computational Efficiency Metrics

The experimental evaluation focuses on evaluating the performance of the platform topology, composed of Kafka spout, split bolt, count bolt, report bolt, and persistent database bolt.

Two relevant metrics are considered for the evaluation: *latency* and *throughput*. Latency evaluates the (intra-worker) communication time within a worker process associated with an executor thread on the same Storm machine/node. Also, when an external service (Kafka broker) interacts with a spout component, the latency evaluates the inter-topology communication time of the response from a Storm node to a Kafka node across the network. Lower latency values mean a better execution time overall. In turn, the throughput evaluates the number of tuples successfully processed, regarding the number of GPS timestamps included in each problem instance. A higher value of throughput represents a better efficiency. Related counters are retrieved from the Storm user interface and used for computing throughput.

4.4 Experimental Results

This subsection presents and discusses the results of the efficiency analysis for the three considered case studies, involving GPS timestamps of 10357 taxi trajectories in Beijing.

Table 1 reports the number of GPS timestamps on each problem instance, the number of tuples successfully processed (*acked*) by the topology, the throughput, the average latency, and the uptime of the system, i.e., the time from the beginning of the experiment until the topology stops emitting tuples. Latency times are reported in milliseconds.

Table 1. Efficiency counters, throughput, latency, and uptime of the topology for the three problem instances studied

Instance	#timestamps	Acked	Throughput	Latency (ms)	Uptime
#1	5742560	5112220	89.02%	325.95	6 h 8 m
#2	12871223	12149800	94.39%	332.12	13 h 35 m
#3	17662984	17490880	99.02%	373.43	19 h 4 m

Results in Table 1 indicate that the topology is capable of processing a significantly large number of the GPS timestamps in each instance in reasonable execution times (considering the low-end computational platform used). Throughput values between 89% and 99% were achieved. The processing of the whole set of GPS timestamps was not attained, mainly because Storm uses three internal queues on a worker node, which generates additional latency. The developed implementation showed good scalability, as demonstrated by the latency values, which did not increase from instance #1 to #2, even though the number of processed GPS increased in a factor of 2.25×. Furthermore, latency only increased a mere 14%, when the problem dimension increased more than three times.

Table 2 reports the number of tuples transferred by a bolt component to the next component in the topology, the throughput, and the latency for each bolt component. The most relevant components are SplitBolt and MySQLBolt because they receive data directly from the spout. Hence, the number of transferred tuples on those bolt components is equal to or lower than the number of GPS timestamps stored on the Kafka topic for each instance. Throughput values for the CountBolt component are not reported because the number of transferred tuples are duplicated by the SplitBolt component, as reported in the transferred column on the table. In turn, throughput values for the ReportBolt component are not reported because the tuples it process and transfer correspond to distance values, not to GPS timestamps.

Table 2. Throughput and latency associated with bolt components

Instance	Bolt	Transferred	Throughput	Latency (ms)
#1	SplitBolt	5402163	94.07%	0.009
	CountBolt	11545907	–	0.003
	ReportBolt	5540620	–	0.003
	MySQLBolt	5363354	93.39%	2.484
#2	SplitBolt	12343030	95.89%	0.012
	CountBolt	25545907	–	0.005
	ReportBolt	12650720	–	0.003
	MySQLBolt	12303074	95.58%	2.662
#3	SplitBolt	17345268	98.20%	0.017
	CountBolt	35280140	–	0.006
	ReportBolt	17139500	–	0.003
	MySQLBolt	17147527	97.08%	2.828

Results in Table 2 indicate that the bolt components of interest (SplitBolt and MySQLBolt) are able to process a significantly large number of timestamps for each instance in a reasonable execution time, using an executor for each task assigned to each bolt component. Throughput values between 93% and 98% were achieved. Ideal throughput values were not obtained due to lost tuples during the processing. The main reason for this loss is that the chosen level of reliability for bolt components does not guarantee complete message processing; it was set focused on efficiency instead. Finally, the bolt component that demanded the larger execution time was the persistent MySQLBolt, mainly due to the response time of network communication with the external database service.

Figure 3 graphically summarizes the latency results. Latency values for the fully completed tuple processed through the topology are reported in Fig. 3a.

In turn, Fig. 3b compares the latency values for each bolt component of the applied Storm topology.

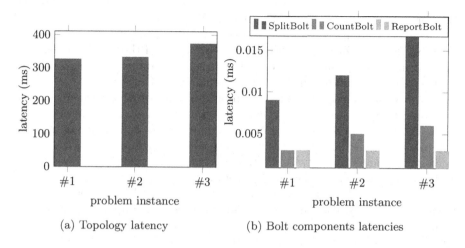

(a) Topology latency   (b) Bolt components latencies

Fig. 3. Latency of the Storm topology and bolt components

Results in Fig. 3a clearly shows the slightly increasing latency behavior when solving problem instances with different sizes. In turn, Fig. 3b shows that the latency of bolt components increases with the number of transferred tuples for the considered problem instances. SplitBolt increases the latency mainly due to the timestamps split task transferred to the next bolt component. The Count-Bolt component has a slight latency increment between different instances sizes in relation to the number of transferred tuples from SplitBolt, mainly because it performs a low-demanding CPU computation (i.e., distance computation). Finally, the latency of ReportBolt had the same value from all problem instances.

Summarizing, results of the experimental evaluation demonstrate that the Storm topology deployed in the proposed open-source big-data platform is capable of processing a significantly large number of the GPS timestamps for each instance in reasonable execution times. Futhermore, the system showed good scalability properties, as latency values slightly increased when processing a significantly large number of GPS timestamps.

5   Conclusions and Future Work

This article presented a distributed open-source big data platform for real-time geolocation data processing in the context of smart cities, particularly for ITS applications.

The proposed platform combines parallel and distributed computing and geolocation to process real-time data for relevant analysis in smart cities. First, the platform collects location GPS timestamps from an IoT device over the MQTT protocol to Mosquitto broker; after that, the MQTT broker publishes the messages into an Apache Kafka topic by using a Confluent connector. Then, a particular Kafka consumer pushes the data into a Storm spout (KafkaSpout), to be processed by bolt components in a parallel topology.

The experimental validation focused on evaluating the efficiency of the proposed big data platform through two relevant metrics of the Storm components (latency and throughput) using real GPS timestamps from 10357 taxi trajectories from Beijing including more than 17 million GPS timestamps.

The main results indicate that the proposed Storm topology is effective for processing problem instances involving a large number of GPS timestamps in reasonable execution times. Accurate throughput values were achieved, between 93% to 98% for the bolt components and between 89% and 99% for the whole topology. A good scalability behavior was also shown, since latency values did not increase significantly when processing more GPS timestamps.

The main lines for future work are oriented to extend the proposed system to compute other essential indicators and statistics of ITS applications, such as public transportation systems from Mexico and Uruguay. Those analysis would certainly be valuable for relevant research such as bus timetable synchronization [17,18], bus network redesign [5], sustainable mobility plans [8], and also private transportation analysis [7,24].

Also, the proposed approach must be compared with other frameworks such as Apache Flink and distributed databases, like Apache Cassandra, to address the analysis in real-time for geolocation transportation tracking in smart cities. In turn, the data collected by the big data platform can be used for analysis through computational intelligence techniques to improve the quality of service of transportation systems.

References

1. Alam, M., Ferreira, J., Fonseca, J.: Introduction to intelligent transportation systems. In: Alam, M., Ferreira, J., Fonseca, J. (eds.) Intelligent Transportation Systems. SSDC, vol. 52, pp. 1–17. Springer, Cham (2016). https://doi.org/10.1007/978-3-319-28183-4_1
2. Batty, M., et al.: Smart cities of the future. Eur. Phys. J. Spec. Top. **214**, 481–518 (2012). https://doi.org/10.1140/epjst/e2012-01703-3
3. Campos, S., et al.: Big data in road transport and mobility research. In: Intelligent Vehicles, pp. 175–205. Butterworth-Heinemann (2018)
4. Ding, W., Zhang, S., Zhao, Z.: A collaborative calculation on real-time stream in smart cities. Simul. Model. Pract. Theory **73**, 72–82 (2017)
5. Fabbiani, E., Nesmachnow, S., Toutouh, J., Tchernykh, A., Avetisyan, A., Radchenko, G.: Analysis of mobility patterns for public transportation and bus stops relocation. Program. Comput. Softw. **44**(6), 508–525 (2018). https://doi.org/10.1134/S0361768819010031
6. Fan, T., Jen, H., Chia, T., Yao, Y., Han, C., Li, C.: Congestion prediction with big data for real-time highway traffic. IEEE Access **6**, 57311–57323 (2018)

7. Winter, H., Serra, J., Nesmachnow, S., Tchernykh, A., Shepelev, V.: Computational intelligence for analysis of traffic data. In: Nesmachnow, S., Hernández Callejo, L. (eds.) ICSC-CITIES 2020. CCIS, vol. 1359, pp. 167–182. Springer, Cham (2021). https://doi.org/10.1007/978-3-030-69136-3_12
8. Hipogrosso, S., Nesmachnow, S.: Analysis of sustainable public transportation and mobility recommendations for Montevideo and Parque Rodó neighborhood. Smart Cities 3(2), 479–510 (2020)
9. Jain, A.: Mastering Apache Storm: Processing Big Data Streams in Real Time. Packt Publishing, Birmingham (2017)
10. Kumar, M., Singh, C.: Building Data Streaming Applications with Apache Kafka. Packt Publishing, Birmingham (2017)
11. Kumar, S., Tiwari, P., Zymbler, M.: Internet of Things is a revolutionary approach for future technology enhancement: a review. J. Big Data 6(1), 1–21 (2019)
12. Laska, M., Herle, S., Klamma, R., Blankenbach, J.: A scalable architecture for real-time stream processing of spatiotemporal IoT stream data-performance analysis on the example of map matching. ISPRS Int. J. Geo-Inf. 7(7), 238 (2018)
13. Li, W., Batty, M., Goodchild, M.: Real-time GIS for smart cities. Int. J. Geogr. Inf. Sci. 34(2), 311–324 (2020)
14. Massobrio, R., Nesmachnow, S.: Urban mobility data analysis for public transportation systems: a case study in Montevideo, Uruguay. Appl. Sci. 10(16), 5400 (2020)
15. Nesmachnow, S., Baña, S., Massobrio, R.: A distributed platform for big data analysis in smart cities: combining intelligent transportation systems and socioeconomic data for Montevideo, Uruguay. EAI Endorsed Trans. Smart Cities 2(5), 320–347 (2017)
16. Nesmachnow, S., Iturriaga, S.: Cluster-UY: collaborative scientific high performance computing in Uruguay. In: Torres, M., Klapp, J. (eds.) ISUM 2019. CCIS, vol. 1151, pp. 188–202. Springer, Cham (2019). https://doi.org/10.1007/978-3-030-38043-4_16
17. Nesmachnow, S., Muraña, J., Goñi, G., Massobrio, R., Tchernykh, A.: Evolutionary approach for bus synchronization. In: Crespo-Mariño, J.L., Meneses-Rojas, E. (eds.) CARLA 2019. CCIS, vol. 1087, pp. 320–336. Springer, Cham (2020). https://doi.org/10.1007/978-3-030-41005-6_22
18. Nesmachnow, S., Risso, C.: Exact and evolutionary algorithms for synchronization of public transportation timetables considering extended transfer zones. Appl. Sci. 11(15), 7138 (2021)
19. Rodrigue, J.: The Geography of Transport Systems. Routledge, London (2020)
20. Sharma, N., Shamkuwar, M.: Big data analysis in cloud and machine learning. In: Mittal, M., Balas, V.E., Goyal, L.M., Kumar, R. (eds.) Big Data Processing Using Spark in Cloud. SBD, vol. 43, pp. 51–85. Springer, Singapore (2019). https://doi.org/10.1007/978-981-13-0550-4_3
21. Targio, I., et al.: The role of big data in smart city. Int. J. Inf. Manag. 36(5), 748–758 (2016)
22. Wang, F., Hu, L., Zhou, D., Sun, R., Hu, J., Zhao, K.: Estimating online vacancies in real-time road traffic monitoring with traffic sensor data stream. Ad Hoc Netw. 35, 3–13 (2015)
23. Widhalm, P., Yang, Y., Ulm, M., Athavale, S., González, M.C.: Discovering urban activity patterns in cell phone data. Transportation 42(4), 597–623 (2015). https://doi.org/10.1007/s11116-015-9598-x
24. Winter, H., Serra, J., Nesmachnow, S., Tchernykh, A., Shepelev, V.: Computational intelligence for analysis of traffic data. In: Smart Cities, pp. 167–182 (2021)

25. Yuan, J., Zheng, Y., Xie, X., Sun, G.: Driving with knowledge from the physical world. In: Proceedings of the 17th ACM SIGKDD International Conference on Knowledge Discovery and Data Mining, KDD 2011, pp. 316–324. Association for Computing Machinery, New York (2011)
26. Zhou, L., Chen, N., Chen, Z.: Efficient streaming mass spatio-temporal vehicle data access in urban sensor networks based on Apache Storm. Sensors **17**(4), 815 (2017)

Using Open Data to Analyze Public Bus Service from an Age Perspective: Melilla Case

Jamal Toutouh[1] , Irene Lebrusán[2] , and Christian Cintrano[1(✉)]

[1] University of Málaga, Málaga, Spain
{jamal,cintrano}@lcc.uma.es
[2] GISMAT, University Complutense of Madrid, Madrid, Spain
ilebrusan@ucm.es

Abstract. The increase in life expectancy is undoubtedly a social achievement. If we want an inclusive and integrating society, the inclusion of the age perspective is key when planning the city and its services. Accordingly, this is reflected in the Sustainable Development Goals (SDGs), especially in SDG 11.2, which aims to provide and expand access to public transport with special attention to the needs of the elderly. In general, the data required to evaluate public transportation is managed by the bus operators and/or other entities that decide whether (or not) to share it. This hardnesses the independent evaluation of the bus service by third-party stakeholders. Thus, this article aims to objectively assess the bus network's quality of service, relying exclusively on available socio-demographic and mobility open data, highlighting the elderly as target users in the city of Melilla (Spain). The open data available allowed the computation of indicators, such as journey times estimation or bus stop distribution to evaluate the universality in access to public transport. However, it has been noted that the lack of available data prevents the calculation of other age-friendly indicators. The main result of this research is that bus service provides a considerable reduction in journey times for the elderly than for non-elderly.

Keywords: Open data · Public transport · Bus service · Elderly

1 Introduction

The most commonly used mean of transportation in modern cities is the private vehicle, which is causing major environmental problems [9]. The noise and polluting gases associated with road transportation are having a direct impact on people's health [24,33]. According to the European Commission, air pollution is the principal health hazard for European citizens [12]. Besides, according to the European Environment Agency, exposure to high noise levels generates a health risk, causing some 12,100 premature deaths per year on the continent [13].

Reducing road traffic in urban areas is a relevant issue, which can be addressed by improving the quality of public transport system, such as urban

© Springer Nature Switzerland AG 2022
S. Nesmachnow and L. Hernández Callejo (Eds.): ICSC-Cities 2021, CCIS 1555, pp. 223–239, 2022.
https://doi.org/10.1007/978-3-030-96753-6_16

buses [15]. It is necessary to have a public transport network that allows moving along the urban areas minimizing the use of private transport. However, citizens often perceive the bus service as unreliable, with unpredictable travel times and schedules [5].

Different studies have been published identifying causes that impact the quality of the public urban bus system, such as poor design. The quality of bus service can be measured in terms of travel time, frequency, passenger comfort, price, and vehicle safety [4,8,18,28]. Besides, providing a high quality, efficient, and effective bus service is a very complex problem. Thus, several authors have applied computational intelligence to bus network/service design [14,20,22,30,32].

Open data is becoming essential in the development of Smart Cities [1]. Open data allows the evaluation of different aspects of the city and the quality of life of its inhabitants [23–25]. Besides, it can be used to design applications that assist both citizens and managers to improve dwellers life [3,11]. This paper explores the use of open data to perform an independent evaluation of the bus service in a city, focusing on elderly citizens' perspective. The case of study is Melilla in Spain. Our main motivation is that having a high quality bus system positively impacts on the relationship between the elderly and the urban spaces [26].

The main contributions of this work are: *i)* selecting and proposing a set of indicators to evaluate the quality of bus service that only rely on available open data, *ii)* analyzing the public bus service in Melilla with special emphasis on the service provided to the elderly, and iii) pointing out the main issues faced on performing the bus network evaluation using only open data.

The rest of this manuscript is organized as follows. Next section explores the importance of public transport to remain independent and participate in society for the elderly, as well as the international compromise to do so. Section 3 introduces the context of the use case taken into account in this paper, the city of Melilla and the public bus service provided there. Section 4 presents the materials and methods applied in the analysis of the bus service. Section 5 evaluates the public bus transport service according to the shared open data. Section 6 discusses the main limitations of this study due to the open data scarcity. Finally, Sect. 7 presents the conclusions and the main lines of future work.

2   Towards Inclusive Aging: Public Transport Matters

Access to public transport is key to the establishment of social connections, especially of fundamental age-related connections during old age [34] contributing to maintaining independence when age-related constraints make driving difficult in later life. However, the prioritization of the use of public vehicles over public transport is one of the problems detected in the process of integrated aging in our cities [26,27] which can limit social interactions and have negative consequences on their health [2] and may even produce undesired mobility (expulsion) from the urban area in which they wish to live [26].

These issues, and especially the need to pay attention to public transport from an age perspective, have begun to receive attention in international agreements: The 2030 Agenda for Sustainable Development established the importance of transport to make cities and human settlements inclusive, safe, resilient, and sustainable (Goal 11), pointing specifically that by 2030, cities should provide access to safe, affordable, accessible and sustainable transport systems for all, improving road safety, notably by expanding public transport, with special attention to the needs of those in vulnerable situations, women, children, people with disabilities and elderly (target 11.2).

3   Use Case: Public Bus Service in Melilla

This section introduces the use case of this study: Melilla city in Spain and the public bus network provided in the city.

3.1   Melilla City

The city of Melilla is the smallest autonomous territory in extension of Spain with a surface of $12\,km^2$ and a population of 87076 inhabitants in the year 2020. These numbers make its population density (6035 inhabitants per square kilometer) superior to population densities of cities like Madrid (5518 people per square kilometer). This is especially relevant in Spain with low density (national average of 91.4 inhabitants per square kilometer) [16].

Melilla is located in the north of Morocco (Africa). It is bordered by Morocco (by land) and by the Alboran Sea. The administrative division is composed of eight districts, 25 neighborhoods and 35 census segments. Figure 1 shows the location of the districts and their segments.

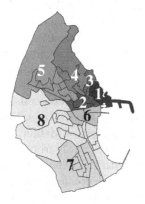

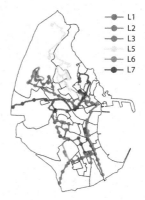

Fig. 1. Location of the districts and sections in Melilla.

Fig. 2. Bus stops and lines distributed through the city.

Table 1 summarizes the main socioeconomic variables taken into account in this study. The metrics are aggregated by district because we have not been able to access to the same in other resolution (i.e., grouped by census segments). The table shows the area, the number of houses (housing), the number of inhabitants (population), the ratio of elderly population, i.e., citizens with age greater than 65, (elderly ratio), and the number of inhabitants per km^2 (pop. density)

If we analyze the ratio between the number of people over 65 and the number of people under 16 in provincial capitals and/or municipalities with more than 50,000 inhabitants, Melilla is the second city in Spain with the lowest aging ratio (44.05% compared to 254.43% in El Ferrol and a national average of 129.17%).

Table 1. Socioeconomic data evaluated per district (# indicates *number of*).

District id	Area (km^2)	Housing (# houses)	Population (# people)	Elderly ratio (% of elderly)	Pop. density (people/km^2)	Poverty ratio (% of people)
1	0.30	770	3117	11.3	10390.0	34.4
2	0.46	1455	5517	16.8	11993.5	48.1
3	0.06	676	2744	13.7	45733.3	48.1
4	0.56	1665	8941	8.6	15966.1	50.1
5	1.14	3206	15484	8.6	13582.5	69.5
6	0.58	1113	4782	12.6	8244.8	34.3
7	1.46	2025	12943	9.5	8865.1	29.6
8	3.25	7016	30229	10.6	9301.2	17.1

3.2   Public Bus Service

Public passenger transport in Melilla is provided only by the taxi service (run by various private companies) and the public bus network provided by the *Cooperativa Omnibus de Autobuses* (COA). COA provides six urban bus lines, articulated by a fleet of 21 vehicles plus reserve vehicles for special needs.

Table 2 summarizes the data for the main bus service during the weekdays when the bus usage is the highest. The distance that the line travels (distance in kilometers), the number of installed bus stops (bus stops), and the frequency in terms of time between the departure from the first stop of two consecutive buses of the same line (bus departure frequency), and the service time. Figure 2 shows the bus lines and stops distribution along the districts of Melilla.

As Table 2 shows, COA offers six bus lines that operate mostly from 7:00 h to 22:00 h. Line L2, which connects the Central Market with the Benienzar Border, is the one that offers the highest frequency. Line L1, which connects the Central Market with Barrio Chino Border, is the longest route (it has 40 stops) and runs along the roads of districts 2, 6, 8, and 7. It should be noted that both L1 and L2 are mainly used by cross-border visitors that enter the city every day.

Table 2. Melilla bus service summary.

Line	Distance (km)	Bus stops	Bus departure frequency	Service time
L1	9.6	37	Every 20/30 min	7:00–22:00
L2	7.6	21	Every 10/15 min	7:00–22:00
L3	14.3	43	Every 20/30 min	7:00–22:00
L5	8.8	20	Every 30 min	7:00–22:00
L6	7.0	29	Every 40 min	7:00–22:00
L7	7.1	15	Every 15/20 min	7:00–21:00

Although Melilla is a small territory, the bus service suffers from deficiencies related to the regularity of service and accessibility of the buses (on which we have not obtained information). One of the biggest challenges is that the buses do not have their bus lanes, so the buses suffer from traffic jams during rush hour, which limits the quality of the bus service. This causes the vast majority of the population to opt for private transport (93%), with only 7% of the population using the bus service regularly [7].

The main aim of this paper is to evaluate the bus service provided by COA using open data. The idea is to become aware of how important it is to have this type of data available to get objective measures about the quality of the bus service, without having to conduct extensive user survey campaigns or employ expensive monitoring systems. In turn, this paper research on elderly citizens, a segment of the population in cities that is particularly vulnerable.

4   Materials and Methods

This section is organized as follows: first, it describes the open data used to perform the analysis of the public bus service of Melilla; second, it presents the metrics evaluated in study; and third, it introduces the methods applied to evaluate the metrics and the computational tools used.

4.1   Open Data Used to Evaluate the Public Bus Service of Melilla

When carrying out any study on mobility over a given city, it is necessary to have real data. Nowadays, municipalities have developed portals where they publish a multitude of open data. In addition to the official open data portals, there are several initiatives in which a community of users is responsible for collecting and publishing open data, e.g., Open Street Maps (OSM) [31]. We now describe the open data sources used in this research.

The data reported in Table 1 was obtained from the municipal census of the National Institute of Statistics and the open reports published by the European Network for the Fight against Poverty and Social Exclusion in Melilla [10]. The areas covered by the districts (and segments) in Melilla were obtained from the geographic information systems (GIS) provided by the National Institute of Statistics [17] (see Fig. 1). The information about the bus transport reported in Table 2 and Fig. 2 is freely available on the official website of COA [6].

There is no available open data on mobility (e.g., roads average speeds, pedestrian paths or affluence, etc.) or on bus network (e.g., the average time a bus needs to perform one whole cycle per bus line or the number of buses per line). This information would be handy for calculations on different bus mobility indicators. The OSM data was used to estimate several mobility metrics useful to compute the bus quality of service indicators to mitigate the lack of data.

4.2 Metrics Evaluated

This article aims to use open data to study the quality of service of the Melilla bus system, emphasizing the service provided to elderly users. Even though the indicators exist in the literature [18,28], they have been computed/estimated by relying only on available open data. The metrics evaluated are presented below:

- *Travel time*: It evaluates the travel time in minutes when the inhabitants travel between any pairs of census segments. Two travel times are computed: *a)* citizens move only by foot and *b)* the users use the public bus service.
- *Improvement when using public bus service*: It represents the reduction ratio in travel time required when using the bus service compared to walking.
- *Travel times difference between elderly and non-elderly*: It compares the travel times of these two types of citizens by computing the ratio of travel time increase of the elderly over non-elderly.
- *Walking distance during the bus trip*: It measures the length of the walking part of a bus trip. This distance includes walking from/to bus stops when starting and finishing the travel. But it also considers the walking required to perform bus transfers, if it is needed.
- *Bus stops density*: It is computed as the number of bus stops installed per square kilometer for each district. This metric allows studying the accessibility of the bus system. In turn, the bus stops density gives an overview of how effectively the bus network is distributed throughout the city.
- *Walking distance to the closest bus stop*: It measures how long (in meters) a citizen has to walk to access the bus network. This walking distance is important because it may impact the use of the bus system, especially for people with mobility difficulties, such as elderly people.

Travel time, bus stop density, and walking distance to the closest bus stop are metrics found in the literature. The improvements when using the bus, the travel times difference between elderly and non-elderly, and the walking distance during the bus trip have not been found in previous research works.

4.3 Methods and Tools for the Evaluation

Most of the evaluated metrics rely on the computation of routes between the segments. The lack of mobility data has motivated the development of a method to model the citizens' trips to estimate the required metrics for our analysis. The routes are computed between the centroids of all the census segments. There are two types of trips: *a)* on foot-only and *b)* getting on the bus. These computations rely on a graph created by using OSM data, which represent the whole city of Melilla including all the walking paths, roads, bus stop locations, etc.

When computing on foot-only trips, the street network of the city is modeled as an undirected graph (named walking graph), in which the edge weights represent the walking time between the nodes (i.e., computed as distance divided by walking speed). The pedestrian trips between two segments are modeled by selecting the shortest path between the centroids of the segments according to the Dijkstra algorithm (minimizing travel time). According to the literature, the walking speed is 1.25 meters per second (m/s) for non-elderly people, and the walking speed is 0.97 m/s for the elderly [19].

To compute the getting on the bus travel, new directional edges that link bus stops are added to the walking graph to represent the bus itinerary (named bus edges). The directionality of the bus edges depends on the direction in which the bus travels, and the weight is the trip time between the bus stops (the bus speed is considered 14.5 km/h [29]). Thus, the algorithm may select walking or bus edges when applying Dijkstra to compute the shortest path between the segments, considering the route by foot from/to the bus stop plus the journey using the bus. Besides, Dijkstra takes into account trips that the user may change the bus or even walk from a given bus stop to the other while on the move (to represent the case of bus transfer).

The bus travel times are affected by the number of bus stops (because they have to wait for passengers to get on or off) and by the frequency (i.e., the time between the departure of two consecutive buses) that impacts the waiting time to get on bus. Thus, the Dijkstra algorithm has been modified to add these times when computing the trips. Each bus stop during the journey adds a travel time of 30 s. This time value has been set after meetings with 12 bus drivers. Besides, every time the user has to get on the bus (either for starting the trip or transfer to another line), a random amount of time (modeled applying a Poisson process of intensity equal to the frequency of the bus line) is also added.

Figure 3 illustrates an example of how the trips are computed. The algorithm consider two trips (among others): *Trip 1* and *Trip 2*. On the one hand, the *Trip 1* time considers the walking time to the bus stop, the random waiting time to get on the bus, the bus trip time to the closest bus stop to the end of the trip, and the walking time from the bus stop to the end. On the other hand, the *Trip 2* time considers the time required to walk to the endpoint of the trip.

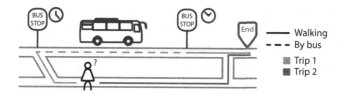

Fig. 3. An example of two trips to compute the routes.

The walking parts of the bus routes make the main difference between the non-elderly and elderly people computations. This is because the criterion applied by the devised method to select the trips minimizes the total required time without considering the path length. Thus, for the same origin and destination, there are cases that non-elderly do not use the bus service because they walk at enough speed to make the travel times shorter than when using the bus. Still, the elderly take the bus because their walking speed is slower.

In order to compute the bus stop density, the information about the polygons provided by the National Institute of Statistics and the information about the location of the buses is used.

The software required for the computations has been developed by using Python. The data analysis has been implemented using Numpy, scikit-learn, and Pandas. The GIS computations rely on Geopandas and Arcpy. Finally, the routes are computed by using libraries for working with graphs OSMnx and NetworkX.

5   Analysis

This section evaluates walking trips, analyzes bus travels, examines the bus stop distribution through the city.

5.1   Walking Through the City

This section evaluates the walking mobility in the city of Melilla. The main goal is to realize the importance of having a public bus transportation service, even for small-sized urban areas. Table 3 presents the mean and standard deviation (mean $\pm$ std) and maximum (max) of the length in meters and the times in min for the trips on foot between all census sections (grouped by district).

Table 3. Distances in meters between the districts and walking times in minutes.

District	Distance		Non-elderly walking time		Elderly walking time	
	mean $\pm$ std	max	mean $\pm$ std	max	mean $\pm$ std	max
1	2072.6 $\pm$ 849.3	4258.4	32.8 $\pm$ 14	69.5	42.2 $\pm$ 19	89.6
2	1589.9 $\pm$ 759.1	3680.5	26.6 $\pm$ 13	60.9	34.3 $\pm$ 17	78.5
3	1946.3 $\pm$ 902.0	4080.1	30.9 $\pm$ 15	67.3	39.8 $\pm$ 20	86.8
4	2278.9 $\pm$ 1073.5	5114.9	37.8 $\pm$ 18	80.0	48.7 $\pm$ 23	103.1
5	2274.5 $\pm$ 1080.2	5110.8	40.7 $\pm$ 19	92.8	52.4 $\pm$ 24	119.6
6	1606.4 $\pm$ 705.1	3721.4	27.5 $\pm$ 13	62.7	35.4 $\pm$ 16	80.9
7	2389.8 $\pm$ 1171.0	5043.7	41.0 $\pm$ 20	92.8	52.8 $\pm$ 26	119.6
8	1951.7 $\pm$ 936.2	5114.9	34.1 $\pm$ 16	82.2	44.0 $\pm$ 20	105.9

The inhabitants of district 7 are farthest away (longer walking distances with an average of 2389.8 m), and therefore need more time to move through the city. Districts 2 and 6 located in the city downtown (see Fig. 1) are those whose residents have the shortest walking distances, average distances of 1589.9 and 1606.4 m, respectively.

There is a remarkable difference in the walking times between elderly and non-elderly people, even for a small-sized city (see Table 3). The longest trips are the ones between district 5 and district 7, which are the most separated peripheral ones (see Fig. 1). The non-elderly citizens require up to 92.8 min to walk between these two districts. The elderly need up to almost two hours for the exact travel (119.6 min).

According to the walking speed considered, elderly people require 22.39% longer times to travel between the census sections. Thus, one would expect the bus service to provide competitive solutions to mitigate this travel time difference with non-elderly while reducing the walking distances.

5.2 Travel Times When Using the Bus Service

This section discusses the quality of bus service in terms of travel time improvement compared to walking. Thus, the travel time using bus transport between all the census sections of the city is estimated for both non-elderly and elderly users by using the method presented in Sect. 4.3. The trip through the city considers *walking-bus multi-modal* and bus transfers, i.e., the user can walk, get on a bus, walk again and get on another bus at another stop, etc. The simulated bus users select the route to minimize the travel time over all possible combinations that may exist from the origin to the destination (including walking to/from several different bus stops, using various bus lines, etc.).

Tables 4 and 5 presents the travel times between all the sections of the city in terms of mean and standard deviation (mean ± std) grouped by districts. These two tables are non-symmetric because parts of the bus trips are carried out through different (one-way) roads depending on the direction of the line.

Table 4. Bus travel times between districts in min for the non-elderly (mean ± std).

Dest.	Origin							
	1	2	3	4	5	6	7	8
1	15.4 ± 0	20.8 ± 8	13.0 ± 7	27.7 ± 8	29.1 ± 4	27.3 ± 3	31.6 ± 4	32.1 ± 8
2	22.9 ± 6	20.3 ± 1	19.1 ± 6	26.0 ± 4	23.4 ± 3	22.4 ± 2	26.9 ± 3	27.0 ± 8
3	16.0 ± 9	19.1 ± 6	3.8 ± 0	21.4 ± 10	25.1 ± 3	23.5 ± 2	28.2 ± 3	27.9 ± 8
4	29.3 ± 7	26.0 ± 4	23.3 ± 9	26.2 ± 5	26.8 ± 6	28.2 ± 5	32.9 ± 5	32.6 ± 9
5	30.4 ± 3	24.1 ± 2	26.6 ± 2	27.8 ± 6	24.0 ± 6	27.2 ± 2	32.0 ± 4	31.7 ± 8
6	25.3 ± 8	20.3 ± 4	24.0 ± 2	27.6 ± 5	25.5 ± 3	18.9 ± 9	27.5 ± 4	26.9 ± 10
7	32.8 ± 4	27.1 ± 3	29.0 ± 3	32.2 ± 5	29.8 ± 4	27.7 ± 4	16.8 ± 10	29.4 ± 8
8	32.5 ± 8	26.7 ± 8	28.7 ± 8	32.6 ± 9	30.7 ± 9	27.2 ± 9	29.5 ± 8	29.2 ± 13

Table 5. Bus travel times between districts in min for the elderly (mean $\pm$ std).

Dest.	Origin							
	1	2	3	4	5	6	7	8
1	19.9 ± 0	23.6 ± 8	19.1 ± 10	33.5 ± 7	32.3 ± 4	30.5 ± 4	34.8 ± 5	36.2 ± 11
2	25.6 ± 6	21.7 ± 1	20.6 ± 6	28.4 ± 5	25.1 ± 3	24.1 ± 2	28.6 ± 4	29.5 ± 10
3	18.3 ± 9	20.6 ± 6	4.8 ± 0	26.1 ± 10	27.2 ± 4	25.5 ± 3	30.3 ± 4	30.7 ± 10
4	33.1 ± 7	28.3 ± 5	25.9 ± 10	33.4 ± 5	29.9 ± 6	30.9 ± 6	36.7 ± 7	36.1 ± 11
5	33.8 ± 4	25.9 ± 3	28.8 ± 3	30.6 ± 7	26.4 ± 6	29.5 ± 3	34.3 ± 4	34.7 ± 10
6	28.6 ± 8	22.2 ± 4	26.1 ± 2	30.5 ± 6	27.7 ± 4	21.1 ± 10	29.7 ± 5	30.7 ± 11
7	36.2 ± 5	29.1 ± 4	31.2 ± 4	35.1 ± 6	32.0 ± 5	30.0 ± 5	19.1 ± 11	32.5 ± 11
8	36.5 ± 11	29.4 ± 10	31.5 ± 10	36.3 ± 12	33.7 ± 11	30.1 ± 11	32.6 ± 11	32.9 ± 16

Results in Tables 4 and 5 show that in general, there is an improvement (travel time reduction) when the citizen uses the bus to travel through the city. The maximum mean travel time occurs when the users move from district 7 to district 4, which is 32.9 min and 36.7 min for non-elderly and elderly, respectively.

Focusing on the trips between districts 5 and 7 (which represent the furthest districts), there is a significant reduction in the travel time when the bus is taken. For example, elderly users go down from requiring 83.8 min to walk from district 5 to district 7 to only 32.0 min, which implies a time reduction of 62%.

In order to have a global view of the quality of service (in terms of travel time improvements regarding walking time) provided by the public bus transport, Table 6 summarizes the bus trip time and the percentage of travel time reduction (i.e., the improvement) by showing the mean and standard deviation (mean $\pm$ std) and maximum (max) values, for non-elderly and elderly people.

Table 6. Travel times between districts when the citizens use the bus (in min) and the time reduction (% of improvement) regarding the same trip by foot.

District	Non-elderly users				Elderly users			
	Travel time		Improvement (%)		Travel time		Improvement (%)	
	mean $\pm$ std	max	mean $\pm$ std	max	mean $\pm$ std	max	mean $\pm$ std	max
1	27.7 ± 9	63.1	12.9 ± 14	47.6	31.9 ± 10	76.0	20.3 ± 17	56.1
2	22.3 ± 8	55.1	12.9 ± 17	48.5	25.6 ± 9	67.6	20.6 ± 20	57.6
3	24.4 ± 8	58.2	17.1 ± 17	52.9	27.5 ± 9	69.8	25.5 ± 20	61.4
4	28.5 ± 9	69.8	20.7 ± 19	58.1	32.4 ± 10	83.3	28.7 ± 21	65.3
5	27.7 ± 7	65.7	30.7 ± 22	66.9	30.7 ± 9	78.4	39.3 ± 22	73.2
6	23.8 ± 8	58.7	11.6 ± 15	50.5	27.4 ± 9	70.1	19.1 ± 18	59.5
7	29.1 ± 6	61.5	30.4 ± 20	60.9	32.2 ± 8	79.2	39.3 ± 21	67.8
8	28.5 ± 9	68.5	17.8 ± 17	57.9	32.3 ± 11	81.8	26.9 ± 19	65.4

Table 6 shows that trips from peripheral districts (i.e., districts 5 and 7) are the ones that reduce travel times the most. For example, elderly mean improvements for districts 5 and 7 are 30.7% and 30.4%, respectively. In contrast, trips from districts 1, 2, and 6 (located in the city's downtown) reduce the travel times least. This lower travel time improvement is mainly because their geographical location makes that moving by foot requires less than 35 min on average.

Figure 4 illustrates the percentage of travel time reduction when using the bus services to travel between all the census sections in a heat map. Darker blues represent higher reductions. The labels in the ticks of the x-axis and y-axis are different. But the two axes have the same ticks and are symmetrical, i.e. the x-axis represents the same census segments as the y-axis. The black axis tick labels represent the segment ids, while the bold red labels the district ids.

In general, when comparing Fig. 4a (non-elderly users) against Fig. 4b (elderly users), the second one shows darker blue, which indicates more improvements (higher time reduction). There is not any cell in the heat-map in Fig. 4a that contains a darker blue than the same cell in the heat map Fig. 4b. Besides, two dark areas (located at the left-bottom and right-top) represent the improvements when travelling between the census segments in the district 5 and 7.

The results in Fig. 4 are in line with the improvement columns in Table 6. The quality of the bus service in terms of travel time reductions is higher for the elderly users and for travelling between the peripheral districts.

When comparing the improvements in Table 6, it is observed that elderly citizens reduce their travel times more than non-elderly ones. The mean time reductions are 29.90% and 21.41% for elderly and non-elderly, respectively. This is a significant outcome because the bus network is expected to improve the most those users who have more limitations getting around the city. Focusing

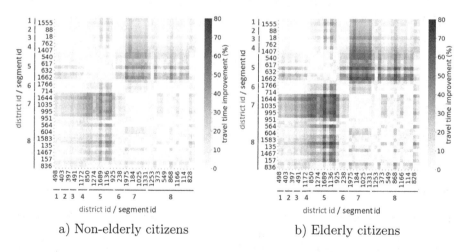

a) Non-elderly citizens   b) Elderly citizens

Fig. 4. Travel time improvements on trips between city sections. (Color figure online)

on elderly, districts 7, 5, and 4 show the most significant improvements, which are the districts with the lowest elderly ratio in the city.

Table 7 presents the percentage of additional time required by the elderly citizens to move from a given district regarding the same by the non-elderly people when both types of evaluated users take the bus. According to the results in Sect. 5.1, elderly people require 22.39% longer times to walk among the census segments than the non-elderly. The results in Table 7 show that percentage is significantly reduced when the bus system is used. On average, when the bus is taken elderly spend 9.97% longer times than non-elderly. Thus, it can be seen that the improvements over the travel time when using the bus network mitigate the mobility differences between the travel times of the two types of users studied.

Table 7. Travel time difference between non-elderly and elderly users when using the bus (percentage of additional time required by the elderly).

District	1	2	3	4	5	6	7	8
Time difference	12.2%	9.0%	11.3%	12.2%	9.4%	9.2%	8.4%	10.3%

Focusing on the walking part of the trip, it has been observed that elderly users select routes that require walking shorter distances than non-elderly. Table 8 presents the percentage of reduction of the length traveled on foot of the elderly over non-elderly users grouped by the origin district of the route.

Table 8. Length of the walking part difference between non-elderly and elderly when using the bus (reduction percentage of the walking distance by the elderly).

District	1	2	3	4	5	6	7	8
Walking distance reduction	2.3%	3.9%	3.8%	3.1%	6.4%	2.1%	2.1%	1.0%

Thus, results in Tables 7 and 8 show that the bus system mitigates the differences in travel times that exist between non-elderly and elderly citizens while offering more comfortable routes (i.e., needing shorter walks) to the elderly.

5.3 Bus Stops Distribution

The distribution of the bus stops has a direct impact on the distance users have to walk to get the bus network, travel times (more stops longer times because the buses stop more often), and the cost of operations (more stops increases costs) [14,32]. This section is focused on the first aspect of the bus stop distribution, the walking distance because it is essential for elderly users.

Table 9 shows that as the districts increase in size (see Table 1), the number of bus stops installed in them also increases. Pearson's correlation analysis confirms this statement with a resulting correlation of 0.86 (i.e., high correlation). A similar correlation can be seen between the number of inhabitants of the districts and the number of stops installed, obtaining a Pearson coefficient of 0.91 (i.e., high correlation). This may lead us to realize better access to the bus system in the larger and more populated districts. However, considering elderly people (i.e., the number of elderly citizens in the district) and the density of bus stops, the Pearson coefficient is -0.02, which indicates that the distribution of the bus stops does not take into account where the elderly population of Melilla live.

Table 9 summarizes the bus stop distribution by including the number of bus stops per square kilometer for each district and the distance in meters to the closest bus stops for all the segments for each district.

Table 9. Density of bus stops and walking distance to the closest stop (meters).

District id	Bus stops per km^2	Distance to the closest bus stop		
		mean $\pm$ std	min	max
1	0.0	489.7 $\pm$ 205.6	284.1	695.3
2	34.8	131.2 $\pm$ 49.6	62.5	178.1
3	16.7	197.7 $\pm$ 133.2	64.4	330.9
4	26.8	339.5 $\pm$ 243.1	132.5	748.2
5	24.6	176.5 $\pm$ 125.5	24.2	456.1
6	10.3	231.4 $\pm$ 85.8	127.4	337.6
7	17.8	201.3 $\pm$ 51.8	121.5	299.8
8	11.1	354.1 $\pm$ 466.6	89.5	424.4

There is significant variability in the density of bus stops installed in the different districts (see Table 9). District 1 has no bus stops, and district 2 has 34.8 bus stops per km^2. Thus, when the citizens of district 1 need to take a bus have to walk about 500 m to find the closest bus stop (district 1 is the smallest district with the lowest population size). However, inhabitants of district 2 need to walk only 131 m. This is because district 2 is located in the city's downtown, and most bus lines operate through the downtown.

Considering this quality of service metric, the peripheral districts (districts 5 and 7) are ranked in the middle with 24.6 and 17.8 bus stops per km^2. However, this does not affect travel times, because as it has been discussed in Sect. 5.2, they are the districts with the most significant improvement when using the bus.

6   Analysis Limitations Due to Lack of Open Data

This research tries to propose evaluating the public bus system in a city from an age perspective based solely and exclusively on open data. The idea is to show the results and the challenges found when carrying out this independent analysis by third parties (other than the concessionary bus company itself or the public bodies involved that manage valuable information about the bus service).

A comprehensive assessment of the bus network would require metrics and indicators such as comfort, cleanliness, and crowding of the bus, ease of access stops, noise, vibration, and temperature on the bus, security against crimes on the bus and at stops, among others [28]. However, these indicators usually are private or difficult to calculate. The indicators selected in this article have the particularity of using only open data (one of the objectives of this study) rather than private or on-site collected data [18].

The evaluation presented in Sect. 5 has been performed by using data found on various websites (e.g., the COA official website) and official reports (e.g., the census of the National Institute of Statistics), but anything from official open data portals. This absence of data on official portals shows the lack of concern of public institutions for making relevant information about public transport available to citizens, which limits the task of an independent evaluation.

Estimating travel times and distances rely on the calculation of routes (on foot and by bus), which suffer from the lack of information on urban mobility (e.g., speeds at which buses move in different situations, use of private transport in the city, what are the most common mobility patterns of citizens, etc.). Therefore, a method for route estimation had to be implemented (see Sect. 4.3). The accuracy of the method is limited because it considers that the buses and citizens move with constant speed, the time waiting for the next bus is modeled by using Poisson processes, the time stop time does not depend on the bus stop or the hour of the day, etc. Besides, the indicators computations consider all possible trips between any census segments for the computations of the indicators. Having information on the mobility and affluence (e.g., most typical trips) would allow the weighting of trips by importance to provide a fairer indicator evaluation. Therefore, incorporating new real data and using a realistic urban simulator such as SUMO [21] may improve the computation of these indicators.

Incorporating information on the distances users are willing to walk to get a bus would allow knowing if there are disconnected users. Getting data on the bus service fares and the cost of operating the bus system would allow an economic evaluation of the system by getting information on the costs of using the service and the efficiency of the service maintenance. Finally, knowing whether buses are adapted for users with special needs (such as the elderly) would improve the evaluation of the system from an aging perspective.

7   Conclusion and Future Work

This work is motivated by the need to provide an efficient and effective public bus system that represents an alternative to private transport, emphasizing the service provided to the elderly because public transport allows independence, enhances well-being, and improves their relationship with urban spaces. Specifically, we analyze the case of Melilla. The main aim is to perform an objective and independent assessment of the bus network relying only on available open data. Thus, the main limitations of such analysis because of the lack of valuable open data have been discussed.

According to the results, the public bus service reduces travel times more for the elderly than non-elderly. This reduction in trip times is higher for districts with the lowest elderly ratio. In turn, it has been shown that the bus system mitigates the differences in travel times between non-elderly and elderly citizens while offering more comfortable routes (i.e., needing shorter walks). However, the distribution of the bus stops does not consider the areas where the most elderly people live, making the elderly have to walk long distances to reach the nearest bus stop. These results indicate that the bus service of Melilla provides a competitive service, but a new distribution of bus stops (or lines) may improve the service with an aging perspective.

The limitation of the proposed study due to the scarcity of open data dictates some of the future research lines. These future works include: *i)* including socioeconomic aspects, bus fares, and cost of operating to extend the analysis; *ii)* considering a collaboration with other stakeholders (such as the COA bus company) to get new (not-open) data such as the types of buses, the bus mobility, the influx on the different bus lines, the number of buses per line, etc. to include new indicators; *iii)* getting information about the location of the most used facilities and ordinary trips of elderly for social/recreational reasons to evaluate the service provided to that specific travels; *iv)* taking into account mobility limitations to find possible disconnected passengers; and *v)* using SUMO urban simulator to improve the accuracy of the evaluated travels.

Acknowledgments. The research of J. Toutouh and C. Cintrano is partially funded by the Universidad de Málaga and MCIN/AEI/10.13039/501100011033 under grant number PID 2020-116727RB-I00 (HUmove).

References

1. Barns, S.: Smart cities and urban data platforms: designing interfaces for smart governance. City Cult. Soc. **12**, 5–12 (2018)
2. Buffel, T., Phillipson, C., Scharf, T.: Ageing in urban environments: developing 'age-friendly' cities. Crit. Soc. Policy **32**(4), 597–617 (2012)
3. Camero, A., Toutouh, J., Stolfi, D.H., Alba, E.: Evolutionary deep learning for car park occupancy prediction in smart cities. In: Battiti, R., Brunato, M., Kotsireas, I., Pardalos, P.M. (eds.) LION 12 2018. LNCS, vol. 11353, pp. 386–401. Springer, Cham (2019). https://doi.org/10.1007/978-3-030-05348-2_32
4. Carrion, C., Levinson, D.: Value of travel time reliability: a review of current evidence. Transp. Res. Part A Policy Pract. **46**(4), 720–741 (2012)
5. Chen, X., Yu, L., Zhang, Y., Guo, J.: Analyzing urban bus service reliability at the stop, route, and network levels. Transp. Res. Part A Policy Pract. **43**(8), 722–734 (2009)
6. COA Melilla: Cooperativa Omnibus de Autobuses de Melilla (2021). https://coamelilla.com/. Accessed 05 Jan 2021

7. Conserjería de Medio Ambiente y Sostenibilidad, Ciudad autónoma de Melilla: El sistema de transporte público de Melilla (2020). https://medioambientemelilla.es/el-sistema-de-transporte-publico/

8. Diab, E.I., Badami, M.G., El-Geneidy, A.M.: Bus transit service reliability and improvement strategies: integrating the perspectives of passengers and transit agencies in North America. Transp. Rev. **35**(3), 292–328 (2015)

9. Dirección General de Tráfico (DGT): El impacto medioambiental del tráfico (2014). https://www.dgt.es/PEVI/documentos/catalogo_recursos/didacticos/did_adultas/impacto.pdf

10. EAPN Melilla: Red Europea de Lucha contra la Pobreza y la Exclusión Social en Melilla (2021). https://eapnmelilla.wordpress.com/. Accessed 05 Jan 2021

11. Estrada, E., Maciel, R., Peña Pérez Negrón, A., López Lara, G., Larios, V., Ochoa, A.: Framework for the analysis of smart cities models. In: Mejia, J., Muñoz, M., Rocha, Á., Peña, A., Pérez-Cisneros, M. (eds.) CIMPS 2018. AISC, vol. 865, pp. 261–269. Springer, Cham (2019). https://doi.org/10.1007/978-3-030-01171-0_24

12. European Environment Agency: Noise pollution is a major environmental health concern in europe. Collection - Environment and health (2018). https://www.eea.europa.eu/themes/human/noise/noise-2

13. European Environment Agency: Health risks caused by environmental noise in Europe (2020). https://www.eea.europa.eu/publications/health-risks-caused-by-environmental

14. Fabbiani, E., Nesmachnow, S., Toutouh, J., Tchernykh, A., Avetisyan, A., Radchenko, G.: Analysis of mobility patterns for public transportation and bus stops relocation. Program. Comput. Softw. **44**(6), 508–525 (2018)

15. González, F., Valdivieso, V., De Grange, L., Troncoso, R.: Impact of the dedicated infrastructure on bus service quality: an empirical analysis. Appl. Econ. **51**(55), 5961–5971 (2019)

16. Instituto Nacional de Estadística: Padrón, población por municipios (2021). https://www.ine.es. Accessed 05 Jan 2021

17. Instituto Nacional de Estadística (INE): Melilla: Población por municipios y sexo (2020). https://www.ine.es/jaxiT3/Datos.htm?t=2909

18. Jomnonkwao, S., Ratanavaraha, V.: Measurement modelling of the perceived service quality of a sightseeing bus service: an application of hierarchical confirmatory factor analysis. Transp. Policy **45**, 240–252 (2016)

19. Knoblauch, R.L., Pietrucha, M.T., Nitzburg, M.: Field studies of pedestrian walking speed and start-up time. Transp. Res. Rec. **1538**(1), 27–38 (1996)

20. Köksal Ahmed, E., Li, Z., Veeravalli, B., Ren, S.: Reinforcement learning-enabled genetic algorithm for school bus scheduling. J. Intell. Transp. Syst., 1–19 (2020)

21. Krajzewicz, D.: Traffic simulation with sumo-simulation of urban mobility. In: Barceló, J. (ed.) Fundamentals of Traffic Simulation. International Series in Operations Research & Management Science, vol. 145, pp. 269–293. Springer, New York (2010). https://doi.org/10.1007/978-1-4419-6142-6_7

22. Kumar, A., Srikanth, P., Nayyar, A., Sharma, G., Krishnamurthi, R., Alazab, M.: A novel simulated-annealing based electric bus system design, simulation, and analysis for Dehradun Smart City. IEEE Access **8**, 89395–89424 (2020)

23. Lebrusán, I., Toutouh, J.: Car restriction policies for better urban health: a low emission zone in Madrid, Spain. AQAH **14**, 333–342 (2020)

24. Lebrusán, I., Toutouh, J.: Using smart city tools to evaluate the effectiveness of a low emissions zone in Spain: Madrid central. Smart Cities **3**(2), 456–478 (2020)

25. Lebrusán, I., Toutouh, J.: Smart city tools to evaluate age-healthy environments. In: Nesmachnow, S., Hernández Callejo, L. (eds.) ICSC-CITIES 2020. CCIS, vol. 1359, pp. 285–301. Springer, Cham (2021). https://doi.org/10.1007/978-3-030-69136-3_20
26. Lebrusán Murillo, I.: La vivienda en la vejez: problemas y estrategias para envejecer en sociedad. La vivienda en la vejez, pp. 1–243 (2019)
27. Lebrusán Murillo, I.: Las dificultades para habitar en la vejez. Documentación Social 1(1), 1 (2020)
28. Mahmoud, M., Hine, J.: Measuring the influence of bus service quality on the perception of users. Transp. Plan. Technol. 39(3), 284–299 (2016)
29. Nesmachnow, S., et al.: Traffic lights synchronization for bus rapid transit using a parallel evolutionary algorithm. Int. J. Transp. Sci. Technol. 8(1), 53–67 (2019)
30. Nguyen, T., Nguyen-Phuoc, D.Q., Wong, Y.D.: Developing artificial neural networks to estimate real-time onboard bus ride comfort. Neural Comput. Appl. 33(10), 5287–5299 (2020). https://doi.org/10.1007/s00521-020-05318-3
31. OpenStreetMap contributors: Planet dump retrieved from https://planet.osm.org. https://www.openstreetmap.org (2017)
32. Rossit, D.G., Nesmachnow, S., Toutouh, J.: Multiobjective design of sustainable public transportation systems. In: 1st International Workshop on Advanced Information and Computation Technologies and Systems, pp. 152–159. CEUR-WS (2021)
33. Soni, N., Soni, N.: Benefits of pedestrianization and warrants to pedestrianize an area. Land Use Policy 57, 139–150 (2016)
34. Walters, P., Bartlett, H.: Growing old in a new estate: establishing new social networks in retirement. Ageing Soc. 29(2), 217–236 (2009)

Hybrid GRASP+VND for Flexible Vehicle Routing in Smart Cities

Lucía Barrero, Rodrigo Viera, Franco Robledo, Claudio Risso[⊠],
and Sergio Nesmachnow

Universidad de la República, Montevideo, Uruguay
{lucia.barrero,rodrigo.viera,frobledo,crisso,sergion}@fing.edu.uy

Abstract. This article presents a metaheuristic resolution approach for a variant of the Vehicle Routing Problem considering heterogeneous fleet and flexible time windows. This problem variant solved considers extended time windows for delivering products to customers, modeling a realistic situation for logistics in smart cities. The proposed metaheuristic follows an hybrid approach, combining well known search procedures. Accurate results are reported for problem instances built by extending existing benchmarks in the literature. The proposed model is competitive with previous results and was able to compute better solutions in ten problem instances.

Keywords: Smart logistics · Vehicle routing · Smart cities

1 Introduction

Vehicle routing is a classical optimization problem that has received a renewed interest due to the importance of logistics for the new Industry 4.0 paradigm. The capabilities of providing supply chains with accurate, coordinated, real-time tool for vehicle scheduling and routing is very relevant for acquiring decisive advantages on supply chain management and business [3,5].

The term Vehicle Routing Problem (VRP) embraces a whole class of problems aimed at determining a set of routes for a fleet of vehicles that must visit and deliver products to a set of customers. The main goal of the problem is computing a minimum cost routing schedule for each vehicle to deliver products to customers according to their demands, operation times, and other constraints [8].

VRP is among the most studied combinatorial optimization problems in operations research. Unlike other traditional combinatorial optimization problems, like the Traveling Salesman Problem (TSP), where exact solvers can be applied to optimally solve instances with thousand of customers, the VRP is intrinsically more complex, as instances with more than one hundred customers can be hard to solve [1].

This article focuses on a specific variant of the VRP that considers flexible time windows for delivering goods to customers. The flexibility allows modeling

© Springer Nature Switzerland AG 2022
S. Nesmachnow and L. Hernández Callejo (Eds.): ICSC-Cities 2021, CCIS 1555, pp. 240–255, 2022.
https://doi.org/10.1007/978-3-030-96753-6_17

realistic scenarios and problem instances that account for situations where it is preferable for the route planner to use a reduced number of vehicles, even paying a penalization for late arrivals in certain customers.

In this line of work, this article presents an hybrid metaheuristic approach combining Greedy Randomized Adaptive Search Procedure (GRASP) and Variable Neighborhood Search (VNS) for solving the VRP with heterogeneous fleet and flexible time windows. The experimental evaluation of the proposed model is performed on realistic problem instances, specifically designed by extending existing VRP benchmarks from literature.

Accurate results are reported for the proposed hybrid metaheuristic model. Despite applying a simple pattern for exploration and exploitation of the search space, the combination of GRASP and VNS computed comparable results with baseline methods in the related literature, and improved existing results in ten problem instances.

The article is organized as follows. Section 2 describes the flexible vehicle routing problem in smart cities and presents its mathematical formulation. Section 3 summarizes relevant related works. Section 4 describes the hybrid algorithmic approach to solve the problem combining GRASP and VND. Section 5 reports the experimental evaluation on standard scenarios and problem instances. Finally, Sect. 6 presents the conclusions and formulate the main lines for future work.

2   Flexible Vehicle Routing in Smart Cities

This section describes the flexible vehicle routing problem and presents its mathematical formulation.

2.1   Problem Description

The proposed problem is a specific variant of the VRP considering time windows for deliveries and heterogeneous vehicles (i.e., vehicles with different transportation capacities) [7]. The main goal is to compute solutions that minimize the cost, the objective function of the problem which is related to the time needed to deliver the products to all customers.

The proposed problem variant relax the standard formulation by considering *flexible* time windows. Flexible time windows operates as follows: i) early arrivals (i.e., before the start of the time window for a customer) are penalized by adding the waiting time to the cost function, whereas ii) late arrivals (i.e., after the end of the time window for a customer) are allowed within a certain tolerance, and a penalty is added to the cost function in order to take into account the extra time (after the end of the time window). Introducing flexible time window provides the studied problem with many additional interesting solutions, by elastically computing different routes accounting for different attention times within the tolerance for each customer.

The mathematical formulation of the considered problem variant is detailed in the next subsection.

2.2   Mathematical Formulation

A linear programming formulation is defined for the Heterogeneous Flexible Vehicle Routing Problem with Time Windows (HFVRPTW).

The problem is defined on a complete graph $G(V, A)$, considering the following elements [2]:

- $V = \{0, 1, ..., n\}$ is the set of nodes. Node 0 represents the deposit (an special node from where all vehicles start their routes), whereas nodes $N = \{1, ..., n\}$ represent the customers.
- $A = \{(i, j) : 0 \leq i, j \leq n, i \neq j\}$ is the set of edges that represent the connections between the nodes.
- t_{ij} is the travel time associated with arc (i, j).

All customers must be visited in a feasible solution. Each customer $i \in N$ has specific attributes that provide known information for the problem formulation:

- d_i is the fixed demand of customer i.
- s_i represents the service time demanded by a vehicle while delivering products to the customer i.
- $[e_i, l_i]$ is the time window of customer i. e_i is the earliest time and l_i is the latest time of the time window for customer i. The considered time windows are of the *soft* type: a vehicle is allowed to reach the customer before the earliest time and also after the end of its time window. In both cases, the solution cost is penalized.
- ot_i is the *overtime* allowed in customer i (i.e., the tolerance after the end of its time window). ot_i is computed as $ot_i = (l_i - e_i) \times w$, with $0 \leq w \leq 1$ being a known constant value. Therefore, for each customer i, a new *flexible* time window is defined, of the form $[e_i, l_i + ot_i]$. The vehicle cost is penalized if it reaches the customer in the interval $[l_i, l_i + ot_i]$.

Specific information is also known for the deposit:

- $[e_0, l_0] = [E, L]$ is the time window of the deposit.
- $d_0 = s_0 = 0$, because there is no demand or service time in the deposit.

The set of vehicles is modeled by set $K = \{1, ..., k\}$. In turn, C represents the set of vehicle types and S_c is the set of vehicles of type $c \in C$. For each vehicle of type $c \in C$, the following information is known:

- q_c is the capacity of a vehicle of type $c \in C$ (i.e., how many product the vehicle can transport when full).
- f_c is the fixed cost of a vehicle of type $c \in C$.
- α_c is the variable cost of a vehicle of type $c \in C$.
- n_c is the number of available vehicles of type $c \in C$.

The decision variables of the problem are:

- x_{ij}^k is a binary variable that takes value 1 if vehicle k passes through edge (i, j) in the graph, and takes value 0 otherwise.

- a_{ik} is the time of arrival of vehicle k to customer i.
- o_{ik} is the time that the vehicle k exceeds the time range of the customer i (referred as "the overtime of vehicle k in the customer i").

Other relevant elements include:

- ρ is the penalty term associated with the overtime of a vehicle in a customer.
- ω is the (percentage) deviation allowed for the time windows of customers. ω is used to define ot_i for each customer i.
- $M = \max(l_i + ot_i + t_{ij} + s_i - e_j), (i, j \in V)$ is the maximum possible time for a vehicle to move from customer i to customer j.

The mathematical formulation of the HFVRPTW is as follows:

$$\min \sum_{c \in C} f_c \sum_{k \in S_c} \sum_{j \in N} x_{0j}^k + \sum_{c \in C} \alpha_c \sum_{k \in S_c} \sum_{\substack{i, j \in V, \\ i \neq j}} t_{ij} x_{ij}^k + \sum_{k \in K, i \in N} o_{ik} * \rho \quad (1)$$

subject to:

$$\sum_{k \in K} \sum_{\substack{j \in V, \\ i \neq j}} x_{ij}^k = 1 \ \forall \ i \in N \quad (2)$$

$$\sum_{j \in N} x_{0j}^k \leq 1 \ \forall \ k \in K \quad (3)$$

$$\sum_{i \in N} x_{i0}^k \leq 1 \ \forall \ k \in K \quad (4)$$

$$\sum_{i \in V} x_{ij}^k = \sum_{i \in V} x_{ji}^k \ \forall \ j \in V, \ k \in K \quad (5)$$

$$\sum_{i \in N} d_i \sum_{\substack{j \in V, \\ i \neq j}} x_{ij}^k \leq q_c \ \forall \ k \in S_c, \ c \in C \quad (6)$$

$$a_{ik} + s_i + t_{ij} - M(1 - x_{ij}^k) \leq a_{jk} \ \forall \ k \in K, \ i \in N, \ j \in V, \ i \neq j \quad (7)$$

$$t_{0i} * x_{0i}^k \leq a_{ik} \ \forall \ k \in K, \ i \in N \quad (8)$$

$$a_{ik} \leq (l_i + ot_i) \sum_{\substack{j \in V, \\ i \neq j}} x_{ij}^k \ \forall \ k \in K, \ i \in N \quad (9)$$

$$e_i \sum_{\substack{j \in V, \\ i \neq j}} x_{ij}^k \leq a_{ik} \leq (l_i + ot_i) \sum_{\substack{j \in V, \\ i \neq j}} x_{ij}^k \ \forall \ k \in K, \ i \in N \quad (10)$$

$$E \leq a_{0k} \leq L + ot_0 \ \forall \ k \in K \quad (11)$$

$$\sum_{k \in S_c} \sum_{j \in N} x_{0j}^k \leq n_c \ \forall \ c \in C \quad (12)$$

$$o_{ik} \geq \max(0, a_{ik} - l_i) \geq 0 \; \forall \; k \in K, \; i \in V \tag{13}$$

$$a_{ik} \geq 0 \; \forall \; k \in K, \; i \in N \tag{14}$$

$$x_{ij}^k \in \{0,1\} \; \forall \; k \in K, \; (i,j) \in A \tag{15}$$

The objective function of the problem (Eq. 1) proposes minimizing the total routing cost. Three terms are considered: the sum of fixed costs and the sum of variable costs of the vehicles that conform each route, as well as the sum of penalties for all those vehicles that arrives with overtime.

Equations 2–15 formulate the problem constraints, which corresponds to:

- The constraint in Eq. 2 guarantees that all customers are visited only once (by one vehicle).
- Equations 3–5 are routing constraints, which forces that every used vehicle departs and returns to the depot using only one route: the vehicle cannot return from the same edge and the route must be a continuous path.
- Equation 6 is a capacity constraint, establishing that for each route, the accumulated demand for any customer cannot exceed the capacity of the vehicle.
- The constraint in Eq. 7 establishes the precedence relationship between the arrival times of the vehicles to the customers in each route. This constraint is the linearization of $x_{ij}^k(a_{ik} + s_i + t_{ij} - a_{jk}) = 0 \; \forall \; k \in K, \; i \in N, \; j \in V, \; i \neq j$.
- The constraint in Eq. 8 establishes the earliest arrival time at the first node of the path. Equations 9–11 impose the constraints set by the time windows for customers and the deposit, whereas the constraint in Eq. 12 limits the number of vehicles available for each type.
- Finally, the constraints in Eq. 13–15 restrict the values that the decision variables can take.

The proposed problem is a relaxation of the heterogeneous VRP with time windows proposed by Jiang et al. [7].

3   Related Work

VRP is a classic optimization problem introduced by Dantzig and Ramser [4]. VRP can be defined as the problem of determining a series of delivery routes for a fleet of vehicles, departing from one or several depots, to deliver products to a set of geographically dispersed customers [6].

VRP is a problem with NP-Hard complexity, as a generalization of the Travelling Salesman Problem [9]. Solomon [16] studied the VRP with time windows and several heuristic methods for its resolution: i) n intuitive method that places all customers in a single route, disregarding the time windows, and after that divides the route into different shorter routes to fulfill the time windows constraints; ii) heuristics based on different movements to define neighborhoods (Nearest-Neighbor, Insertion, Sweep, and Time-Oriented Insertion); and iii) list heuristics, following a waiting time limit approach. In the comparative empirical evaluation, the Time-Oriented Insertion heuristic computed the best results.

This method is based on selecting a seed customer between those most distant from the depot or those with the earliest time for delivering, and then building an initial route to those customers. After that, routes are building by adding other customers to the initial route, properly observing their time windows, until the vehicle capacity is reached or until the end of the delivering time period.

On the one hand, several exact methods have been proposed for different VRP variants. One of the most comprehensive related works was presented by Baldacci et al. [1], who proposed a framework to compute exact solutions to VRP problem, including the variant with time windows, based on modeling partition problems with additional constraints. Efficient results were reported in comparison with previous exact methods.

On the other hand, many articles have proposed heuristic and metaheuristic approaches [11] to solve different VRP variants. Regaring the VRP with time windows and heterogeneous fleet, Tabu Search (TS) methods have been applied by Semet and Taillard [15] and Rochat ans Semet [14]. Yepes and Medina [18] applied probabilistic variable neighborhood local searches for the problem. The most relevant related work is by Jiang et al. [7], which proposed an exact formulation for the VRP with time windows and heterogeneous fleet and a two-stages heuristic method based on TS. The method computed accurate results, even for larger problem instances.

Many other articles have studied specific cases of the VRP with time windows and heterogeneous fleet, focused on the real routing applications; e.g. bi-objective multi-depot VRP [19], and heterogeneous VRP with time windows and a limited number of resources [10]. However, no recent articles have addressed the problem variant where flexible deadlines are considered, to account for the trade-off between cost and quality of service.

Our previous work [2] studied the flexible VRP variant with heterogeneous fleet and time windows. A MILP formulation was presented and an exact resolution approach was developed and implemented in CPLEX. The proposed exact model was able to solve 146 out of 148 problem instances, but just 16 of them to optimality. The exact approach was not evaluated with problem instances including 100 customers, due to the large execution times required.

The research reported in this article contributes to this line of work by developing an hybrid metaheuristic approach combining GRASP and VND to solve problem instances for which the previous exact method was unable to compute solutions in reasonable execution times.

4 The Proposed GRASP+VND for Flexible Vehicle Routing

This section describes the hybrid metaheuristic approach combining GRASP and VND to solve the HFVRPTW.

4.1 Overall Description

The proposed metaheuristic approach to solve the HFVRPTW follows an hybrid approach. Hybridization is a common technique for improving the search capabilities of metaheuristic algorithms [17]. In this context, hybridization refers to include problem-dependent knowledge in the search mechanism or combine several methods, trying to take advantage of the features of each one of them to improve the search efficiency and/or accuracy of the resulting hybrid method. The common approach is to organize the hybrid in a master method that controls the application of a given (or a set of) subordinate metaheuristics. The hybrid metaheuristic defines a new search pattern that determines when each algorithm is applied and how each algorithm reports its results to the other [11].

The pseudocode in Algorithm 1 presents the overall description of the proposed hybrid GRASP+VND metaheuristic for the HFVRPTW. A standard approach is applied: a solution is built using a constructive procedure, and a VND operator is applied for improving the solution.

Algorithm 1: Proposed GRASP+VND for the HFVRPTW

---

1 noImprov = 0
2 data ← ReadData()
3 vehicles ← SortVehicles(datos)
4 bestSol ← ϕ
5 **for** $k = 1$ to maxIter **do**
6   initSol ← Construction(data, vehicles)
7   improvedSol ← VND(solucionInicial)
8   **if** cost(bestSol) > cost(improvedSol) **then**
9 | bestSol ← improvedSol
10   **else**
11 | noImprov = noImprov + 1
12   **end**
13   **if** noImprovement ≥ maxIterWithoutImpr **then**
14 | **break**
15   **end**
16 **end**
17 **return** bestSol

Two stopping criteria are considered in Algorithm 1: a fixed effort stopping criterion defined by a maximum number of iterations (maxIter) and a stagnation criterion defined by a maximum number of iterations without improvement (maxIterWithoutImpr) of the best solution found.

Before starting the iterative process, function SortVehicles() sorts each of the vehicles types according to a specific criterion. For each dataset that defines a problem instance, two values are computed: the average customer demand $\bar{d}$ and the average travel time $\bar{t}$ between all nodes (depot and customers). Let q be the capacity of each type of vehicle, it is possible to compute the number of customers that can be attended by that type of vehicle, that is, the number of customers on the average route: $customers = \lfloor q/\overline{d} \rfloor$. Therefore, for each vehicle type, the average demand for the average route is $demand = customers \times \overline{d}$, and the average travel time for the average route is $time = (customers + 2) \times \overline{t}$ (the +2 term accounts for two additional segments when departing from/returning to the depot). Using these data, and the fixed (f_c) and variable costs (α_c) for the vehicle type, a specific metric for each type of vehicle is defined by Eq. 16. The different types of vehicles are added to a list K in increasing order of priority according to the defined metric.

$$\frac{f_c}{demand} + \alpha_c \times time \tag{16}$$

Construction Phase. Two stages are involved in the construction phase: vehicle selection and construction of the route for the selected vehicle.

For vehicle selection, a list of customers that have not yet been included in the solution is maintained. When creating a new route to be added to the solution, the available vehicle type with the highest priority is selected.

After that, a route is assembled for the selected vehicle, always including the depot as initial node. A list of candidate customers to be included as the next node is defined, checking that they generate a feasible route. Then, the incremental cost associated with each candidate is calculated as follows: being t the travel time from the current node of the route under construction to the candidate customer, at the arrival time to the candidate, ot_i the time that the time window of the candidate is exceeded, ρ the penalty for the late arrival, the incremental cost is calculated as $incr(i) = \alpha * t + ot_i \times \rho + at_i$. This incremental cost does not represent the real cost to be summed if that candidate is added to the route, since the time of arrival to the candidate is also weighted, trying to include as soon as possible in the route those customers with high priority (i.e., with the earliest time windows).

Once the incremental cost are computed, a restricted candidate list (RCL) is built by selecting from the candidate list those that verify $incr(cand) \leq min(incr) + \alpha(max(incr) - min(incr))$, with $\alpha = 0,2$ (computed in preliminary experiments). Then, an element from the RCL is randomly selected and added to the partial route, updating both the list of customers not included in the solution and the candidate set, and reevaluating the incremental costs. When the capacity of the vehicle is reached or the list of candidates is empty (i.e., there is no customer to add to the solution generating a feasible route), the current route is closed by adding the deposit. In case there are customers not visited, another vehicle is selected to create a new route.

Algorithm 2 describes the construction procedure. Function `Getcustomers` returns the set of customers for a problem instance and `GetCapacity` returns the capacity of a vehicle. Function `SelectVehicle`, given a list of vehicle types ordered according to the defined metric, returns an available vehicle of the type with the lowest metric and updates the availability for that type of vehicle. Function `CreateRoute` initializes a route by associating a vehicle and a path.

Given a route and a customer, function IsFeasible determines if is possible to add the customer at the end of the path of the route, by checking if the demand of the customer does not exceed the available capacity of the vehicle and that the arriving time to the customer is within its extended time window. Finally, function SelectRandom returns an element of the RCL, selected according to a uniform distribution probability.

Local Search Phase. The local search phase applies a VND metaheuristic to explore different neighborhoods of the solution constructed in the previous phase. Five neighborhood structures are considered, four of them taken from the related literature: Exchange, Relocate, 2-opt, and 3-opt. They are explored in that order, according to their cardinality [13].

In addition, a new operator is applied: fleet-opt. The main goal of this operator is creating a neighborhood that allows exploring the allocation of vehicles on each route of a given solution. This way a fifth neighborhood is defined by applying the fleet-opt operator in two different ways:

- *A movement*: For all routes in the solution, pairs of two different routes p and q are selected. If their associated vehicles v_p and v_q are of different types, their are exchanged (route p is associated with vehicle v_q and route q is associated with vehicle v_p, as illustrated in Fig. 1(a).
- *B movement*: This movement requires knowing the available vehicles v_d, not included in the solution. For each route p of the solution, the associated vehicle v_p is replaced by each of the v_d with a different type, as illustrated in Fig. 1(b).

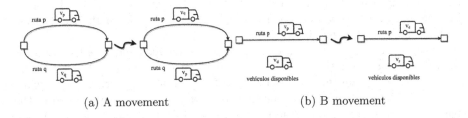

(a) A movement   (b) B movement

Fig. 1. Fleet-opt operator

The proposed fleet-opt neighborhood has a smaller cardinality than that of the other neighborhood structures, therefore, it is applied first.

The diagram in Fig. 2 describes the structure of the proposed VND metaheuristic algorithm applied as local search operator in the proposed algorithm and the order of exploration of each neighborhood.

Algorithm 2: Construction phase of the proposed GRASP+VND for the HFVRPTW

1	solution ← φ
2	customers ← GetCustomers(datos) ▷ Initialize customers list
3	newRoute ← true ▷ Define new route initialization
4	**while** customers ≠ φ **do**
5	candidates ← φ ▷ Initialize candidate list
6	**if** *newRoute* **then**
7	path ← depot ▷ Initialize path
8	vehicle ← SelectVehicle(vehicles) ▷ Select vehicle
9	q ← GetCapacity(vehicle) ▷ Initialize vehicle capacity
10	route ← CreateRoute(vehicles,path) ▷ Initialize route
11	newRoute ← false
12	**end**
13	**for** cust ∈ customers **do**
14	**if** IsFeasible(route, cust) **then**
15	candidates ← candidates ∪ {cli} ▷ Insert candidate
16	**end**
17	**end**
18	**if** candidates ≠ φ **then**
19	**for** cand ∈ candidates **do**
20	incr(cand) ▷ Compute incremental cost
21	**end**
22	i^{min} ← min{incr(cand)	cand ∈ candidates}
23	i^{max} ← max{incr(cand)	cand ∈ candidates}
24	RCL ← {cand ∈ candidates	incr(e) ≤ i^{min} + α(i^{max} − i^{min})}
25	customer ← SelectRandom(RCL)
26	path ← path ∪ {customer} ▷ Add customer to path
27	Update(path,route) ▷ Update path in route
28	q = q− GetDemand(customer) ▷ Update capacity
29	customers ← customers \ {customer} ▷ Update customers list
30	**end**
31	**if** candidates = φ OR q = 0 **then**
32	path ← path ∪ {depot} ▷ Add depot to path
33	Update(path,route) ▷ Update path in route
34	Add(route,solution) ▷ Add route to solution
35	newRoute ← true
36	**end**
37	**end**
38	**return** solution

---

5 Experimental Evaluation

This section reports the experimental evaluation of the proposed hybrid meta-heuristic algorithmic approach to solve the HFVRPTW.

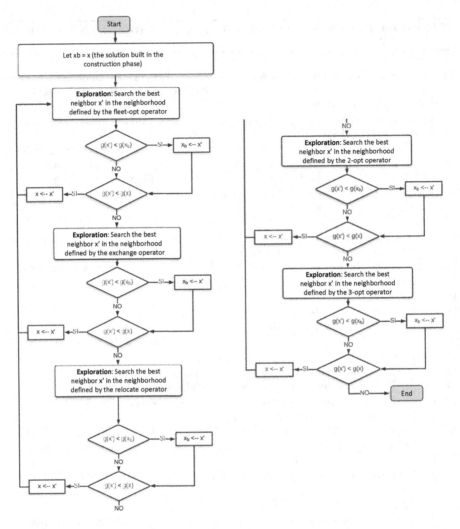

Fig. 2. Diagram of the proposed VND search

5.1   Problem Instances

The evaluation of the proposed hybrid metaheuristic approach is performed using a set of benchmark instances built over existing ones for the classic VRP problem (with homogeneous vehicles) and including specific features of the proposed HFVRPTW model, namely heterogeneous vehicles and flexible time windows. These problem instances are described next.

Regarding topological data, the proposed dataset extends VRP benchmark with homogeneous vehicles by Solomon [16]. Information of these instances include: locations, demands, time windows, and service times of customers and the depot. The benchmark is organized in six classes:

- Classes C1 and C2 are defined considering grouped customers.
- Classes R1 and R2 are defined considering evenly distributed locations on a square area,
- Classes RC1 and RC2 are defined considering both customers grouped and location distributed.

Problem instances with narrow windows and small vehicle capacities (classes C1, R1, and RC1) and also with wide time windows and large vehicle capacities (classes C2, R2, and RC2) are considered. Fixed and variable costs are defined as proposed by Jiang et al. [7]. The defined cost structure assigns higher fixed and variable costs to vehicles with larger capacities. Six new classes are generated: HC1, HC2, HR1, HR2, HRC1 and HRC2 (the 'H' stands for heterogeneous). Four classes (HC1, HC2, HR2, and HRC2) include two types of vehicles, with different capacities, costs, and different cost/capacity ratios. Other two classes (HR1 and HRC1) include three types of vehicles, with similar cost/capacity ratios. Regarding flexibility of customers and time windows, the value of ω is set to 0.3, providing a reasonable level of flexibility for delivering products.

Table 1 reports the data of new heterogeneous problem instances. Information reported in the table include the number of vehicles, their type, capacities, and both fixed and variable costs.

Table 1. Data of the considered problem instances classes

Class	Vehicle type	# vehicles	Capacity	Fixed cost	Variable cost
HC1	A	20	100	30	1.0
	B	5	200	80	1.2
HC2	A	20	400	100	1.0
	B	5	500	140	1.2
HR1	A	10	50	80	1.0
	B	15	80	140	1.2
	C	10	120	250	1.4
HR2	A	10	300	45	1.0
	B	5	400	70	1.2
HRC1	A	10	40	60	1.0
	B	20	80	150	1.2
	C	10	150	300	1.4
HRC2	A	10	100	150	1.0
	B	5	200	350	1.2

5.2 Methodology

Development and Execution Platform. The proposed GRASP+VND meta-heuristic was implemented in C. The experimental evaluation was performed in a HP ProLiant DL380 G9 with Intel Xeon Gold 6138 processor and 128 GB RAM, from National Supercomputing Center, Uruguay (Cluster-UY) [12].

Parameters Setting. For the proposed GRASP+VND, parameter values for the stopping criteria were set to maxIter = 100 and maxIterWithoutImpr = 20, after a preliminary analysis that concluded that this values allowed a proper exploration of the search space of the problem.

Results Comparison. Results computed with the proposed GRASP+VND approach are compared with previous reference results by the TS of Jiang et al. [7] for non-flexible problem instances with 100 customers.

5.3 Numerical Results of the Hybrid Metaheuristic Approach

Table 2 reports the results computed for VRP instances with 00 customers and the comparison with the previous TS approach by Jiang et al. [7] for the non-flexible version of the problem. The gap metric reports the relative difference between the cost of solutions computed by GRASP+VND and the previous TS.

Results in Table 2 indicate that the proposed hybrid metaheuristic approach combining GRASP and VND is able to compute competitive results when compared with state-of-the-art results for the heterogeneous VRP with time windows. Although the average gap is over 14.1% for instances class HC1, significantly lower values were obtained for the other studied problem classes. The best results were computed for problem classes HR! and HR2, where the gaps between the proposed GRASP+VND and the reference TS [7] were 0.93% and 1.68% respectively. In those problem classes, GRASP+VND computed nine better solutions (four in class HR1 and five in class HR2), with improvement up to 10.75% in problem instance HR202. In turn, another better solution was computed for problem instance HC207.

The best solutions computed for classes HR1 and HR2 suggest that the proposed hybrid metaheuristic approach is useful to solve both problem instances with narrow windows and small vehicle capacities, and also with wider time windows and large vehicle capacities, using different types of vehicles.

Table 2. Results computed by the proposed GRASP+VND (GVND) and comparison with Jiang et al. [7] heterogeneous instances with 100 customers

Instance	GVND	TS [7]	Δ cost	Gap	Instance	GVND	TS, [7]	Δ cost	Gap
HC101	2285.12	1885.33	399.79	17.50%	HR201	1661.63	1765.74	−104.11	−6.27%
HC102	2136.37	1890.66	245.71	11.50%	HR202	1387.66	1536.81	−149.15	−10.75%
HC103	2109.95	1908.04	201.91	9.57%	HR203	1240.21	1337.39	−97.18	−7.84%
HC104	2098.63	1809.78	288.85	13.76%	HR204	1111.87	1114.94	−3.07	−0.28%
HC105	2209.49	1854.73	354.76	16.06%	HR205	1375.37	1263.91	111.46	8.10%
HC106	2184.47	1880.64	303.83	13.91%	HR206	1263.93	1180.44	83.49	6.61%
HC107	2170.92	1839.52	331.4	15.27%	HR207	1191.44	1102.06	89.38	7.50%
HC108	2160.83	1826.49	334.34	15.47%	HR208	1072.93	1007	65.93	6.14%
HC109	2096.88	1799.22	297.66	14.20%	HR209	1242.66	1119.04	123.62	9.95%
					HR210	1243.48	1307.53	−64.05	−5.15%
					HR211	1127.61	1010.22	117.39	10.41%
Avg.	−	−	306.47	14.14%	*Avg.*	−	−	−	1.68%
HC201	1355.96	1313.28	42.68	3.15%	HRC101	6032.29	5703.97	328.32	5.44%
HC202	1380.24	1283.58	96.66	7.00%	HRC102	5841.77	5556.02	285.75	4.89%
HC203	1390.66	1259.97	130.69	9.40%	HRC103	5819.42	5438.89	380.53	6.54%
HC204	1274.94	1256.09	18.85	1.48%	HRC104	5728.36	5331.41	396.95	6.93%
HC205	1371.87	1325.84	46.03	3.36%	HRC105	5906.44	5705.79	200.65	3.40%
HC206	1382.84	1263.63	119.21	8.62%	HRC106	5898.69	5528.42	370.27	6.28%
HC207	1278.11	1307.35	−29.24	−2.29%	HRC107	5767.87	5451.31	316.56	5.49%
HC208	1331.29	1190.81	140.48	10.55%	HRC108	5733.73	5322.31	411.42	7.18%
Avg.	−	−	−	5.16%	*Avg.*	−	−	−	5.77%
HR101	4979.38	5125.52	−146.14	−2.93%	HRC201	4951.2	4501.65	449.55	9.08%
HR102	4752.87	4982.39	−229.52	−4.83%	HRC202	4766.55	4408.53	358.02	7.51%
HR103	4555.72	4661.22	−105.50	−2.32%	HRC203	4598.44	4321.87	276.57	6.01%
HR104	4393.14	4530.55	−137.41	−3.13%	HRC204	4511.08	4306.65	204.43	4.53%
HR105	4707.31	4570.39	136.92	2.91%	HRC205	4633.37	4452.88	180.49	3.90%
HR106	4564.32	4431.31	133.01	2.91%	HRC206	4696.54	4419.09	277.45	5.91%
HR107	4485.23	4391.14	94.09	2.10%	HRC207	4562.1	4343.55	218.55	4.79%
HR108	4410.89	4280.05	130.84	2.97%	HRC208	4442.41	4276.15	166.26	3.74%
HR109	4540.24	4339.86	200.38	4.41%					
HR110	4419.36	4272.25	147.11	3.33%					
HR111	4467.47	4366.32	101.15	2.26%					
HR112	4403.84	4252.71	151.13	3.43%					
Avg.	−	−	−	0.93%	*Avg.*	−	−	−	5.68%

6   Conclusions and Future Work

This article presented an hybrid metaheuristic approach to solve the VRP with heterogeneous fleet and flexible time windows. The addressed problem variant considers extended time windows for delivering products to customers, and models interesting situations in smart cities, considering the renewed interesting on smart logistics under the Industry 4.0 paradigm.

An hybrid metaheuristic approach is applied to solve the problem. combining GRASP and VND, two well-known search procedures for optimization. Different operators and neighborhood structures are proposed for the search.

The experimental evaluation is performed on a set of problem instances with 100 customers, built by extending existing benchmarks in the literature. Regarding the quality of the computed solutions, the GRASP+VND approach was competitive when compared with a previous TS method applied to the non-flexible version of the problem and was able to compute better solutions in ten problem instances.

The main lines for future work are related to extend the experimental validation of the proposed approach, by considering an extended set of problem instances and improving the exploration/exploitation procedures to compute better solutions. The problem model can also be extended to consider a multiobjective formulation to compute accurate trade-off solutions for the simultaneous optimization of the total cost and the quality of service offered to customers.

References

1. Baldacci, R., Bartolini, E., Mingozzi, A., Roberti, R.: An exact solution framework for a broad class of vehicle routing problems. CMS **7**(3), 229–268 (2010). https://doi.org/10.1007/s10287-009-0118-3
2. Barrero, L., Viera, R., Robledo, F., Risso, C., Nesmachnow, S., Tchernykh, A.: Exact resolution of the vehicle routing problem with flexible time windows. In: International Conference of Production Research, pp. 658–672 (2020)
3. Brekalo, L., Albers, S.: Effective logistics alliance design and management. Int. J. Phys. Distrib. Logist. Manag. **46**(2), 212–240 (2016)
4. Dantzig, G., Ramser, J.: The truck dispatching problem. Manag. Sci. **6**(1), 80–91 (1959)
5. Díaz-Madroñero, M., Peidro, D., Mula, J.: A review of tactical optimization models for integrated production and transport routing planning decisions. Comput. Ind. Eng. **88**, 518–535 (2015)
6. Golden, B., Magnanti, T., Nguyen, H.: Implementing vehicle routing algorithms. Networks **7**(2), 113–148 (1977)
7. Jiang, J., Ng, K.M., Poh, K.L., Teo, K.M.: Vehicle routing problem with a heterogeneous fleet and time windows. Expert Syst. Appl. **41**(8), 3748–3760 (2014)
8. Laporte, G.: Fifty years of vehicle routing. Transp. Sci. **43**(4), 408–416 (2009)
9. Lenstra, J., Rinnooy, A.: Complexity of vehicle routing and scheduling problems. Networks **11**(2), 221–227 (1981)
10. Molina, J., Salmeron, J., Eguia, I., Racero, J.: The heterogeneous vehicle routing problem with time windows and a limited number of resources. Eng. Appl. Artif. Intell. **94**, 103745 (2020)
11. Nesmachnow, S.: An overview of metaheuristics: accurate and efficient methods for optimisation. Int. J. Metaheuristics **3**(4), 320–347 (2014)
12. Nesmachnow, S., Iturriaga, S.: Cluster-UY: collaborative scientific high performance computing in Uruguay. In: Torres, M., Klapp, J. (eds.) ISUM 2019. CCIS, vol. 1151, pp. 188–202. Springer, Cham (2019). https://doi.org/10.1007/978-3-030-38043-4_16

13. Pop, P.C., Fuksz, L., Marc, A.H.: A variable neighborhood search approach for solving the generalized vehicle routing problem. In: Polycarpou, M., de Carvalho, A.C.P.L.F., Pan, J.-S., Woźniak, M., Quintian, H., Corchado, E. (eds.) HAIS 2014. LNCS (LNAI), vol. 8480, pp. 13–24. Springer, Cham (2014). https://doi.org/10.1007/978-3-319-07617-1_2

14. Rochat, Y., Semet, F.: A tabu search approach for delivering pet food and flour in Switzerland. J. Oper. Res. Soc. **45**(11), 1233–1246 (1994)

15. Semet, F., Taillard, E.: Solving real-life vehicle routing problems efficiently using tabu search. Ann. Oper. Res. **41**(4), 469–488 (1993). https://doi.org/10.1007/BF02023006

16. Solomon, M.: Algorithms for the vehicle routing and scheduling problems with time window constraints. Oper. Res. **35**(2), 254–265 (1987)

17. Talbi, E.G.: A taxonomy of hybrid metaheuristics. J. Heuristics **8**(5), 541–564 (2002). https://doi.org/10.1023/A:1016540724870

18. Yepes, V., Medina, J.: Economic heuristic optimization for heterogeneous fleet VRPHESTW. J. Transp. Eng. **132**(4), 303–311 (2006)

19. Zhou, Z., Ha, M., Hu, H., Ma, H.: Half open multi-depot heterogeneous vehicle routing problem for hazardous materials transportation. Sustainability **13**(3), 1262 (2021)

A Practical Approach for Sustainable Transit Oriented Development in Montevideo, Uruguay

Silvina Hipogrosso$^{(\boxtimes)}$ ⓘ and Sergio Nesmachnow$^{(\boxtimes)}$ ⓘ

Universidad de la República, Montevideo, Uruguay
{silvina.hipogrosso,sergion}@fing.edu.uy

Abstract. The need for a proper development of transportation systems in modern smart cities is motivated and driven by relevant factors, including conceiving territorial and transportation planning as part of an unified urban activity. In this line of work, this article presents an empirical analysis of sustainable mobility under the Transit Oriented Development paradigm, focuses on properly capturing the relationships between urban environment, activities, and mobility, by analyzing diverse indicators. As a relevant case study, the article analyzes the current situation regarding sustainable mobility and Transit Oriented Development in the area surrounding Engineering Faculty, in Parque Rodó Neighborhood, Montevideo, Uruguay. Specific recommendations are provided to improve sustainable mobility under the studied paradigm.

Keywords: Sustainable mobility · Transit-Oriented Development · Public transportation · Smart cities

1 Introduction

Mobility is a crucial component of modern smart cities, allowing daily activities social participation of citizens on urban areas [21]. The relationship of mobility with sustainable development has been recognized as one of the main issues to achieve the 2030 Sustainable Development Goals (SDG), as defined by the United Nation, since mobility is part of the great environmental challenges existing nowadays. Several of the defined SDG are related to sustainable mobility, including relevant issues as health and road safety, affordable and clean energy, economic growth, resilient infrastructure for sustainable cities, access to transportation modes and expanded public transportation, and sustainable consumption and production. Thus, promoting sustainable mobility has been a major concern and one of the toughest environmental and social challenges.

The main concepts of sustainability and sustainable development have been applied to conceive new approaches and models to guarantee mobility with a reduced environmental impact. Sustainable mobility is defined as the ability to "meet the needs of society to move freely, gain access, communicate, trade and

© Springer Nature Switzerland AG 2022
S. Nesmachnow and L. Hernández Callejo (Eds.): ICSC-Cities 2021, CCIS 1555, pp. 256–270, 2022.
https://doi.org/10.1007/978-3-030-96753-6_18

establish relationships without sacrificing other essential human or ecological values, today or in the future" [29]. Three main pillars support the sustainable mobility paradigm: environmental, social, and economic [15]. These pillars must be properly respected to develop positive contributions, by collaborative efforts by public and private sectors, suitably considering citizens and their participation. Transit-Oriented Development (TOD) [7,22] is a paradigm for urban planning and development that has revitalized city urbanization, by combining the renewal of suburban spaces and friendly walkable environments in neighborhoods. Although TOD has been successfully applied in USA, Europe, and Asia to ensure sustainable mobility and economic development, few proposals have applied the paradigm in Latin America.

In this line of work, this article presents a practical approach for analyzing and developing sustainable mobility initiatives under the TOD paradigm. The analysis is focused on properly capturing the relationships between urban environment, activities, and mobility. The main contributions of the research reported in this article are: the evaluation of the area surrounding Engineering Faculty, in Parque Rodó neighborhood using TOD indicators and the analysis of mobility demand through quantitative indicators and the formulation of several suggestions and recommendations to improve sustainable mobility in the studied zone, applying the TOD paradigm.

The article is organized as follows. Next section introduces the main concepts regarding sustainable mobility and TOD. A review of related works is presented in Sect. 3. The methodology applied for the analysis of the studied zone is reported in Sect. 4. Results and discussion of the analysis are presented in Sect. 5, and specific suggestions and recommendations to improve sustainable mobility under the TOD paradigm in the studied area are presented in Sect. 6. Finally, Sect. 7 presents the conclusions and the main lines for future work.

2 TOD Approach

In the last thirty years, sustainability has been a major concern of modern society. The concept of sustainable development, i.e., development to fulfill important roles of nowadays without compromising the future, has been promoted to build a more equitable, environment friendly, and inclusive model of society.

The sustainable mobility paradigm integrates many relevant concepts, including those related with their impacts on environment and society [2]. Overall, the main idea is to consider mobility as a valued activity regarding environmental, social, and economic concerns [19]. One of the most studied aspects has been the impact of mobility on the environment, with the main idea of conceiving new transportation paradigms accounting for cleaner means, accessibility, and integration of people. Other important aspects have also been analyzed, including the impact on economy, and the overall quality of life (safety, health, etc.). Raising awareness and involving citizens are key aspects for sustainable mobility. In turn, technology has been identified as one of the most valuable tools to help developing environmental friendly sustainable mobility. Different methods and indicators have been proposed to analyze means of transportation [12] and other important issues related to sustainable mobility.

In turn, the TOD paradigm for urban planning is a trendy model for planning sustainable urban communities by creating dense, walkable communities that greatly reduce the need for driving and energy consumption. The goal TOD is ensuring sustainable mobility and economic development, while protecting global energy. TOD has become a great prominence for urban planning and transport since the first proposals by Calthorpe [7] and Newman and Kenworthy [22] in the 1990s. The approach was later supported by the empirical works of Bertolini et al. [3, 4] and Cervero et al. [8, 9], among other authors.

TOD is the key to more sustainable, efficient, and equitable communities because it works under the "3Cs" concepts (compact, coordinated, and connected). In turn, it is related to other five principles for decision makers and urban planners strengthen their communities according to the TOD standard:

1. *Compactness*: The closer the activities are located between each other in a compact city/district, the less time consuming and energy is required.
2. *Density*: Instead of building out to increase the urban sprawl, TOD supports building up to create dense cities in a more compact way.
3. *Transit–public transportation*: Public transportation connects and integrates many distant areas around the city. A good public transportation planning that contemplate all area of a city creates an equitable and accessible city.
4. *Connectivity*: Create dense networks of streets and paths for pedestrians and cyclists as well as public transportation.
5. *Mix*: Plan for mix use in order to create shorter trips and more lively neighborhoods.
6. *Cycling*: Prioritize non-motorized transport networks. Cycling provides people an efficient and convenient way to travel for short/medium distances, increase accessibility as well as coverage of transit.
7. *Shift (to sustainable transportation modes)*: Closer locations between activities and a good transportation network do not imply people shift to sustainable transportation modes. Other actions are needed, such as regulating car parking and road use, to discourage the use of non-sustainable means.
8. *Walk*: Develop neighborhoods that promote walking creating vibrant, active streets where people feel safe.

In the related literature, TOD is conceived to hold urban sprawl, prioritizing sustainable mobility as well as driving to environmentally and economically-balanced growth TOD is closely related to the *smart growth* and *new urbanist* approaches [6] conceiving walkable, compact, pedestrian-oriented, and mixed-use communities centered around high quality public transport systems [26] reducing, in this way, the utilization of automobiles.

Several articles have defined a buffer of 400 m as the walkable distance to get to a bus stop and a buffer of 800 m as the walkable distance to get to a rail station [23, 24]. According to these radius, urban designers and planners design mixed used areas around bus stops and rail stations to promote sustainable mobility. Accessibility also plays an important role when designing a project based on TOD principles. The interaction between urban structure, accessibility, and travel behavior has been discussed for several authors [23].

Based on the TOD approach, this article presents an analysis of the zone surrounding Engineering Faculty in Parque Rodó neighborhood, describing the mixed uses of land (services, public spaces, open spaces, pedestrian paths and bike lanes, maintainance condition of the built environment and green places, bicycle parking facilities and transport nodes.) The data collected was examinated by some factors to characterize the built environment.

Furthermore, an empirical approach is followed to consider subjective opinions, based on personal questionnaires to people traveling from/to the area. The resulting data are processed and analyzed following a urban data approach, in order to extract useful information and elaborate specific suggestions towards a sustainable mobility plan in the studied area.

3   Related Work

Sustainabile mobility has been an important concern for researchers in the last twenty years. Litman and Burwell [17] recognized that sustainable transportation initiatives must be developed considering a broad point of view, for properly capturing the interrelations between economic and social welfare, energy efficiency, ecological integrity, human health, and proper land use. The authors proposed a paradigm shift for rethinking transportation, considering different integrated solutions for sustainable transportation systems. Some of the proposed indicators for detecting trends, assessing and comparing activities, and evaluating policies related to sustainable transportation, are those considered in TOD principles.

The main concepts in TOD are strongly related to sustainability. One the one hand, successful examples of applying TOD in USA, Europe, and Asia, are commonly associated to mass rail systems. On the other hand, in Latin America, most of the TOD-related initiatives have been implemented on Bus Rapid Transit (BRT) or similar public transportation systems, which allow providing a cost-effective service more adapted to the economic reality of developing countries.

Hasibuana et al. [13] studied the applicability of TOD ideas for improving urban mobility in a case study in Jabodetabek, Indonesia, with more than 27 million population. The main results of the analysis showed that TOD concepts can definitely contribute to restructuring urban land use and growth, improving the modal share of public transportation and the quality of the urban environment. Loo and Verle [18] proposed a sustainable mobility approach oriented on people and places. Three lines were proposed for TOD planning: improving the built environment at both neighborhood and city scales; improving walking and related urban planning/design related to public spaces; and encouraging non-uniform designs for different neighborhoods. A case study in Hong Kong, China, analyzed several indicators for five different neighborhood types. The authors recognized that further efforts are needed to quantify and fostering both direct and indirect benefits associated with TOD, benefits beyond traditional impacts on transportation. Tsigdinos et al. [27] studied surrounding zones of metro stations (line 4) in Athens, Greece, regarding several TOD features (density, walkability, public transportation, land uses, and public spaces). Spatial analysis, indicators for categorizing TOD regions, multi-criteria analysis and geo-visualization were applied to identify differences between categories and contrast between central ans suburban stations. The authors found important limitations of the studied areas and common weaknesses of more than a half of the studied stations, which hinders the implementation of integrated transportation and urban planning strategies. Specific suggestions for improving the identified weaknesses were also proposed.

Woo [28] evaluated TOD features in Seoul, Korea, to characterize subway station areas and their neighborhoods, for a urban rail transit. Accessibility analysis and clustering methods were applied to categorize TOD types using the targeted 246 subway station areas at the neighborhood level. The main results of the analysis grouped the studied zones in four categories: (1) high-density mixed-use areas for residential and retail purposes, which have good accessibility; (2) moderate-density, with average accessibility and high-mixed land use; (3) compact business, mainly offices and commerce, with high accessibility and a high transit demand; and (4) compact housing with high-rise buildings, mostly used for residences. The study concluded that the period of urban development significantly affects the main features of each identified category. And category (2) offers the best option for urban redesign under TOD concepts.

In Latin America, TOD-related developments have been scarce. The region mostly focused on building and developing infrastructures based on mass transit corridors and BRT systems. Some articles argued that BRT systems, even though applying a more restricted paradigm, are able to produce a similar impact on land utilization than TOD strategies [9]. However, Moscoso et al. [20] stated that Latinamerican cities have considered BRT as a mobility solution, without integrating key TOD concepts to promote compact, dense, and well-connected urban development. Nevertheless, the most well-known BRT development in Latin America (Curitiba, Brazil) is also a model of TOD, due to a long-term integration of transportation and land use planning, which was crucial for the success of the mobility model. The land development impacts of BRT have been also studied in other Latinamerican cities, such as Bogota and Quito [5, 25].

Other analysis of sustainable transportation considering TOD-based indicators have been developed for specific cases, such as the study for universities in the Guadalajara metropolitan area, Mexico, by de Alba et al. [1].

The analysis of related works allows concluding that few articles have studied TOD analysis and characterization for specific cases in Latin America. This article contributes in this line of research, by proposing a TOD-based sustainable mobility analysis in a specific zone of Montevideo, Uruguay.

4 TOD-Based Sustainable Mobility Analysis for Engineering Faculty, Montevideo, Uruguay

This section describes the analysis of sustainable mobility and urban structure in the area surrounding Engineering Faculty, Montevideo, Uruguay, considering TOD-related indicators.

4.1 Motivation and Objectives of the Study

The objective of the study is to analyze how the studied area can be transformed in a walkable, compact, pedestrian-oriented, and mixed-use community, where people want to live and work, built around sustainable public transportation.

Since global concern of environmental pollution appeared, only few initiatives have been proposed towards sustainable mobility in Montevideo. Most of the recent initiatives focused on public transportation, e.g., electric buses were introduced in the system, and a few private initiatives, e.g., a leasing plan to acquire electric vans for last mile distribution of people and goods.

The studied area (called *The Isle*) is located nearby Engineering Faculty, in Montevideo. It is an area of $0.25\,\text{km}^2$ surrounded by about $1\,\text{km}^2$ of green areas (Parque Rodó/Rodó Park). Although The Isle is a residential area, where more than 5.000 people live, it has high daily flow of people traveling to/from services, institutions, green and recreation areas, and other places located in the zone. In this regard, this area creates opportunities for multi-modal travel, sustainable mobility and urban planning development based in TOD approach.

The studied area includes four avenues: Herrera y Reissig, where Engineering Faculty is located, Sarmiento, Sosa, and Bulevar Artigas. In 2021, Engineering Faculty has more than 10 000 students, 1 000 professors, and 200 employees. In addition, students and professors of other faculties also assist to lectures in Aulario Massera, a large classroom building nearby Engineering Faculty.

4.2 Methodology

The main details of the applied methodology are described next.

Overall Description. The study is based on two methodological stages: i) applying urban data analysis to develop a spatial-functional definition of the study area; and ii) characterizing the current mobility in the studied area;

The proposed methodology combines different quantitative elements and analysis to identify the mixed uses of land in the area, transportation connectivity, and infrastructure for bikers and pedestrians, in order to improve accessibility and create opportunities for sustainable development in the area.

Data Collection. Three main sources of data were considered in the study.

First, data from Google Maps (in JSON format) and from personal inspection (from photographs taken in the area) were collected to identify a spatial-functional definition in the studied area. The collected data include the following information about the environment: infrastructure for non-motorized traveling mode (pedestrian-only paths, bicycle paths, accessible ramps for sidewalks); land uses (commercial, residential, institutional); semi-public spaces (restaurants, education center, health center, sport centers); open spaces (green areas, parks, squares); the maintenance condition of the built environment and green spaces (bus stop shelters, sidewalks, bicycle paths); and parking facilities and transportation nodes (bicycle parking, and bus stops).

The study defines two areas for the analysis: The Isle, located within 400 m of Engineering Faculty, and an extended area delimited by a radius of 800 m from Engineering Faculty (mostly in directions North and East).

Second, the study gathered operational data (e.g., bus lines that operates in the zone, timetables, etc.) and also information about the available infrastructure (e.g., bus stops, bicycle lanes and bicycle parking facilities.) either from open data sources or by personal inspection.

Third, a survey was performed in-situ in the studied area, to gather data for the analysis and characterize sustainable public transportation in Montevideo [14]. Data from 617 persons were collected: 79 living in the area and 538 commuting from other zones of the city. The study identified four relevant groups of people: students of Engineering Faculty and attending Aulario Massera professors and employees of Engineering Faculty, people living in the neighborhood, and people working in the neighborhood [14].

The survey focused on gathering mobility information for the four groups of people. The study reported in this article includes the most relevant information for the analysis: origin/destination of trips and relevant aspects of transportation mode(s) used for commuting. Interviews were performed in November–December 2019, from Monday to Friday, from 8:00 to 19:00. Weekend trips were not surveyed, as the mobility demand is significantly lower than working days trips.

Indicators/Metrics. For the analysis of urban infrastructure, the study examined the surveyed area through different metrics, including:

- The existence and total distance of infrastructure for non-motorized traveling modes, including pedestrian paths and bicycle paths;
- The existence of different elements, such as ramps, on sidewalks that provide universal accessibility;
- To evaluate the land uses, the total area of commercial, residential, educational, recreation and green areas;
- The number of commercial areas in both areas, separated in public places (supermarkets, mini markets or food store) and semi-public places (restaurants, utility shops, health centers, and pharmacies);
- The number of bicycle parkings and bus shelters;
- The maintenance condition of the built environment (bus shelters condition, sidewalks, bicycle paths and green areas, evaluated in three qualitative categories (low, medium, and high). The analysis considers 'The 8 principles of sidewalks' [11] as reference for design and construction of sidewalks and the NACTO Urban Bikeway Design Guide as reference for bicycle paths.

For the mobility analysis in the studied area, two relevant (quantitative) sustainable mobility indicators proposed by the World Business Council for Sustainable Development were used:

- Distance between origin and destination of trips: the real distances that people travel, considering the zones that originate trips to the studied area and also the destination of trips that initiate in the studied area.
- Commuting travel time: the average time spent by a person when traveling from/to the studied area. The average walking speed is assumed to be 5 km/h. For bus, the commuting travel time includes the time for a person to walk to the bus stop and the time waiting for the bus to arrive. For bicycles, the average speed is 13.5 km/h.

Methodology for Data Analysis. For the analysis of urban infrastructure, distances were computed using the Google Maps service, and both green and residential areas were computed using the Google Maps Area Calculator tool. The area of institutions and commercial buildings were measured by personal inspection, using a laser device. Furthermore, bus stops, bike roads, and bicycle parking were also identified by personal inspection to evaluate their maintenance conditions.

The overall characteristics of mobility demand in the area were studied in a previous article [14] using quantitative mobility indicators to evaluate the opportunities that the studied area offers for communication with other zones of Montevideo. According to Calthorpe [7], TOD is conceived to promote non-motorized transportation modes or public transportation instead. However, some studies [10,16] that travel behavior are more associated to human attitudes than to land use characteristics, influenced by certain factors as income, or household composition. On the other hand, Papa and Bertolini [23] stated that the travel behavior can change if other urban characteristics significantly change too (e.g., universal accessibility, good connectivity, safe neighborhoods and attractive streets that promote walking, etc.).

5 Sustainable TOD Analysis

The studied area was analyzed through TOD principles followed by decision makers and urban planners to strengthen their communities, and relevant indicators for sustainable development [24].

Compactness and Mix. Citizens prefer traveling shorter distances to perform their activities, which implies the closer the activities are from each other, the less time required. The study identified that residents have first-needs stores only a few blocks away from home. Maps in Fig. 1 present accurate information about the location of different services, bus stops, bicycle parking, pedestrian only paths, and also identified land uses in the studied area. The upper map reports the information for the studied area (buffer area of 400 m), whereas the map at the bottom reports services in the extended area (buffer area of 800 m).

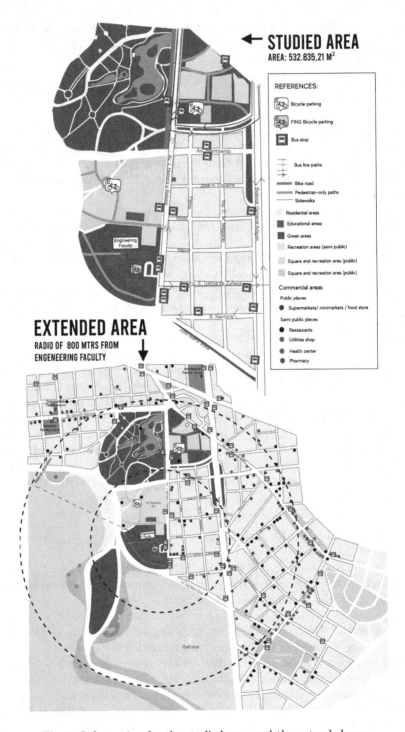

Fig. 1. Information for the studied area and the extended area

Public Spaces. Public spaces contribute to enhance the beauty and environmental quality of neighborhoods, and also contribute to socialization and sustainability. The studied zone provides $0.217\,km^2$ of green areas, which corresponds to 40.6% of the overall land. The average distance for residents walk to a green area is 200 m. Regarding maintenance conditions, municipal workers are responsible for keeping green and public recreation areas clean and in proper conditions.

Density. Urban density is a fundamental principle of sustainable development. Dense development sustains public transportation, shortens travel distances and keeps travel cost affordable. For dense cities, the TOD paradigm supports building up instead of building out to avoid urban sprawl. In this regard, the study analyzed two criteria: residential density and commercial activities density. The residential density correspond to 13.18 residents/ha, and the commercial activities density (over total uses) is 0.1%. These figures confirm that the studied area is most a residential (rather than commercial) area of the city.

Transit–Public Transportation. A good public transportation service should connect many distant areas, creating a more accessible and equitable city. High bus frequencies and the existence of a bus stop in the proximity of residential areas is one of the principles of the TODs approach. The study identified 17 bus stops in the studied area, and residents can walk to them in less than 5 min from their homes. During working days, the bus service operates with a mean frequency of 12 to 17 min on peak hours (7:00 to 22:00), 25 to 35 min from 22:00 to 0:00, and low frequency between 0:00 and 5:00. On weekend days the demand is lower and so the frequency. In general, the maintenance conditions of bus shelters is low. The original design presents a sitting bench, a roof, a commercial panel, lighting, bus line signage and a trash bin. However, the majority of commercial panels, lightening and bus line signage are damaged; 7 out of 10 have the sitting bench, 15 out of 17 already have the roof, and the trash bin is missing in all of them. Moreover, 8 bus shelters are located closer the corner of the street, blocking the visibility for pedestrian that are crossing the street.

Connectivity and Cycling. Safety and comfortable walking and cycling contribute to the TOD approach. Relevant indicators to evaluate those sustainable mobility means are the proportion of pedestrian and cycling routes, intersections density, and the network connectivity. The proportion of cycling and pedestrian routes over the total road network is just 0.2%, a very small proportion. The intersection density in the area is 0.2 and the gamma index connectivity is 0.3, which are reasonable values for a residential neighborhood.

Infrastructure for Pedestrians and Walkability. Regarding design and maintenance conditions of sidewalks, the study analyzed the area through guidelines provided by municipal technicians and city planners to facilitate the design and construction of sidewalks [11], to encourage people to walk more in their daily routine. Overall, sidewalks on the studied area present a proper width that provides pedestrians a comfort and safety walking. Also, the studied area offers universal accessibility with curb ramps in every corner and at the entrance of pedestrian-only paths, providing easy access for people with reduced mobility (e.g., elderly and wheelchair users), people with temporary limitations, pregnant women, or parents with baby strollers. Public lightening is located in all sidewalks in the area, increasing the sensation of security while walking. In turn, vegetation is plentiful in the studied area, motivating people to walk and occupy urban public spaces. However, the connections of sidewalks to other means of transportation presents some issues, such as the lack of crosswalks, poor quality paving, crude design of urban furniture and vegetation, no tactile surfaces integrated into the sidewalks and few informative signage. Furthermore, the studied area present few initiatives to discourage the use of car in the area.

The bicycle path width in the studied area is 2.0 m (two-way bicycle lines with a yellow center line), well below the minimum recommended of 2.5 m. For the intersection crossing markings, color pavement is used to increase visibility within conflict areas or across entire intersections. Elephant feet marks are also used as an alternative to dotted line extensions, to offer increased visibility. Relevant examples of bicycle path design in the studied area are shown in Fig. 2.

Bike lane signs and symbols   Crossing lane

Fig. 2. Bicycle lane design in the studied area (Herrera y Reissig Avenue) (Color figure online)

Shift. To promote sustainable mobility, parking and road use must be regulated to discourage the use of car. According to the guide by NACTO, the maximum recommended speed limits are 15 km/h for shared streets or alleys, 30 km/h for minor streets, and 60 km/h for major streets that have well-protected lines for pedestrians and bicycles. Car speed limit in the studied area is 45 km/h on streets and 60 km/h on avenues. There are no parking restrictions and no fee is charged for parking on the streets. Furthermore, there are three free car parking areas and many open places to park in. Overall, the studied area does not meet with the recommended speed limit and with other policies regulations in order to reduce the use of car and increase sustainable mobility.

Travel Distances and Percentage of Trips. Regarding the number of trips from/to the studied zone, the main findings of the analysis is that many people travel from/to near locations: one third commute from/to less than 3 km away, and 60% from a maximum distance of 5 km). This tendency suggests that the impact of implementing sustainable mobility initiatives following the TOD approach, specially focused on accessibility to nearby locations, will be notable. Furthermore, the study also revealed that 95% of people make a round trip and more than 90% commute from/to the same location at least three times a week. These results demonstrate that mobility demands in the studied zone are regular and steady.

Commuting Travel Time. In line with the analysis of travel distances, Table 1 reports the average commuting travel times from/to the five most demanded origin/destination of trips to/from the studied zone, which are less than 4 km away from the studied zone. One neighborhood that is far away (Prado, 8 km from the studied zone) is also included to analyze the scalability to larger distances (no walking travels were registered for Prado).

Table 1. Commuting travel time to Engineering Faculty from the five most frequent neighborhoods as origin/destination of trips (in minutes).

Neighborhood (average distance)	Bus	Bicycle	Walking	Car
Parque Rodó (~1.0 km)	–	4.4	12.0	5.7
Cordón (~2.5 km)	18.9	11.0	30.0	12.0
Tres Cruces (~3.0 km)	21.2	13.3	36.0	15.2
Pocitos (~3.5 km)	28.4	15.5	42.0	17.0
Centro (~3.7 km)	24.4	21.4	44.4	20.8
Prado (8.0 km)	44.4	35.5	n/a	28.8

For nearby neighborhoods (up to 3.5 km from Engineering Faculty) bicycle is the fastest transportation mode. This is a relevant result, since a large percentage of travels have origin/destination in closer neighborhoods. Up to 8.0 km, car has similar travel time than bicycle and both are faster then bus, suggesting that public transportation is not optimized to provide an appropriate travel time. Even though bicycle is the most convenient traveling mode, the length of bicycle-only lanes in the studied area is not appropriate, as previously commented.

6 Suggestions and Recommendations to Improve Sustainable Mobility Under the TOD Paradigm

From the obtained results, there is evidence to confirm that sustainable mobility in the studied area can be enhanced considering specific TOD-related actions.

Extend the Bicycle Network. The studied area offers a very short bicycle network. The analysis suggest it should be extended along main avenues. This way, the studied area would be connected with relevant places by extending bicycle lanes: seaside (through Sarmiento), other faculties (through Ramirez and Herrera y Reissig), shopping center (through Sosa) and other major neighborhoods and the Terminal Bus Station in Montevideo (through Bulevar Artigas).

Signal Locations for Safe Pedestrian Crossing. A proper signaling of crossings improves walkability, pedestrian safety, and also promotes a better pedestrian behavior. The study also recommend installing a pedestrian crosswalk in front of Engineering Faculty, to improves accessibility for students.

Reallocate Bus Shelters for Safe Crossing. The study recommend reallocating eight bus shelters that are installed closer to corners, in order to improve pedestrian visibility when crossing. Car parking should be prohibited or discouraged in those locations where it implies a risk to pedestrians and other vehicles.

Re-pavement Damaged Sidewalks. The study recommend re-paving low-quality sidewalks, especially those damaged by tree roots, which pose a serious risk for universal accessibility. Also, this issue must be considered for the selection of trees, to avoid them cracking and raising the sidewalks. Sidewalk surfaces must be firm and leveled, for a proper use of wheelchairs, the elder, or people with temporary o permanent walking limitations.

Add Tactile Surfaces to Guide Blind or Visually Impaired People. The area does not provide elements to allow safe walking of visually impaired people. Guides are also missing on bus stops and other relevant locations and they must be properly installed to provide and improve universal accessibility.

Improve Bus Shelters. Comfort on bus shelter improves the image of public transportation. The study recommends an appropriate design to prevent bus shelter being so vulnerable to vandalism, using concrete or other highly resistant materials. Also, the design must provide better protection for adverse climate conditions (e.g., strong wind and rainy days). Every bus shelter must provide a garbage bin and a proper bench for people wait for the bus to arrive.

Promote Walking and Interaction with the Environment. The study demonstrated that sidewalks play an important role in encouraging the interaction between people and the urban environment. Several actions must be developed to provide a better and more pleasant experience: improve information to guide pedestrian to reach destination, provide better and more functional urban furniture and vegetation (planter boxes, garbage bins, benches, etc.), to make the environment more attractive and improve the walking experience.

7   Conclusions and Future Work

This article presented an empirical analysis of sustainable mobility under the TOD paradigm in the area surrounding Engineering Faculty, Universidad de la República, Montevideo, Uruguay. Several relevant indicators were studied to determine the reality and relationships between territory, activities, and mobility.

The study applied urban data analysis to identify a spatial/functional definition of the studied area, using operational data, personal inspection, and a survey performed in/situ in the original and an extended area.

The main findings of the analysis are related on the characterization of several TOD concepts and metrics, related to sustainable mobility. Based on the results of the analysis, specific recommendations are provided to develop a TOD-based approach to improve sustainable mobility in the studied area. The main goals of the proposed suggestions are related to improve the walking experience, provide universal accessibility, promote walking and bicycle, and the interaction with public transportation. This is a direct contribution oft he reported research, since no previous similar studies have been developed in Montevideo.

The main lines for future work are related to extend the analysis to consider other relevant TOD concepts and indicators to better characterize sustainable mobility and the impact of recommended actions in the studied zone.

References

1. Alba, H., Grindlay, A., Ochoa, G.: (In)equitable accessibility to sustainable transport from universities in Guadalajara metropolitan area, México. Sustainability **13**, 55 (2020)
2. Banister, D.: The sustainable mobility paradigm. Transp. Policy **15**, 73–80 (2008)
3. Bertolini, L.: Nodes and places: complexities of railway station redevelopment. Eur. Plan. Stud. **4**(3), 331–45 (1996)
4. Bertolini, L., Curtis, C., Renne, J.: Station area projects in Europe and beyond: towards transitoriented development. Built Environ. **38**(1), 31–50 (2012)
5. Bocarejo, J., Portilla, I., Pérez, M.: Impact of transmilenio on density, land use, and land value in Bogotá. Res. Transp. Econ. **40**(1), 78–86 (2013)
6. Burchell, R., Listokin, D., Galley, C.: Smart growth: more than a ghost of urban policy past, less than a bold new horizon. Hous. Policy Debate **11**, 821–879 (2000)
7. Calthorpe, P.: The Next American Metropolis: Ecology, Community and the American Dream. Princeton Architectural Press, Hudson (1993)
8. Cervero, R.: Transit-oriented development's ridership bonus: a product of self-selection and public policies. Environ. Plan. A Econ. Space **39**(9), 2068–2085 (2007)
9. Cervero, R., Dai, D.: BRT TOD: leveraging transit oriented development with bus rapid transit investments. Transp. Policy **36**, 127–138 (2014)
10. De Vos J., Van Acker V., W.F.: The influence of attitudes on transit oriented development: an explorative analysis. Transp. Policy **35**(5), 326–329 (2014)
11. Dos Santos, P., Caccia, L., Barbosa, A., Zoppaas, L.: The 8 Principles of Sidewalks. World Resources Institute (2019)
12. Gudmundsson, H., Hall, R.P., Marsden, G., Zietsman, J.: High-speed rail in England. In: Sustainable Transportation. STBE, pp. 233–250. Springer, Heidelberg (2016). https://doi.org/10.1007/978-3-662-46924-8_9

13. Hasibuan, H.S., Soemardi, T.P., Koestoer, R., Moersidik, S.: The role of Transit Oriented Development in constructing urban environment sustainability, the case of Jabodetabek, Indonesia. Procedia Environ. Sci. **20**, 622–631 (2014)
14. Hipogrosso, S., Nesmachnow, S.: Analysis of sustainable public transportation and mobility recommendations for Montevideo and Parque Rodó neighborhood. Smart Cities **3**(2), 479–510 (2020)
15. Jeon, C., Amekudzi, M.: Addressing sustainability in transportation systems: definitions, indicators, and metrics. Infrastruct. Syst. **11**(1), 31–50 (2005)
16. Kitamura, R., Mokhtarian, P.: A micro-analysis of land use and travel in five neighborhoods in the San Francisco Bay area. Transportation **24**, 125–158 (1997)
17. Litman, T., Burwell, D.: Issues in sustainable transportation. Int. J. Global Environ. Issues **6**(4), 331–347 (2006)
18. Loo, B., Du Verle, F.: Transit-oriented development in future cities: towards a two-level sustainable mobility strategy. Urban Sci. **21**, 54–67 (2016)
19. Marshall, S.: The challenge of sustainable transport. In: Layard, A., Davoudi, S., Batty, S. (eds.) Planning for a Sustainable Future, pp. 131–147. Spon Press, London (2001)
20. Moscoso, M., van Laake, T., Quiñones, L. (eds.): Sustainable Urban Mobility in Latin America: Assessment and Recommendations for Mobility Policies. Despacio, Bogotá (2019)
21. Neckermann, L.: Smart Cities, Smart Mobility: Transforming the Way We Live and Work. Troubador Publishing Ltd. (2017)
22. Newman, P., Kenworthy, J.: The land use-transport connection: an overview. Land Use Policy **13**, 1–22 (1995)
23. Papa, E., Bertolini, L.: Accessibility and transit-oriented development in European metropolitan areas. J. Transp. Geogr. **47**, 70–83 (2015)
24. Renne, J.: From transit-adjacent to transit-oriented development. Local Environ. **14**(1), 1–15 (2009)
25. Rodriguez, D., Vergel, E.: Urban development around bus rapid transit stops in seven cities in Latin-America. J. Urban. Int. Res. Placemaking Urban Sustain. **11**(2), 175–201 (2017)
26. Sung, H., Oh, J.: Transit-oriented development in a high-density city: identifying its association with transit ridership in Seoul. Cities **28**, 70–82 (2011)
27. Tsigdinos, S., Paraskevopoulos, Y., Rallatou, N.: Transit Oriented Development (TOD). Challenges and perspectives; the case of Athens' Metro Line 4. In: European Transport Conference (2019)
28. Woo, J.: Classification of TOD typologies based on pedestrian behavior for sustainable and active urban growth in Seoul. Sustainability **13**(6), 3047 (2021)
29. World Business Council for Sustainable Development: The sustainable mobility project (2002)

Internet of Things, Smart Energy
and Smart Grid

Development and Improvement of a Data Storage System in a Microgrid Environment with HomeAssistant and MariaDB

Oscar Izquierdo-Monge$^{(\boxtimes)}$, Gonzalo Martin-Jimenez, and Paula Peña-Carro

CEDER-CIEMAT, Autovía de Navarra A15 salida 56, 422290 Lubia (Soria), Spain
{oscar.izquierdo,paula.pena}@ciemat.es

Abstract. In a microgrid environment, it's suitable to store data obtained from the different devices that make up the microgrid in order to have the ability to perform a detailed data analysis later. This article will detail the process followed to store the data that has been collected through the monitoring and control software 'Home Assistant' in the microgrid of the CEDER-CIEMAT (Renewable Energy Center in Soria, Spain). The structure of the storage system created for a robust storage of data in the DBMS (Database Management System) MariaDB will be detailed and how to correct the different typical errors that are made in the development process of this storage system. Aspects the operation of the connection between Home Assistant and MariaDB, the configuration to establish communication with each other correctly and the organization of the different structures to be formed in the database created using the programming language SQL (Structured Query Language). It will detail the performance offered by this system together with the transformed data that has been generated for further analysis. Due to the emergence of new storage systems that are better adapted to the field of microgrids, the different alternatives that can be used will be described, which may replace the system developed to improve it.

Keywords: Microgrids · Data storage · Home Assistant · MariaDB · Data analytics · SCADA

1 Introduction

In recent years, IoT (Internet of Things) technology has become increasingly popular, this type of technology can be seen as it is applied in homes with the so-called domotics, applied to energy saving in the home, security and comfort, among others. It is also applied in modern cities with the 'Smart Cities' concept, facilitating mobility, improving the environment and the way of life for citizens. It can also be applicable to the industry to achieve greater efficiency in production and obtain analysis of the different processes that are carried out in order to obtain a series of improvements in the production process.

© Springer Nature Switzerland AG 2022
S. Nesmachnow and L. Hernández Callejo (Eds.): ICSC-Cities 2021, CCIS 1555, pp. 273–284, 2022.
https://doi.org/10.1007/978-3-030-96753-6_19

274   O. Izquierdo-Monge et al.

The term 'Internet of Things' has come to represent electrical or electronic devices, of varying sizes and capabilities, that are connected to the Internet. The scope of the connections is ever broadening to beyond just machine-to-machine communication (M2M) [1]. All those devices are seamlessly integrated into the information network, and where the physical objects can become active participants in business processes. Services are available to interact with these 'smart objects' over the Internet, query their state and any information associated with them [2].

IoT technology can also be applied in the energy sector, obtaining various benefits and advantages, i.e., in energy supply, transmission and distribution, and demand. IoT can be employed for improving energy efficiency, increasing the share of renewable energy, and reducing environmental impacts of the energy use. Energy systems are on the threshold of a new transition era, the need for efficient use of energy calls for system-wide, integrated approaches to minimize the socio-economic-environmental impacts of energy systems. In this respect, modern technologies such as IoT can help the energy sector transform from a central, hierarchical supply chain to a decentralized, smart, and optimized system [3,4]. The advancements in computational intelligence capabilities can evolve an intelligent IoT system by emulating biological nervous systems with cognitive computation, streaming and distributed analytics including at the edge and device levels [5].

Knowing the advantages that IoT technology has in the energy sector, as a logical consequence it is possible to apply it in an energy distribution and storage system, thus obtaining the concept of an intelligent electrical microgrid, which is defined as a local smaller electricity systems that can operate independently and separated from the main electricity grid. Microgrids provide improved security and availability for the electrical distribution system while reducing the carbon emissions [6]. A smart grid is an electricity network that can intelligently integrate the actions of all users connected to it - generators, consumers and those that assume both roles - in order to efficiently deliver sustainable, economic and secure electricity supplies. A smart grid employs innovative products and services together with intelligent monitoring, control, communication and self-healing technologies. Wired and wireless technology based integrated, robust and reliable communication network is needed for real time monitoring and control of microgrids [7,8].

Once the connection of the microgrid has been made, with all the elements connected to each other and to be able to monitor the different variables in real time and to be able to have control over the devices, the next step to follow will be to store the acquired data in order to carry out a precise analysis subsequently. The data storage is controlled by a DBMS, with a stable infrastructure that allows to save large amounts of data with a fast read/write speed to be able to make queries to the database easily.

Traditional database systems used SQL database which has supported all the user requirements along with simplicity, robustness, flexibility, scalability, performance. But the main limitation they are facing is their static schema which is making RDBMS (Relational Database Management System) not suitable for IoT applications. On the other hand, NoSQL (non SQL) databases emerging in market have claimed to perform better than SQL database. With the emergence of IoT and Big Data, NoSQL databases now represent an alternative to traditional relational databases in terms of simpler design and faster operations on large data volumes [9–11]. It is worth highlighting within the non-relational databases the real-time databases that are gaining increasing popularity in recent years, these databases save the values in time series (timestamps) and allow different functions to be performed with the data, all oriented to IoT applications [12].

The software and hardware used in this use case is detailed in Sects. 2 and 3 explains the operation of data storage in 'Home Assistant', Sect. 4 explains the connection between Home Assistant and MariaDB, in Sect. 5 the various steps to follow for the configuration of the MariaDB server are detailed to start operating the database, then in Sect. 6 the structure of the data stored by default in Home Assistant is exposed along with the transformation of these as convenient in Sect. 7, in Sect. 8 the results obtained thanks to the implementation of the database in the whole monitoring system and the benefits of storing data for subsequent analysis are exposed and finally in Sect. 9 the conclusions are narrated, where the importance of having a robust database in microgrids will be exposed, in addition to the next line of work in the field of data storage in the center's microgrid.

2   Materials and Methods

To carry out the work, the data storage system will be implemented in the CEDER-CIEMAT (Renewable Energy Center in Soria, Spain, as shown in Fig. 1) microgrid, data will be stored in a relational database such as MariaDB [13], where it will be periodically stored for later analysis.

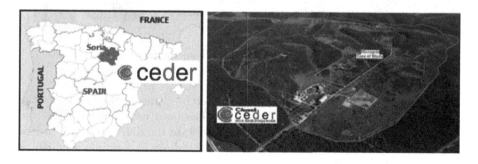

Fig. 1. CEDER-CIEMAT location.

CEDER grid is connected to a 45 kV distribution network and transforms at its input to 15 kV. Eight transformation centres make up the grid, reducing the voltage to 400 V. The centre has various non-controllable renewable (photo-voltaic and wind), controllable renewable (hydraulic turbine), and non-renewable (diesel generator) generation systems, several storage systems, mechanical (pumping system with tanks at different levels) and electrochemical (lithium-ion and Pb-acid batteries), as well as various consumption elements connected to each of the transformation centres monitored with grid analyzers (PQube) installed in the low voltage part of each of the transformation centres [14].

To carry out the tests it will be used a Raspberry Pi 4 Model B (Broadcom BCM2711, Quad core Cortex-A72 (ARM v8) 64-bit SoC @ 1.5 GHz, LPDDR4-3200 SD RAM, 64 GB Micro-SD card, 5 V DC) [15], obtaining all the data related to performance and consumption to be able to carry out an analysis with processing times. The system will be developed using two Raspberry computers, each with its corresponding dedicated software (Home Assistant and MariaDB), although this design decision is optional.

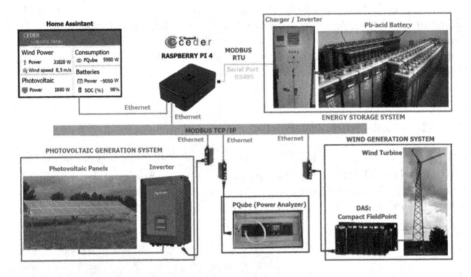

Fig. 2. Example of device connection in CEDER microgrid with Home Assistant.

For the monitoring and control of the different elements that make up the microgrid, the Home Assistant software [16] has been used., as shown in the diagram of the Fig. 2. This software allows to obtain the different values in real time of different elements and save them in a database in a simple way. Home Assistant can support more than 1000 devices, allowing to control and automate them, with a wide variety of extensions, security, smartphone support and power manager. For the development of this system, version 2021.8.8 of this software has been used.

For data storage, the DBMS MariaDB is used, a relational-type database that it's made by the original developers of MySQL and guaranteed to stay open source. It is part of most cloud offerings and the default in most Linux distributions. It is built upon the values of performance, stability, and openness

[13]. For the development of this system, version v10.3.29-MariaDB-0 + deb10u1 of this software has been used.

3   Data Storage Behavior in Home Assistant

In order to store the data that is being monitored by the Home Assistant software, it is necessary to have a database in order to achieve robust, reliable data storage that allows high-speed read/write operations.

Home Assistant stores the data thanks to the integration called 'recorder' by default the data is stored in its own database located in the configuration directory of the Home Assistant itself using SQLite as the database engine, this database is automatically generated in a file with the extension '.db'. Home Assistant uses SQLAlchemy, a Python SQL toolkit and Object Relational Mapper that provides the application with support for all types of operations in relational databases. This communication flow is explained in Fig. 3. With Home Assistant and SQLAlchemy, the supported relational databases are SQLite, MySQL, PostgreSQL, and MS SQL Server. In this use case, the MariaDB database will be used, since the default database, SQLite has several limitations such as limiting the maximum to 264 rows for a table or advanced and complex functions in SQL that are not supported, therefore that it will be mandatory to use the another database management system.

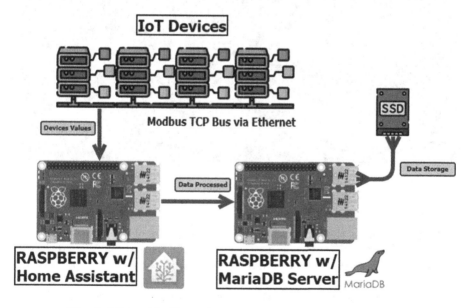

Fig. 3. Microgrid - Home Assistant - MariaDB flow connection.

This database can be installed both on the device/server on which Home Assistant is running as well as on another independent device/server, for this use case the implementation will be carried out through the second option, as it is advisable to build the system following the modularization-oriented micro-services architecture for better performance and security.

It is also advisable to use storage systems other than the microSD card that Raspberry uses by default, it is possible to connect an external hard drive through the USB inputs, even an external SSD (Solid-State Drive), this being the most recommended option and the one used in this use case. Different advantages are obtained with this system since the data read/write transmission speed is much higher compared to a microSD and the life expectancy and reliability is greater since microSD cards are not designed to perform operations constantly or to store large amounts of data.

4   Setting Up the Connection Between Home Assistant and MariaDB

To use MariaDB it is necessary to install the server of this software on a device, to connect it and be able to link it with Home Assistant it will be necessary to modify the configuration file.

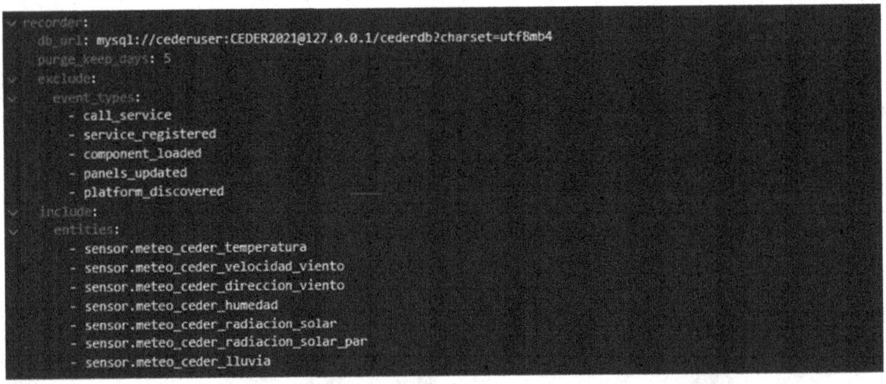

```
recorder:
  db_url: mysql://cederuser:CEDER2021@127.0.0.1/cederdb?charset=utf8mb4
  purge_keep_days: 5
  exclude:
    event_types:
      - call_service
      - service_registered
      - component_loaded
      - panels_updated
      - platform_discovered
  include:
    entities:
      - sensor.meteo_ceder_temperatura
      - sensor.meteo_ceder_velocidad_viento
      - sensor.meteo_ceder_direccion_viento
      - sensor.meteo_ceder_humedad
      - sensor.meteo_ceder_radiacion_solar
      - sensor.meteo_ceder_radiacion_solar_par
      - sensor.meteo_ceder_lluvia
```

Fig. 4. Recorder integration in the home assistant configuration file.

This file declares the connection with the IP address of the device where the database is located, the port it uses, the name of the database where it will operate, along with the username and password with the necessary permissions to perform the operations. An example of this configuration is shown in Fig. 4.

In this configuration file, with the "recorder" integration we can also declare the variables that we want to be stored, thanks to this it is possible to separate the monitored variables and the subset of them that are going to be saved.

With this connection we indicate that the database is of type MySQL and that the database called "cederdb" located at IP address 10.10.103.80 will be accessed, accessing with the user "cederuser" and its password "cederpass". Once the "recorder" integration is configured, other integrations such as "loogbook" or "hystorygraph" will be enabled, which will allow the Home Assistant web environment to view the changes in the variables and historical graphs of the different variables. An example of a monitored variable is shown in the graph in the Fig. 5.

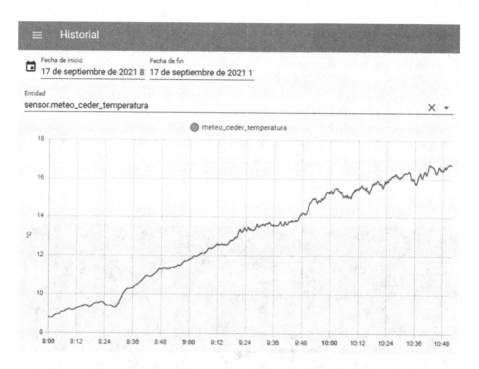

Fig. 5. History graph integration in Home Assistant.

5 Installation and Configuration of the MariaDB Server

In order to start using the database, it will be necessary to install the MariaDB server using the "apt" tool, in this case in its stable version v10.3.29-MariaDB-0 + deb10u1, in the repository, this package is called "mariadb-server". You will also need a Python client that performs the operations such as "pymysql" or "mysqlclient". When working as independent modules there can be no conflict between the version of Home Assistant and MariaDB, so there is no problem about which version each software uses for compatibility. Once the server is installed, the database and a user will be created, which will serve as access for the connection between the database and the Home Assistant application. To do this using the command "sudo mysql -u root", with which you access the mysql command line interpreter, three different commands will be executed:

A database schema is created, on which it is going to operate, with the name 'homeassistant' using the following command:

"$ *CREATE DATABASE cederdb;*"

A user is created with the name "cederuser" who can access from any device on the network and whose password is "CEDER2021". With this user you can access and operate Home Assistant with the database. To carry out this operation it is necessary to enter the following command:

"$ *CREATE USER 'cederuser'@'*' IDENTIFIED BY 'cederpass';*"

Permissions are given to the "cederuser" user from any device on the network to perform any type of operation on any of the available schemes and tables by means of the following command:

"$ *GRANT ALL PRIVILEGES ON '*'.'*' TO 'cederuser'@'*';*"

And the privileges of the users will be updated by the command:

"$ *FLUSH PRIVILEGES;*"

The next step will be to configure the MariaDB server by modifying the configuration file, for this the 'nano' tool will be used, which is a text editor, indicating the path of the configuration file itself:

"*/etc./mysql/mariadb.conf.d/50-server.cnf*"

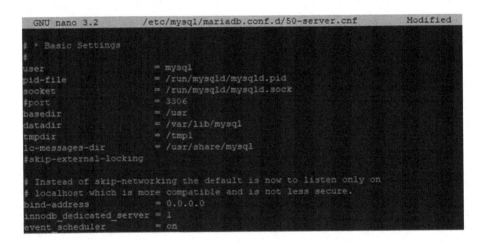

Fig. 6. MariaDB configuration file.

Inside the configuration file, a variable will be modified and two new ones will be added: In order for the server to be accessible from any device on the network, it will be necessary to modify the variable "bind-address", which by default its value is 127.0.0.1 (localhost), it will be changed to the value 0.0.0.0 so that the server is accessible for all devices on the network. It is also possible to add a list of IP addresses so that only certain devices can operate with the database, indicating the desired list of IP addresses. There is a default example of this configuration on the config file of Fig. 6.

By means of the variable "innodbdedicatedserver" the server is indicated that the device that is running the server, in this case a raspberry, is only dedicated to running this database service, which will automatically assign some memory values, buffer and cache that allow to take advantage of the maximum efficiency of the device for the MariaDB server.

Regarding the execution of events on the MariaDB server, it is disabled by default, that is, we can only execute events through the command line, but not schedule them for a certain date and that they are executed at that moment, to enable this function it will be necessary create the variable "event_scheduler" with a default value of "on".

6 Structure of the Default Data Storage in Home Assistant

By default, Home Assistant stores the data in the database to which it is automatically connected, this data has a certain structure optimized for recording and graphic representation in Home Assistant, but it is quite ineffective for a later analysis carried out with third-party software.

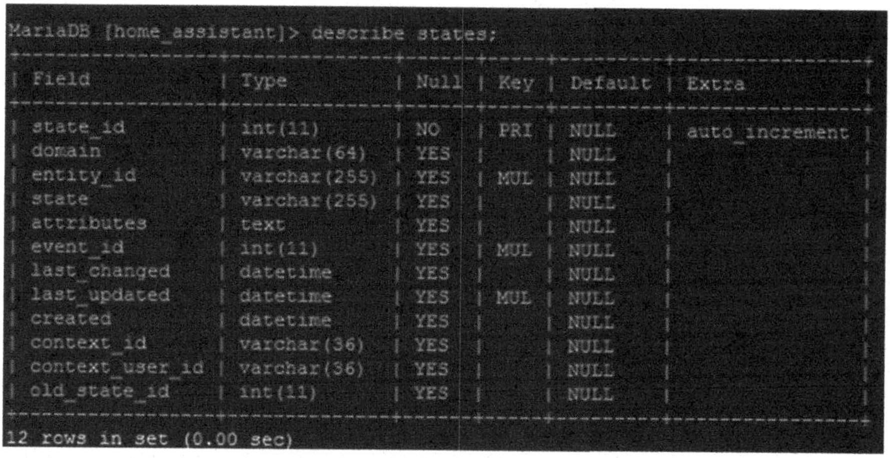

```
MariaDB [home_assistant]> describe states;
+----------------+--------------+------+-----+---------+----------------+
| Field          | Type         | Null | Key | Default | Extra          |
+----------------+--------------+------+-----+---------+----------------+
| state_id       | int(11)      | NO   | PRI | NULL    | auto_increment |
| domain         | varchar(64)  | YES  |     | NULL    |                |
| entity_id      | varchar(255) | YES  | MUL | NULL    |                |
| state          | varchar(255) | YES  |     | NULL    |                |
| attributes     | text         | YES  |     | NULL    |                |
| event_id       | int(11)      | YES  | MUL | NULL    |                |
| last_changed   | datetime     | YES  |     | NULL    |                |
| last_updated   | datetime     | YES  | MUL | NULL    |                |
| created        | datetime     | YES  |     | NULL    |                |
| context_id     | varchar(36)  | YES  |     | NULL    |                |
| context_user_id| varchar(36)  | YES  |     | NULL    |                |
| old_state_id   | int(11)      | YES  |     | NULL    |                |
+----------------+--------------+------+-----+---------+----------------+
12 rows in set (0.00 sec)
```

Fig. 7. Default data structure in Home Assistant

The structure of the stored data, described on Fig. 7 is quite ineffective for a later analysis of them, so we will proceed to transform this structure into a more adequate one. The structure provided is as follows:

An example of a tuple stored in this table is as follows:

```
id: 71530000
last_changed: 2021-08-14 02:12:34
last_updated: 2021-08-14 02:12:34
created: 2021-08-14 02:12:40
event_id: 71527383
old_state_id: 71527387
domain: sensor
entity_id: sensor.pqube7pepaiiiturbina500
state: 294
unitofmeasurement: W
friendlyname: PQUBE7PEPAIIITURBINA500
```

These tuples store three important values that will be used in the new structure, which are the name of the monitored variable ('state_id', in this case "sensor.pqube7pepaiiiturbina500"), the value of that variable ("state", in this case 294 Watts/hour of active power) and the instant of time in which the variable has changed its value ("last_updated", in this case 2021-08-14 02:12:34); the other values are totally unnecessary for the treatment and analysis to be carried out, so they will be ignored in the new table structure created from it.

7   Data Structure Transformation

In the new structure, a new row will not be generated with each change in the value of a variable, but rather each row will correspond to one second in the given time, that is, each day we will have 86,400 rows, which correspond to the seconds that a day has . In each row the value of all the variables at that instant of time will be saved. The instants of time in which there has been no change in value will be filled in with the previous value of the specific variable.

In this new structure, only the values of the devices are stored every second in time, resulting in tuples with an identifier number, date and the values of all the devices at that instant of time.

From this table, a new one will be generated with the values in 15-minute averages, which will serve for a subsequent analysis of the data. These data in averages of 15 min will be saved forever in the database and the data will be eliminated from the table in seconds for better performance and efficiency in database storage.

The insertion of data in the new tables is carried out through events automatically, every day after 00:00 the necessary insertions and calculations will be made to introduce the data values of the previous day into the tables.

To operate with large amounts of data as is this case, it is necessary to use different mechanisms, so that the database engine uses all the hardware of the equipment, the equipment will be limited to the operation of the database service as It is indicated in the installation process and to handle the numerous queries made, "HASH"-type indexes specialized in equality queries will be used. With all this, the database is capable of processing 2.5 million daily operations in 30 min.

8 Different Methods of Data Analysis

Once the data is monitored and stored, it is time to perform an analysis on that data, for this, in this case the data will be exported through automated SQL queries daily in an Excel sheet to obtain a unified view of them.

These excel sheets can be modified using MACROS to obtain a transformation of these daily data into graphs and tables that offer a quick overview of the values obtained.

It is also possible to use other data analysis methods using business intelligence technology and the software associated with this technology, such as PowerBI, Tableau, Domo, Grafana, etc. With this software we will be able to connect with the database created and collect the data through queries to create graphs in a simple way.

9 Conclusions

Thanks to the inclusion of the database in the monitoring system, it is possible to use additional integrations offered by Home Assistant such as a record and time series graphs, this allows obtaining a quick visualization of the values of a variable without leaving the web environment by Home Assistant. Apart from this advantage, the data is automatically saved in a database in which it is possible to access a history of data since it has been stored. In the field of microgrids it is quite important to have historical data available to be able to make a concrete analysis of them in posterity.

The Home Assistant tool allows you to easily store the data, although it is designed to support a couple of weeks of data by default, it is possible to transform this data to save it in a database independent of the system that allows you to save the data historically without limits, Even so, Home Assistant offers different integrations that save the data in periods of time but do not allow to choose the way of grouping that data.

In recent years a good type of database has been used in the field of IoT technology, which are time series databases, you can find different managers such as InfluxDB, Prometheus, Timescale, DBGraphite, etc. This type of database is ideal for storing data in the field of microgrids since their main values to save are the value of a variable and the instant of time in which this variable has changed its value, in addition to a a large number of advanced functions to perform statistical calculations, that is why the center will migrate data to this new time series DBMS to implement it in the already developed system and obtain a data reading/writing time greater and less use of storage space.

References

1. Miraz, M.H., Ali, M., Excell, P.S., Picking, R.: A review on internet of things (IOT), internet of everything (IOE) and internet of Nano things (IONT). In: 2015 Internet Technologies and Applications (ITA), pp. 219–224 (2015). https://doi.org/10.1109/ITechA.2015.7317398
2. Weber, R.H., Weber, R.: Introduction, pp. 1–22. Springer, Heidelberg (2010). https://doi.org/10.1007/978-3-642-11710-7_1
3. Hossein Motlagh, N., Mohammadrezaei, M., Hunt, J., Zakeri, B.: Internet of things (IOT) and the energy sector. Energies 13(2), 404 (2020). https://doi.org/10.3390/en13020494. https://www.mdpi.com/1996-1073/13/2/494
4. Liu, X., Ansari, N.: Toward green IoT: energy solutions and key challenges. IEEE Commun. Mag. 57(3), 104–110 (2019). https://doi.org/10.1109/MCOM.2019.1800175
5. Bedi, G., Venayagamoorthy, G.K., Singh, R., Brooks, R.R., Wang, K.C.: Review of internet of things (IoT) in electric power and energy systems. IEEE Internet of Things J. 5(2), 847–870 (2018). https://doi.org/10.1109/JIOT.2018.2802704
6. Zubieta, L.E.: Power management and optimization concept for DC microgrids. In: 2015 IEEE First International Conference on DC Microgrids (ICDCM), pp. 81–85 (2015). https://doi.org/10.1109/ICDCM.2015.7152014
7. Islam, M., Lee, H.H.: Microgrid communication network with combined technology. In: 2016 5th International Conference on Informatics, Electronics and Vision (ICIEV), pp. 423–427 (2016). https://doi.org/10.1109/ICIEV.2016.7760039
8. Hatziargyriou, N.: The microgrids concept. In: Microgrids: Architectures and Control, pp. 1–24 (2014). https://doi.org/10.1002/9781118720677.ch01
9. Asiminidis, C., Georgiadis, I., Syndoukas, D., Kokkonis, G., Kontogiannis, S.: Performance evaluation on encrypted - non encrypted database fields containing IOT data. In: Proceedings of the 23rd International Database Applications and Engineering Symposium, IDEAS 2019. Association for Computing Machinery, New York, NY, USA (2019). https://doi.org/10.1145/3331076.3331097
10. Rautmare, S., Bhalerao, D.M.: MySQL and NoSQL database comparison for IOT application. In: 2016 IEEE International Conference on Advances in Computer Applications (ICACA), pp. 235–238 (2016). https://doi.org/10.1109/ICACA.2016.7887957
11. Reetishwaree, S., Hurbungs, V.: Evaluating the performance of SQL and NoSQL databases in an IOT environment. In: 2020 3rd International Conference on Emerging Trends in Electrical, Electronic and Communications Engineering (ELECOM), pp. 229–234 (2020). https://doi.org/10.1109/ELECOM49001.2020.9297028
12. Ming, D., Tian, X., Lei, W.: Research of real-time database system for microgrid. In: The 2nd International Symposium on Power Electronics for Distributed Generation Systems, pp. 708–712 (2010). https://doi.org/10.1109/PEDG.2010.5545839
13. Mariadb foundation (2019). https://mariadb.org/
14. Izquierdo-Monge, O., et al.: Conversion of a network section with loads, storage systems and renewable generation sources into a smart microgrid. Appl. Sci. 11(11), 5012 (2021). https://doi.org/10.3390/app11115012. https://www.mdpi.com/2076-3417/11/11/5012
15. Pi, R.: Raspberry Pi 4 model B specifications. https://www.raspberrypi.org/products/raspberry-pi-4-model-b/specifications/
16. Home Assistant. https://www.home-assistant.io/

P2P Energy Trading Model for a Local Electricity Community Considering Technical Constraints

Fernando García-Muñoz[1(✉)], Francisco Díaz-González[2], and Cristina Corchero[1]

[1] IREC Catalonia Institute for Energy Research, C. Jardins de les Dones de Negre, 1, Pl. 2a, 08930 Sant Adrià del Besòs, Spain
fernando.garciam@usach.c
[2] Departament d'Enginyeria Elèctrica, Universitat Politècnica de Catalunya ETS d'Enginyeria Industrial de Barcelona, Avinguda Diagonal, 647, Pl. 2, 08028 Barcelona, Spain

Abstract. This article proposes a new formulation to model the energy traded among peers into a distribution network (DN) with high distributed energy resources (DERs) penetration, considering a centralized market design. The goal is to minimize the energy purchased to the grid and quantify the savings when exchanging energy among prosumers and consumers. The technical constraints are based on DC power flow equations, while the graph theory is used to model the local energy market (LEM). The proposed formulation is tested under two modified IEEE 5 and 33 bus systems, reporting savings in both study cases.

Keywords: Peer-to-peer energy trading · Distributed energy resources · Local energy markets · Smart grids

Nomenclature

$i \in \mathbb{B}$	Set of buses.
$t \in \mathbb{T}$	Set of time periods.
$d \in \mathbb{D}$	Set of types of flexible demand resources.
$(i,j) \in \mathbb{L}$	Set of lines, such that $\mathbb{L} = \{(i,j); i,j \in \mathbb{B}\}$.
PG_t^{max}	Maximum active power available at the period t in [%].
$PL_{i,t}$	Non-flexible active load of the bus i at the period t [kW].
V^{min}	Minimum voltage allowed for the bus i [p.u.].
V^{max}	Maximum voltage allowed for the bus i [p.u.].
$S_{i,j}^{max}$	Maximum apparent power of the line between buses i and j [kVA].
SOC^{min}	Minimum state of charge of battery [%].
SOC^{max}	Maximum state of charge of battery [%].
β_i^p	Maximum rated power of generator of the bus i [kW].
β_i^{bt}	Capacity of the Battery of the bus i [kWh].
I_i^{pg}	Binary parameters; 1 if bus i has generation, 0 otherwise.

© Springer Nature Switzerland AG 2022
S. Nesmachnow and L. Hernández Callejo (Eds.): ICSC-Cities 2021, CCIS 1555, pp. 285–296, 2022.
https://doi.org/10.1007/978-3-030-96753-6_20

I_i^{bt}	Binary parameters; 1 if bus i has battery, 0 otherwise.
φ	Efficiency of battery [%].
M^{bt}	Maximum charge/discharge for battery in a period [kW].
λ_t^{bg}	Electricity price bought to the grid at the period t [kW].
λ_t^{sg}	Electricity price sold to the grid at the period t [kW].
λ_t^{bm}	Electricity price bought to the market at the period t [kW].
λ_t^{sm}	Electricity price sold to the market at the period t [kW].
Pfd^d	Load for the flexible demand type d [kW].
Nfd_i^d	Total number of hours that Pfd^d should be active in a period of time.
$pg_{i,t}$	Active power injected from the generator in the bus i at period t [kW].
$v_{i,t}$	Voltage of the bus i at the period t [p.u].
$\theta_{i,t}$	Angle of the bus i at the period t [p.u].
$p_{i,j,t}$	Active power in line between buses i and j at the period t [kW].
$ch_{i,t}$	Power absorbed by the battery of the bus i at the period t [kW].
$ds_{i,t}$	Power injected from the storage to the bus i at the period t [kW].
$soc_{i,t}$	State of charge of battery of the bus i at the period t [kWh].
$w_{i,t}$	Binary variable: 1 if the battery is charging in bus i at period t, 0 otherwise.
$p_{i,t}^{sc}$	Self-consumption energy by the bus i at the period t [kW].
$p_{i,t}^{bg}$	Energy bought to the grid by the bus i at the period t [kW].
$p_{i,t}^{sg}$	Energy sold to the grid by the bus i at the period t [kW].
$p_{i,t}^{bm}$	Energy bought to the market by the bus i at the period t [kW].
$p_{i,t}^{sm}$	Energy sold to the market by the bus i at the period t [kW].
$pl_{i,t}$	Total electricity load of bus i at the period t [kW].
$\tau_{i,t}^d$	Binary variable: 1 if the flexible demand type d is activated, 0 otherwise.

1   Introduction

Newmarket structures have emerged as an alternative to face an increasing penetration of distributed energy resources (DERs) in low voltage distribution networks (LVDN), where some more empowered, aware and active consumers have opted for self-consumption and to include storage energy systems to reduce the electricity bill and their dependence from the grid [14]. Peer-to-peer energy trading belongs to this new structure that seeks to increase self-generated energy efficiency by selling and buying its surplus within of small-scale smart-grid community. The residential areas composed of prosumers and consumers willing to exchange surplus energy are the baseline of this local energy market (LEM) [13]. However, the design of a platform that allows this new paradigm's correct operation is still under research, becoming the focus of many works over the last years [1–9].

The work done by [5] establishes a framework for local energy trading, presenting definitions and classification of market players and the different market-clearing approaches in the literature. Likewise, a state-of-the-art and perspective are presented in [6], discussing the critical aspect for a proper P2P energy trading, which are: trading platforms, physical infrastructure, policy, market design, information and communication technology (ICT) infrastructure. Under the market design aspect (the focus of the model proposed in this article), there are three subcategories: centralized, decentralized or distributed markets. The first one could maximize the community's social welfare because a coordinator decides the energy amount exchange. In the decentralized market, the users have complete control over their devices, and they decide when selling or buying; however, the total community efficiency is affected. The distributed market design is between the two above, where a coordinator provides accurate information about pricing and the community requirement, and the peer decides when sell/buy, generating better coordination between them than decentralized design [6].

Two approaches are presented in [2] to compare the community-based and decentralized market based on optimal power flow (OPF) and continuous double auction (CDA), respectively. The work in [3] presents a bidding-based Hierarchical P2P energy transaction optimization model, which considers the prosumer's objective in terms of standard and green energy preference. The authors in [4] propose a bi-level optimization model for the decentralized P2P energy market without considering technical constraints; however, the proposed method in [4] achieves proper peers coordination without sacrificing privacy. A multi-class energy management concept is used in [9] to presents a P2P energy platform that allows coordinate trading among peers with preferences beyond the typical financial criteria, minimizing losses and battery depreciation. A game-theoretic approach is applied by [7] and [1] for P2P energy trading using the cooperative and the noncooperative game, respectively. However, both studies are not based on the power flow equations, and therefore, they do not include technical constraints in their formulation. The work done by [8] proposes a decentralized market clearing mechanism for the P2P energy trading considering the agents' privacy, power losses, and the utilization fees for using the third-party-owned network, where the fees are proportional to the electrical distance between producers and consumers.

The article's major contribution is a scalable and new P2P energy trading model, based on graph theory and the power flow equations, for a small-scale community local energy market with a centralized market design, considering high DERs penetration and flexible demand.

The rest of the paper is organized as follows. Section 2 describes the mixed-linear programming problem. Section 3 presents the computational results under two cases of study. Finally, the following steps to expand the model are discussed in Sect. 4.

2   Peer-to-Peer Energy Trading Model

The formulation presented in this article pretends to model a small local community market with penetration of rooftop PV systems, batteries and flexible demand. Through the purchase and sale of energy exchanged among peers, the community minimize the electricity purchased to the grid and maximize the use of the DERs, considering the following assumptions:

- The information related to the power loaded, generated and stored by peers is known.
- There is a safety mechanism to buy and sell energy within the small local market.
- The community is connected to an external grid which provides the remaining energy.
- The community buy and sell energy under a global internal market price and not an individual price.
- The peers seek to minimize their cost and maximize their benefits.
- The energy bought/sold to the grid is connected to the respective bus (not to slack bus), such that the power flow within the lines is only the energy exchanged among peers and not the energy from/to the grid.
- The power flow equations have been considered in their linear form (DC).

The last two assumptions aim to simplify the formulation, at least in this first approach, to improve the model's explanation, operation and results. Specifically, when the energy bought/sold to the grid is considered in the bus and does not in the slack-bus, all energy flows in the system belongs to the local market. Thus, the mixed-linear programming problem (MILP) is the following:

$$minimize \quad z = \sum_{i \in \mathbb{B}} \sum_{t \in \mathbb{T}} \lambda_t^{bg} p_{i,t}^{bg} - \lambda^{sg} p_{i,t}^{sg} + \lambda_t^{bm} p_{i,t}^{bm}$$
$$-\lambda_t^{sm} p_{i,t}^{sm} + \sum_{(i,j) \in \mathbb{L}} \sum_{t \in \mathbb{T}} p_{i,j,t}. \tag{1}$$

The objective function in (1) comprises, from left to right: the energy bought (p^{bg}) and sold (p^{sm}) to the grid, the energy traded within the local market (p^{bm}, p^{sm}) (where the Lambdas indicates the respective trading prices), and the energy flow among peers ($p_{i,j,t}$). Thus, (1) is subject to the following constraints:

Nodes constraints; $\forall i \in \mathbb{B}, \forall t \in \mathbb{T}$

$$\sum_{(i,j) \in \mathbb{L}} p_{i,j,t} = pg_{i,t} - pl_{i,t} + p_{i,t}^{bg} - p_{i,t}^{sg} + (ds_{i,t} - ch_{i,t}). \tag{2}$$

Under the assumption of the DC version of the OPF, the constraints of the lines possess the following structure; $\forall (i,j) \in \mathbb{L}, \forall t \in \mathbb{T}$

$$p_{i,j,t} = \frac{\theta_{i,t} - \theta_{j,t}}{x_{i,j}}. \tag{3}$$

Equation (2) represents, from left to right, the power injected by the PV systems (pg), the load (pl), power bought/sold to the grid, and the power injected (ds) or absorbed (ch) by the storage system. Equation (3) is the classic DC-OPF for the branches, and it does not present any variation.

The power injected limits by the rooftop system, the voltages, and the flow between nodes are explained as follows:

Power injected by the PV system; $\forall i \in \mathbb{B}$

$$0 \leq pg_{i,t} \leq I_i^{pg} \ \beta_i^p \ PG_t^{max}. \tag{4}$$

Voltage limits; $\forall i \in \mathbb{B}, \forall t \in \mathbb{T}$

$$V^{min} \leq v_{i,t} \leq V^{max}. \tag{5}$$

Energy flow among peers; $\forall (i,j) \in \mathbb{L}, \forall t \in \mathbb{T}$

$$p_{i,j,t} \leq S_{i,j}^{max}. \tag{6}$$

In Eq. (4), the power injected by the rooftop system is bounded by; a binary vector (I_i^{pg}) that indicates if there is a PV system installed in the bus; the power system capacity (β_i^p); and the maximum power (PG_t^{max}) that can be injected by the system into a specific period t (see Sect. 3).

The battery behaviour is represented through the follows constraints; $\forall i \in \mathbb{B}, \forall t \in \mathbb{T}$

$$soc_{i,t+1} = soc_{i,t} + (\varphi \ ch_{i,t} - \frac{ds_{i,t}}{\varphi})\Delta t, \tag{7}$$

$$I_i^{bt} \ \beta_i^b \ SOC_t^{min} \leq soc_{i,t} \leq I_i^{bt} \ \beta_i^b \ SOC_t^{max}, \tag{8}$$

$$ch_{i,t} \leq M^{bt}w_{i,t}, \tag{9}$$

$$ds_{i,t} \leq M^{bt}(1 - w_{i,t}) - M^{bt}(1 - I^{bt}), \tag{10}$$

$$w_{i,t} \leq I^{bt}. \tag{11}$$

Equation (7) indicates the state of charge of the battery, which is bounded in Eq. (8) by the battery capacity, multiplied by its minimum/maximum operating range and multiplied by a binary vector (I^{bt}) which is 1 when a bus possesses a storage system installed. Likewise, Eq. (9) indicates the charge power of the battery, such that when it is charging, $w_{i,t}$ takes value 1; otherwise, the battery is discharging through Eq. (10). If there is no battery installed $(I^{bt} = 0)$, $w_{i,t}$ must be zero (see Eq.(11)), and the other battery constraints are also zero.

Flexible Demand, Therefore; $\forall i \in \mathbb{B}, \forall t \in \mathbb{T}$

$$pl_{i,t} = PL_{i,t} + \sum_{d \in \mathbb{D}} \tau_{i,t}^d Pf d^d. \tag{12}$$

Therefore; $\forall i \in \mathbb{B}, \forall d \in \mathbb{D}$

$$\sum_{d \in \mathbb{D}} \tau_{i,t}^d = Nf d_i^d. \tag{13}$$

The total electricity load in Eq. (12) is composed of unmanageable demand $(PL_{i,t})$ and flexible demand (Pfd^d), which could be activated at any time t depend on the generation and consumption level, in order to minimize the energy purchased to the grid. Thus, the binary variable $\tau_{i,t}^d$ is 1 when the flexible load is activated and zero otherwise, allowing different types of flexible loads activated in the same period t, such as air conditioner, wash, and dish machine. Eq (13) indicates the total numbers of hours that a type of demand must be activated at a certain time horizon.

The local energy market is modelled through the following set of constraints. Therefore; $\forall i \in \mathbb{B}, \forall t \in \mathbb{T}$

$$pg_{i,t} + ds_{i,t} = p_{i,t}^{sc} + p_{i,t}^{sm} + p_{i,t}^{sg} + ch_{i,t}, \tag{14}$$

$$p_{i,t}^{sm} + p_{i,t}^{sg} \leq (pg_{i,t} + ds_{i,t} - pl_{i,t}) + M(1 - y1_{i,t}), \tag{15}$$

$$p_{i,t}^{sm} + p_{i,t}^{sg} \leq y1_{i,t} + M(1 - y2_{i,t}), \tag{16}$$

$$y1_{i,t} + y2_{i,t} = 1, \tag{17}$$

$$\sum_{(i,j)\in\mathbb{L}} p_{i,j,t} \leq p_{i,t}^{sm}, \tag{18}$$

$$\sum_{(j,i)\in\mathbb{L}} p_{j,i,t} \leq p_{i,t}^{bm}. \tag{19}$$

Equation (14) represents the relation between i) the power injected from the generator plus the battery (power available to use), with ii) how to assign this power to: meet the load $(p_{i,t}^{sc})$, sell the remaining energy to the local market $(p_{i,t}^{sm})$ /grid $(p_{i,t}^{sg})$, or charge the battery $(ch_{i,t})$. Equations (15)–(17) represents the energy amount that can be sold by a user (peer) at a specific time. Specifically, Eqs. (15) and (16) explain: if the user has generation and/or energy stored, this energy must satisfy first its electricity load. Once the load is complete, the remaining energy can be sold in the local market; otherwise, the power sold to the grid or the market must be zero. Equation (17) is composed of two sets of binary variables that allow the proper operation of the Eqs. (15) and (16) supported by M, which is a significant positive number. Thus, $y1$ takes the value 1 when the generator's power plus the power injected from the battery is greater than the electricity load, and in the case when the load is greater than the power available to use, $y2$ takes the value 1. Equation (18) indicates that all the energy that leaves node i is energy sold to the market, and Eq. (19) that all the energy reaching node i is energy bought to the market.

Market clearing constraint; $\forall t \in \mathbb{T}$

$$\sum_{i\in\mathbb{B}} p_{i,t}^{sm} = \sum_{i\in\mathbb{B}} p_{i,t}^{bm}. \tag{20}$$

Equation (13) indicates that the total energy sold to the local market must be bought. Therefore, following the market constraints already explained, a user (peer) with a self-consumption system is under the following scenarios:

a) if $pg_{i,t} + ds_{i,t} > pl_{i,t}$,   sell to   Market: $p_{i,t}^{sm} = p_{i,t}^{bm}$
Grid: Remaining

b) if $pg_{i,t} + ds_{i,t} < pl_{i,t}$,   bought to   Market: $p_{i,t}^{bm} = p_{i,t}^{sm}$
Grid: Remaining

c) if $pg_{i,t} + ds_{i,t} = pl_{i,t}$,   nothing.

In the first scenario, if the self-generation is greater than the load, the remaining energy could be sold to the grid or the local market, such that the energy available to sell within the community must be equal to the market load. However, for selling within the market to make sense, the pricing should be under the following pattern:

$$\lambda_t^{sg} \leq \lambda_t^{sm} \leq \lambda_t^{bg}, \quad \lambda_t^{sm} = \lambda_t^{bm}. \tag{21}$$

Therefore, the user would prefer to sell its remaining energy to the market before the grid because the internal market price is always greater than λ_t^{sg}. On the other hand, the users always would choose to buy energy to the internal market than the grid because it is cheaper than λ_t^{bg}. Under this context, the objective function must be rewritten as follows:

$$z = \sum_{i \in B} \sum_{t \in T} \lambda_t^{bg} p_{i,t}^{bg} - \lambda^{sg} p_{i,t}^{sg} + \sum_{(i,j) \in L} \sum_{t \in T} p_{i,j,t}. \tag{22}$$

In Eq. (22), the local market's energy traded has been deleted because the energy sold and bought always are equal in amount and price.

3   Computational Results

This section presents the data used to test the model under two IEEE bus systems with their respective results. The first network, corresponding to the IEEE 5-bus system, is used as a slight case of study to facilitate the results explanations and show clearly the data type obtained from the model and its operation before being tested in a second case study corresponding to the 33 nodes distribution network. The two study cases compare the total energy bought when there is no energy traded among peers and when it is. The aim is to quantify the savings produced by the energy exchange among peers with PV and storage systems. The formulation has been programmed in Pyomo-Python using CPLEX as the solver.

3.1   Data

The load profiles have been taken from [10], the energy price [11], and the PV power output from [12], where the weather conditions belong to Barcelona, Spain. Figure 1 shows the relationship between these curves such that everyone has been normalized to be in function of the maximum power capacity. i.e., if the power capacity of the PV system is 10 kW, then every hour of the PV normalized curve (between 0 and 1) represents the power than can be injected into the system at that hour. Thus the PV curve in Fig. 1 is the PG max vector used in the formulation. Likewise, the normalized curves belonging to the load profiles are multiplied by the maximum power load at every bus to obtain the load at every hour. The price to sell energy to the grid has been assumed in 1/3 of the buy price.

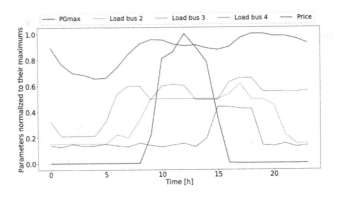

Fig. 1. Profiles used in the first case of study

3.2 IEEE 5 Bus System

The small case study [16] considers five nodes, six lines, and three buses with load profiles where buses 2, 3, and 4 possess a maximum power of 7, 5, and 3.5 kW, respectively. Besides, node 2 and 4 have installed a rooftop PV system of 10 and 5 kW, and bus 4 has a storage device of 10 kWh with a power charge/discharge of 5 kW which start charged at 50%. Two types of flexible demand are included: a consumption of 1.5 and 2.5 kWh, which must be activated within the 24 h time horizon.

Table 1 shows the results for bus 4 that includes self-generation and battery. Thus, it is easy to observe the following behaviour:

- Hour 1: The load is composed only by unmanageable demand that is fulfilled with energy from the battery, which means that the load is equal to the self-consumption.
- Hour 2–7: There is not battery discharged, and therefore the energy is bought to the grid.
- Hour 10–16: There is power generated from the PV system, which in hour 10 generate 1.1 kW, of which 0.5 kW are for self-consumption; the remaining is summed to the 2.1 kW discharged from the battery to sell 2.7 kW to the market. In hour 13, the power generated reaches 5 kW, of which 3 kW belong to self-consumption composed of a fixed load of 0.5 kW and a flexible demand of 2.5 kW; the remaining 2 kW are used to charge the battery with 1.5 kW and sell to the market 0.5 kW.

– Hour 17–24: In the remaining hours, the battery supplies the energy to meet the load. Thus, the only hours when bus 4 buy energy to the grid is when the electricity price is the lowest (see Fig. 1).

Figure 2 shows schematically how the nodes exchange energy into the local market at hour 12. Bus 3 is a consumer without flexible devices or PV system, while nodes 2 and 4 are prosumer, which sells the remaining energy to node 3, showing the energy flow in Fig. 2.

Table 3 shows a final comparison between three different scenarios: (**A**) System without DERs penetration, (**B**) System with DERs but without energy traded among peers, and (**C**) System with DERs and energy traded. Thus, in case (**B**) the energy bought to the grid is 102.8 kW, corresponding to 67.68% of the total demand; however, when there are energy traded, the energy from the grid is 78.6 kW, 51.7% of the total load, which means that the community local market has reduced the grid dependence in 23.6%. In saving terms, the community electricity bill for 24 h arise to 9.15€ in scenario (A); however, under (B) scenario, the cost decreases to 5.68€ and considering energy traded among peers 4.79€, which means a 15.7% in saving regarding the scenario (B) and 47.6% of the scenario (A) (Table 2).

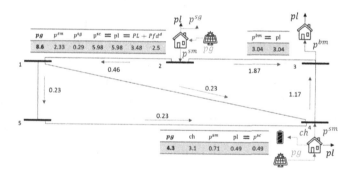

Fig. 2. IEEE 5 bus system: energy traded, 12 am

3.3   IEEE 33 Bus System

The second case of study considers the IEEE 33 bus system [15], which has been modified to includes a high DERs penetration, i.e., the PVs and Batteries power installed represents 61.8% and 70.9%, respectively, of the total power demanded. The DN has 33 nodes, 32 lines, and 32 load points, where the load profiles used in Fig. 1 has been replicated to the 33 bus system.

Table 3 shows the comparison results for the same scenarios explained in the previous section. Thus, the internal market; traded 10% of the total load; the self-consumption round the 27% for scenarios (B) and (C); the batteries provide 8% of the energy to meet the load; and the scenario (C) shows a lower dependence from the external grid purchasing 12% less than the scenario with

Table 1. 5-test system case: bus 4 results

Hour	pg	p^{sc}	p^{bg}	p^{sg}	p^{bm}	p^{sm}	soc	ch	ds	pl	PL	Pfd
1	0	0.5	0	0	0	0	5	0	0.5	0.5	0.5	0
2	0	0	0.4	0	0	0	4.5	0	0	0.4	0.4	0
3	0	0	0.5	0	0	0	4.5	0	0	0.5	0.5	0
4	0	0	0.5	0	0	0	4.5	0	0	0.5	0.5	0
5	0	0	0.5	0	0	0	4.5	0	0	0.5	0.5	0
6	0	0	0.5	0	0	0	4.5	0	0	0.5	0.5	0
7	0	0	0.5	0	0	0	4.5	0	0	0.5	0.5	0
8	0	0.4	0	0	0	0	4.5	0	0.4	0.4	0.4	0
9	0	0.5	0	0	0	0	4	0	0.5	0.5	0.5	0
10	1.1	0.5	0	0	0	2.7	3.4	0	2.1	0.5	0.5	0
11	4	1.9	0	0	0	1.5	1	0.6	0	1.9	0.4	1.5
12	4.3	0.5	0	0	0	0.7	1.5	3.1	0	0.5	0.5	0
13	5	3	0	0	0	0.5	4.3	1.5	0	3	0.5	2.5
14	4.5	1.9	0	0	0	0	5.7	2.6	0	1.9	0.4	1.5
15	3.9	0.7	0	0	0	2.1	8	1.1	0	0.7	0.7	0
16	1.7	1.5	0	0	0	0.2	9	0	0	1.5	1.5	0
17	0	1.5	0	0	0	0	9	0	1.5	1.5	1.5	0
18	0	1.5	0	0	0	0	7.3	0	1.5	1.5	1.5	0
19	0	1.5	0	0	0	0	5.7	0	1.5	1.5	1.5	0
20	0	0.5	0	0	0	0	4.1	0	0.5	0.5	0.5	0
21	0	0.5	0	0	0	0	3.5	0	0.5	0.5	0.5	0
22	0	0.5	0	0	0	0	3	0	0.5	0.5	0.5	0
23	0	0.4	0	0	0	0	2.4	0	0.4	0.4	0.4	0
24	0	0.5	0	0	0	0.5	1.9	0	0.9	0.5	0.5	0

Table 2. 5-test system case: summary table results

	pg	p^{sc}	p^{bg}	p^{sg}	p^{bm}	p^{sm}	sc	ds	pl	PL	Pfd
(A)	0	0	151.9	0	0	0	0	0	151.9	131.9	20
(B)	73.7	49.1	102.8	26.7	0	0	8.4	10.4	151.9	131.9	20
(C)	73.7	47	78.6	2.4	26.4	26.4	8.9	10.9	151.9	131.9	20

DERs but without energy traded. In terms of savings, scenario (C) continues been the most efficient because it paid 9.13% less than scenario (B) and 39.7% less than scenario (A). These results are aligned with the first case of study, and they are consistent with the expected values for an energy local trading market.

Table 3. 33-test system case: summary table results

	pg	p^{sc}	p^{bg}	p^{sg}	p^{bm}	p^{sm}	sc	ds	pl	PL	Pfd
(A)	0	0	990.7	0	0	0	0	0	990.7	925.7	65
(B)	403	275.4	715.3	151.9	0	0	55.5	79.7	990.7	925.7	65
(C)	403	255.6	296.5	66.1	105.5	105.5	55.4	79.7	990.7	925.7	65

4 Discussion and Next Steps

The model presented in this paper allows computing the efficiency obtained when a community network with high DERs penetration exchange energy among peers to met the load, minimizing the energy purchased to an external grid. Besides, the formulation proposed could favour creating local energy markets identifying and quantifying every user share, addressing one of the main barriers of this new market structures. However, the formulation presents several assumptions that could relax to improve significantly the model proposed. For example:

- Use the AC power flow equations to represents more realistic technical constraints.
- Consider the slack bus like interconnection point among peers to sell or buy energy to the grid, and size possible congestion level produced by the energy exchanged.
- Include electric vehicles and observe their role when they are connected and operate like flexible service to the users.
- Change the global internal trading price to a competitive price to move toward a decentralized market design, where the model proposed to act as a master problem to identify the energy amount that should be traded, and a subproblem could establish the final price for every user that could buy or sell energy into the local market.

References

1. Paudel, A., Chaudhari, K., Long, C., Gooi, H.: Peer-to-peer energy trading in a prosumer-based community microgrid: a game-theoretic model. IEEE Trans. Indust Electron. **66**, 6087–6097 (2019)
2. Guerrero, J., Chapman, A., Verbič, G.: Local energy markets in LV networks: community based and decentralized P2P approaches. In: 2019 IEEE Milan PowerTech, PowerTech 2019, pp. 1–6 (2019)
3. Park, D., Park, Y., Roh, J., Lee, K., Park, J.: A hierarchical peer-to-peer energy transaction model considering prosumer's renewable energy preference. IFAC-PapersOnLine. **52**, 312–317 (2019). https://doi.org/10.1016/j.ifacol.2019.08.228
4. Wang, Z., Yu, X., Mu, Y., Jia, H.: A distributed Peer-to-Peer energy transaction method for diversified prosumers in urban community microgrid system. Appl. Energy **260**, 114327 (2020). https://doi.org/10.1016/j.apenergy.2019.114327
5. Khorasany, M., Mishra, Y., Ledwich, G.: Market framework for local energy trading: a review of potential designs and market clearing approaches. IET Gener. Trans. Distrib. **12**, 5899–5908 (2018)

6. Zhou, Y., Wu, J., Long, C., Ming, W.: State-of-the-art analysis and perspectives for peer-to-peer energy trading. Engineering **6**, 739–753 (2020). https://doi.org/10.1016/j.eng.2020.06.002

7. Tushar, W., Saha, T., Yuen, C., Morstyn, T., McCulloch, M., Poor, H., Wood, K.: A motivational game-theoretic approach for peer-to-peer energy trading in the smart grid. Appl. Energy **243**, 10–20 (2019). https://doi.org/10.1016/j.apenergy.2019.03.111

8. Paudel, A., Sampath, L., Yang, J., Gooi, H.: Peer-to-peer energy trading in smart grid considering power losses and network fees. IEEE Trans. Smart Grid **11**, 4727–4737 (2020)

9. Morstyn, T., McCulloch, M.: Multiclass energy management for peer-to-peer energy trading driven by prosumer preferences. IEEE Trans. Power Syst. **34**, 4005–4014 (2019)

10. OpenEI Open Energy Information (2020). https://openei.org/datasets/files/961/pub/

11. Omie Iberian Electricity Market Operator (2020). https://www.omie.es/en/market-results/daily/daily-market/daily-hourly-price

12. Commission, E.: Photovoltaic Geographical Information System (2019). https://re.jrc.ec.europa.eu/pvg-tools/en/tools.html

13. Mengelkamp, E., Staudt, P., Garttner, J., Weinhardt, C.: Trading on local energy markets: a comparison of market designs and bidding strategies. In: International Conference on the European Energy Market, EEM (2017)

14. IRENA Electricity trading arrangements (2020). https://www.youtube.com/watch?v=UDv04q3U6e0

15. Selvan, M., Swarup, K.: Distribution system load flow using object-oriented methodology. In: 2004 International Conference on Power System Technology, POWERCON 2004, vol. 2, pp. 1168–1173 (2004)

16. Saharuddin, N., Abidin, I., Mokhlis, H., Abdullah, A., Naidu, K.: A power system network splitting strategy based on contingency analysis. Energies **11**, 434 (2018)

Design and Installation of an IoT Electricity and Water Technological and Monitoring Solution

Ponciano J. Escamilla-Ambrosio$^{(\boxtimes)}$ ⓘ, Maria G. Pulido-Navarro ⓘ,
Marco A. Ramírez-Salinas ⓘ, Marco A. Moreno-Ibarra ⓘ,
and J. Humberto Sossa-Azuela ⓘ

Instituto Politécnico Nacional, Centro de Investigación en Computación,
Ciudad de México, México
{pescamilla,mars,marcomoreno,hsossa}@cic.ipn.mx

Abstract. Nowadays, monitoring electricity and water usage is becoming very important to obtain consumption baselines towards establishing savings goals. Therefore, this work details the design and implementation of electricity and water monitoring networks installed to monitor electricity and water consumption at three research and academic buildings of Instituto Politécnico Nacional. Internet of Things is also implemented as it allows the systems to send the gathered information to the cloud using an Internet connection for analysis purposes. The main objective of this development is to have an electricity and water usage data repository and visualization tool to make users aware of these resources consumptions and then make changes in the infrastructure that will produce better usage and savings. This design included the installation of electricity and water consumption meters. Also, data concentrators are used to send the information obtained from the meters to monitoring software. A technical memory was documented, demonstrating the components and activities carried out in each monitoring point—finally, the collected data allowed to estimate the electricity and water consumption baselines on the considered instances. As the main objective, all the information gathered will form a baseline on which improvement and political proposals will be generated to implement saving actions on energy and water handling in these buildings.

Keywords: Water and electricity monitoring · Data concentration · IoT system

1 Introduction

This paper presents the technical aspects that were considered in the design and installation of a monitoring network for electricity and water consumption at three facilities of Instituto Politécnico Nacional (IPN): Centro de Investigación en Computación (CIC), Centro de Innovación y Desarrollo Tecnológico en Cómputo (CIDETEC), and Escuela Superior de Cómputo (ESCOM). The results generated from the initial planning and corresponding monitoring of the project are presented. Additionally, the visualization

S. Nesmachnow and L. Hernández Callejo (Eds.): ICSC-Cities 2021, CCIS 1555, pp. 297–310, 2022.
https://doi.org/10.1007/978-3-030-96753-6_21

of the data, generated through the activation of the Strategic System for the Evaluation and Performance for Sustainability (SEEDS) technological platform, is shown. All the information gathered has been used to determine the consumptions baseline to state new policies and rules that could be implemented in the future to make improvements and savings in energy and water usage. Internet of Things (IoT) is also implemented to collect data and for their analysis. An IoT architecture is a system that allows communication between smart devices that use wireless communication and Internet technologies [1]. In this way, devices can collect and transmit data efficiently.

In the IoT ecosystem, communication between devices is done in different ways. For example, multi-hop short-range communication (Zigbee, Bluetooth, and RF) [2, 3]. In [4, 5], the authors report a home energy management system in a wireless sensor network using the Zigbee protocol to communicate with sensor nodes. The sensor network monitors energy consumption data and sends control signals to end nodes when peak loads are detected. Another example of reducing energy expenses is presented in [6]; in this article, the authors propose a cost modeling scheme for optimization-based energy management. The authors consider many scenarios such as local energy generation capacity, peak load hours, length of cycle of appliances, time of use, and tariffs have been taken into consideration. In [7], for example, the authors used Zigbee technology with a mesh topology. They were able to construct a network for intercommunicating devices allowing maximum effectiveness when receiving and sending data. Another system for water monitoring [8] was built in a city based on the platform Bristol Is Open; here, the authors used WiFi due to its long-range (up to 100 m).

For this project, the activities carried out in the research and academic centers considered are shown from the initial planning of the requirements to the start-up of the electrical energy and water monitoring systems. An effective approach to persuading energy usage and engaging in sustainable practice is by providing people with information about their consumption habits [9]. As said by [10] a study in developing countries, more than 16 billion cubic meters of treated water from urban supply systems are lost every year. That is why information on water usage brings along possible irregularities in water consumption such as leaks, meter failure, warning situations, peak water use, for example. All this data can be used as feedback for planning and policy implementation concerns. Similarly, according to [11], if consumers have a display that offers real-time feedback on their energy and water consumption, it could help people make better decisions about their usage behavior and might inspire them to use less water and electricity. According to [12–14], automated accounting monitoring of electricity and water consumption in some countries has already shown efficacy.

The monitoring systems used in this work aim to facilitate the design of strategies for the efficient use of electricity and water. These systems have meters, data concentrators, single board computers, routers, modems, etc. Monitoring systems make it possible to have an alert system when energy and water consumption present atypical behaviors; equally, it is expected to incorporate automation and control mechanisms to optimize the use and saving of resources. In order to obtain the baselines of energy and water consumption, the following actions were carried out that made it possible to measure the consumption of electricity and water:

- Activation of the SEEDS technological platform.
- Installation of a monitoring network for electricity and water consumption.
- Quantification of potential energy, economic and environmental savings.
- Substitution of infrastructure and equipment for efficient consumption.
- Development of measurement systems (meter, data concentrator, and transmission module).

Once the initial information was analyzed, some actions were taken for energy and water savings purposes. For instance, changes to provide savings were recommended, such as turning off computing systems whenever they were not in use; it was detected that, over time, they consume more energy than a microwave oven (which consumes lots of energy but only during a short time). Other actions were taken, as the replacement of devices with high consumption energy for devices that present energy savings, such as replacing lamps, replacing hand dryers, and replacing air conditioning units. New policies were devised once these high-consumption devices were detected and replaced. Moreover, once energy and water consumption baselines were determined, they were used as a starting point to plan and install solar photovoltaic systems in the parking lot and rooftop of the CIC, CIDETEC, and ESCOM; the outline of these systems' analysis and installation can be found in [15].

The realization of the presented project is explained in the following sections. Section 2 shows the network architecture, recording the energy and water consumption data sent to a data concentrator. Section 3 details the installation of the monitoring system for energy and water consumption for the three academic buildings. Results on the monitoring and quantification of energy and water consumption baselines at the three buildings are shown in Sect. 4. Finally, conclusions are presented in Sect. 5.

2   Network Architecture

The measurement systems installed in the IPN facilities have seven basic components [16]:

1. Energy meters.
2. Water meters.
3. Analog pulse transmitting antennas.
4. System for data acquisition.
5. Information processing systems.
6. Components for sending data.
7. Information display system.

Figure 1 shows the general architecture of the monitoring network. The first step consisted of installing the electricity and water meters in the available water and energy supply connections. In the second step, transmitting and receiving antennas were enabled to send the information to the data acquisition system. Then, in the third step, these meters were connected to the data acquisition system to enable the reception and sending of electricity and water consumption records. The fourth step consisted of sending the data

300   P. J. Escamilla-Ambrosio et al.

according to the type of connection available (Ethernet, Wi-Fi or 3G). Finally, a screen was installed so that general users could monitor electricity and water consumption in real-time.

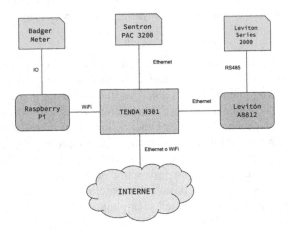

Fig. 1. Network architecture diagram.

2.1 Measurement of Electrical Energy Consumption

The electrical energy monitoring network has four types of meters. The most widely used meter is the Siemens Sentron PAC3200 [17]. This meter permits obtaining energy consumption measurements and energy quality parameters such as harmonic distortion, real, reactive, and apparent powers, phase unbalance, frequency, among other parameters. It has a digital display to show energy consumption and over 50 parameters. The meter can send the electrical system's current consumption information through a twisted pair cable that connects to a data concentrator. According to the scope established for this project, the installation of individual meters or a series of meters was considered. Such meters were located according to the requirements to have the general electricity consumption measurements of the buildings.

2.2 Measurement of Water Consumption

Measurement of water consumption is done with Badger Meter volumetric nutating disc or turbine meters [18]. These varied according to the characteristics of the facilities in the different buildings. The meters have an additional register type HR-LCD 4–20 (High Resolution 4–20 scaled/unscaled register); this device is entirely electronic in solid-state; unlike its predecessors, it does not have moving parts. Solid-state drives generate a scaled/unscaled output signal and a pulse in the 4–20 mA range over a two-wire/passive cable. The meters that were considered according to the project requirements are:

- Thermoplastic Disc Type Recordall Cold Water Meter Certified ANSI/NSF Standard 61 Size DN15 mm (5/8″)

- Recordall thermoplastic disc type cold water meter Size DN20 mm (3/4″) Certified ANSI/NSF Standard 61
- Thermoplastic Disc Type Recordall Cold Water Meter Size DN25 mm (1″) Certified ANSI/NSF Standard 61

These three meters work on the same principle. The water flows through the filter of the meter to reach the measurement chamber, where it causes nutation of the disc. The disc moves freely, never on its sphere, guided by a push roller. A magnetic coupling transmits the movement of the disc to a follower magnet located within the permanently sealed register. The follower magnet is connected to the register gear train. The gear train converts disk rotations to units of totalized volume displayed on the register panel.

2.3 Data Acquisition System

In order to export the information to a server, it is necessary to use a data concentrator (see Fig. 2). This data concentrator can receive digital signals (Modbus, RS485, and RTU) and analog signals such as pulses, XYZ pulses, 0–10 V. The Data Hub (EMH) can connect metering equipment as gas, water, electricity, and others. Up to 32 different devices can be connected by the RS485 communication Modbus and 8 resistive, analog, and pulse output devices. This connection can be digital or analog; this will always depend on the meter's manufacturer. In both cases, it is always important to consider the distance between the data concentrator and the meters; one more good thing about the system is that the link can be made by wiring the equipment or wirelessly with transceiver devices (Mod-Hopper).

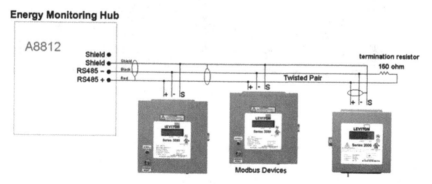

Fig. 2. Connecting the Leviton Series 2000 m to the data concentrator.

Before connecting to the concentrator, each meter must be connected with a different configuration to the electric power transmission lines, which will be the object of study. The following configuration is available for the Leviton meter, Series 2000 model. It is necessary to assign a network node for each EMH hub. The system provides the necessary materials, but the voice and data network administrators must provide the IP addresses and enable the network to send data.

3   Installation of Monitoring Systems

3.1   Installation of Monitoring Systems at CIC

Electric Power

CIC has an electric power supply contract in conjunction with ESCOM and CIDETEC and, therefore, only one meter. Hence, the primary substation receives electrical energy at 23,000 V in medium voltage and distributes 120/220 V to the named institutions. The CIC substation, located in the basement parking lot, receives energy from the primary substation. This energy goes through a 500 kVA transformer to obtain the 1600 A general distribution panel, which distributes energy at 120/220 V to all the spaces that make up the property. In this sense, the CIC's electrical connection is where the real-time energy monitoring system was installed (see Fig. 3).

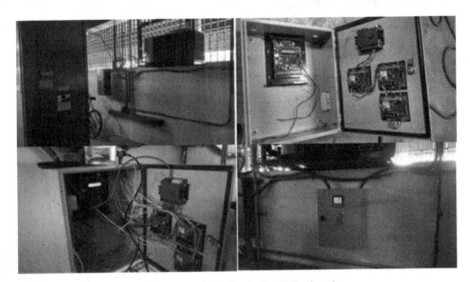

Fig. 3. Meter installation in the CIC substation.

Water

For the real-time water metering system, a 3″ Badger Meter turbine meter was installed in the drinking water connection, located in the central cistern of the building. This meter is connected to the data concentrator through an antenna (Modhopper), see Fig. 4.

3.2   Installation of Monitoring System at CIDETEC

Electric Power

CIDETEC has an electricity supply contract in conjunction with ESCOM and CIC and, therefore, only one meter. A primary substation receives electrical energy at 23,000 V in medium voltage. It distributes to said institutions at 120/220 V. However, CIDETEC has its own substation located on one side of the building. It receives energy from the primary substation through a 225 kVA transformer that derives 800 A to the distribution

Fig. 4. Water meter installed in the CIC.

panel. From this panel, the 120/220 V energy distribution gets to all the spaces that make up the property. The general panel is located at the back of the stairs in the main hall, where the real-time energy monitoring system was installed, as is shown in Fig. 5.

Fig. 5. General dashboard and energy monitoring system at CIDETEC.

Water

A 3″ Badger Meter turbine meter was installed in the drinking water connection, located next to the CIC connection for the real-time water metering system. This meter will be connected to the data concentrator through an antenna (Modhopper) see Fig. 6.

Fig. 6. Water meter installed at CIDETEC.

3.3   Installation of Monitoring Systems at ESCOM

Electric Power

ESCOM has a contract for electricity supply in conjunction with CIC and CIDETEC, which means there is only one meter. A primary substation receives electrical energy at 23,000 V in medium voltage that is in charge of distributing 120/220 V to said institutions. However, ESCOM has its own substation located in building 5. It receives energy from the primary substation, which through two 500 kVA transformers 1600 A are derived to two distribution panels with their capacity thermomagnetic switches. They are in charge of distributing energy in 120/220 V to all the spaces that make up the property. In this sense, ESCOM's electrical connection is where the real-time energy monitoring system was installed (see Fig. 7).

Fig. 7. ESCOM general dashboard and energy monitoring system.

Water

A 3″ Badger Meter turbine meter was installed in the drinking water connection for the real-time water metering system. This meter was connected to the data concentrator through an antenna (Modhopper), as is shown in Fig. 8.

Fig. 8. ESCOM water monitoring system.

4   Monitoring and Quantification of Electricity and Water Consumption Baselines

4.1   Consumption Baselines at CIC

Electricity

Derived from the analysis of the information collected by the monitoring systems, the CIC baseline consumption of electricity through the SEEDS Platform was obtained. Figure 9 shows a view of the information recorded in the SEEDS system about the electricity consumption (KWh) of CIC on a particular day, in this case, 12/18/2018.

The electrical energy consumption (KWh) per day of CIC, which has been obtained from the SEEDS platform, corresponding to November 2018, December 2018, January 2019, and February 2019, are shown in Fig. 10.

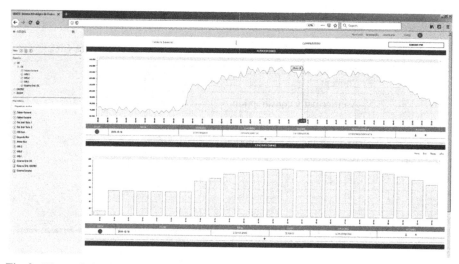

Fig. 9. View of the information that is recorded in the SEEDS system on the electricity consumption (KWh) of the CIC on a particular day, in this case 12/18/2018.

The average daily and monthly electricity consumption values were obtained using the data collected from the monitoring network over the four months considered before an average annual consumption was estimated. The values obtained are shown in Table 1.

4.2   Consumption Baseline at CIDETEC

Electricity

From the analysis of the information collected by the monitoring systems, the CIDE-TEC baseline electricity consumption through the SEEDS Platform was obtained. From Fig. 11, the information recorded in the SEEDS system about the electricity consumption (KWh) of CIDETEC on a particular day (for example, 01/22/2019) can be observed.

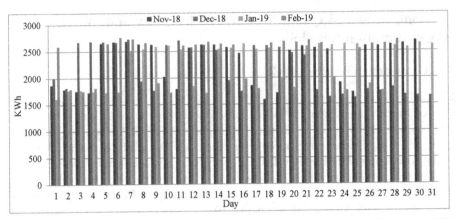

Fig. 10. Electric energy consumption per day (KWh) in the CIC in the months of November 2018, December 2018, January 2019 and February 2019.

Table 1. Average daily, monthly, and annual electricity consumption in the CIC.

Concept	Value in KWh
Average daily consumption	2,285
Average monthly consumption	68,453
Average annual consumption (estimated)	821,436

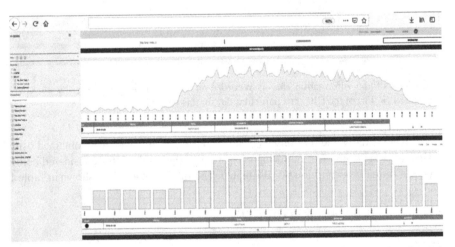

Fig. 11. View of the information that is recorded in the SEEDS system on the electricity consumption (KWh) of CIDETEC on a particular day, in this case 01/22/2019.

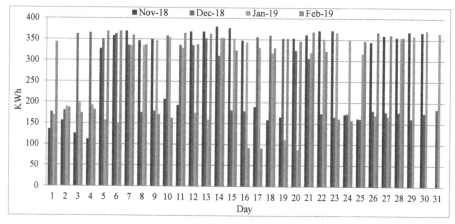

Fig. 12. Electric energy consumption per day (KWh) in CIDETEC in the months of November 2018, December 2018, January 2019 and February 2019.

The electrical energy consumption (KWh) per day of CIDETEC, obtained from the SEEDS platform, corresponding to November 2018, December 2018, January 2019, and February 2019, are shown in Fig. 12.

The average daily and monthly electricity consumption were obtained using the data collected from the monitoring network over the four months considered. After that, an estimate of the average annual consumption was made. The values obtained are shown in Table 2.

Table 2. Average daily, monthly and annual electricity consumption in the CDETEC.

Concept	Value in KWh
Average daily consumption	276
Average monthly consumption	8,279
Average annual consumption (estimated)	99,348

4.3   Consumption Baselines at ESCOM

Electricity

From the analysis of the information collected by the monitoring systems, the ESCOM baseline consumption of electricity through the SEEDS Platform was obtained. Figure 13 shows a view of the information recorded in the SEEDS system about the electricity consumption (KWh) of the ESCOM on a particular day (for example, in this case, the date 04/01/2019).

The electrical energy consumption (KWh) per day of the ESCOM, which has been obtained from the SEEDS platform, corresponding to November 2018, December 2018, January 2019, and February 2019, are shown in Fig. 14.

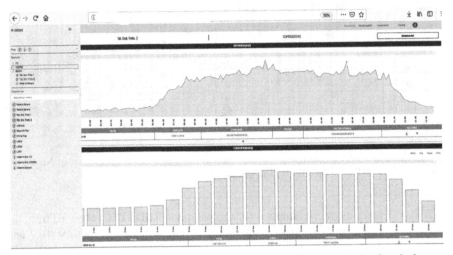

Fig. 13. View of the information that is recorded in the SEEDS system on the electrical energy consumption (KWh) of the ESCOM on a particular day, in this case 04/01/2019.

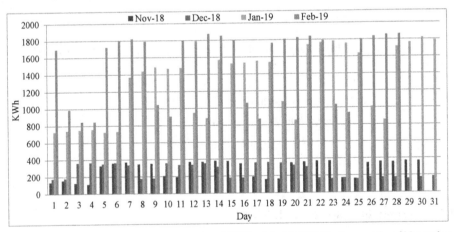

Fig. 14. Electric energy consumption per day (KWh) of the ESCOM in the months of November 2018, December 2018, January 2019 and February 2019.

The average daily and monthly electricity consumption were obtained using the data collected from the monitoring network over the four months considered. Then, an estimate of the average annual consumption was made. The values obtained are shown in Table 3.

Table 3. Average daily, monthly and annual electricity consumption in the ESCOM.

Concept	Value in KWh
Average daily consumption	1,383
Average monthly consumption	41,341
Average annual consumption (estimated)	496,094

5 Conclusions

This work presented a whole project from planning to the installation of an electrical and water monitoring network based on the SEEDS technological platform. IoT was also implemented for remote monitoring, which allowed the three systems to send the collected data to the cloud to be analyzed. The systems were implemented at three research and academic units of the Instituto Politécnico Nacional (IPN): CIC, CIDETEC, and ESCOM. The system included changes in the infrastructure, such as the installation of electricity and water consumption meters and the IoT implementation for data collection. The generated data helped estimate the electricity and water consumption baselines on the considered instances. For example, the baseline electricity consumption per year, estimated based on the collected data, at CIC is 821,436 KW, at CIDETEC is 99,348 KW, and at ESCOM is 496,094 KW. These baselines served as the basis for implementing saving actions in these research and academic units. With the above information, it was possible to integrate data that allowed us to know the consumption pattern of these resources in real-time. Identifying possibilities for savings with the implementation of operational measures and technological substitutions would lead to a lower environmental impact and reduce the carbon footprint of the three instances considered.

References

1. Abedin, S., Alam, G., Haw, R., Hong, C.: A system model for energy efficient green-IoT network. In: International Conference on Information Networking (ICOIN), pp. 177–182. IEEE (2015)
2. Miorandi, D., Sicari, S., De Pellegrini, F., Chlamtac, I.: Internet of things: vision, applications and research challenges. Ad Hoc Netw. **10**, 1497–1516 (2012)
3. Gubbi, J., Buyya, R., Marusic, S., Palaniswami, M.: Internet of things (IoT): vision, architectural elements, and future directions. Futur. Gener. Comput. Syst. **29**, 1645–1660 (2013)
4. Abo-Zahhad, M., Ahmed, S., Farrag, M., Ahmed M., Ali, A.: Design and implementation of building energy monitoring and management system based on wireless sensor networks. In: Tenth International Conference on Computer Engineering and Systems (ICCES), pp. 230–233 (2015)
5. Nguyen, N., Tran, Q., Leger, J. Vuong, T.: A real-time control using wireless sensor network for intelligent energy management system in buildings. In: IEEE Workshop on Environmental Energy and Structural Monitoring Systems, pp. 87–92 (2010)

6. Erol-Kantarci, M., Mouftah, H.: Wireless sensor networks for cost-efficient residential energy management in the smart grid. IEEE Trans. Smart Grid **2**, 314–325 (2011)
7. Marais, J., Malekian, R., Ye, N., Wang, R.: A review of the topologies used in smart water meter networks: a wireless sensor network application. Hindawi LTD **9857568**, 1–12 (2016)
8. Chen, Y., Han, D.: Water quality monitoring in smart city: a pilot project. Elsevier Sci. BV **89**, 307–316 (2018)
9. Peterson, D., Steele, J., Wilkerson, J.: WattBot: A Residential Electricity Monitoring and Feedback System. ACM 978–1–60558–247 Student Design Competition (2009)
10. Kingdom, B., Liemberger, R., Marin, P.: The challenge of reducing nonrevenue water (NRW) in developing countries. How the private sector can help: a look at performance-based service contracting, World Bank Group 8 (2006)
11. Chetty, M., Tran, D., Grinter, R.: Getting to green: understanding resource consumption in the home. Proc. UbiComp (2008)
12. Ikramov, N., Majidov, T., Kan, E., Mukhammadjonov, A.: Monitoring system for electricity consumption at pumping stations. IOP Conf. Ser.: Mater. Sci. Eng. **883** 012101 (2020)
13. Singh, P., Kansal, A.: Energy and GHG accounting for wastewater infrastructure. Resour. Conser. Recycl. **128**, 499–507 (2018)
14. Bessa, J., Alves, M.: Data-driven predictive energy optimization in a wastewater pumping station. Appl. Energ. **252**, 113423 (2019)
15. Escamilla-Ambrosio, P.J., Ramírez-Salinas, M.A., Espinosa-Sosa, O., Gallegos-García, G., Morales-Olea, M., Hernández-Callejo, L.: IPN sustainability program: solar photovoltaic electricity generation and consumption reduction. In: Nesmachnow, Sergio, Callejo, Luis Hernández (eds.) ICSC-CITIES 2019. CCIS, vol. 1152, pp. 109–120. Springer, Cham (2019). https://doi.org/10.1007/978-3-030-38889-8_9
16. Leviton Homepage. https://www.leviton.com. Accessed on 1 Sept 2019
17. PAC3200 Power Meter, Siemens. https://www.downloads.siemens.com/download-center/Download.aspx?pos=download&fct=getasset&id1=BTLV_50409. Accessed on 1 Sept 2019
18. Badger Meter Home page. https://www.badgermeter.com/es-us. Accessed on 1 Sept 2019

Integration of Internet of Things Technologies in Government Buildings Through Low-Cost Solutions

Miguel Aybar-Mejía$^{(\boxtimes)}$ (iD), Deyslen Mariano-Hernández (iD), Jesús Coronado Marte (iD), Adrián Contreras (iD), and Jimmy Arias (iD)

Área de Ingeniería, Instituto Tecnológico de
Santo Domingo, Santo Domingo, Dominican Republic
`miguel.aybar@intec.edu.do`

Abstract. Buildings have an untapped efficiency potential, being, on many occasions, government buildings present the most significant potential for energy savings. With the help of building energy management systems, this potential can be exploited, but due to the high cost that represents the implementation of these systems are not used in many buildings. This article aims to present a low-cost building energy management system based on Internet of Things technologies that can help take advantage of the efficiency potential that buildings have. The system implemented in this investigation consisted of a monitoring system that monitored different variables in real-time such as temperature, humidity, air quality, luminous intensity, and energy consumption. This system was implemented in a government building in the Dominican Republic, where the results showed opportunities for improvement. Many of these opportunities for improvement were impossible to know before the system implementation because there was no practical way to monitor them.

Keywords: Internet of things · IoT · Energy efficiency · Building energy management system · Monitoring system

1 Introduction

Energy efficiency is an issue that has gained critical pertinence in the preceding decade of the XXI century due to its significant environmental and economic role. Several nations have presented energy-effective techniques in their public-use buildings due to the increment in energy needs [1]. Energy efficiency levels have increased in the last years, but there is a critical unexploited energy efficiency potential in the building sector.

Buildings offer energy-saving opportunities with extraordinary potential since their performance level is far beneath current efficiency potentials [2]. The buildings sectors consumed 36% of the worldwide energy and almost 40% of CO_2 emission [3, 4].

Over the years, the search for systems to better manage energy has become mandatory. The development of energy management systems has been increasing due to improving energy consumption [5]. The work of building energy management systems

© Springer Nature Switzerland AG 2022
S. Nesmachnow and L. Hernández Callejo (Eds.): ICSC-Cities 2021, CCIS 1555, pp. 311–319, 2022.
https://doi.org/10.1007/978-3-030-96753-6_22

(BEMS) is known and significant since these systems can contribute to saving energy and reducing costs [6].

Internet of things (IoT) is a communication paradigm that imagines a future world-view where day-to-day existence items will be outfitted with a microcontroller and some communication protocol. For an IoT-based solution to be executed, it should be energy efficient, ready to communicate and share information across continued coverage [7].

The innovation of IoT has been generally evolved, and its utilization has been stretched out to buildings, security, business, social networks, and medical care. The innovations joining the IoT-based smart monitoring, for example, energy consumption [8] and environment monitoring, with human cooperation, have made a massive possibility inside a smart city setting to assist with working on human wellbeing and prosperity [9].

The sensor normalization in BEMS through IoT technologies and their coupling to more intelligent control systems are shaping the premise of smart buildings, giving better approaches to work on both reliability and performance [10].

There are successful studies that have integrated IoT technology into BEMS for the monitoring of different variables. Kelly et al. [11] presented an efficient implementation for IoT utilized for monitoring normal building conditions through a minimal expense pervasive detecting framework. Stavropoulos et al. [12] introduced a system for developing a university application, fusing an energy-effective sensor and actuator network, and a suitable Information Integration. Lehrer et al. [13] exhibited the efficacy of constant information observing and interactive information visualization in buildings to increase energy efficiency. Rahman et al. [14] proposed an architecture for a distributed blockchain-based IoT network for the smart building. Xing et al. [15] presented an intelligent energy-saving monitoring system for buildings based on the IoT.

This paper aims to present a methodology to implement a low-cost monitoring system based on IoT for building energy management systems in government buildings.

The rest of the paper is organized as follows. Section 2 shows the materials and methods used for the development of this research, Sect. 3 presents the case study, Sect. 4 discusses the results obtained by the systems, and Sect. 5 presents the conclusions.

2 Materials and Methods

Based on the literature review on studies using IoT and BEMS, which controllers were used were investigated. Before selecting the controller, the sensors were selected due to the need to know which types of sensors can measure variables such as temperature, humidity, air quality, light intensity, voltage, and the current was available.

Once the hardware to be used was selected, the components were programmed through Python. Additionally, the Firebase platform was used to develop the application that would allow the monitoring system to be viewed in real-time and to record the measurements made by the sensors.

2.1 System Architecture

The architecture of the monitoring system is shown in Fig. 1. This research decided to create two subsystems using two single-board computers (SBC) to monitor the variables.

One of the subsystems is in charge of the environmental variables, while the other subsystem is in charge of the electrical variables.

The environmental subsystem is composed of a single-board computer, a multiplexer for the I2C serial communication protocol, a light intensity sensor, and an environmental sensor to measure the variables of temperature, humidity, and air quality. In the case of the electrical subsystem, it is composed of an analog-to-digital converter, a voltage sensor, and a current sensor.

Both subsystems are connected wirelessly to the internal network of the building, which is connected to the internet. Through this connection, the monitoring system can be remotely viewed through a user interface.

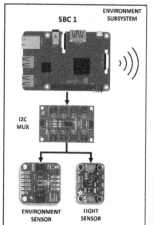 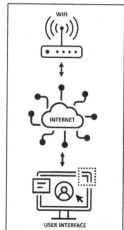 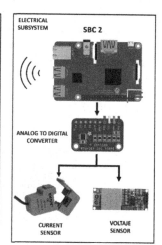

Fig. 1. Monitoring system architecture overview.

2.2 Hardware Description

The hardware selected for the monitoring system was the following:

- The SBC used was a Raspberry Pi 3B for both subsystems, which has a Quad-Core 1.2 GHz Broadcom BCM2837 64bit CPU, 1 GB RAM, BCM43438 wireless LAN and Bluetooth low energy onboard, and 40-pin extended GPIO.
- Sparkfun TCA9548A MUX is an 8 channel multiplexer that enables communication with multiple I2C devices with the same address.
- Adafruit TSL2591 is a digital light sensor configured to detect light ranges from 188 µLux up to 88,000 lx.
- Sparkfun BME680, an environment sensor that allows measuring temperature, humidity, and indoor air quality. With an operating range of $-40\,°C–85\,°C$ for temperature, $0\%–100\%$ for humidity, and resolution of gas sensor resistance of $0.05\%–0.11\%$.
- Adafruit ADS1115, an analog-to-digital converter with 16-bit precision at 860 samples/second over I2C.

- YHDC SCT-013-000, a split-core current transformer that allows measuring a maximum current of 100 A.
- ANGEEK ZMPT101B, a voltage sensor that can measure AC within 250 V.

2.3 Software Programming

For the programming of the system, the steps shown in Fig. 2 were followed. First, the libraries required for the operation of the devices were imported. Second, the necessary functions for the connection of the devices were activated, such as activating the multiplexer ports. Third, the variables for all sensors were defined, and they were assigned to the controller's physical port. Fourth, the values received for the different sensors were normalized to be related to the measured variables. Fifth, the connection between the Firebase platform and the SBCs was made to store the data collected by the sensors and subsequently access them. Finally, a web application was programmed for users to view the data obtained by the monitoring system in real-time.

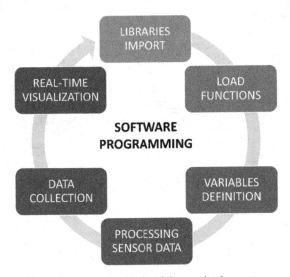

Fig. 2. Programming cycle of the monitoring system.

2.4 Real-Time Data Visualization

Through the Firebase platform, a web interface was created in which users could view in real-time the different variables recorded by the monitoring system. The user interface (see Fig. 3) consists of three display sections, (1) shows a trend graph of the selected variable, (2) shows a bar graph with the average value of each month, and (3) shows a table with the data recorded by the sensors.

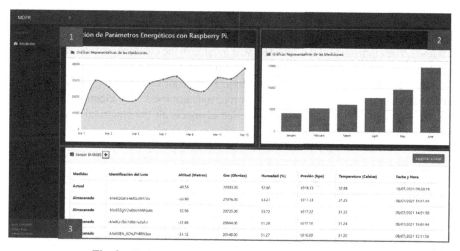

Fig. 3. Firebase user interfaces for real-time visualization.

3 Case of Study

3.1 General Description

In collaboration with the Ministerio de Trabajo (MT) of the Dominican Republic, a pilot application was carried out at the main headquarters. The MT is located at the following coordinates 18° 26′58.5″N, 69° 55′37.8″W and has five levels of which, the first level is used for citizen service, and the other four are intended for offices (see Fig. 3).

For the case study, the customer service area located on the first level of the building was selected; the working hours of this area are Monday through Friday from 8:00 AM to 4:00 PM. This area was selected because it is the area with the highest circulation of people. The monitoring system was placed to measure the different variables during customer service hours to save energy and have better resources management.

Fig. 4. Location of the building for the case study.

The data collection was carried out from June to July 2021. Figure 4 presents the physical location of the subsystems, which were located in two different areas of the first level. The environmental subsystem was located in the customer service department, which has an area of 195 m^2; the walls are made of cement with translucent windows that allow seeing the exterior of the building. For the air conditioning of the customer service area, two air conditioners units of five tons are used. The electrical subsystem was located next to the distribution panel that connects all the electrical loads, located in the first level's electrical room (Fig. 5).

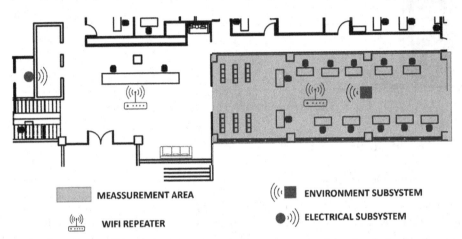

MEASSUREMENT AREA   ENVIRONMENT SUBSYSTEM

WIFI REPEATER   ELECTRICAL SUBSYSTEM

Fig. 5. The physical location of the environmental subsystem and the electrical subsystem.

4 Results and Discussion

In the case of the air quality index, the higher the value, the higher the level of air pollution. According to the Air Quality Index Basics for Ozone and Particle Pollution [16], if the air quality value is 50 or below, the air quality is satisfactory. Figure 6 shows the data captured by the air quality sensor where it can be seen that the air quality index remains between 11–12 indicating good air quality.

Figure 7 shows the values obtained from the temperature and humidity sensors, where it can be seen that the temperature during the operation of the system was between 30 °C and 33 °C. It was verified if it was a system error, but after several validations, it was observed that within the area, there were problems with some windows that made the air conditioning units not achieve the desired temperature in the area.

Figure 8 shows the recorded average voltage line to line values and phase voltage (line to neutral) with the study area. Both voltages present a voltage drop of approximately 20% of the nominal value. This voltage drop is far above the approved value of 3% that exposes the electric code of the Dominican Republic for charges interconnected in electrical panels [17]. In the same figure, it is seen as the voltage drop begins to increase as it starts the working day of the customer service area due to the electrical equipment that is used in that area.

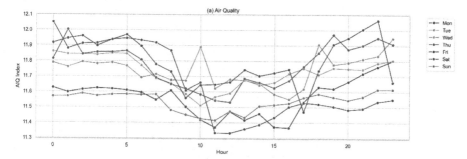

Fig. 6. Average air quality record for each hour of each day of the week.

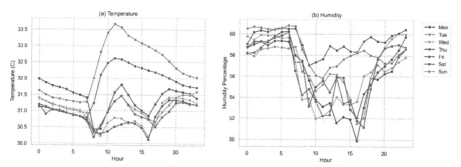

Fig. 7. (a) Average temperature and (b) average humidity for each hour of each day of the week.

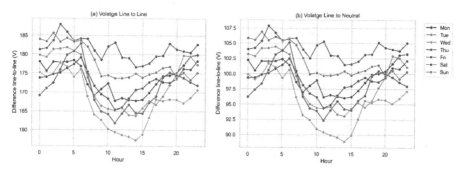

Fig. 8. (a) Average voltage line to line and (b) Average voltage line to neutral for each hour of each day of the week.

Figure 9 presents the values of electrical currents registered in each of the connected lines to the monitoring system. The behavior of the average current is observed for 24 h. In the same way, an imbalance exists between phase A and the other phases (B-C) due to the excess load connected therein. This registered load imbalance is one of the factors that affects the voltage drop recorded in the study area.

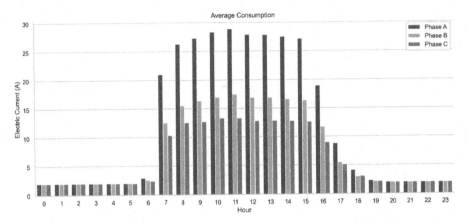

Fig. 9. Average consumption of the three phases for each hour of each day of the week.

5 Conclusions

This case study demonstrated the advantages of applying an IoT system for energy management systems in government buildings. Although it is known that there are IoT technologies for EMS applications, but in the proposed case, it is present as an integrated system in government buildings that can use to record information on the state of energy quality and environmental conditions. The measurements showed the importance of using EMS systems in government buildings since they allow managers and those in charge of building maintenance to detect areas where energy infrastructure improvements should be proposed.

Integrating the IoT system and the EMS allows seeing in real-time the consumption conditions of the building, allowing to detect energy consumption outside service hours, achieving a better demand management system within a specific area of any government building. This information served as a decision tool since they have presented some weaknesses in their energy system within the customer service area.

As future work remains, the integration of the IoT system to a 3G to 5G network allows, in case of failures or latency of the data network of the building, subsequent degradation, the system can continue to send the information to the database.

Acknowledgment. Ministerio de Trabajo (MT) of the Dominican Republic for allowing this case study to be carried out in one of its service areas, in addition to the complementary information on the selected area.

References

1. de la Cruz-Lovera, C., Perea-Moreno, A.-J., de la Cruz-Fernández, J.-L., Alvarez-Bermejo, J., Manzano-Agugliaro, F.: Worldwide research on energy efficiency and sustainability in public buildings. Sustainability **9**(8), 1294 (2017). https://doi.org/10.3390/su9081294

2. Sheikhnejad, Y., Gonçalves, D., Oliveira, M., Martins, N.: Can buildings be more intelligent than users? - The role of intelligent supervision concept integrated into building predictive control. Energy Rep. **6**, 409–416 (2020). https://doi.org/10.1016/j.egyr.2019.08.081

3. Sun, Y., Haghighat, F., Fung, B.C.M.: A review of the state-of-the-art in data-driven approaches for building energy prediction. Energy Build. **221**, 110022 (2020). https://doi.org/10.1016/j.enbuild.2020.110022

4. Vishwanath, A., Chandan, V., Saurav, K.: An IoT-based data-driven precooling solution for electricity cost savings in commercial buildings. IEEE Internet Things J. **6**(5), 7337–7347 (2019). https://doi.org/10.1109/JIOT.2019.2897988

5. Bonilla, D., Samaniego, M.G., Ramos, R., Campbell, H.: Practical and low-cost monitoring tool for building energy management systems using virtual instrumentation. Sustain. Cities Soc. **39**, 155–162 (2018). https://doi.org/10.1016/j.scs.2018.02.009

6. Doukas, H., Patlitzianas, K.D., Iatropoulos, K., Psarras, J.: Intelligent building energy management system using rule sets. Build. Environ. **42**(10), 3562–3569 (2007). https://doi.org/10.1016/j.buildenv.2006.10.024

7. Sheng, T.J., et al.: An Internet of Things based smart waste management system using LoRa and tensorflow deep learning model. IEEE Access **8**, 148793–148811 (2020). https://doi.org/10.1109/ACCESS.2020.3016255

8. Al-Ali, A.R., Zualkernan, I.A., Rashid, M., Gupta, R., Alikarar, M.: A smart home energy management system using IoT and big data analytics approach. IEEE Trans. Consum. Electron. **63**(4), 426–434 (2017). https://doi.org/10.1109/TCE.2017.015014

9. Hossain, M., Weng, Z., Schiano-Phan, R., Scott, D., Lau, B.: Application of IoT and BEMS to visualise the environmental performance of an educational building. Energies **13**(15), 4009 (2020). https://doi.org/10.3390/en13154009

10. Linder, L., Vionnet, D., Bacher, J.-P., Hennebert, J.: Big building data - a big data platform for smart buildings. Energy Procedia **122**, 589–594 (2017). https://doi.org/10.1016/j.egypro.2017.07.354

11. Bala, R., Aravind, S.: Towards the implementation of IoT for environmental vStatus Verification in homes. Indian J. Public Heal. Res. Dev. **10**(8), 591 (2019). https://doi.org/10.5958/0976-5506.2019.01950.8

12. Stavropoulos, T.G., Tsioliaridou, A., Koutitas, G., Vrakas, D., Vlahavas, I.: System architecture for a smart university building. In: Diamantaras, K., Duch, W., Iliadis, L.S. (eds.) ICANN 2010. LNCS, vol. 6354, pp. 477–482. Springer, Heidelberg (2010). https://doi.org/10.1007/978-3-642-15825-4_64

13. Lehrer, D., Vasudev, J.: Visualizing Energy Information in Commercial Buildings: A Study of Tools, Expert Users, and Building Occupants. Final Report to California Energy Commission Program, pp. 41-p (2011)

14. Rahman, A., Nasir, M.K., Rahman, Z., Mosavi, A., Shahab, S., Minaei-Bidgoli, B.: DistBlock-Building: a distributed blockchain-based SDN-IoT network for smart building management. IEEE Access **8**, 140008–140018 (2020). https://doi.org/10.1109/ACCESS.2020.3012435

15. Xing, L., Jiao, B., Du, Y., Tan, X., Wang, R.: Intelligent energy-saving supervision system of urban buildings based on the internet of things: a case study. IEEE Syst. J. **14**(3), 4252–4261 (2020). https://doi.org/10.1109/JSYST.2020.2995199

16. AirNow: AQI Basics|AirNow.gov (2019)

17. Superintendencia de Electricidad, de la C. Calidad, I.D.: Codigo Eléctrico Nacional de la República Dominicana. SIE-056-2016-MEMI. Santo Domingo, Distrito Nacional (2016). https://sie.gob.do/images/sie-documentos-pdf/marco-legal/resoluciones-sie/2016/RESOLUCIONSIE-056-2016-MEMIEMISIONCODIGOELECTRICONACIONAL-1-_merged2_merged2.pdf

Author Index

Printed in the United States
by Baker & Taylor Publisher Services